Advanced Global Illumination

Advanced Global Illumination

Second Edition

Philip Dutré
Kavita Bala
Philippe Bekaert

A K Peters, Ltd.
Wellesley, Massachusetts

Editorial, Sales, and Customer Service Office

A K Peters, Ltd.
888 Worcester Street, Suite 230
Wellesley, MA 02482
www.akpeters.com

Library of Congress Cataloging-in-Publication Data

Dutré, Philip
    Advanced global illumination / Philip Dutré, Kavita Bala, Philippe Bekaert.
        p. cm.
    Includes bibliographical references and index.
    ISBN 13: 978-1-56881-307-3 (alk. paper)
    ISBN 10: 1-56881-307-4 (alk. paper)
        1. Computer graphics. I. Bala, Kavita II. Bekaert, Philippe III. Title.

T385.D89 2006
006.6'93–dc22

                                                    2006044831

Printed in India
10 09 08 07 06   10 9 8 7 6 5 4 3 2 1

To my family. —Phil

To Andrew, Vivek, and Ravi. —KB

To Annelies, Lotte, and Fien. —Philippe

Foreword

There have been tremendous advances in the realism of computer-generated images over the last twenty years. This is the result of a great deal of research and is documented in thousands of technical papers. While this effort has resulted in many algorithmic and mathematical tools, it has also resulted in a vast and somewhat impenetrable literature. This literature has conflicting terms, symbols, and often advocates approaches that are simply not practical. As a result, it is very difficult for new people to "get up to speed" and begin developing software to generate realistic images. The most technical part of realistic image generation is dealing with "global illumination." The word "global" refers to the fact that the appearance of an object depends on the light it receives from all other objects. So in this sense, computing lighting even at a single point requires computation using the entire model of the scene. While this might seem like overkill, the visual richness of an image created using a global illumination program is simply not possible with simpler local illumination programs.

This book breaks down the barrier to entry and describes global illumination concepts and algorithms from a modern viewpoint using consistent terms and symbols. While there are good books on specific global illumination topics, this is the first book to address global illumination techniques as a whole. The authors are ideal for such an ambitious project; they have a broad background in rendering and have done significant research in all of the major global illumination topics.

Most of the major theoretical advances in global illumination took place in the 1980s. These included the development of both radiosity and Monte Carlo ray tracing. In the 1990s, it became apparent that none of these algorithms were practical when applied in a straightforward manner. In that time, a more quiet revolution took place as techniques were developed to make global illumination practical for real-world models. The authors were key players in that revolution, and this book stresses techniques that have been shown to work in the field. The approach of the book has been fine-tuned in a course on global illumination taught by the authors at the annual SIGGRAPH conference, and this has resulted in a clean progression of ideas.

Since *Advanced Global Illumination* was published, it has become my default reference for points related to advanced rendering. I also recommend it to new students at my university who need to absorb twenty years of rendering research without wading through hundreds of dense papers that often have conflicting terminology or, worse, advance concepts that have since been discredited. Rendering images with realistic illumination effects is very rewarding, and it is not hard once the basic concepts are clearly understood. This book describes all of those concepts, and it is a passport to making beautiful and realistic images. Enjoy!

Peter Shirley
May 2006

Table of Contents

Preface

This book is the result of our experience while teaching a course of the same name at the annual ACM SIGGRAPH conference during 2001 and 2002, as well as teaching various graduate-level courses and seminars covering advanced photorealistic rendering topics. When setting up these courses, we always felt that covering the fundamentals gives a much broader insight into how to design a global illumination algorithm, instead of presenting the student with a number of recipes and ready-to-compile code. By explaining the basic building blocks and underlying theory, the reader should be more able to design and implement his own photorealistic rendering algorithms.

We chose *Advanced Global Illumination* as the title because we present topics which are of a more fundamental nature than those which are usually understood by the term *global illumination* or *photorealistic rendering* by the computer graphics enthusiast. Too often, classic ray tracing with some extensions for handling area light sources, or with some heuristics added for indirect illumination, are categorized as global illumination algorithms. In order to know why such approaches fail to cover all possible illumination effects, and exactly why this is the case, it is necessary to understand the fundamental and advanced concepts of the most advanced global illumination algorithms available. The adjective "advanced" is to be read in this way. The professional researcher or Ph.D. student who spends several years of research studying global illumination algorithms may not judge the topics in this book to be "advanced" in this sense, but we think that the majority of computer graphics practitioners will discover many topics here not covered by other books.

However, this does not imply that this book only covers theoretical concepts. Various sections deal with practical issues on how to implement the different building blocks needed to build your own global illumination algorithm. We hope that the researcher, the graduate and undergraduate student, and the computer graphics enthusiast will find this book interesting to read.

We would like to thank the people from A K Peters, who have been more than helpful during the process of publishing this book, and who have been very patient and encouraging. Especially, we would like to thank Alice Peters, Heather Holcombe, and Jonathan Peters for their understanding in us taking more time to finish this manuscript than originally intended.

We would also like to thank the various research groups and institutions, at which we found the time to work on this book and who gave us the opportunity to teach computer graphics and photorealistic rendering: The Program of Computer Graphics at Cornell University, USA; the Max Planck Institut für Informatik in Saarbrücken, Germany; the Department of Computer Science at the University of Leuven, Belgium; and the Expertise Centre for Digital Media at the University of Limburg, also in Belgium.

The students in our various computer graphics courses over the past years provided us with valuable additional insight on how to adequately explain various topics related to photorealistic rendering. Student feedback in an educational setting is very worthwhile, and we wish to thank them all. We also wish to thank the attendees of our global illumination courses at the ACM SIGGRAPH conferences for the criticism and encouragement they provided.

Last but not least, we would like to thank our families and close friends, who supported us throughout the huge task of writing this book.

Philip Dutré
Philippe Bekaert
Kavita Bala

Leuven, Hasselt, and Ithaca, January 2003

Preface to the Second Edition

Since the first edition of this book was published almost three years ago, we have received quite some feedback. We were very happy to hear that *Advanced Global Illumination* has been used as a textbook in various universities and are grateful for the constructive comments from our readers.

During the last years, the field of global illumination has expanded, and as a result, some new sections have been added. Chapter 5 contains a small section about environment maps. Moreover, we extended Chapters 7 and 8 to include some of the newest developments in scalable rendering and precomputed radiance transfer.

The most significant change probably is the inclusion of exercises at the end of each chapter. We often received requests about homeworks for courses using this book, and so we included a selection of homeworks we have used ourselves during the past years.

Specifically for this second edition of the book, we would like to thank all readers who have provided us with valuable feedback and criticism. Partly due to their comments, various sections in this book have been amended and improved. We especially thank the following persons: Tomas Akenine-Möller, Andreas Baerentzen, Dave Beveridge, Bryan Cool, Jeppe Revall Frisvad, Michael Goesele, Vlastimil Havran, Magnus Jonneryd, Jaroslav Křivánek, Nelson Max, Rick Speer, Derek Young, Koen Yskout. Our apologies to anyone who has contributed but is not mentioned in this list. We would like to thank Bruce Walter for providing us with the images for the book cover.

We would like to thank all the staff at A K Peters, and in particular Alice Peters, who has provided us with the opportunity to publish a second edition of this book. Also, we especially thank our editor Kevin Jackson-Mead, who has assisted us greatly in preparing the final manuscript and managed us skillfully throughout the whole process.

All three of us would also like to thank our families and close friends for making this a rewarding and fun experience; without their support this book would not have been possible.

Philip Dutré
Kavita Bala
Philippe Bekaert

Leuven, Ithaca, and Hasselt, March 2006

1

Introduction

1.1 What Is Realistic Image Synthesis?

Realistic image synthesis is a domain in the field of computer graphics that generates new images from other data. Typically, one starts from a complete description of a three-dimensional scene, specifying the size and location of objects, the material properties of all surfaces of solid objects in the scene, and the position and emission characteristics of light sources. From this data, a new picture is generated, as seen from a virtual camera placed in the scene. The aim is to make these pictures as photorealistic as possible, such that the difference with a real photograph (if the virtual scene would be constructed in reality) is not noticeable. This requires the underlying physical processes regarding materials and the behavior of light to be precisely modeled and simulated. Only by knowing exactly what one is trying to simulate does it become possible to know where simplifications can be introduced in the simulation and how this will affect the resulting pictures.

Generating photorealistic pictures is a very ambitious goal, and it has been one of the major driving forces in computer graphics over the last decades. Visual realism has always been a strong motivation for research in this field, and it is a selling point for many graphics-related, commercially available products. It is expected that this trend will continue in the coming years and that photorealism will remain one of the core fields in rendering.

Photorealistic rendering is not the only rendering paradigm that is used in computer graphics, nor is it the best solution for all rendering applications. Especially in the last couple of years, non-photorealistic rendering has become a field in itself, providing viable alternatives for the photorealistic rendering style. Non-photorealistic rendering (or NPR, as it is commonly called) uses a wide variety of drawing styles that are suited for a more artistic, technical, or educational approach. Drawing styles covered by NPR include pen-and-ink drawings, cartoon-style drawings, technical illustrations, watercolor painting, and various artistic styles such as impressionism, pointillism, etc. The possibilities are virtually limitless, and the algorithms are driven by trying to recreate a certain style rather than by trying to simulate a physical process found in nature. While there is clearly room for NPR, a variety of applications are interested in the physical simulation of reality.

1.1.1 The Importance of Realistic Image Synthesis

Photorealistic rendering is a rendering style that has many applications in various fields. Early applications were limited by the amount of time it took to compute a single image (usually measured in hours), but recently, interactive techniques have broadened the scope of photorealistic image synthesis considerably.

Film and Visual Effects

Visual effects in the film industry have always been a driving force for the development of new computer graphics techniques. Depending on the rendering style used, feature animations can benefit from global illumination rendering, although this might be limited to a few scenes where more complex lighting configurations are used. Movies with live footage can benefit too, especially when virtual elements are added. In this case, a consistent lighting between the real and virtual elements in the same shot needs to be achieved, in order to avoid implausible lighting effects. Global illumination is necessary to compute the light interaction between those different elements.

Architecture

Architectural design is often quoted as one of the most beneficial applications of photorealistic rendering. It is possible to make visualizations, whether they be still images or interactive walk-throughs, of buildings yet to be constructed. Not only can indoor illumination due to interior lighting be simulated, but outdoor lighting can be considered as well, e.g., the building can be illuminated using various atmospheric conditions at different times of the year, or even various times during the day.

Ergonomic Design of Buildings and Offices

Although not strictly a computer graphics application, the ergonomic design of office rooms or factory halls is very much related to global illumination. Given the design of a building, it is possible to compute the various illumination levels in different parts of the building (e.g., desks, workstations, etc.), and the necessary adjustments can be made to reach the minimum legal or comfortable requirements by changing the color of paint on the walls, the repositioning of windows, or even the replacement of walls.

Computer Games

Most computer games revolve around fast and interactive action, coupled with a suspension of disbelief in a virtual world. As such, photorealistic rendered imagery probably is a strong cue to draw players into the environments in which their virtual characters are acting. Since interactivity is more important in a gaming context than realistic images, the use of global illumination in games is still somewhat limited but will undoubtedly become more important in the near future.

Lighting Engineering

The design of lights and light fixtures can also benefit from global illumination algorithms. Specific designs can be simulated in virtual environments, such that the effect of the emission patterns of light bulbs can be studied. This requires an accurate measurement and modeling of the characteristics of the emission of the light sources, which is a whole field of study by itself.

Predictive Simulations

Predictive simulations encompass much more than just simulating the look of buildings as described above. Other areas of design are important as well: car design, appliances, consumer electronics, furniture, etc. This all involves designing an object and then simulating how it will look in a real or virtual environment.

Flight and Car Simulators

Simulators used for training, such as flight and car simulators, benefit from having an as accurate as possible visual simulation, e.g., aspects of street lighting are important in car simulators, accurate atmospheric visual simulation is important when designing a flight simulator, etc. Other types of training simulators also use or might use realistic imagery in the future; armed combat, ship navigation, and sports are a few examples.

Advertising

Producing accurate imagery of yet-to-be-produced products is probably a good tool for the advertising world. Not only does the customer have the ability to see what the product looks like when generated using photorealistic rendering, but he would benefit if he could place the product in a known environment, e.g., furniture could be placed, with consistent illumination, in a picture of your own living room.

1.1.2   History of Photorealistic Rendering

This section provides a brief history of photorealistic rendering algorithms and the quest for visual realism. Some more extensive background and history on specific algorithms can also be found in the relevant chapters.

Photorealism in the Precomputer Age

The history of photorealistic rendering, or the quest for visual realism, can be traced throughout the history of art. Although we are mainly interested here in the computer-driven photorealistic rendering programs, it might be useful to look at how the understanding of realistic rendering evolved in the course of history. Medieval and premedieval art is very much iconic in nature: persons and objects are displayed in simplified, often two-dimensional forms, and sizes and shapes are used to reflect the importance of the person displayed, relative positioning in a scene, or other properties.

The real beginning of realistic rendering probably starts with the first use and study of perspective drawings. Especially in Italy during the Renaissance period, various artists were involved in discovering the laws of perspective. Brunelleschi (1377–1446), da Vinci (1452–1519), and Dürer (1471–1528) (to name a few) are well known for their contributions. Later, painters also started to pay attention to the shading aspects. By carefully studying shadows and light reflections, very accurate renderings of real scenes could be produced using classic artistic materials.

Much of the knowledge of photorealistic painting was collected by British landscape artist Joseph Turner (1775–1851), appointed Professor of Perspective at the Royal Academy of Arts in London. He designed a course of six lectures, covering principles such as accurate drawing of light, reflections, and refractions. Some of his sketches show reflections in mirrored and transparent spheres, a true precursor of ray tracing almost 300 years later. In his book, *Secret Knowledge*, British artist David Hockney [73] develops an interesting thesis: Starting in the 15th century, artists began using optical tools to display reality very accurately. Mostly using a camera lucida, they projected imagery onto the canvas and traced the silhouettes and outlines very carefully. Afterwards, several such drawings were composed in a bigger painting, which explains the different perspectives found in various well-known paintings of the era.

It is certainly no coincidence that the trend and developments towards more photorealism in art were somewhat halted with the invention of photography at the beginning of the 19th century (Nicéphore Niépce, 1765–1833). Capturing an image accurately is suddenly not a difficult process anymore. After the invention of photography, art evolved into modern art, with its various novel ways, not necessarily photorealism, of looking at reality (pointillism, impressionism, cubism, etc.).

Primitive Shading Algorithms

The birth of computer graphics is usually accredited to *SketchPad* [188], the Ph.D. thesis of Ivan Sutherland at the Massachusetts Institute of Technology (M.I.T.) in 1963. Early computer graphics were mostly line drawings, but with the advent of raster graphics, shading algorithms became widely available. Primitive shading algorithms usually attributed a single color to a single polygon, the color being determined by the incident angle of light on the surface. This type of shading gives some cues about shape and orientation but is far away from realistically illuminated objects.

A breakthrough was achieved by Henri Gouraud and Bui Tui Phong, who realized that by interpolation schemes, additional realism in shading can be easily achieved. Gouraud shading [58] computes illumination values at vertices and interpolates these values over the area of a polygon. Phong shading [147] interpolates the normal vectors over the area of a polygon and computes illumination values afterwards, thus better preserving highlights caused by nondiffuse reflection functions. Both techniques are longstanding shading algorithms in computer graphics and are still widely used.

Another major breakthrough for more realism in computer-generated imagery was the use of texture mapping. Using a local two-dimensional coordinate system on an object, it is possible to index a texture map and attribute a color to the local coordinate. Integration in the rendering process involves a two-dimensional coordinate transform from the local coordinate system on the object to the local coordinate system of the texture map. Once texture mapping was able to change the color of points on a surface, it was fairly straightforward to change other attributes as well. Thus, the techniques of bumpmapping, displacement mapping, environment mapping, etc., were added. Texturing remains one of the building blocks for rendering in general.

Additional research was also performed in the area of light-source modeling. Originally only point light sources or directional light sources were used in the earliest rendering algorithms, but fairly soon spotlights, directional lights, and other types of light sources, sometimes emulating those found in lighting design, were introduced. Together with the modeling of light sources, the accurate portrayal of shadows has received much attention. When using point light sources, the computation of shadows can be reduced to a simple visibility problem from a single point of view, but the shadows are sharp and hard. The use of shadow volumes and shadow maps are among the best-known algorithms and still receive attention for improvement.

Ray Tracing

In 1980, *ray tracing*, probably the most popular algorithm in rendering, was introduced by Turner Whitted [194]. Although the principle of tracing rays was used before to generate correct perspective and shadows in the conventional arts, the tracing of rays in computer graphics was a major idea for generating all sorts of photorealistic effects. The original paper used rays for determining visibility through a single pixel (also known as *ray casting*) but also used rays to compute direct illumination and perfect specular and refractive illumination effects. As such, this seminal paper described a major new tool in generating images.

The ray-tracing algorithm has been researched and implemented extensively during the last two decades. Initially, much attention was on efficiency, using well-known techniques such as spatial subdivision and bounding volumes. More and more, the focus was also on lighting effects themselves. By treating ray tracing as a tool for computing integrals, effects such as diffuse reflections and refractions, motion blur, lens effects, etc. could be computed within a single framework. For a nice overview, the reader is referred to [52].

The original paper did not solve the entire global illumination problem but was very influential for later developments. To make a distinction with more modern ray-tracing algorithms, the first algorithm is sometimes referred to as *Whitted-style ray tracing* or *classic ray tracing*. Many present-day global illumination algorithms at the core are ray tracers, in the sense that the basic tool still is a procedure that traces a ray through a three-dimensional scene.

Since a basic ray tracer is rather easy to implement, it is a very popular algorithm to serve as the first step into photorealistic rendering. It is traditional to have undergraduate students implement a ray tracer in many graphics courses. Many computer graphics enthusiasts post their ray tracers on the internet, and many of the more popular rendering packages have ray-tracing roots.

Radiosity

With ray tracing being well underway in the first half of the eighties as the algorithm of choice for realistic rendering, it became clear that ray tracing also had severe limitations. Indirect illumination effects such as color bleeding and diffuse reflections were very difficult to simulate. It was clear that a solution needed to be found if one wanted to produce photorealistic pictures. The answer came in the form of a finite-element method called *radiosity*, named after the radiometric quantity that was computed. The algorithm was developed originally at Cornell University

[56] but, as was the case with ray tracing, spawned many research papers and received lots of attention.

One of the early advantages of radiosity was that it was a scene-based method, as opposed to ray tracing, which is an image-based method. In radiosity, the distribution of light is computed by subdividing the scene into surface elements and computing for each element the correct radiometric value. Once the radiosity value for each surface element was known, the solution could be displayed with existing graphics hardware, using Gouraud shading for smoothing out the radiosity values computed at each vertex or polygon. This made radiosity an algorithm of choice for interactive applications such as scene walk-throughs.

Early radiosity research was centered around computing a faster solution for the linear system of equations that expressed the equilibrium of the light distribution in the scene. Several relaxation techniques were introduced and more or less subdivided the radiosity solvers into *"gathering"* and *"shooting"* algorithms.

Early on, radiosity was limited to diffuse surfaces, and the accuracy of the method was set by the choice of surface elements. Finer details in the shading at a frequency higher than the initial mesh could not be displayed. Hierarchical radiosity proved to be a major step forwards, since the algorithm was now able to adapt its underlying solution mesh to the actual shading values found on those surfaces. Discontinuity meshing was similarly used to precompute accurate meshes that followed the discontinuity lines between umbra and penumbra regions caused by area light sources. The algorithm was also extended by subdividing the hemisphere around surfaces in a mesh as well, such that glossy surfaces could also be handled. On the other side of hierarchical radiosity, clustering algorithms were introduced to compute the illumination for disjunct objects in single clusters. Overall, radiosity has received wide attention comparable to ray tracing but, due to the somewhat more complex underlying mathematics, has not been as popular.

The Rendering Equation

One of the most important concepts for global illumination algorithms, the rendering equation, was introduced by Kajiya in 1986 [85], although in a different form than is used today. In this seminal paper, for the first time, the complete transport equation describing the distribution of light in a scene was described in a computer graphics context. The importance of the rendering equation is that all light transport mechanisms are described using a recursive integral equation, whose kernel contains the various material properties and the visibility function.

Formulating the global illumination problem as the rendering equation allows for a unified approach when computing images. It now became possible to apply any sort of integration mechanism to numerically evaluate the rendering equation. Also, because the recursive nature of the rendering equation required recursive algorithms, and thus stopping conditions, it was more obvious which successive light reflections were ignored, approximated only up to a certain depth, etc. Also, ray-tracing and radiosity algorithms could now be considered as different integration procedures trying to solve the rendering equation. Ray tracing basically could be written down as a succession of recursive quadrature rules, and radiosity algorithms expressed a finite element solution to the same equation.

One of the most influential consequences of the rendering equation was the development of stochastic ray tracing or Monte Carlo ray tracing. Monte Carlo integration schemes use random numbers to evaluate integrals, but they have the nice property that the expected value of the result equals the exact value of the integral. Thus, it became possible, in theory, to compute correct photorealistic images, assuming the algorithm ran long enough.

Multipass Methods

At the end of the eighties, there were two big families of global illumination algorithms: those that used a ray-tracing approach, computing a single color for every pixel on the screen, and those that were based on the radiosity approach, computing a scene-based solution, only generating an image as a post-process. The first class of algorithms is good for mostly specular and refractive indirect illumination, while the second class is better suited for computing diffuse interreflections and allows interactive manipulation.

It was therefore inevitable that a *"best-of-both-worlds"* approach would be developed, using ray tracing and radiosity characteristics in the same algorithm. These algorithms usually consist of multiple passes, hence the name *multipass methods*. Many different variants have been published (e.g., [24], [209], [171]). A multipass method usually consists of a radiosity pass computing the indirect diffuse illumination, followed by a ray-tracing pass computing the specular light transport, while picking up radiosity values from the first pass. Care has to be taken that some light transport modes are not computed twice, otherwise the image would be too bright in some areas. More than two passes are possible, each pass dedicated to computing a specific aspect of the total light transport.

Algorithms that store partial solutions of the light distribution in the scene, such as the *RADIANCE* algorithm [219] or photon mapping, can be considered multipass algorithms as well. The photon mapping algorithm has especially received a lot of attention in research literature and is widely considered to be an efficient and accurate algorithm to solve the global illumination problem.

Current Developments

Currently, lots of attention is given to interactive applications using global illumination algorithms. These usually involve a clever combination of storage and reuse of partial solutions, multipass algorithms, etc.

Also, more and more use is made of photographs of real objects or scenes, which are integrated into virtual environments. The problem is that one wants to keep a consistent illumination, and image-based lighting techniques have proposed some elegant solutions.

As far as the authors can see, global illumination and photorealistic rendering will likely remain a major influence in computer graphics developments of the future.

1.1.3 A Framework for Global Illumination Algorithms

When looking at the development of global illumination algorithms over the past 20 years, one sees a collection of widely different approaches, as well as variants of the same approach. Especially for the light transport simulation, one can make a distinction between different paradigms: pixel-oriented versus scene-oriented, diffuse versus specular surfaces, deterministic versus Monte Carlo integration, shooting versus gathering, etc. These differences are important because they affect the accuracy of the final image, but a wider framework for a complete global illumination pipeline also involves other aspects such as data acquisition and image display.

A framework for realistic image synthesis that combines these different aspects was described in a paper by the same name by Greenberg et al. [59]. The framework presented in this paper encompasses different aspects of a full photorealistic rendering system and provides a general overview of how photorealistic rendering algorithms have evolved over time.

A photorealistic rendering system can be thought of as consisting of three main stages: measurement and acquisition of scene data, the light transport simulation, and the visual display.

Measurement and Acquisition

This part of the framework includes measuring and modeling the BRDF of materials to be used in the virtual scene, as well as emission characteristics of light sources. By comparing the goniometric data, one is able to verify the accuracy of the models and measurements.

Light Transport

The light transport phase takes the data describing the geometry of the
scene, materials, and light sources and computes the distribution of light
in the scene. This is the main bulk of what is usually called a global
illumination algorithm. The result is radiometric values in the image plane,
which can be verified by, for example, comparing real photographs with
computed pictures.

Visual Display

The matrix of radiometric values needs to be displayed on a screen or
printer. A tone-mapping operator is necessary to transform the raw radiometric data into pixel colors. This transformation uses a model of the
human visual system, such that the same visual sensation is caused by
looking at the displayed picture as by looking at the real scene.

If it is known what error can be tolerated in last stage, this error can
be translated into tolerances for the light transport phase, and eventually
to the measurement phase. The critical notion of this framework is that
perceptual accuracy on the part of the human observer, not radiometric
accuracy, should be the driving force when designing algorithms.

1.2 Structure of this Book

As mentioned before, the content of this book is geared towards understanding the fundamental principles of global illumination algorithms. The
division of the content into several chapters reflects this. We strongly believe that only by treating the fundamental and basic building blocks in
a thorough way can a full understanding of photorealistic rendering be
achieved.

The chapters are organized as follows:

- Chapter 1 provides a general introduction to global illumination, outlines the importance of global illumination in the field of computer
  graphics, and provides a short history of global illumination algorithms.

- Radiometry and the rendering equation are covered in Chapter 2.
  A good understanding of radiometry is necessary for understanding
  global illumination algorithms. We only cover those aspects that we
  need to design global illumination software. The characteristics and
  nature of the bidirectional reflectance distribution function (BRDF)

are covered in detail, as well as how the definition of the BRDF gives rise to the rendering equation.

- Chapter 3 explains the principle of Monte Carlo integration, a versatile technique that is used in almost all recent global illumination algorithms. The key concepts are explained, but again, only to the level that we need to understand and adequately explain the chapters that follow.

- Chapter 4 puts the rendering equation in a somewhat broader context and gives some general insights into several strategies on how a global illumination algorithm can be designed.

- Chapter 5 gives all the details about stochastic ray tracing. Starting from the rendering equation and using Monte Carlo integration as a tool, several algorithms are deduced for computing various lighting effects. Special attention is given to the computation of direct illumination.

- Stochastic radiosity is covered in Chapter 6 and complements the previous chapter. It offers a very profound overview on the various Monte Carlo radiosity approaches that matured only recently.

- Chapter 7 provides an overview of hybrid methods, which builds on the principles of stochastic ray tracing and radiosity. Various algorithms are explained in detail, with references for further study.

- Chapter 8 covers a number of topics that receive attention in current research, including participating media, subsurface scattering, tone mapping, human visual perception, and strategies for computing global illumination very rapidly.

- Appendix A describes an API for global illumination, a set of object classes that encapsulates and hides the technical details of material and geometry representation and ray casting. This API allows concise and efficient implementations of the algorithms discussed in this book. An example implementation of a light tracer, a path tracer, and a bidirectional path tracer are given.

- Appendix B gives a review of solid angles and hemispherical geometry.

- Appendix C contains technical details omitted from Chapter 6.

1.3   How to Use this Book

This book is the result of teaching various classes about advanced rendering algorithms, and we think that if this book is used as a textbook, it should be a course at the graduate level.

Students that wish to take a class that uses this book should have taken at least one other computer graphics course. One course might be a general introduction to computer graphics, while another course might be project-oriented and focus on some aspects of animation, ray tracing, or modeling. Also, familiarity with probability theory and calculus is required, since otherwise the concepts of the rendering equation and Monte Carlo integration will be hard to explain. Some knowledge about physics might help, although we usually found it was not strictly necessary.

We have added exercises to each chapter in this edition. These exercises are based on assignments we have used ourselves when teaching this course at the graduate level and so have gone through some scrutiny as to whether they have the appropriate difficulty level.

In all of our assignments for our own courses, we provided the students with a basic ray-tracing framework. This skeleton ray tracer is kept very simple, such that the focus can be put entirely on implementing physically correct algorithms. Having the students themselves implement a (basic) ray tracer from scratch is, in our opinion, not a good assignment, since students will be mostly bothered by the nuts and bolts of ray-object intersections, parsing an input file, image viewing, etc.

In case the instructor wants to put together his or her own assignments, here are some suggestions based on our experience:

- Homework 1 might include some problems on radiometry to make students familiar with the concepts of radiometry and make them think about the definition of radiance. A typical exercise could be to compute the radiance reaching earth from the sun, or the radiosity value incident on a square surface under various conditions.

- Homework 2 could be a programming exercise in which students are provided with a basic ray-tracing program. The students would then have to add a specific BRDF model and render a few pictures.

- Homework 3 would extend on the ray tracer from Homework 2. Students could be allowed to add specific lighting effects, such as various ways of computing direct illumination. Also, they could be asked to experiment with different sampling techniques and see what the effect is on the resulting images.

- A number of problems about which global illumination algorithm to use in specific situations could be the subject of Homework 4. For example, scenes could be given with a high number of light sources, a significant amount of specular materials, some unusual geometric configuration, etc. This could be a written exercise, in which the student does not necessarily have to implement his or her ideas, but merely sketch them on paper. Thus, students can design any algorithm they wish without the burden of actually implementing it.

- Studying and presenting a recent research paper would be a good topic for Homework 5 and would also be a good conclusion of the entire course.

Additionally, various problems discussed in the different chapters can be used as homework assignments or can serve as a problem to start a class discussion.

2

The Physics of Light Transport

The goal of rendering algorithms is to create images that accurately represent the appearance of objects in scenes. For every pixel in an image, these algorithms must find the objects that are visible at that pixel and then display their "appearance" to the user. What does the term "appearance" mean? What quantity of light energy must be measured to capture "appearance"? How is this energy computed? These are the questions that this chapter will address.

In this chapter, we present key concepts and definitions required to formulate the problem that global illumination algorithms must solve. In Section 2.1, we present a brief history of optics to motivate the basic assumptions that rendering algorithms make about the behavior of light (Section 2.2). In Section 2.3, we define radiometric terms and their relations to each other. Section 2.4 describes the sources of lights in scenes; in Section 2.5, we present the bidirectional distribution function, which captures the interaction of light with surfaces. Using these definitions, we present the rendering equation in Section 2.6, a mathematical formulation of the equilibrium distribution of light energy in a scene. We also formulate the notion of importance in Section 2.7. Finally, in Section 2.8, we present the measurement equation, which is the equation that global illumination algorithms must solve to compute images. In the rest of this book, we will discuss how global illumination algorithms solve the measurement equation.

2.1 Brief History

The history of the science of optics spans about three thousand years of human history. We briefly summarize relevant events based mostly on the history included by Hecht and Zajac in their book *Optics* [68]. The Greek philosophers (around 350 B.C.), including Pythagoras, Democritus, Empedocles, Plato, and Aristotle among others, evolved theories of the nature of light. In fact, Aristotle's theories were quite similar to the ether theory of the nineteenth century. However, the Greeks incorrectly believed that vision involved emanations from the eye to the object perceived. By 300 B.C. the rectilinear propagation of light was known, and Euclid described the law of reflection. Cleomedes (50 A.D.) and Ptolemy (130 A.D.) did early work on studying the phenomenon of refraction.

The field of optics stayed mostly dormant during the Dark Ages with the exception of the contribution of Ibn-al-Haitham (also known as Al-hazen); Al-hazen refined the law of reflection specifying that the angles of incidence and reflection lie in the same plane, normal to the interface. In fact, except for the contributions of Robert Grosseteste (1175–1253) and Roger Bacon (1215–1294) the field of optics did not see major activity until the seventeenth century.

Optics became an exciting area of research again with the invention of telescopes and microscopes early in the seventeenth century. In 1611, Johannes Kepler discovered total internal reflection and described the small angle approximation to the law of refraction. In 1621, Willebrord Snell made a major discovery: the *law of refraction*; the formulation of this law in terms of sines was later published by René Descartes. In 1657, Pierre de Fermat rederived the law of refraction from his own *principle of least time*, which states that a ray of light follows the path that takes it to its destination in the shortest time.

Diffraction, the phenomenon where light "bends" around obstructing objects, was observed by Grimaldi (1618–1683) and Hooke (1635–1703). Hooke first proposed the wave theory of light to explain this behavior. Christian Huygens (1629–1695) considerably extended on the wave theory of light. He was able to derive the laws of reflection and refraction using this theory; he also discovered the phenomenon of *polarization* during his experiments.

Contemporaneously, Isaac Newton (1642–1727) observed *dispersion*, where white light splits into its component colors when it passes through a prism. He concluded that sunlight is composed of light of different colors, which are refracted by glass to different extents. Newton, over the course of his research, increasingly embraced the emission (corpuscular) theory of light over the wave theory.

Thus, in the beginning of the nineteenth century, there were two conflicting theories of the behavior of light: the particle (emission/corpuscular) theory and the wave theory. In 1801, Thomas Young described his *principle of interference* based on his famous double-slit experiment, thus providing experimental support for the wave theory of light. However, due to the weight of Newton's influence, his theory was not well-received. Independently, in 1816, Augustin Jean Fresnel presented a rigorous treatment of diffraction and interference phenomena showing that these phenomena can be explained in terms of the wave theory of light. In 1821, Fresnel presented the laws that enable the intensity and polarization of reflected and refracted light to be calculated.

Independently, in the field of electricity and magnetism, Maxwell (1831–1879) summarized and extended the empirical knowledge on these subjects into a single set of mathematical equations. Maxwell concluded that light is a form of electromagnetic wave. However, in 1887, Hertz accidentally discovered the *photoelectric effect*: the process whereby electrons are liberated from materials under the action of radiant energy. This effect could not be explained by the wave model of light. Other properties of light also remained inexplicable in the wave model: black body radiation (the spectrum of light emitted by a heated body), the wavelength dependency of the absorption of light by various materials, fluorescence[1], and phosphorescence[2], among others. Thus, despite all the supporting evidence for the wave nature of light, the particle behavior of light had to be explained.

In 1900, Max Karl Planck introduced a universal constant called Planck's constant to explain the spectrum of radiation emitted from a hot black body: black body radiation. His work inspired Albert Einstein, who, in 1905, explained the photoelectric effect based on the notion that light consists of a stream of quantized energy packets. Each quantum was later called a photon. Each photon has a frequency ν associated with it. The energy associated with a photon is $E = \hbar\nu$, where $\hbar$ is Planck's constant.

The seemingly conflicting behavior of light as a stream of particles and waves was only reconciled by the establishment of the field of *quantum mechanics*. By considering submicroscopic phenomena, researchers such as Bohr, Born, Heisenberg, Schrödinger, Pauli, de Broglie, Dirac, and others were able to explain the dual nature of light. Quantum field theory and quantum electrodynamics further explained high-energy phenomena; Richard Feynman's book on quantum electrodynamics (QED) [49] gives an intuitive description of the field.

2.2 Models of Light

The models of light used in simulations try to capture the different behaviors of light that arise from its dual nature: certain phenomena, for example, diffraction and interference, can be explained by assuming that

---

[1]Fluorescence is the phenomenon by which light absorbed at one frequency is emitted at a different frequency.

[2]Phosphorescence is the phenomenon by which light absorbed at one frequency at some time is emitted at a different frequency and time.

light is a wave; other behavior, such as the photoelectric effect, can be better explained by assuming that light consists of a stream of particles.

2.2.1 Quantum Optics

Quantum optics is the fundamental model of light that explains its dual wave-particle nature. The quantum optics model can explain the behavior of light at the submicroscopic level, for example, at the level of electrons. However, this model is generally considered to be too detailed for the purposes of image generation for typical computer graphics scenes and is not commonly used.

2.2.2 Wave Model

The wave model, a simplification of the quantum model, is described by Maxwell's equations. This model captures effects, such as diffraction, interference, and polarization, that arise when light interacts with objects of size comparable to the wavelength of light. These effects can be observed in everyday scenes, for example, in the bright colors seen in oil slicks or birds' feathers. However, for the purposes of image generation in computer graphics, the wave nature of light is also typically ignored.

2.2.3 Geometric Optics

The geometric optics model is the simplest and most commonly used model of light in computer graphics. In this model, the wavelength of light is assumed to be much smaller than the scale of the objects that the light interacts with. The geometric optics model assumes that light is emitted, reflected, and transmitted. In this model, several assumptions are made about the behavior of light:

- Light travels in straight lines, i.e., effects such as diffraction where light "bends around" objects are not considered.

- Light travels instantaneously through a medium; this assumption essentially requires light to unrealistically travel at infinite speed. However, it is a practical assumption because it requires global illumination algorithms to compute the steady-state distribution of light energy in scenes.

- Light is not influenced by external factors, such as gravity or magnetic fields.

In most of this book, we ignore effects that arise due to the transmission of light through participating media (for example, fog). We also do not consider media with varying indices of refraction. For example, mirage-like effects that arise due to varying indices of refraction caused by temperature differentials in the air are not considered. How to deal with these phenomena is discussed in Section 8.1.

2.3 Radiometry

The goal of a global illumination algorithm is to compute the steady-state distribution of light energy in a scene. To compute this distribution, we need an understanding of the physical quantities that represent light energy. Radiometry is the area of study involved in the physical measurement of light. This section gives a brief overview of the radiometric units used in global illumination algorithms.

It is useful to consider the relation between radiometry and photometry. Photometry is the area of study that deals with the quantification of the perception of light energy. The human visual system is sensitive to light in the frequency range of 380 nanometers to 780 nanometers. The sensitivity of the human eye across this visible spectrum has been standardized; photometric terms take this standardized response into account. Since photometric quantities can be derived from the corresponding radiometric terms, global illumination algorithms operate on radiometric terms. However, Section 8.2 will talk about how the radiometric quantities computed by global illumination algorithms are displayed to an observer.

2.3.1 Radiometric Quantities

Radiant Power or Flux

The fundamental radiometric quantity is radiant power, also called flux. Radiant power, often denoted as Φ, is expressed in watts (W) (joules/sec). This quantity expresses how much total energy flows from/to/through a surface per unit time. For example, we can say that a light source emits 50 watts of radiant power, or that 20 watts of radiant power is incident on a table. Note that flux does not specify the size of the light source or the receiver (table), nor does it include a specification of the distance between the light source and the receiver.

Irradiance

Irradiance (E) is the incident radiant power on a surface, per unit surface area. It is expressed in watts/m^2:

$$E = \frac{d\Phi}{dA}. \tag{2.1}$$

For example, if 50 watts of radiant power is incident on a surface that has an area of 1.25 m^2, the irradiance at each surface point is 40 watts/m^2 (assuming the incident power is uniformly distributed over the surface).

Radiant Exitance or Radiosity

Radiant exitance (M), also called radiosity (B), is the exitant radiant power per unit surface area and is also expressed in watts/m^2:

$$M = B = \frac{d\Phi}{dA}. \tag{2.2}$$

For example, consider a light source, of area 0.1 m^2, that emits 100 watts. Assuming that the power is emitted uniformly over the area of the light source, the radiant exitance of the light is 1000 W/m^2 at each point of its surface.

Radiance

Radiance is flux per unit projected area per unit solid angle (watts/(steradian $\cdot$ m^2)). Intuitively, radiance expresses how much power arrives at (or leaves from) a certain point on a surface, per unit solid angle, and per unit projected area. Appendix B gives a review of solid angles and hemispherical geometry.

Radiance is a five-dimensional quantity that varies with position x and direction vector Θ, and is expressed as $L(x, \Theta)$ (see Figure 2.1):

$$L = \frac{d^2\Phi}{d\omega dA^\perp} = \frac{d^2\Phi}{d\omega dA \cos\theta}. \tag{2.3}$$

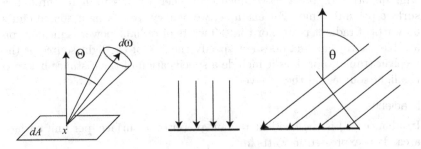

Figure 2.1. Definition of radiance $L(x, \Theta)$: flux per unit projected area $dA^\perp$ per unit solid angle $d\omega$.

Radiance is probably the most important quantity in global illumination algorithms because it is the quantity that captures the "appearance" of objects in the scene. Section 2.3.3 explains the properties of radiance that are relevant to image generation.

Intuition for cosine term. The projected area $A^\perp$ is the area of the surface projected perpendicular to the direction we are interested in. This stems from the fact that power arriving at a grazing angle is "smeared out" over a larger surface. Since we explicitly want to express power per (unit) projected area and per (unit) direction, we have to take the larger area into account, and that is where the cosine term comes from. Another intuition for this term is obtained by drawing insights from transport theory.

Transport Theory

This section uses concepts from transport theory to intuitively explain the relations between different radiometric terms (see Chapter 2, [29]). Transport theory deals with the transport or flow of physical quantities such as energy, charge, and mass. In this section, we use transport theory to formulate radiometric quantities in terms of the flow of "light particles" or "photons."

Let us assume we are given the density of light particles, $p(x)$, which defines the number of particles per unit volume at some position x. The number of particles in a small volume dV is $p(x)dV$. Let us consider the flow of these light particles in some time dt across some differential surface area dA. Assume that the velocity of the light particles is $\vec{c}$, where $|\vec{c}|$ is the speed of light and the direction of $\vec{c}$ is the direction along which the particles are flowing. Initially, we assume that the differential surface area dA is perpendicular to the flow of particles. Given these assumptions, in time dt, the particles that flow across the area dA are all the particles included in a volume $cdtdA$. The number of particles flowing across the surface is $p(x)cdtdA$.

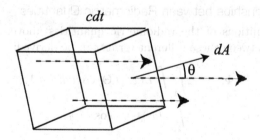

Figure 2.2. Flow of particles across a surface.

We now relax the assumption that the particle flow is perpendicular to the surface area dA (as shown in Figure 2.2). If the angle between the flow of the particles and dA is θ, the perpendicular area across which the particles flow is $dA \cos \theta$. Now, the number of particles flowing across the surface is $p(x)cdtdA \cos \theta$.

The derivation above assumed a fixed direction of flow. Including all possible directions (and all possible wavelengths) along which the particles can flow gives the following number of particles N that flow across an area dA,

$$N = p(x, \omega, \lambda)cdtdA \cos \theta d\omega d\lambda,$$

where $d\omega$ is a differential direction (or solid angle) along which particles flow and the density function p varies with both position and direction.

Flux is defined as the energy of the particles per unit time. In this treatment, flux is computed by dividing the number of particles by dt and computing the limit as dt goes to zero:

$$\Phi \propto p(x, \omega, \lambda)dA \cos \theta d\omega d\lambda,$$

$$\frac{\Phi}{dA \cos \theta d\omega} \propto p(x, \omega, \lambda)d\lambda.$$

Let us assume these particles are photons. Each photon has energy $E = \hbar \nu$. The wavelength of light λ is related to its frequency by the following relation: $\lambda = c/\nu$, where c is the speed of light in vacuum. Therefore, $E = \frac{\hbar c}{\lambda}$. Nicodemus [131] defined radiance as the radiant energy per unit volume, as follows:

$$L(x, \omega) = \int p(x, \omega, \lambda)\hbar \frac{c}{\lambda}d\lambda.$$

Relating this equation with the definition of Φ above, we get a more intuitive notion of how flux relates to radiance, and why the cosine term arises in the definition of radiance.

2.3.2 Relationships between Radiometric Quantities

Given the definitions of the radiometric quantities above, the following relationships between these different terms can be derived:

$$\Phi = \int_A \int_\Omega L(x \rightarrow \Theta) \cos \theta d\omega_\Theta dA_x, \tag{2.4}$$

$$E(x) = \int_\Omega L(x \leftarrow \Theta) \cos \theta d\omega_\Theta, \tag{2.5}$$

$$B(x) = \int_\Omega L(x \rightarrow \Theta) \cos \theta d\omega_\Theta, \tag{2.6}$$

where A is the total surface area and Ω is the total solid angle at each point on the surface.

We use the following notation in this book: $L(x \rightarrow \Theta)$ represents radiance leaving point x in direction Θ. $L(x \leftarrow \Theta)$ represents radiance arriving at point x from direction Θ.

Wavelength Dependency

The radiometric measures and quantities described above are not only dependent on position and direction but are also dependent on the wavelength of light energy. When wavelength is explicitly specified, for example, for radiance, the corresponding radiometric quantity is called spectral radiance. The units of spectral radiance are the units of radiance divided by meters (the unit of wavelength). Radiance is computed by integrating spectral radiance over the wavelength domain covering visible light. For example,

$$L(x \rightarrow \Theta) = \int_{spectrum} L(x \rightarrow \Theta, \lambda)d\lambda.$$

The wavelength dependency of radiometric terms is often implicitly assumed to be part of the global illumination equations and is not mentioned explicitly.

2.3.3 Properties of Radiance

Radiance is a fundamental radiometric quantity for the purposes of image generation. As seen in Equations 2.4–2.6, other radiometric terms, such as flux, irradiance, and radiosity, can be derived from radiance. The following properties of radiance explain why radiance is important for image generation.

Property 1: Radiance is invariant along straight paths.

Mathematically, the property of the invariance of radiance is expressed as

$$L(x \rightarrow y) = L(y \leftarrow x),$$

which states that the radiance leaving point x directed towards point y is equal to the radiance arriving at point y from the point x. This property assumes that light is traveling through a vacuum, i.e., there is no participating medium.

This important property follows from the conservation of light energy in a small pencil of rays between two differential surfaces at x and y, respectively. Figure 2.3 shows the geometry of the surfaces. From the definition of radiance, the total (differential) power leaving a differential surface area dA_x, and arriving at a differential surface area dA_y, can be written as

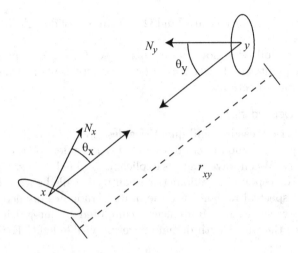

Figure 2.3. Invariance of radiance.

$$L(x \rightarrow y) \;=\; \frac{d^2\Phi}{(\cos\theta_x dA_x)d\omega_{x \leftarrow dA_y}}; \qquad (2.7)$$

$$d^2\Phi \;=\; L(x \rightarrow y)\cos\theta_x d\omega_{x \leftarrow dA_y} dA_x, \qquad (2.8)$$

where we use the notation that $d\omega_{x \leftarrow dA_y}$ is the solid angle subtended by dA_y as seen from x.

The power that arrives at area dA_y from area dA_x can be expressed in a similar way:

$$L(y \leftarrow x) \;=\; \frac{d^2\Phi}{(\cos\theta_y dA_y)d\omega_{y \leftarrow dA_x}}; \qquad (2.9)$$

$$d^2\Phi \;=\; L(y \leftarrow x)\cos\theta_y d\omega_{y \leftarrow dA_x} dA_y. \qquad (2.10)$$

The differential solid angles are:

$$d\omega_{x \leftarrow dA_y} = \frac{\cos\theta_y dA_y}{r_{xy}^2};$$

$$d\omega_{y \leftarrow dA_x} = \frac{\cos\theta_x dA_x}{r_{xy}^2}.$$

We assume that there are no external light sources adding to the power arriving at dA_y. We also assume that the two differential surfaces are in a vacuum; therefore, there is no energy loss due to the presence of participating media. Then, by the law of conservation of energy, all energy leaving dA_x in the direction of the surface dA_y must arrive at dA_y,

$$L(x \rightarrow y) \cos \theta_x d\omega_{x \leftarrow dA_y} dA_x = L(y \leftarrow x) \cos \theta_y d\omega_{y \leftarrow dA_x} dA_y;$$

$$L(x \rightarrow y) \cos \theta_x \frac{\cos \theta_y dA_y}{r_{xy}^2} dA_x = L(y \leftarrow x) \cos \theta_y \frac{\cos \theta_x dA_x}{r_{xy}^2} dA_y,$$

and thus,

$$L(x \rightarrow y) = L(y \leftarrow x). \tag{2.11}$$

Therefore, radiance is invariant along straight paths of travel and does not attenuate with distance. This property of radiance is only valid in the absence of participating media, which can absorb and scatter energy between the two surfaces.

From the above observation, it follows that once incident or exitant radiance at all surface points is known, the radiance distribution for all points in a three-dimensional scene is also known. Almost all algorithms used in global illumination limit themselves to computing the radiance values at surface points (still assuming the absence of any participating medium). Radiance at surface points is referred to as surface radiance by some authors, whereas radiance for general points in three-dimensional space is sometimes called field radiance.

Property 2: Sensors, such as cameras and the human eye, are sensitive to radiance.

The response of sensors (for example, cameras or the human eye) is proportional to the radiance incident upon them, where the constant of proportionality depends on the geometry of the sensor.

These two properties explain why the perceived color or brightness of an object does not change with distance. Given these properties, it is clear that radiance is the quantity that global illumination algorithms must compute and display to the observer.

2.3.4 Examples

This section gives a few practical examples of the relationship between the different radiometric quantities that we have seen.

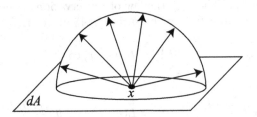

Figure 2.4. Diffuse emitter.

Example (Diffuse Emitter)

Let us consider the example of a diffuse emitter. By definition, a diffuse emitter emits equal radiance in all directions from all its surface points (as shown in Figure 2.4). Therefore,

$$L(x \rightarrow \Theta) = L.$$

The power for the diffuse emitter can be derived as

$$
\begin{aligned}
\Phi &= \int_A \int_\Omega L(x \rightarrow \Theta) \cos\theta d\omega_\Theta dA_x \\
&= \int_A \int_\Omega L \cos\theta d\omega_\Theta dA_x \\
&= L(\int_A dA_x)(\int_\Omega \cos\theta d\omega_\Theta) \\
&= \pi L A,
\end{aligned}
$$

where A is the area of the diffuse emitter, and integration at each point on A is over the hemisphere, i.e., Ω is the hemisphere at each point (see Appendix B).

The radiance for a diffuse emitter equals the power divided by the area, divided by π. Using the above equations, it is straightforward to write down the following relationship between the power, radiance, and radiosity of a diffuse surface:

$$\Phi = LA\pi = BA. \tag{2.12}$$

Example (Nondiffuse Emitter)

Consider a square area light source with a surface area measuring 10×10 cm^2. Each point on the light source emits radiance according to the following distribution over its hemisphere:

$$L(x \to \Theta) = 6000 \cos \theta \ (\text{W/sr} \cdot \text{m}^2).$$

Remember that the radiance function is defined for all directions on the hemisphere and all points on a surface. This specific distribution is the same for all points on the light source. However, for each surface point, there is a fall-off as the direction is farther away from the normal at that surface point.

The radiosity for each point can be computed as follows:

$$
\begin{aligned}
B &= \int_\Omega L(x \to \Theta) \cos \theta d\omega_\Theta \\
&= \int_\Omega 6000 \cos^2 \theta d\omega_\Theta \\
&= 6000 \int_0^{2\pi} \int_0^{\pi/2} \cos^2 \theta \sin \theta d\theta d\phi \\
&= 6000 \cdot 2\pi \cdot \left[\frac{-\cos^3 \theta}{3} \right]_0^{\pi/2} \\
&= 4000\pi \ \text{W/m}^2 \\
&= 12566 \ \text{W/m}^2.
\end{aligned}
$$

The power for the entire light source can then be computed as follows:

$$
\begin{aligned}
\Phi &= \int_A \int_\Omega L(x \to \Theta) \cos \theta d\omega_\Theta dA_x \\
&= \int_A (\int_\Omega L \cos \theta d\omega_\Theta) dA_x \\
&= \int_A B(x) dA_x \\
&= 4000\pi \ \text{W/m}^2 \cdot 0.1 \ \text{m} \cdot 0.1 \ \text{m} \\
&= 125.66 \ \text{W}.
\end{aligned}
$$

Example (Sun, Earth, Mars)

Now let us consider the example of an emitter that is very important to us: the Sun. One might ask the question, if the radiance of the Sun is the same irrespective of the distance from the Sun, why is the Earth warmer than Mars?

Consider the radiance output from the Sun arriving at the Earth and Mars (see Figure 2.5). For simplicity, let us assume that the Sun is a

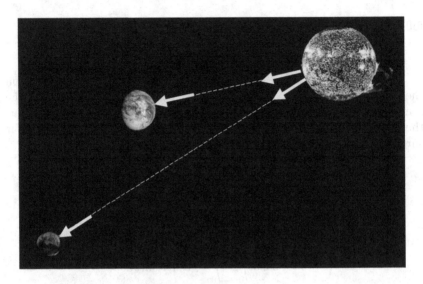

Figure 2.5. Relationship between the Earth, Mars, and the Sun.

uniform diffuse emitter. As before, we assume that the medium between the Earth, Sun, and Mars is a vacuum. From Equation 2.12,

$$\Phi = \pi L A.$$

Given that the total power emitted by the Sun is 3.91×10^{26} watts, and the surface area of the Sun is 6.07×10^{18} m^2, the Sun's radiance equals

$$L(Sun) = \frac{\Phi}{A\pi} = \frac{3.91 \times 10^{26}}{\pi 6.07 \times 10^{18}} = 2.05 \times 10^7 \ \text{W/sr} \cdot \text{m}^2.$$

Now consider a 1×1 m^2 patch on the surface of the Earth; the power arriving at that patch is

$$P(Earth \leftarrow Sun) = \int_A \int_\Omega L \cos \theta d\omega dA.$$

Let us also assume that the Sun is at its zenith (i.e., $\cos \theta = 1$), and that the solid angle subtended by the Sun is small enough that the radiance can be assumed to be constant over the patch:

$$P(Earth \leftarrow Sun) = A_{patch} L \omega.$$

The solid angle ω subtended by the Sun as seen from the Earth is

$$\omega_{Earth \leftarrow Sun} = \frac{A^{\perp}_{Sun_{disk}}}{distance^2} = 6.7 \times 10^{-5} \text{ sr}.$$

Note that the area of the Sun considered for the computation of the radiance of the Sun is its surface area, whereas the area of the Sun in the computation of the solid angle is the area of a circular section (disc) of the Sun; this area is 1/4th the surface area of the Sun:

$$
\begin{aligned}
P(Earth \leftarrow Sun) &= (1 \times 1 \text{ m}^2)(2.05 \times 10^7 \text{ W}/(\text{sr} \cdot \text{m}^2))(6.7 \times 10^{-5} \text{ sr}) \\
&= 1373.5 \text{ W}.
\end{aligned}
$$

Similarly, consider a 1×1 m^2 patch on the surface of Mars, the power arriving at that patch can be computed in the same way. The solid angle subtended by the Sun as seen from Mars is

$$\omega_{Mars \leftarrow Sun} = \frac{A^{\perp}_{Sun_{disk}}}{distance^2} = 2.92 \times 10^{-5} \text{ sr}.$$

The total power incident on the patch on Mars is given by

$$
\begin{aligned}
P(Mars \leftarrow Sun) &= (1 \times 1 \text{ m}^2)(2.05 \times 10^7 \text{ W}/(\text{sr} \cdot \text{m}^2))(2.92 \times 10^{-5} \text{ sr}) \\
&= 598.6 \text{ W}.
\end{aligned}
$$

Thus, even though the radiance of the Sun is invariant along rays and is the same as seen from the Earth and Mars, the solid angle measure ensures that the power arriving at the planets drops off as the square of the distance (the familiar inverse square law). Therefore, though the Sun will appear equally bright on the Earth and Mars, it will look larger on the Earth than on Mars and, therefore, warm the planet more.

Example (Plate)

A flat plate is placed on top of Mount Everest with its normal pointing up (See Figure 2.6). It is a cloudy day, and the sky has a uniform radiance of 1000 W/(sr $\cdot$ m^2). The irradiance at the center of the plate can be computed as follows:

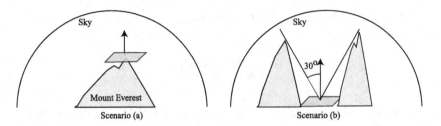

Figure 2.6. Plate with different constraints on incoming hemisphere. Scenario
(a): plate at top of peak; Scenario (b): plate in valley with 60° cutoff.

$$
\begin{aligned}
E &= \int L(x \leftarrow \Theta) \cos\theta d\omega \\
&= 1000 \int\int \cos\theta \sin\theta d\theta d\phi \\
&= 1000 \int_0^{2\pi} d\phi \int_0^{\pi/2} \cos\theta \sin\theta d\theta \\
&= 1000 \cdot 2\pi \cdot \left[-\frac{\cos^2\theta}{2} \right]_0^{\pi/2} \\
&= 1000 \cdot 2\pi \cdot \frac{1}{2} \\
&= 1000 \cdot \pi \ \text{W/m}^2.
\end{aligned}
$$

Now assume the plate is taken to an adjoining valley where the surrounding
mountains are radially symmetric and block off all light below 60°. The
irradiance at the plate in this situation is

$$
\begin{aligned}
E &= \int L(x \leftarrow \Theta) \cos\theta d\omega \\
&= 1000 \int\int \cos\theta \sin\theta d\theta d\phi \\
&= 1000 \int_0^{2\pi} d\phi \int_0^{\pi/6} \cos\theta \sin\theta d\theta \\
&= 1000 \cdot 2\pi \cdot \left[-\frac{\cos^2\theta}{2} \right]_0^{\pi/6} \\
&= 1000 \cdot \pi \cdot \left(1 - \frac{3}{4} \right) \\
&= 250 \cdot \pi \ \text{W/m}^2.
\end{aligned}
$$

2.4   Light Emission

Light is electromagnetic radiation produced by accelerating a charge. Light can be produced in different ways; for example, by thermal sources such as the sun, or by quantum effects such as fluorescence, where materials absorb energy at some wavelength and emit the energy at some other wavelength. As mentioned in previous sections, we do not consider a detailed quantum mechanical explanation of light for the purposes of computer graphics. In most rendering algorithms, light is assumed to be emitted from light sources at a particular wavelength and with a particular intensity.

The computation of accurate global illumination requires the specification of the following three distributions for each light source: spatial, directional, and spectral intensity distribution. For example, users, such as lighting design engineers, require accurate descriptions of light source distributions that match physical light bulbs available in the real world. Idealized spatial distributions of lights assume lights are point lights; more realistically, lights are modeled as area lights. The directional distributions of typical luminaires is determined by the shape of their associated light fixtures. Though the spectral distribution of light could also be simulated accurately, global illumination algorithms typically simulate RGB (or a similar triple) for efficiency reasons. All these distributions could be specified either as functions or as tables.

2.5   Interaction of Light with Surfaces

Light energy emitted into a scene interacts with the different objects in the scene by getting reflected or transmitted at surface boundaries. Some of the light energy could also be absorbed by surfaces and dissipated as heat, though this phenomenon is typically not explicitly modeled in rendering algorithms.

2.5.1   BRDF

Materials interact with light in different ways, and the appearance of materials differs given the same lighting conditions. Some materials appear as mirrors; others appear as diffuse surfaces. The reflectance properties of a surface affect the appearance of the object. In this book, we assume that light incident at a surface exits at the same wavelength and same time. Therefore, we are ignoring effects such as fluorescence and phosphorescence.

In the most general case, light can enter some surface at a point p and incident direction Ψ and can leave the surface at some other point q and exitant direction Θ. The function defining this relation between the

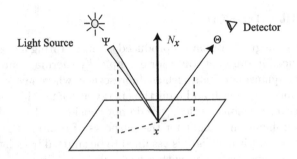

Figure 2.7. Bidirectional reflectance distribution function.

incident and reflected radiance is called the bidirectional surface scattering reflectance distribution function (BSSRDF) [131]. We make the additional assumption that the light incident at some point exits at the same point; thus, we do not discuss subsurface scattering, which results in the light exiting at a different point on the surface of the object.

Given these assumptions, the reflectance properties of a surface are described by a reflectance function called the bidirectional reflectance distribution function (BRDF). The BRDF at a point x is defined as the ratio of the differential radiance reflected in an exitant direction (Θ), and the differential irradiance incident through a differential solid angle $(d\omega_\Psi)$. The BRDF is denoted as $f_r(x, \Psi \rightarrow \Theta)$:

$$f_r(x, \Psi \rightarrow \Theta) \quad = \quad \frac{dL(x \rightarrow \Theta)}{dE(x \leftarrow \Psi)} \qquad (2.13)$$

$$= \quad \frac{dL(x \rightarrow \Theta)}{L(x \leftarrow \Psi)\cos(N_x, \Psi)d\omega_\Psi}, \qquad (2.14)$$

where $\cos(N_x, \Psi)$ is the cosine of the angle formed by the normal vector at the point x, N_x, and the incident direction vector Ψ.

Strictly speaking, the BRDF is defined over the entire sphere of directions (4π steradians) around a surface point. This is important for transparent surfaces, since these surfaces can "reflect" light over the entire sphere. In most texts, the term BSDF (bidirectional scattering distribution function) is used to denote the reflection and transparent parts together.

2.5.2 Properties of the BRDF

There are several important properties of a BRDF:

1. **Range.** The BRDF can take any positive value and can vary with wavelength.

2. Dimension. The BRDF is a four-dimensional function defined at each point on a surface; two dimensions correspond to the incoming direction, and two dimensions correspond to the outgoing direction.

   Generally, the BRDF is anisotropic. That is, if the surface is rotated about the surface normal, the value of f_r will change. However, there are many isotropic materials for which the value of f_r does not depend on the specific orientation of the underlying surface.

3. Reciprocity. The value of the BRDF remains unchanged if the incident and exitant directions are interchanged. This property is also called *Helmholtz reciprocity*; intuitively, it means that reversing the direction of light does not change the amount of light that gets reflected:

$$f_r(x, \Psi \to \Theta) = f_r(x, \Theta \to \Psi).$$

   Because of the reciprocity property, the following notation is used for the BRDF to indicate that both directions can be freely interchanged:

$$f_r(x, \Theta \leftrightarrow \Psi).$$

4. Relation between incident and reflected radiance. The value of the BRDF for a specific incident direction is not dependent on the possible presence of irradiance along other incident angles. Therefore, the BRDF behaves as a linear function with respect to all incident directions. The total reflected radiance due to some irradiance distribution over the hemisphere around an opaque, non-emissive surface point can be expressed as:

$$dL(x \to \Theta) \quad = \quad f_r(x, \Psi \to \Theta)dE(x \leftarrow \Psi); \tag{2.15}$$

$$L(x \to \Theta) \quad = \quad \int_{\Omega_x} f_r(x, \Psi \to \Theta)dE(x \leftarrow \Psi); \tag{2.16}$$

$$L(x \to \Theta) \quad = \quad \int_{\Omega_x} f_r(x, \Psi \to \Theta)L(x \leftarrow \Psi)\cos(N_x, \Psi)d\omega_\Psi. \tag{2.17}$$

5. Energy conservation. The law of conservation of energy requires that the total amount of power reflected over all directions must be less than or equal to the total amount of power incident on the surface (excess power is transformed into heat or other forms of energy). For any distribution of incident radiance $L(x \leftarrow \Psi)$ over the hemisphere, the total incident power per unit surface area is the total irradiance over the hemisphere:

$$E = \int_{\Omega_x} L(x \leftarrow \Psi)\cos(N_x, \Psi)d\omega_\Psi. \tag{2.18}$$

The total reflected power M is a double integral over the hemisphere. Suppose we have a distribution of exitant radiance $L(x \rightarrow \Theta)$ at a surface. The total power per unit surface area leaving the surface, M, is

$$M = \int_{\Omega_x} L(x \rightarrow \Theta) \cos(N_x, \Theta) d\omega_\Theta. \qquad (2.19)$$

From the definition of the BRDF, we know

$$dL(x \rightarrow \Theta) = f_r(x, \Psi \rightarrow \Theta) L(x \leftarrow \Psi) \cos(N_x, \Psi) d\omega_\Psi.$$

Integrating this equation to find the value for $L(x \rightarrow \Theta)$ and combining it with the expression for M gives us

$$M = \int_{\Omega_x} \int_{\Omega_x} f_r(x, \Psi \rightarrow \Theta) L(x \leftarrow \Psi) \cos(N_x, \Theta) \cos(N_x, \Psi) d\omega_\Psi d\omega_\Theta. \qquad (2.20)$$

The BRDF satisfies the constraint of energy conservation for reflectance at a surface point if, for all possible incident radiance distributions $L(x \leftarrow \Psi)$, the following inequality holds: $M \leq E$, or

$$\frac{\int_{\Omega_x} \int_{\Omega_x} f_r(x, \Psi \rightarrow \Theta) L(x \leftarrow \Psi) \cos(N_x, \Theta) \cos(N_x, \Psi) d\omega_\Psi d\omega_\Theta}{\int_{\Omega_x} L(x \leftarrow \Psi) \cos(N_x, \Psi) d\omega_\Psi} \leq 1. \qquad (2.21)$$

This inequality must be true for any incident radiance function. Suppose we take an appropriate δ-function for the incident radiance distribution, such that the integrals become simple expressions:

$$L(x \leftarrow \Psi) = L_{in} \delta(\Psi - \Theta),$$

then, the above equation can be simplified to

$$\forall \Psi : \int_{\Omega_x} f_r(x, \Psi \rightarrow \Theta) \cos(N_x, \Theta) d\omega_\Theta \leq 1. \qquad (2.22)$$

The above equation is a necessary condition for energy conservation, since it expresses the inequality for a specific incident radiance distribution. It is also a sufficient condition because incident radiance from two different directions do not influence the value of the BRDF; therefore, conservation of energy is valid for any combination of incident radiance values. If the value of the BRDF is dependent on the intensity of the incoming light, the more elaborate inequality from Equation 2.21 holds.

Global illumination algorithms often use empirical models to characterize the BRDF. Great care must be taken to make certain that these empirical models are a good and acceptable BRDF. More specifically, energy conservation and Helmholtz reciprocity must be satisfied to make an empirical model physically plausible.

Satisfying Helmholtz reciprocity is a particularly important constraint for bidirectional global illumination algorithms; these algorithms compute the distribution of light energy by considering paths starting from the light sources and paths starting from the observer at the same time. Such algorithms explicitly assume that light paths can be reversed; therefore, the model for the BRDF should satisfy Helmholtz's reciprocity.

2.5.3 BRDF Examples

Depending on the nature of the BRDF, the material will appear as a diffuse surface, a mirror, or a glossy surface (see Figure 2.8). The most commonly encountered types of BRDFs are listed below.

Diffuse Surfaces

Some materials reflect light uniformly over the entire reflecting hemisphere. That is, given an irradiance distribution, the reflected radiance is independent of the exitant direction. Such materials are called diffuse reflectors, and the value of their BRDF is constant for all values of Θ and Ψ. To an observer, a diffuse surface point looks the same from all possible directions. For an ideal diffuse surface,

$$f_r(x, \Psi \leftrightarrow \Theta) = \frac{\rho_d}{\pi}. \tag{2.23}$$

The reflectance ρ_d represents the fraction of incident energy that is reflected at a surface. For physically-based materials, ρ_d varies from 0 to 1. The reflectance of diffuse surfaces is used in radiosity calculations as will be seen in Chapter 6.

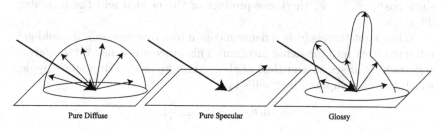

Pure Diffuse   Pure Specular   Glossy

Figure 2.8. Different types of BRDFs.

Specular Surfaces

Perfect specular surfaces only reflect or refract light in one specific direction.

Specular reflection. The direction of reflection can be found using the law of reflection, which states that the incident and exitant light direction make equal angles to the surface's normal, and lie in the same plane as the normal. Given that light is incident to the specular surface along direction vector Ψ, and the normal to the surface is N, the incident light is reflected along the direction R:

$$R = 2(N \cdot \Psi)N - \Psi. \tag{2.24}$$

A perfect specular reflector has only one exitant direction for which the BRDF is different from 0; the implication is that the value of the BRDF along that direction is infinite. The BRDF of such a perfect specular reflector can be described with the proper use of δ-functions. Real materials can exhibit this behavior very closely, but are nevertheless not *ideal reflectors* as defined above.

Specular refraction. The direction of specular refraction is computed using Snell's law. Consider the direction T along which light that is incident from a medium with refractive index η_1 to a medium with refractive index η_2 is refracted. Snell's law specifies the following invariant between the angle of incidence and refraction and the refractive indices of the media:

$$\eta_1 \sin \theta_1 = \eta_2 \sin \theta_2, \tag{2.25}$$

where θ_1 and θ_2 are the angles between the incident and transmitted ray and the normal to the surface.

The transmitted ray T is given as:

$$
\begin{aligned}
T &= -\frac{\eta_1}{\eta_2}\Psi + N(\frac{\eta_1}{\eta_2}\cos\theta_1 - \sqrt{1 - (\frac{\eta_1}{\eta_2})^2(1 - \cos\theta_1^2)}), \\
&= -\frac{\eta_1}{\eta_2}\Psi + N(\frac{\eta_1}{\eta_2}(N \cdot \Psi) - \sqrt{1 - (\frac{\eta_1}{\eta_2})^2(1 - (N \cdot \Psi)^2)}), \quad (2.26)
\end{aligned}
$$

since $\cos\theta_1 = N \cdot \Psi$, the inner product of the normal and the incoming direction.

When light travels from a dense medium to a rare medium, it could get refracted back into the dense medium. This process is called *total internal reflection*; it arises at a critical angle θ_c, also known as Brewster's angle, which can be computed by Snell's law:

$$
\begin{aligned}
\eta_1 \sin \theta_c &= \eta_2 \sin \frac{\pi}{2}; \\
\sin \theta_c &= \frac{\eta_2}{\eta_1}.
\end{aligned}
$$

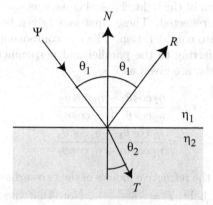

Figure 2.9. Perfect specular reflection and refraction.

We can derive the same condition from Equation 2.26, where total internal reflection occurs when the term under the square root, $1 - (\frac{\eta_1}{\eta_2})^2(1 - \cos\theta_1^2)$, is less than zero.

Figure 2.9 shows the geometry of perfect specular reflections and refractions.

Reciprocity for transparent surfaces. One has to be careful when assuming properties about the transparent side of the BSDF; some characteristics, such as reciprocity, may not be true with transparent surfaces as described below. When a pencil of light enters a dense medium from a less dense (rare) medium, it gets compressed. This behavior is a direct consequence of Snell's law of refraction (rays "bend" towards the normal direction). Therefore, the light energy per unit area perpendicular to the pencil direction becomes higher; i.e., the radiance is higher. The reverse process takes place when a pencil of light leaves a dense medium to be refracted into a less dense medium. The change in ray density is the square ratio of the refractive indices of the media [203, 204]: $(\eta_2/\eta_1)^2$. When computing radiance in scenes with transparent surfaces, this weighting factor should be considered.

Fresnel equations. The above equations specify the angles of reflection and refraction for light that arrives at a perfectly smooth surface. Fresnel derived a set of equations called the *Fresnel equations* that specify the amount of light energy that is reflected and refracted from a perfectly smooth surface.

When light hits a perfectly smooth surface, the light energy that is reflected depends on the wavelength of light, the geometry at the surface, and the incident direction of the light. Fresnel equations specify the fraction of light energy that is reflected. These equations (given below) take the polarization of light into consideration. The two components of the polarized light, r_p and r_s, referring to the parallel and perpendicular (*senkrecht* in German) components, are given as

$$r_p = \frac{\eta_2 \cos\theta_1 - \eta_1 \cos\theta_2}{\eta_2 \cos\theta_1 + \eta_1 \cos\theta_2};$$ (2.27)

$$r_s = \frac{\eta_1 \cos\theta_1 - \eta_2 \cos\theta_2}{\eta_1 \cos\theta_1 + \eta_2 \cos\theta_2},$$ (2.28)

where η_1 and η_2 are the refractive indices of the two surfaces at the interface.

For unpolarized light, $F = \frac{|r_p|^2 + |r_s|^2}{2}$. Note that these equations apply for both metals and nonmetals; for metals, the index of refraction of the metal is expressed as a complex variable: $n + ik$, while for nonmetals, the refractive index is a real number and $k = 0$.

The Fresnel equations assume that light is either reflected or refracted at a purely specular surface. Since there is no absorption of light energy, the reflection and refraction coefficients sum to 1.

Glossy Surfaces

Most surfaces are neither ideally diffuse nor ideally specular but exhibit a combination of both reflectance behaviors; these surfaces are called glossy surfaces. Their BRDF is often difficult to model with analytical formulae.

2.5.4 Shading Models

Real materials can have fairly complex BRDFs. Various models have been suggested in computer graphics to capture the complexity of BRDFs. Note that in the following description, Ψ is the direction of the light (the input direction) and Θ is the direction of the viewer (the outgoing direction).

Lambert's model. The simplest model is Lambert's model for idealized diffuse materials. In this model, the BRDF is a constant as described earlier:

$$f_r(x, \Psi \leftrightarrow \Theta) = k_d = \frac{\rho_d}{\pi},$$

where ρ_d is the diffuse reflectance (see Section 2.5.3).

Phong model. Historically, the Phong shading model has been extremely popular. The BRDF for the Phong model is:

$$f_r(x, \Psi \leftrightarrow \Theta) = k_s \frac{(R \cdot \Theta)^n}{N \cdot \Psi} + k_d,$$

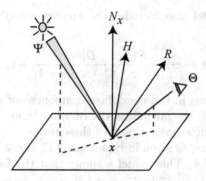

Figure 2.10. Shading models geometry.

where the reflected vector R can be computed from Equation 2.24.

Blinn-Phong model. The Blinn-Phong model uses the half-vector H, the halfway vector between Ψ and Θ, as follows:

$$f_r(x, \Psi \leftrightarrow \Theta) = k_s \frac{(N \cdot H)^n}{N \cdot \Psi} + k_d.$$

Modified Blinn-Phong model. While the simplicity of the Phong model is appealing, it has some serious limitations: it is not energy conserving, it does not satisfy Helmholtz's reciprocity, and it does not capture the behavior of most real materials. The modified Blinn-Phong model addresses some of these problems:

$$f_r(x, \Psi \leftrightarrow \Theta) = k_s(N \cdot H)^n + k_d.$$

Physically Based Shading Models

The modified Blinn-Phong model is still not able to capture realistic BRDFs. Physically based models, such as Cook-Torrance [33] and He [67], among others, attempt to model physical reality. We provide a brief description of the Cook-Torrance model below. For details, refer to the original paper [33]. The He model [67] is, to date, the most comprehensive and expensive shading model available; however, it is beyond the scope of this book to present this model.

Cook-Torrance model. The Cook-Torrance model includes a microfacet model that assumes that a surface is made of a random collection of small smooth planar facets. The assumption in this model is that an incoming ray randomly hits one of these smooth facets. Given a specification of the distribution of microfacets for a material, this model captures the shadowing effects of these microfacets. In addition to the facet distribution, the

Cook-Torrance model also includes the Fresnel reflection and refraction terms:

$$f_r(x, \Psi \leftrightarrow \Theta) = \frac{F(\beta)}{\pi} \frac{D(\theta_h)G}{(N \cdot \Psi)(N \cdot \Theta)} + k_d,$$

where the three terms in the nondiffuse component of the BRDF are the Fresnel reflectance F, the microfacet distribution D, and a geometric shadowing term G. We now present each of these terms.

The Fresnel terms, as given in Equations 2.27 and 2.28, are used in the Cook-Torrance model. This model assumes that the light is unpolarized; therefore, $F = \frac{|r_p|^2 + |r_s|^2}{2}$. The Fresnel reflectance term is computed with respect to the angle β, which is the angle between the incident direction and the half-vector: $\cos \beta = \Psi \cdot H = \Theta \cdot H$. By the definition of the half-vector, this angle is the same as the angle between the outgoing direction and the half-vector.

The distribution function D specifies the distribution of the microfacets for the material. Various functions can be used to specify this distribution. One of the most common distributions is the distribution by Beckmann:

$$D(\theta_h) = \frac{1}{m^2 \cos^4 \theta_h} e^{-(\frac{\tan \theta_h}{m})^2},$$

where θ_h is the angle between the normal and the half-vector and $\cos \theta_h = N \cdot H$. Also, m is the root-mean-square slope of the microfacets, and it captures surface roughness.

The geometry term G captures masking and self-shadowing by the microfacets:

$$G = \min\{1, \frac{2(N \cdot H)(N \cdot \Theta)}{\Theta \cdot H}, \frac{2(N \cdot H)(N \cdot \Psi)}{\Theta \cdot H}\}.$$

Empirical Models

Models such as Ward [221] and Lafortune [105] are based on empirical data. These models aim at ease of use and an intuitive parameterization of the BRDF. For isotropic surfaces, the Ward model has the following BRDF:

$$f_r(x, \Psi \leftrightarrow \Theta) = \frac{\rho_d}{\pi} + \rho_s \frac{e^{\frac{-tan^2 \theta_h}{\alpha^2}}}{4\pi\alpha^2 \sqrt{(N \cdot \Psi)(N \cdot \Theta)}},$$

where θ_h is the angle between the half-vector and the normal.

The Ward model includes three parameters to describe the BRDF: ρ_d, the diffuse reflectance; ρ_s, the specular reflectance; and α, a measure of the surface roughness. This model is energy conserving and relatively intuitive to use because of the small set of parameters; with the appropriate parameter settings, it can be used to represent a wide range of materials.

Lafortune et al. [105] introduced an empirically based model to represent measurements of real materials. This model fits modified Phong lobes to measured BRDF data. The strength of this technique is that it exploits the simplicity of the Phong model while capturing realistic BRDFs from measured data. More detailed descriptions of several models can be found in Glassner's books [54].

2.6 Rendering Equation

Now we are ready to mathematically formulate the equilibrium distribution of light energy in a scene as the rendering equation. The goal of a global illumination algorithm is to compute the steady-state distribution of light energy. As mentioned earlier, we assume the absence of participating media. We also assume that light propagates instantaneously; therefore, the steady-state distribution is achieved instantaneously. At each surface point x and in each direction Θ, the rendering equation formulates the exitant radiance $L(x \rightarrow \Theta)$ at that surface point in that direction.

2.6.1 Hemispherical Formulation

The hemispherical formulation of the rendering equation is one of the most commonly used formulations in rendering. In this section, we derive this formulation using energy conservation at the point x. Let us assume that $L_e(x \rightarrow \Theta)$ represents the radiance emitted by the surface at x and in the outgoing direction Θ, and $L_r(x \rightarrow \Theta)$ represents the radiance that is reflected by the surface at x in that direction Θ.

By conservation of energy, the total outgoing radiance at a point and in a particular outgoing direction is the sum of the emitted radiance and the radiance reflected at that surface point in that direction. The outgoing radiance $L(x \rightarrow \Theta)$ is expressed in terms of $L_e(x \rightarrow \Theta)$ and $L_r(x \rightarrow \Theta)$ as follows:

$$L(x \rightarrow \Theta) = L_e(x \rightarrow \Theta) + L_r(x \rightarrow \Theta).$$

From the definition of the BRDF, we have

$$f_r(x, \Psi \rightarrow \Theta) = \frac{dL_r(x \rightarrow \Theta)}{dE(x \leftarrow \Psi)},$$

$$L_r(x \rightarrow \Theta) = \int_{\Omega_x} f_r(x, \Psi \rightarrow \Theta) L(x \leftarrow \Psi) \cos(N_x, \Psi) d\omega_\Psi.$$

Putting these equations together, the rendering equation is

$$L(x \to \Theta) = L_e(x \to \Theta) \hspace{4cm} (2.29)$$
$$+ \int_{\Omega_x} f_r(x, \Psi \to \Theta) L(x \leftarrow \Psi) \cos(N_x, \Psi) d\omega_\Psi.$$

The rendering equation is an integral equation called a Fredholm equation of the second kind because of its form: the unknown quantity, radiance, appears both on the left-hand side of the equation, and on the right, integrated with a kernel.

2.6.2 Area Formulation

Alternative formulations of the rendering equation are sometimes used depending on the approach that is being used to solve for global illumination. One popular alternative formulation is arrived at by considering the surfaces of objects in the scene that contribute to the incoming radiance at the point x. This formulation replaces the integration over the hemisphere by integration over all surfaces visible at the point.

To present this formulation, we introduce the notion of a ray-casting operation. The ray-casting operation, denoted as $r(x, \Psi)$, finds the point on the closest visible object along a ray originating at point x and pointing in the direction Ψ. Efficient ray-casting techniques are beyond the scope of this book; hierarchical bounding volumes, octrees, and BSP trees are data structures that are used to accelerate ray casting in complex scenes [52].

$$r(x, \Psi) = \{y : y = x + t_{intersection} \Psi\};$$
$$t_{intersection} = \min\{t : t > 0, x + t\Psi \in A\},$$

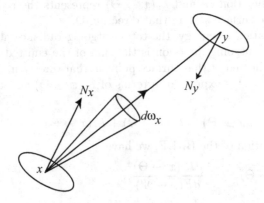

Figure 2.11. Area formulation of the rendering equation.

where all the surfaces in the scene are represented by the set A. The visibility function $V(x, y)$ specifies the visibility between two points x and y and is defined as follows:

$$\forall x, y \in A : V(x, y) = \begin{cases} 1 & \text{if } x \text{ and } y \text{ are mutually visible,} \\ 0 & \text{if } x \text{ and } y \text{ are not mutually visible.} \end{cases}$$

The visibility function is computed using the ray-casting operation $\mathbf{r}(x, \Psi)$: x and y are mutually visible if there exists some Ψ such that $r(x, \Psi) = y$.

Using these definitions, let us consider the terms of the rendering equation from Equation 2.29. Assuming nonparticipating media, the incoming radiance at x from direction Ψ is the same as the outgoing radiance from y in the direction $-\Psi$:

$$L(x \leftarrow \Psi) \;=\; L(y \rightarrow -\Psi).$$

Additionally, the solid angle can be recast as follows (see Appendix B):

$$d\omega_\Psi = d\omega_{x \leftarrow dA_y} = \cos(N_y, -\Psi) \frac{dA_y}{r_{xy}^2}.$$

Substituting in Equation 2.29, the rendering equation can also be expressed as an integration over all surfaces in the scene as follows:

$$L(x \rightarrow \Theta) = L_e(x \rightarrow \Theta)$$
$$+ \int_A f_r(x, \Psi \rightarrow \Theta) L(y \rightarrow -\Psi) V(x, y) \frac{\cos(N_x, \Psi)\cos(N_y, -\Psi)}{r_{xy}^2} dA_y.$$

The term $G(x, y)$, called the geometry term, depends on the relative geometry of the surfaces at point x and y:

$$G(x, y) \;=\; \frac{\cos(N_x, \Psi)\cos(N_y, -\Psi)}{r_{xy}^2};$$

$$L(x \rightarrow \Theta) \;=\; L_e(x \rightarrow \Theta)$$
$$+ \int_A f_r(x, \Psi \rightarrow \Theta) L(y \rightarrow -\Psi) V(x, y) G(x, y) dA_y.$$

This formulation recasts the rendering equations in terms of an integration over all the surfaces in the scene.

2.6.3 Direct and Indirect Illumination Formulation

Another formulation of the rendering equation separates out the direct and indirect illumination terms. Direct illumination is the illumination that arrives at a surface directly from the light sources in a scene; indirect illumination is the light that arrives after bouncing at least once off another surface in the scene. It is often efficient to sample direct illumination using the area formulation of the rendering equation, and the indirect illumination using the hemispherical formulation.

Splitting the integral into a direct and indirect component gives the following form of the rendering equation:

$$L(x \to \Theta) = L_e(x \to \Theta) + L_r(x \to \Theta);$$

$$L_r(x \to \Theta) = \int_{\Omega_x} f_r(x, \Psi \to \Theta) L(x \leftarrow \Psi) \cos(N_x, \Psi) d\omega_\Psi$$

$$= L_{direct} + L_{indirect};$$

$$L_{direct} = \int_A f_r(x, \overrightarrow{xy} \to \Theta) L_e(y \to \overrightarrow{yx}) V(x, y) G(x, y) dA_y;$$

$$L_{indirect} = \int_{\Omega_x} f_r(x, \Psi \to \Theta) L_i(x \leftarrow \Psi) \cos(N_x, \Psi) d\omega_\Psi;$$

$$L_i(x \leftarrow \Psi) = L_r(r(x, \Psi) \to -\Psi).$$

Thus, the direct term is the emitted term from the surface y visible to the point x along direction $\overrightarrow{xy}$: $y = r(x, \overrightarrow{xy})$. The indirect illumination is the reflected radiance from all points visible over the hemisphere at point x: $r(x, \Psi)$.

2.7 Importance

The problem that a global illumination algorithm must solve is to compute the light energy that is visible at every pixel in an image. Each pixel functions as a sensor with some notion of how it responds to the light energy that falls on the sensor. The *response function* captures this notion of the response of the sensor to the incident light energy. This response function is also called the *potential function* or *importance* by different authors.

The *response function* is similar in form to the rendering equation:

$$W(x \to \Theta) = W_e(x \to \Theta) \hfill (2.30)$$

$$+ \int_{\Omega_x} f_r(x, \Psi \leftarrow \Theta) W(x \leftarrow \Psi) \cos(N_x, \Psi) d\omega_\Psi.$$

Importance flows in the opposite direction as radiance. An informal intuition for the form of the response function can be obtained by considering two surfaces, i and j. If surface i is visible to the eye in a particular image, then $W_e(i)$ will capture the extent to which the surface is important to the image (some measure of the projected area of the surface on the image). If surface j is also visible in an image and surface i reflects light to surface j, then, due to the importance of j, i will indirectly be even more important. Thus, while energy flows from i to j, importance flows from j to i.

2.8 The Measurement Equation

The rendering equation formulates the steady-state distribution of light energy in the scene. The importance equation formulates the relative importance of surfaces to the image. The *measurement equation* formulates the problem that a global illumination algorithm must solve. This equation brings the two fundamental quantities, importance and radiance, together as follows.

For each pixel j in an image, M_j represents the measurement of radiance through that pixel j. The measurement function M is

$$M_j = \int W(x \leftarrow \Psi) L(x \leftarrow \Psi) \cos(N_x, \Psi) dA_x d\omega_\Psi. \qquad (2.31)$$

We assume here that the sensors are part of the scene so that we can integrate over their surface.

2.9 Summary

This chapter presented the formulation of the fundamental problems that global illumination must solve: the rendering equation and the measurement equation. We discussed a model of the behavior of light, definitions from radiometry, and a description of how light interacts with materials in a scene. For more details on the behavior of light, refer to standard physics textbooks in the field of optics [68]. References for radiative transport theory are Chandrasekhar's *Radiative Transfer* [22] and Ishimaru's *Wave Propagation and Scattering in Random Media* [75]. Glassner's books [54] present a range of different shading models used in computer graphics.

2.10 Exercises

1. A flat plate (measuring 0.5 meter by 0.5 meter) is placed on the highest mountain in the landscape, exactly horizontal. It is a cloudy

day, such that the sky has a uniform radiance of 1000 W/m^2sr. What is the irradiance at the center point of the plate?

2. The plate has a uniform Lambertian reflectance $\rho = 0.4$. What is the exitant radiance leaving the center point of the plate in a direction 45 degrees from the normal? In a direction normal to the surface?

3. Consider the sun being a diffuse light source with a diameter of $1.39 \cdot 10^9$ meters at a distance of $1.5 \cdot 10^{11}$ meters and emitting a radiance of $8 \cdot 10^6$ W/m^2sr. What is the radiance at the center point of the plate, expressed as a function of the angle between the position of the sun and the normal to the plate (the zenith)?

4. Using the Web, look up information on the following: the irradiance spectrum of the sun (irradiance as a function of wavelength) reaching the Earth; and the reflectivity of a chosen material, also as a function of wavelength. Sketch the approximate spectrum of the reflected light from the plate as a function of wavelength.

5. Implement the specular term of the Cook-Torrance BRDF model. For nickel at 689 nm wavelength, use the following parameters: microfacet distribution $m = 0.3$; refractive index $n = 2.14$ and $k = 4.00$. Plot graphs of the following terms: the Fresnel reflectance; the geometry term G; the full BRDF in the plane of incidence. Look up parameters for some additional materials and make similar plots.

3

Monte Carlo Methods

This chapter introduces the concept of Monte Carlo integration and reviews some basic concepts in probability theory. We also present techniques to create better distributions of samples. More details on Monte Carlo methods can be found in Kalos and Whitlock [86], Hammersley and Handscomb [62], and Spanier and Gelbard [183]. References on quasi–Monte Carlo methods include Niederreiter [132].

3.1 Brief History

The term "Monte Carlo" was coined in the 1940s, at the advent of electronic computing, to describe mathematical techniques that use statistical sampling to simulate phenomena or evaluate values of functions. These techniques were originally devised to simulate neutron transport by scientists such as Stanislaw Ulam, John von Neumann, and Nicholas Metropolis, among others, who were working on the development of nuclear weapons. However, early examples of computations that can be defined as Monte Carlo exist, though without the use of computers to draw samples. One of the earliest documented examples of a Monte Carlo computation was done by Comte de Buffon in 1677. He conducted an experiment in which a needle of length L was thrown at random on a horizontal plane with lines drawn at a distance d apart $(d > L)$. He repeated the experiment many times to estimate the probability P that the needle would intersect one of these lines. He also analytically evaluated P as

$$P = \frac{2L}{\pi d}.$$

Laplace later suggested that this technique of repeated experimentation could be used to compute an estimated value of π. Kalos and Whitlock [86] present early examples of Monte Carlo methods.

3.2 Why Are Monte Carlo Techniques Useful?

Consider a problem that must be solved, for example, computing the value of the integration of a function with respect to an appropriately defined measure over a domain. The Monte Carlo approach to solving this problem would be to define a random variable such that the expected value of that random variable would be the solution to the problem. Samples of this random variable are then drawn and averaged to compute an estimate of the expected value of the random variable. This estimated expected value is an approximation to the solution of the problem we originally wanted to solve.

One major strength of the Monte Carlo approach lies in its conceptual simplicity; once an appropriate random variable is found, the computation consists of sampling the random variable and averaging the estimates obtained from the sample. Another advantage of Monte Carlo techniques is that they can be applied to a wide range of problems. It is intuitive that Monte Carlo techniques would apply to problems that are stochastic in nature, for example, transport problems in nuclear physics. However, Monte Carlo techniques are applicable to an even wider range of problems, for example, problems that require the higher-dimensional integration of complicated functions. In fact, for these problems, Monte Carlo techniques are often the only feasible solution.

One disadvantage of Monte Carlo techniques is their relatively slow convergence rate of $\frac{1}{\sqrt{N}}$, where N is the number of samples (see Section 3.4). As a consequence, several variance reduction techniques have been developed in the field, discussed in this chapter. However, it should be noted that despite all these optimizations, Monte Carlo techniques still converge quite slowly and, therefore, are not used unless there are no viable alternatives. For example, even though Monte Carlo techniques are often illustrated using one-dimensional examples, they are not typically the most efficient solution technique for problems of this kind. But there are problems for which Monte Carlo methods are the only feasible solution technique: higher-dimensional integrals and integrals with nonsmooth integrands, among others.

3.3 Review of Probability Theory

In this section, we briefly review important concepts from probability theory. A Monte Carlo process is a sequence of random events. Often, a numerical outcome can be associated with each possible event. For example, when a fair die is thrown, the outcome could be any value from 1 to 6. A *random variable* describes the possible outcomes of an experiment.

3.3.1 Discrete Random Variables

When a random variable can take a finite number of possible values, it is called a discrete random variable. For a discrete random variable, a probability p_i can be associated with any event with outcome x_i.

A random variable x_{die} might be said to have a value of 1 to 6 associated with each of the possible outcomes of the throw of the die. The probability p_i associated with each outcome for a fair die is 1/6.

Some properties of the probabilities p_i are:

1. The probablity of an event lies between 0 and 1: $0 \leq p_i \leq 1$. If an outcome never occurs, its probability is 0; if an event always occurs, its probability is 1.

2. The probability that either of two events occurs is:

$$Pr(Event_1 \text{ or } Event_2) \leq Pr(Event_1) + Pr(Event_2).$$

   Two events are *mutually exclusive* if and only if the occurence of one of the events implies the other event cannot possibly occur. In the case of two such mutually exclusive events,

$$Pr(Event_1 \text{ or } Event_2) = Pr(Event_1) + Pr(Event_2).$$

3. A set of all the possible events/outcomes of an experiment such that the events are mutually exclusive and collectively exhaustive satisfies the following normalization property: $\sum_i p_i = 1$.

Expected Value

For a discrete random variable with n possible outcomes, the expected value, or mean, of the random variable is

$$E(x) = \sum_{i=1}^{n} p_i x_i.$$

For the case of a fair die, the expected value of the die throws is

$$E(x_{die}) = \sum_{i=1}^{6} p_i x_i$$

$$= \sum_{i=1}^{6} \frac{1}{6} x_i = \frac{1}{6}(1+2+3+4+5+6)$$

$$= 3.5.$$

Variance and Standard Deviation

The *variance* σ^2 is a measure of the deviation of the outcomes from the expected value of the random variable. The variance is defined as the expected value of the square difference between the outcome of the experiment and its expected value. The *standard deviation* σ is the square root of the variance. The variance is expressed as

$$\sigma^2 = E[(x - E[x])^2] = \sum_i (x_i - E[x])^2 p_i.$$

Simple mathematical manipulation leads to the following equation:

$$\sigma^2 = E[x^2] - (E[x])^2 = \sum_i x_i^2 p_i - \left(\sum_i x_i p_i\right)^2.$$

In the case of the fair die, the variance is

$$\sigma_{die}^2 = \frac{1}{6}[(1 - 3.5)^2 + (2 - 3.5)^2 + (3 - 3.5)^2 + (4 - 3.5)^2$$
$$+ (5 - 3.5)^2 + (6 - 3.5)^2]$$
$$= 2.91.$$

Functions of Random Variables

Consider a function $f(x)$, where x takes values x_i with probabilities p_i. Since x is a random variable, $f(x)$ is also a random variable whose expected value or mean is defined as

$$E[f(x)] = \sum_i p_i f(x_i).$$

The variance of the function $f(x)$ is defined similarly as

$$\sigma^2 = E[(f(x) - E[f(x)])^2].$$

Example (Binomial Distribution)

Consider a random variable that has two possible mutually exclusive events with outcomes 1 and 0. These two outcomes occur with probability p and $1 - p$, respectively. The expected value and variance of a random variable distributed according to this distribution are

$$
\begin{aligned}
E[x] &= 1 \cdot p + 0 \cdot (1 - p) = p; \\
\sigma^2 &= E[x^2] - E[x]^2 = p - p^2 = p(1 - p).
\end{aligned}
$$

Consider an experiment in which N random samples are drawn from the probability distribution above. Each sample can take a value of 0 or 1. The sum of these N samples is given as

$$
S = \sum_{i=1}^{N} x_i.
$$

The probability that $S = n$, where $n \leq N$, is the probability that n of the N samples take a value of 1, and $N - n$ samples take a value of 0. This probability is

$$
Pr(S = n) = C_n^N p^n (1 - p)^{N-n}.
$$

This distribution is called the binomial distribution. The binomial coefficient, C_n^N, counts the number of ways in which n of the N samples can take a value of 1: $C_n^N = \frac{N!}{(N-n)!n!}$.

The expected value of S is

$$
E[S] = \sum_{i=1}^{N} np_i = \sum nC_n^N p^n (1 - p)^{N-n} = Np.
$$

The variance is

$$
\sigma^2 = Np(1 - p).
$$

This expected value and variance can be computed analytically by evaluating the expression: $a\frac{d}{da}(a+b)^N$, where $a = p$ and $b = (1-p)$. Another possible way to compute the expected value and variance is to treat S as the sum of N random variables. Since these random variables are independent of each other, the expected value of S is the sum of the expected value of each variable as described in Section 3.4.1. Therefore, $E[S] = \sum E[x_i] = Np$.

3.3.2 Continuous Random Variables

We have been discussing discrete-valued random variables; we will now extend our discussion to include continuous random variables.

Probability Distribution Function and Cumulative Distribution Function

For a real-valued (continuous) random variable x, a *probability density function* (PDF) $p(x)$ is defined such that the probability that the variable takes a value x in the interval $[x, x + dx]$ equals $p(x)dx$. A *cumulative distribution function* (CDF) provides a more intuitive definition of probabilities for continuous variables. The CDF for a random variable x is defined as follows:

$$P(y) = Pr(x \leq y) = \int_{-\infty}^{y} p(x)dx.$$

The CDF gives the probability with which an event occurs with an outcome whose value is less than or equal to the value y. Note that the CDF $P(y)$ is a nondecreasing function and is non-negative over the domain of the random variable.

The PDF $p(x)$ has the following properties:

$$\forall x : p(x) \geq 0;$$

$$\int_{-\infty}^{\infty} p(x)dx = 1;$$

$$p(x) = \frac{dP(x)}{dx}.$$

Also,

$$
\begin{aligned}
Pr(a \leq x \leq b) &= Pr(x \leq b) - Pr(x \leq a) \\
&= CDF(b) - CDF(a) = \int_{a}^{b} p(z)dz.
\end{aligned}
$$

Expected Value

Similar to the discrete-valued case, the expected value of a continuous random variable x is given as:

$$E[x] = \int_{-\infty}^{\infty} xp(x)dx.$$

Now consider some function $f(x)$, where $p(x)$ is the probability distribution function of the random variable x. Since $f(x)$ is also a random variable, its expected value is defined as follows:

$$E[f(x)] = \int f(x)p(x)dx.$$

Variance and Standard Deviation

The *variance* σ^2 for a continuous random variable is

$$\sigma^2 = E[(x - E[x])^2] = \int (x - E[x])^2 p(x) dx.$$

Simple mathematical manipulation leads to the following equation:

$$\sigma^2 = E[x^2] - (E[x])^2 = \int x^2 p(x) dx - (\int x p(x) dx)^2.$$

Example (Uniform Probability Distribution)

For concreteness, we consider an example of one of the simplest probability distribution functions: the uniform probability distribution function. For a uniform probability distribution, the PDF is a constant over the entire domain, as depicted in Figure 3.1.

We know that $\int_a^b p(x) dx = 1$. Therefore, the PDF p_u for a uniform probability distribution function is

$$p_u(x) = \frac{1}{b - a}. \tag{3.1}$$

The probability that $x \in [a', b']$ is

$$Pr(x \in [a', b']) = \int_{a'}^{b'} \frac{1}{b - a} dx$$

$$= \frac{b' - a'}{b - a};$$

$$Pr(x \leq y) = CDF(y) = \int_{-\infty}^{y} \frac{1}{b - a} dx$$

$$= \frac{y - a}{b - a}.$$

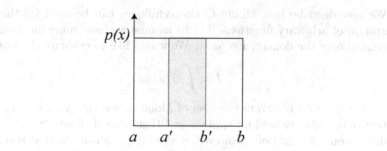

Figure 3.1. Uniform distribution.

For the special case where $a = 0$, $b = 1$:

$$Pr(x \leq y) = CDF(y) = y.$$

3.3.3 Conditional and Marginal Probabilities

Consider a pair of random variables x and y. For discrete random variables, p_{ij} specifies the probability that x takes a value of x_i and y takes a value of y_i. Similarly, a joint probability distribution function $p(x, y)$ is defined for continuous random variables.

The marginal density function of x is defined as

$$p(x) = \int p(x, y) dy.$$

Similarly, for a discrete random variable, $p_i = \sum_j p_{ij}$.

The conditional density function $p(y|x)$ is the probability of y given some x:

$$p(y|x) = \frac{p(x, y)}{p(x)} = \frac{p(x, y)}{\int p(x, y) dy}.$$

The conditional expectation of a random function $g(x, y)$ is computed as

$$E[g|x] = \int g(x, y) p(y|x) dy = \frac{\int g(x, y) p(x, y) dy}{\int p(x, y) dy}.$$

These definitions are useful for multidimensional Monte Carlo computations.

3.4   Monte Carlo Integration

We now describe how Monte Carlo techniques can be used for the integration of arbitrary functions. Let us assume we have some function $f(x)$ defined over the domain $x \in [a, b]$. We would like to evaluate the integral

$$I = \int_a^b f(x) dx. \tag{3.2}$$

We will first illustrate the idea of Monte Carlo integration in the context of one-dimensional integration and then extend these ideas to higher-dimensional integration. However, it should be mentioned that several effective deterministic techniques exist for one-dimensional integration, and Monte Carlo is typically not used in this domain.

3.4.1 Weighted Sum of Random Variables

Consider a function G that is the weighted sum of N random variables $g(x_1), ...g(x_N)$, where each of the x_i has the same probability distribution function $p(x)$. The x_i variables are called *independent identically distributed* (IID) variables. Let $g_i(x)$ denote the function $g(x_i)$:

$$G = \sum_{j=1}^{N} w_j g_j.$$

The following linearity property can easily be proved:

$$E[G(x)] = \sum_{j} w_j E[g_j(x)].$$

Now consider the case where the weights w_j are the same and all add to 1. Therefore, when N functions are added together, $w_j = 1/N$:

$$
\begin{aligned}
G(x) &= \sum_{j=1}^{N} w_j g_j(x) \\
&= \sum_{j=1}^{N} \frac{1}{N} g_j(x) \\
&= \frac{1}{N} \sum_{j=1}^{N} g_j(x).
\end{aligned}
$$

The expected value of $G(x)$ is

$$
\begin{aligned}
E[G(x)] &= \sum_{j} w_j E[g_j(x)] \\
&= \frac{1}{N} \sum_{j=1}^{N} E[g_j(x)] \\
&= \frac{1}{N} \sum_{j=1}^{N} E[g(x)] \\
&= \frac{1}{N} N E[g(x)] \\
&= E[g(x)].
\end{aligned}
$$

Thus, the expected value of G is the same as the expected value of $g(x)$. Therefore, G can be used to estimate the expected value of $g(x)$. G is called an *estimator* of the expected value of the function $g(x)$.

The variance of G is

$$\sigma^2[G(x)] \;=\; \sigma^2[\sum_{i=1}^{N} \frac{g_i(x)}{N}].$$

Variance, in general, satisfies the following equation:

$$\sigma^2[x+y] = \sigma^2[x] + \sigma^2[y] + 2Cov[x,y],$$

with the covariance $Cov[x,y]$ given as

$$Cov[x,y] = E[xy] - E[x] \cdot E[y].$$

In the case of independent random variables, the covariance is 0, and the following linearity property for variance does hold:

$$\sigma^2[x+y] = \sigma^2[x] + \sigma^2[y].$$

This result generalizes to the linear combination of several variables.
The following property holds for any constant a:

$$\sigma^2[ax] \;=\; a^2\sigma^2[x].$$

Using the fact that the x_i in G are independent identically distributed variables, we get the following variance for G:

$$\sigma^2[G(x)] \;=\; \sum_{i=1}^{N} \sigma^2[\frac{g_i(x)}{N}].$$

Therefore,

$$\sigma^2[G(x)] \;=\; \sum_{i=1}^{N} \frac{\sigma^2[g(x)]}{N^2}$$

$$=\; N\frac{\sigma^2[g(x)]}{N^2}$$

$$=\; \frac{\sigma^2[g(x)]}{N}.$$

Thus, as N increases, the variance of G decreases with N, making G an increasingly good estimator of $E[g(x)]$. The standard deviation σ decreases as $\sqrt{N}$.

3.4.2 Estimator

The Monte Carlo approach to computing the integral is to consider N samples to estimate the value of the integral. The samples are selected randomly over the domain of the integral with probability distribution function $p(x)$. The estimator is denoted as $\langle I \rangle$ and is

$$\langle I \rangle = \frac{1}{N} \sum_{i=1}^{N} \frac{f(x_i)}{p(x_i)}.$$

In Section 3.6.1, we explain why samples are computed from a probability distrubtion $p(x)$ as opposed to uniform sampling of the domain of the integration. Let us for now accept that $p(x)$ is used for sampling.

Using the properties described in Section 3.4.1, the expected value of this estimator is computed as follows:

$$
\begin{aligned}
E[\langle I \rangle] &= E[\frac{1}{N} \sum_{i=1}^{N} \frac{f(x_i)}{p(x_i)}] \\
&= \frac{1}{N} \sum_{i=1}^{N} E[\frac{f(x_i)}{p(x_i)}] \\
&= \frac{1}{N} N \int \frac{f(x)}{p(x)} p(x) dx \\
&= \int f(x) dx \\
&= I.
\end{aligned}
$$

Also, from Section 3.4.1, we know that the variance of this estimator is

$$\sigma^2 = \frac{1}{N} \int (\frac{f(x)}{p(x)} - I)^2 p(x) dx.$$

Thus, as N increases, the variance decreases linearly with N. The error in the estimator is proportional to the standard deviation σ; the standard deviation decreases as $\sqrt{N}$. This is a classic result of Monte Carlo methods. In fact one problem with Monte Carlo is the slow convergence of the estimator to the right solution; four times more samples are required to decrease the error of the Monte Carlo computation by half.

Example (Monte Carlo Summation)

A discrete sum $S = \sum_{i=1}^{n} s_i$ can be computed using the estimator $\langle S \rangle = nx$, where x takes the value of each term of the sum s_i with equal probability

$1/n$. We can see that the expected value of the estimator is S. Using the estimator, the following algorithm can be used to estimate the sum S: Randomly select a term s_i where each term has the same chance of being selected $1/n$. An estimate of the sum is the product of the value of the selected term times the number of terms: ns_i.

Since computing sums is clearly a very efficient computation in modern computers, it might appear that the above algorithm is not very useful. However, in cases where the sum consists of complex terms that are time-consuming to compute, this technique of sampling sums is useful. We show how this technique is used in Chapter 6.

Example (Simple MC Integration)

Let us show how Monte Carlo integration works for the following simple integral:

$$I = \int_0^1 5x^4 dx.$$

Using analytical integration, we know that the value of this integral is 1. Assuming samples are computed from a uniform probability distribution

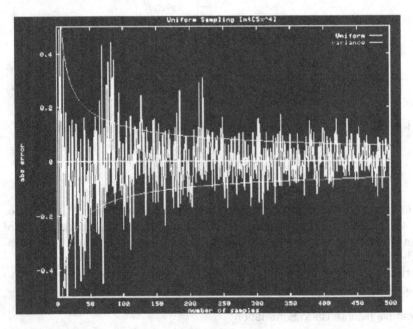

Figure 3.2. Monte Carlo integration of a simple function $5x^4$ including the plot of the variance.

(i.e., $p(x) = 1$ over the domain $[0, 1)$), our estimator would be

$$\langle I \rangle = \frac{1}{N} \sum_{i=1}^{N} 5x_i^4.$$

A possible evaluation of this integral using Monte Carlo techniques is shown in Figure 3.2.

The variance of this function can be analytically computed as follows:

$$\sigma_{est}^2 = \frac{1}{N} \int_0^1 (5x^4 - 1)^2 dx = \frac{16}{9N}.$$

As N increases, we get an increasingly better approximation of the integral.

3.4.3 Bias

When the expected value of the estimator is exactly the value of the integral I (as is the case for the estimator described above), the estimator is said to be *unbiased*. An estimator that does not satisfy this property is said to be biased; the difference between the expected value of the estimator and the actual value of the integral is called *bias*: $B[\langle I \rangle] = E[\langle I \rangle] - I$. The total error on the estimate is typically represented as the sum of the standard deviation and the bias. The notion of bias is important in characterizing different approaches to solving a problem using Monte Carlo integration.

A biased estimator is called *consistent* if the bias vanishes as the number of samples increases; i.e., if $\lim_{N \to \infty} B[\langle I \rangle] = 0$. Sometimes, it is useful to use biased estimators if they result in a lower variance that compensates for the bias introduced. However, we must analyze both variance and bias for these estimators, making the analysis more complicated than for unbiased estimators.

3.4.4 Accuracy

Two theorems explain how the error of the Monte Carlo estimator reduces as the number of samples increases. Remember that these error bounds are probabilistic in nature.

The first theorem is *Chebyshev's Inequality*, which states that the probability that a sample deviates from the solution by a value greater than $\sqrt{\frac{\sigma^2}{\delta}}$, where δ is an arbitrary positive number, is smaller than δ. This inequality is expressed mathematically as

$$Pr[|\langle I \rangle - E[I]| \geq \sqrt{\frac{\sigma_I^2}{\delta}}] \leq \delta,$$

where δ is a positive number. Assuming an estimator that averages N samples and has a well-defined variance, the variance of the estimator is

$$\sigma_I^2 = \frac{1}{N}\sigma_{primary}^2.$$

Therefore, if $\delta = \frac{1}{10000}$,

$$Pr[|\langle I \rangle - E[I]| \geq \frac{100\sigma_{primary}}{\sqrt{N}}] \leq \frac{1}{10000}.$$

Thus, by increasing N, the probability that $\langle I \rangle \approx E[I]$ is very large.

The Central Limit Theorem gives an even stronger statement about the accuracy of the estimator. As $N \to \infty$, the Central Limit Theorem states that the values of the estimator have a normal distribution. Therefore, as $N \to \infty$, the computed estimate lies in a narrower region around the expected value of the integral with higher probability. Thus, the computed estimate is within one standard deviation of the integral 68.3% of the time, and within three standard deviations of the integral 99.7% of the time. As N gets larger, the standard deviations, which vary as $\frac{1}{\sqrt{N}}$, get smaller and the estimator estimates the integral more accurately with high probability.

However, the Central Limit Theorem only applies when N is large enough; how large N should be is not clear. Most Monte Carlo techniques assume that N is large enough; though care should be taken when small values of N are used.

3.4.5 Estimating the Variance

The variance of a Monte Carlo computation can be estimated using the same N samples that are used to compute the original estimator. The variance for the Monte Carlo estimator is

$$\begin{aligned}
\sigma^2 &= \frac{1}{N}\int(\frac{f(x)}{p(x)} - I)^2 p(x)dx \\
&= \frac{1}{N}\int(\frac{f(x)}{p(x)})^2 p(x)dx - I^2 \\
&= \frac{1}{N}\int\frac{f(x)^2}{p(x)}dx - I^2.
\end{aligned}$$

The variance itself can be estimated by its own estimator σ_{est}^2 [86]:

$$\sigma_{est}^2 \approx \frac{\frac{1}{N}\sum_{i=1}^{N}(\frac{f(x_i)}{p(x_i)})^2 - (\frac{1}{N}\sum_{i=1}^{N}\frac{f(x_i)}{p(x_i)})^2}{N-1}.$$

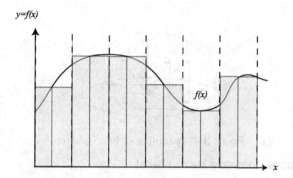

Figure 3.3. Deterministic one-dimensional integration.

3.4.6 Deterministic Quadrature versus Monte Carlo

As a point of comparison, note that a deterministic quadrature rule to compute a one-dimensional integral could be to compute the sum of the area of regions (perhaps uniformly spaced) over the domain (see Figure 3.3). Effectively, one approximation of the integral I would be

$$I \approx \sum_{i=1}^{N} w_i f(x_i) = \sum_{i=1}^{N} \frac{f(x_i)(b-a)}{N}.$$

The trapezoidal rule and other rules [149] are typical techniques used for one-dimensional integration. Extending these deterministic quadrature rules to a d-dimensional integral would require N^d samples.

3.4.7 Multidimensional Monte Carlo Integration

The Monte Carlo integration technique described above can be extended to multiple dimensions in a straightforward manner as follows:

$$I = \int \int f(x,y) dx dy$$

$$\langle I \rangle = \frac{1}{N} \sum_{i=1}^{N} \frac{f(x_i, y_i)}{p(x_i, y_i)}.$$

One of the main strengths of Monte Carlo integration is that it can be extended seamlessly to multiple dimensions. Unlike deterministic quadrature techniques, which would require N^d samples for a d-dimensional integration, Monte Carlo techniques permit an arbitrary choice of N.

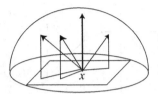

Figure 3.4. Sampling of hemisphere.

Example (Integration over a Hemisphere)

Let us consider a simple example of Monte Carlo integration over a hemisphere. The particular problem we want to solve is to estimate the irradiance at a point by integrating the contribution of light sources in the scene.

Let us consider a light source L. To compute the irradiance due to the light source, we must evaluate the following integral:

$$
\begin{aligned}
I &= \int L_{source} \cos\theta d\omega_\Theta \\
&= \int_0^{2\pi} \int_0^{\frac{\pi}{2}} L_{source} \cos\theta \sin\theta d\theta d\phi.
\end{aligned}
$$

The estimator for irradiance is:

$$
\langle I \rangle = \frac{1}{N} \sum_{i=1}^{N} \frac{L_{source}(\Theta_i) \cos\theta \sin\theta}{p(\Theta_i)}.
$$

We can choose our samples from the following probability distribution:

$$
p(\Theta_i) = \frac{\cos\theta \sin\theta}{\pi}.
$$

The estimator for irradiance is then given as

$$
\langle I \rangle = \frac{\pi}{N} \sum_{i=1}^{N} L_{source}(\Theta_i).
$$

3.4.8 Summary of Monte Carlo

In summary, a Monte Carlo estimator for an integral $I = \int f(x)dx$ is

$$
\langle I \rangle = \frac{1}{N} \sum_{i=1}^{N} \frac{f(x_i)}{p(x_i)}.
$$

The variance of this estimator is

$$\sigma^2 = \frac{1}{N} \int \left(\frac{f(x)}{p(x)} - I\right)^2 p(x) dx.$$

Monte Carlo integration is a powerful, general technique that can handle arbitrary functions. A Monte Carlo computation consists of the following steps:

- Sampling according to a probability distribution function.

- Evaluation of the function at that sample.

- Averaging these appropriately weighted sampled values.

The user only needs to understand how to do the above three steps to be able to use Monte Carlo techniques.

3.5 Sampling Random Variables

We have discussed how the Monte Carlo technique must compute samples from a probability distribution $p(x)$. Therefore, we want to find samples such that the distribution of the samples matches $p(x)$. We now describe different techniques to achieve this sampling.

3.5.1 Inverse Cumulative Distribution Function

To intuitively illustrate the *inverse cumulative distribution function* (CDF) technique, we first describe how to sample according to a PDF for a discrete PDF. We then extend this technique to a continuous PDF.

Discrete Random Variables

Given a set of probabilities p_i, we want to pick x_i with probability p_i. We compute the discrete cumulative probability distribution (CDF) corresponding to the p_i as follows: $F_i = \sum_{j=1}^{i} p_i$. Now, the selection of samples is done as follows. Compute a sample u that is uniformly distributed over the domain $[0, 1)$. Output k that satisfies the property:

$$F_{k-1} \leq u < F_k;$$

$$\sum_{j=1}^{k-1} p_j \leq u < \sum_{j=1}^{k} p_j;$$

$$\sum_{j=1}^{k-1} p_j \leq u < F_{k-1} + p_k.$$

We know from Equation 3.1 for a uniform PDF, $F(a \le u < b) = (b - a)$. Clearly, the probability that the value of u lies between F_{k-1} and F_k is $F_k - F_{k-1} = p_k$. But this is the probability that k is selected. Therefore, k is selected with probability p_k, which is exactly what we want.

The F values can be computed in $O(n)$ time; the look-up of the appropriate value to output can be done in $O(\log_2(n))$ time per sample by doing a binary search on the precomputed F table.

Continuous Random Variables

The approach above can be extended to continuous random variables. A sample can be generated according to a given distribution $p(x)$ by applying the inverse cumulative distribution function of $p(x)$ to a uniformly generated random variable u over the interval $[0, 1)$. The resulting sample is $F^{-1}(u)$. This technique is illustrated in Figure 3.5.

```
Pick u uniformly from [0,1)
Output y  =  F⁻¹(u)
```

The resulting samples have the distribution of $p(x)$ as can be proved below:

$$F(y) = \int_{-\infty}^{y} p(x)dx.$$

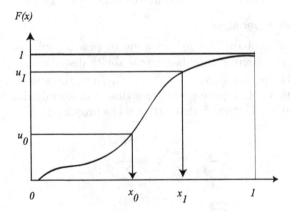

Figure 3.5. Inverse CDF sampling.

We want to prove that

$$Pr[y \leq Y] = \int_{-\infty}^{Y} p(x)dx.$$

Consider the new samples we compute. For every uniform variable u, we compute the sample as $y = F^{-1}(u)$. From Equation 3.1, we know that

$$Pr[u \leq X] = X.$$

Therefore,

$$Pr[F^{-1}(u) \leq F^{-1}(X)] = X$$
$$\text{if } X = F(Y)$$
$$Pr[y \leq Y] = F(Y) = \int_{-\infty}^{Y} p(x)dx.$$

Note that the fact that the cumulative probability distribution function is a monotonically nondecreasing function is important in the proof above. Also note that this method of sampling requires the ability to compute and analytically invert the cumulative probability distribution.

Example (Cosine Lobe)

A cosine weighting factor arises in the rendering equation; therefore, it is often useful to sample the hemisphere to compute radiance using a cosine PDF. We show how the hemisphere can be sampled such that the samples are weighted by the cosine term.

The PDF is

$$p(\theta, \phi) = \frac{\cos \theta}{\pi}.$$

Its CDF is computed as described above:

$$F = \frac{1}{\pi} \int \cos \theta d\omega;$$

$$F(\theta, \phi) = \frac{1}{\pi} \int_0^\phi \int_0^\theta \cos \theta' \sin \theta' d\theta' d\phi'$$

$$= \frac{1}{\pi} \int_0^\phi d\phi' \int_0^\theta \cos \theta' \sin \theta' d\theta'$$

$$= \frac{\phi}{\pi} (-\cos^2 \theta'/2)|_0^\theta$$

$$= \frac{\phi}{2\pi} (1 - \cos^2 \theta).$$

The CDF, with respect to ϕ and θ functions, is separable:

$$F_\phi = \frac{\phi}{2\pi};$$
$$F_\theta = 1 - \cos^2 \theta.$$

Therefore, assuming we compute two uniformly distributed samples u_1 and u_2:

$$\phi_i = 2\pi u_1$$

and

$$\theta_i = \cos^{-1} \sqrt{u_2},$$

where $1 - u$ is replaced by u_2 since the uniform random variables lie in the domain $[0, 1)$. These ϕ_i and θ_i values are distributed according to the cosine PDF.

3.5.2 Rejection Sampling

It is often not possible to derive an analytical formula for the inverse of the cumulative distribution function. Rejection sampling is an alternative that could be used and was one of the primary techniques used in the field in the past. In rejection sampling, samples are tentatively proposed and tested to determine acceptance or rejection of the sample. This method raises the dimension of the function being sampled by one and then uniformly samples the bounding box that includes the entire PDF. This sampling technique yields samples with the appropriate distribution.

Let us see how this works for a one-dimensional PDF whose maximum value over the domain $[a, b]$ to be sampled is M. Rejection sampling raises the dimension of the function by one and creates a two-dimensional function over $[a, b] \times [0, M]$. This function is then sampled uniformly to compute samples (x, y). Rejection sampling rejects all samples (x, y) such that $p(x) < y$. All other samples are accepted. The distribution of the accepted samples is exactly the PDF $p(x)$ we want to sample.

```
Compute sample x_i uniformly from the domain of x
Compute sample u_i uniformly from [0, 1)
if u_i ≤ p(x_i)/M then return x_i
else reject sample
```

One criticism of rejection sampling is that rejecting these samples (those that lie in the unshaded area of Figure 3.6) could be inefficient. The efficiency of this technique is proportional to the probabilty of accepting a proposed sample. This probability is proportional to the ratio of the area

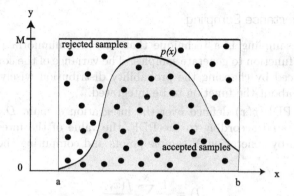

Figure 3.6. Rejection Sampling.

under the function to the area of the box. If this ratio is small, a lot of samples are rejected.

3.5.3 Look-Up Table

Another alternative for sampling PDFs is to use a look-up table. This approach approximates the PDF to be sampled using piecewise linear approximations. This technique is not commonly used though it is very useful when the sampled PDF is obtained from measured data.

3.6 Variance Reduction

Monte Carlo integration techniques can be roughly subdivided into two categories: those that have no information about the function to be integrated (sometimes called blind Monte Carlo), and those that do have some kind of information (sometimes called informed Monte Carlo). Intuitively, one expects that informed Monte Carlo methods are able to produce more accurate results as compared to blind Monte Carlo methods. The Monte Carlo integration algorithm outlined in Section 3.4 would be a blind Monte Carlo method if the samples were generated uniformly over the domain of integration without any information about the function being integrated.

Designing efficient estimators is a major area of research in Monte Carlo literature. A variety of techniques that reduce variance have been developed. We discuss some of these techniques in this section: importance sampling, stratified sampling, multiple importance sampling, the use of control variates, and quasi–Monte Carlo.

3.6.1   Importance Sampling

Importance sampling is a technique that uses a nonuniform probability distribution function to generate samples. The variance of the computation can be reduced by choosing the probability distribution wisely based on information about the function to be integrated.

Given a PDF $p(x)$ defined over the integration domain D, and samples x_i generated according to the PDF, the value of the integral I can be estimated by generating N sample points and computing the weighted mean:

$$\langle I \rangle = \frac{1}{N} \sum_{i=1}^{N} \frac{f(x_i)}{p(x_i)}.$$

As proven earlier, the expected value of this estimator is I; therefore, the estimator is unbiased. To determine if the variance of this estimator is better that an estimator using uniform sampling, we estimate the variance as described in Section 3.4.5. Clearly, the choice of $p(x)$ affects the value of the variance. The difficulty of importance sampling is to choose a $p(x)$ such that the variance is minimized. In fact, a *perfect* estimator would have the variance be zero.

The optimal $p(x)$ for the perfect estimator can be found by minimizing the equation of the variance using variational techniques and Lagrange multipliers as below. We have to find a scalar λ for which the following expression L, a function of $p(x)$, reaches a minimum,

$$L(p) \quad = \quad \int_D (\frac{f(x)}{p(x)})^2 p(x) dx + \lambda \int_D p(x) dx,$$

where the only boundary condition is that the integral of $p(x)$ over the integration domain equals 1, i.e.,

$$\int_D p(x) dx = 1.$$

This kind of minimization problem can be solved using the Euler-Lagrange differential equation:

$$L(p) \quad = \quad \int_D (\frac{f(x)^2}{p(x)} + \lambda p(x)) dx.$$

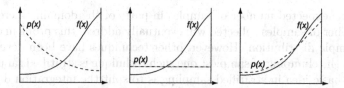

Figure 3.7. Comparing three different importance functions.

To minimize the function, we differentiate $L(p)$ with respect to $p(x)$ and solve for the value of $p(x)$ that makes this quantity zero:

$$0 = \frac{\partial}{\partial p}\left(\frac{f(x)^2}{p(x)} + \lambda p(x)\right)$$

$$0 = -\frac{f^2(x)}{p^2(x)} + \lambda$$

$$p(x) = \frac{1}{\sqrt{\lambda}}|f(x)|.$$

The constant $\frac{1}{\sqrt{\lambda}}$ is a scaling factor, such that $p(x)$ can fulfill the boundary condition. The optimal $p(x)$ is then given by:

$$p(x) = \frac{|f(x)|}{\int_D f(x)dx}.$$

If we use this $p(x)$, the variance will be exactly 0 (assuming $f(x)$ does not change sign). However, this optimal $p(x)$ requires us to know the value of the integral $\int_D f(x)dx$. But this is exactly the integral we want to compute to begin with! Clearly, finding the optimal $p(x)$ is not possible. However, importance sampling can still be a major tool in decreasing variance in Monte Carlo techniques. Intuitively, a good importance sampling function matches the "shape" of the original function as closely as possible. Figure 3.7 shows three different probability functions, each of which will produce an unbiased estimator. However, the variance of the estimator on the left-hand side will be larger than the variance of the estimator shown on the right-hand side.

3.6.2 Stratified Sampling

One problem with the sampling techniques that we have described is that samples can be badly distributed over the domain of integration resulting in a poor approximation of the integral. This clumping of samples can happen irrespective of the PDF used, because the PDF only tells us something about the expected number of samples in parts of the domain. Increasing the number of samples collected will eventually address this problem of uneven sample distribution. However, other techniques have been developed to avoid the clumping of samples: one such technique is stratified sampling.

The basic idea in stratified sampling is to split the integration domain into m disjoint subdomains (also called *strata*) and evaluate the integral in each of the subdomains separately with one or more samples. More precisely,

$$\int_0^1 f(x)dx = \int_0^{\alpha_1} f(x)dx + \int_{\alpha_1}^{\alpha_2} f(x)dx + \ldots$$
$$+ \int_{\alpha_{m-2}}^{\alpha_{m-1}} f(x)dx + \int_{\alpha_{m-1}}^1 f(x)dx.$$

Stratified sampling often leads to a smaller variance as compared to a blind Monte Carlo integration method. The variance of a stratified sampling method, where each stratum receives a number of samples n_j, which are in turn distributed uniformly over their respective intervals, is equal to

$$\sigma^2 = \sum_{j=1}^m \frac{\alpha_j - \alpha_{j-1}}{n_j} \int_{\alpha_{j-1}}^{\alpha_j} f(x)^2 dx - \sum_{j=1}^m \frac{1}{n_j} \left(\int_{\alpha_{j-1}}^{\alpha_j} f(x)dx \right)^2.$$

If all the strata are of equal size ($\alpha_j - \alpha_{j-1} = 1/m$), and each stratum contains one uniformly generated sample ($n_j = 1; N = m$), the above equation can be simplified to:

$$\sigma^2 = \sum_{j=1}^m \frac{1}{N} \int_{\alpha_{j-1}}^{\alpha_j} f(x)^2 dx - \sum_{j=1}^m \left(\int_{\alpha_{j-1}}^{\alpha_j} f(x)dx \right)^2$$
$$= \frac{1}{N} \int_0^1 f(x)^2 dx - \sum_{j=1}^N \left(\int_{\alpha_{j-1}}^{\alpha_j} f(x)dx \right)^2.$$

This expression indicates that the variance obtained using stratified sampling is always smaller than the variance obtained by a pure Monte Carlo sampling scheme. As a consequence, there is no advantage in generating more than one sample within a single stratum, since a simple equal subdivision of the stratum such that each sample is attributed to a single stratum always yields a better result.

This does not mean that the above sampling scheme always gives us the smallest possible variance; this is because we did not take into account

the size of the strata relative to each other and the number of samples
per stratum. It is not an easy problem to determine how these degrees
of freedom can be chosen optimally, such that the final variance is the
smallest possible. It can be proven that the optimal number of samples
in one subdomain is proportional to the variance of the function values
relative to the average function value in that subdomain. Applied to the
principle of one sample per stratum, this implies that the size of the strata
should be chosen such that the function variance is equal in all strata. Such
a sampling strategy assumes prior knowledge of the function in question,
which is often not available. However, such a sampling strategy might be
used in an adaptive sampling algorithm.

Stratified sampling works well when the number of samples required is
known in advance and the dimensionality of the problem is relatively low
(typically less than 20). The number of strata required does not scale well
with an increase in the number of dimensions. For a d-dimensional function,
the number of samples required is N^d, which can be prohibitive for large
values of d. Several techniques can be used to control the increase in the
number of samples with the increase in dimensions. The N-rooks algorithm
keeps the number of samples fixed (irrespective of dimensionality). Quasi–
Monte Carlo sampling uses nonrandom samples to avoid clumping. Both
of these techniques are described below.

3.6.3   N-Rooks or Latin Hypercube Algorithm

As mentioned, one major disadvantage of stratified sampling arises when
it is used for higher-dimensional sampling. Consider, for example, a two-
dimensional function; stratification of both dimensions would require N^2

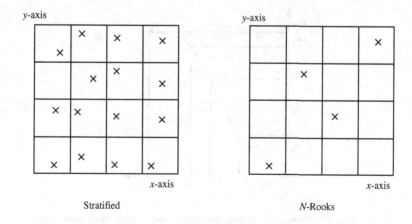

Figure 3.8. Stratified sampling versus N-rooks sampling for two dimensions.

strata with one sample per stratum. The N-rooks algorithm addresses this by distributing N samples evenly among the strata. Each dimension is still subdivided into N subintervals. However, only N samples are needed; these samples are distributed such that one sample lies in each subinterval.

This distribution is achieved by computing permutations of $1..N$ (let us call them $q_0, q_1, ...$), and letting the ith d-dimensional sample be:

$$(\frac{q_0(i) - u_0}{N}, \frac{q_1(i) - u_1}{N}, ..., \frac{q_{d-1}(i) - u_{d-1}}{N}).$$

In two dimensions, this means that no row or column has more than one sample. An example distribution is shown in Figure 3.8.

3.6.4 Combining Stratified Sampling and Importance Sampling

Stratified sampling can easily be integrated with importance sampling: the samples computed from a uniform probability distribution can be stratified, and then these stratified samples are transformed using the inverse cumulative distribution function. This strategy (shown in Figure 3.9) avoids the clumping of samples, while at the same time distributing the samples according to the appropriate probability distribution function.

Example (Stratified Sampling of Discrete Sums)

The following example illustrates how stratification can be combined with importance sampling. Stratification of the following sum, $S = \sum_{i=1}^{n} a_i$, with probabilities p_i, is done using the following code [124]:

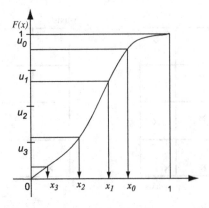

Figure 3.9. Combining stratified sampling and importance sampling.

Compute a uniformly distributed random number u in $[0,1)$
Initialize: $N_{sum} = 0$, $P = 0$
for $i = 1$ to n
  P += p_i
  $N_i = \lfloor P\ n\ +\ u \rfloor\ -\ N_{sum}$
  Sample the ith term of the sum N_i times
  $N_{sum}\ += \ N_i$

A single random number u is computed using the above algorithm. The ith term of the sum is sampled N_i times, where N_i is computed as above.

3.6.5 Combining Estimators of Different Distributions

We have explained that importance sampling is an effective technique often used to decrease variance. The function f could consist of the product of several different functions: importance sampling according to any one of these PDFs could be used. Each of these techniques could be effective (i.e., have a low variance) depending on the parameters of the function. It is useful to combine these different sampling techniques so as to obtain robust solutions that have low variance over a wide range of parameter settings. For example, the rendering equation consists of the BRDF, the geometry term, the incoming radiance, etc. Each one of these different terms could be used for importance sampling. However, depending on the material properties or the distribution of objects in a scene, one of these techniques could be more effective than the other.

Using Variance

Consider combining two estimators, $\langle I_1 \rangle$ and $\langle I_2 \rangle$, to compute an integral I. Clearly, any linear combination $w_1 \langle I_1 \rangle + w_2 \langle I_2 \rangle$ with constant weights $w_1 + w_2 = 1$ will also be an estimator for S. The variance of the linear combination however depends on the weights,

$$\sigma^2[w_1 \langle I_1 \rangle + w_2 \langle I_2 \rangle] = w_1^2 \sigma^2[\langle I_1 \rangle] + w_2^2 \sigma^2[\langle I_2 \rangle] + 2 w_1 w_2 \text{Cov}[\langle I_1 \rangle \langle I_2 \rangle],$$

where $\text{Cov}[\langle I_1 \rangle \langle I_2 \rangle]$ denotes the *covariance* of the two estimators:

$$\text{Cov}[\langle I_1 \rangle \langle I_2 \rangle] = E[\langle I_1 \rangle \cdot \langle I_2 \rangle] - E[\langle I_1 \rangle] \cdot E[\langle I_2 \rangle].$$

If $\langle I_1 \rangle$ and $\langle I_2 \rangle$ are independent, the covariance is zero. Minimization of the variance expression above allows us to fix the optimal combination weights:

$$\frac{w_1}{w_2} = \frac{\sigma^2[\langle I_2 \rangle] - \text{Cov}[\langle I_1 \rangle, \langle I_2 \rangle]}{\sigma^2[\langle I_1 \rangle] - \text{Cov}[\langle I_1 \rangle, \langle I_2 \rangle]}.$$

For independent estimators, the weights should be inversely proportional to the variance. In practice, the weights can be calculated in two different ways:

- Using analytical expressions for the variance of the involved estimators (such as presented in this text).

- Using a posteriori estimates for the variances based on the samples in an experiment themselves [86]. By doing so, a slight bias is introduced. As the number of samples is increased, the bias vanishes: the combination is asymptotically unbiased or *consistent*.

Multiple Importance Sampling

Veach [204] described a robust strategy, called multiple importance sampling, to combine different estimators using potentially different weights for each individual sample, even for samples from the same estimator. Thus, samples from one estimator could have different weights assigned to them, unlike the approach above where the weight depends only on the variance. The *balance heuristic* is used to determine the weights that combine these samples from different PDFs provided the weights sum to 1. The balance heuristic results in an unbiased estimator that provably has variance that differs from the variance of the "optimal estimator" by an additive error term. For complex problems, this strategy is simple and robust.

Let the sample computed from technique i with PDF p_i be denoted $X_{i,j}$, where $j = 1, .., n_i$. The estimator using the balance heuristic is

$$F = \frac{1}{N} \sum_{i=1}^{n} \sum_{j=1}^{n_i} \frac{f(X_{i,j})}{\sum_k c_k p_k(X_{i,j})},$$

where $N = \sum_i n_i$ is the total number of samples and $c_k = n_k/N$ is the fraction of samples from technique k.

The balance heuristic is computed as follows:

```
N  =  ∑_{i=1}^{n} n_i
for i = 1 to n
  for j = 1 to n_i
    X = Sample(p_i)
    d = ∑_{k=1}^{n} (n_k/N) p_k(X)
    F = F + f(X)/d
return F/N
```

3.6.6 Control Variates

Another technique to reduce variance uses *control variates*. Variance could be reduced by computing a function g that can be integrated analytically and subtracted from the original function to be integrated.

$$
\begin{aligned}
I &= \int f(x)dx \\
&= \int g(x)dx + \int f(x) - g(x)dx.
\end{aligned}
$$

Since the integral of the function $\int g(x)dx$ has been computed analytically, the original integral is estimated by computing an estimator for $\int f(x) - g(x)dx$.

If $f(x) - g(x)$ is almost constant, this technique is very effective at decreasing variance. If f/g is nearly constant, g should be used for importance sampling [86].

3.6.7 Quasi–Monte Carlo

Quasi–Monte Carlo techniques decrease the effects of clumping in samples by eliminating randomness completely. Samples are deterministically distributed as uniformly as possible. Quasi–Monte Carlo techniques try to minimize clumping with respect to a measure called the *discrepancy*.

The most commonly used measure of discrepancy is the star discrepancy measure described below. To understand how quasi–Monte Carlo techniques distribute samples, we consider a set of points P. Consider each possible axis-aligned box with one corner at the origin. Given a box of size B_{size}, the ideal distribution of points would have NB_{size} points. The star discrepancy measure computes how much the point distribution P deviates from this ideal situation,

$$
D_N^*(P) = sup_B \left| \frac{NumPoints(P \cap B)}{N} - B_{size} \right|,
$$

where $NumPoints(P \cap B)$ are the number of points from the set P that lie in box B.

The star discrepancy is significant because it is closely related to the error bounds for quasi–Monte Carlo integration. The *Koksma–Hlawka inequality* [132] states that the difference between the estimator and the integral to be computed satisifes the condition:

$$
\left| \frac{1}{N} \sum_{k=1}^{N} f(x_k) - \int_0^1 f(x)dx \right| \leq V_{HK}(f(x))D^*,
$$

i	Reflection about decimal point	$\Phi_{b=2}$ (Base 2)
$1 = 1_2$	$.1_2\ = 1/2$	0.5
$2 = 10_2$	$.01_2\ = 1/4$	0.25
$3 = 11_2$	$.11_2\ = 1/2 + 1/4$	0.75
$4 = 100_2$	$.001_2 = 1/8$	0.125
$5 = 101_2$	$.101_2 = 1/2 + 1/8$	0.625
$6 = 110_2$	$.011_2 = 1/4 + 1/8$	0.375

Table 3.1. Examples of the radical inverse function for base 2.

where the V_{HK} term is the variation in the function $f(x)$ in the sense of Hardy and Krause. Intuitively, V_{HK} measures how fast the function can change. If a function has bounded and continuous mixed derivatives, then its variation is finite.

The important point to take from this inequality is that the error in the MC estimate is directly proportional to the discrepancy of the sample set. Therefore, much effort has been expended in designing sequences that have low discrepancy; these sequences are called *low-discrepancy sequences* (LDS).

There are several low-discrepancy sequences that are used in quasi–Monte Carlo techniques: Hammersley, Halton, Sobol, and Niederreiter, among others. We describe a few of these sequences here.

Halton sequences are based on the radical inverse function and are computed as follows. Consider a number i which is expressed in base b with the terms a_j:

$$i\ =\ \sum_{j=0}^{\infty} a_j(i)b^j.$$

The radical inverse function Φ is obtained by reflecting the digits about the decimal point:

$$\Phi_b(i)\ =\ \sum_{j=0}^{\infty} a_j(i)b^{-j-1}.$$

Examples of the radical inverse function for numbers 1 through 6 in base 2 ($b = 2$) are shown in Table 3.1. To compare the radical inverse function for different bases, consider the number 11 in base 2: $i = 1011_2$. The radical inverse function $\Phi_2(11) = .1101_2 = 1/2 + 1/4 + 1/16 = 0.8125$. In base 3, $\Phi_3(11) = .201_3 = 2/3 + 1/27 = 0.7037$.

The discrepancy of the radical inverse sequence is $O((\log N)/N)$ for any base b. To obtain a d-dimensional low-discrepancy sequence, a different radical-inverse sequence is used in each dimension. Therefore, the ith point in the sequence is given as

$$x_i = (\Phi_{b_1}(i), \Phi_{b_2}(i), \Phi_{b_3}(i), ..., \Phi_{b_d}(i)),$$

where the bases b_j are relatively prime.

The Halton sequence for d dimensions sets the b_i terms to be the first d prime numbers; i.e., 2, 3, 5, 7, ..., and so on. The Halton sequence has a discrepancy of $O((\log N)^d/N)$. Intuitively, the reason the Halton sequence is uniform can be explained as follows: This sequence produces all binary strings of length m before producing strings of length $m+1$. All intervals of size 2^{-m} will be visited before a new point is put in the same interval.

When the number of samples required N is known ahead of time, the Hammersley sequence could be used for a slightly better discrepancy. The ith point of the Hammersley sequence is

$$x_i = (\frac{i}{N}, \Phi_{b_1}(i), \Phi_{b_2}(i), \Phi_{b_3}(i), ..., \Phi_{b_{d-1}}(i)).$$

This sequence is regular in the first dimension; the remaining dimensions use the first $(d-1)$ prime numbers. The discrepancy of the Hammersley point set is $O((\log N)^{d-1}/N)$.

Other sequences, such as the Niederreiter, are also useful for Monte Carlo computations [19].

Why Quasi–Monte Carlo?

The error bound for low-discrepancy sequences when applied to MC integration is $O((\log N)^d/N)$ or $O((\log N)^{d-1}/N)$ for large N and dimension d. This bound could have a substantial potential benefit compared to the $1/\sqrt{N}$ error bounds for pure Monte Carlo techniques. Low-discrepancy sequences work best for low dimensions (about 10-20); at higher dimensions, their performance is similar to pseudorandom sampling. However, as compared to pseudorandom sampling, low-discrepancy sequences are highly correlated; e.g., the difference between successive samples in the van der Corput sequence (a base-2 Halton sequence) is 0.5 half of the time; Table 3.1 shows this.

The upshot is that low-discrepancy sampling gives up randomness in return for uniformity in the sample distribution.

3.7 Summary

In this chapter, we have described Monte Carlo integration techniques and discussed their accuracy and convergence rates. We have also presented variance reduction techniques such as importance sampling, stratified sampling, the use of control variates, multiple importance sampling, and quasi–Monte Carlo sampling. More details on MC methods can be found in Kalos and Whitlock [86], Hammersley and Handscomb [62], and Spanier and Gelbard [183]. References on quasi–Monte Carlo methods include Niederreiter [132].

3.8 Exercises

1. Write a program to compute the integral of a one-dimensional function using Monte Carlo integration. Plot the absolute error versus the number of samples used. This requires that you know the analytic answer to the integral, so use well-known functions such as polynomials.

   Experiment with various optimization techniques such as stratified sampling and importance sampling. Draw conclusions about how the error due to the Monte Carlo integration is dependent on the sampling scheme used.

2. Using the algorithm designed above, try to compute the integral for sine functions with increasing frequencies. How is the error influenced by the various frequencies over the same integration domain?

3. Write a program to compute the integral of a two-dimensional function using Monte Carlo integration. This is very similar to the first exercise, but using two-dimensional functions poses some additional problems. Experiment with stratified sampling versus N-rooks sampling, as well as with importance sampling. Again, plot absolute error versus number of samples used.

4. Implement an algorithm to generate uniformly distributed points over a triangle in the 2D-plane. Start with a simple triangle first (connecting points $(0,0)$, $(1,0)$ and $(0,1)$), then try to generalize to a random triangle in the 2D plane.

   How can such an algorithm be used to generate points on a triangle in 3D space?

5. Pick an interesting geometric solid in 3D: a sphere, cone, cylinder, etc. Design and implement an algorithm to generate uniformly distributed points on the surface of these solids. Visualize your results to make sure the points are indeed distributed uniformly.

4

Strategies for Computing
Light Transport

4.1 Formulation of the Rendering Equation

The global illumination problem is basically a transport problem. Energy
emitted by light sources is transported by means of reflections and refractions in a three-dimensional environment. We are interested in the energy
equilibrium of the illumination in the environment. Since the human eye is
sensitive to radiance values, and since we want to compute photorealistic
images, we are primarily interested in radiance values or average radiance
values computed over certain areas and solid angles in the scene. The latter means that we should compute flux values for several areas of interest,
which will be referred to as sets. The exact geometric shape of these sets can
vary substantially, depending on the requested level of accuracy. As will be
explained in subsequent chapters, ray tracing algorithms define sets as surface points visible through a pixel, with regard to the aperture of the eye.
Radiosity algorithms often define sets as surface patches with the reflecting
hemisphere as the directional component (Figure 4.1). Other algorithms
might follow different approaches, but the common factor is always that for
a number of finite surface elements and solid angle combinations, average
radiance values need to be computed.

As explained in Chapter 2, the fundamental transport equation used to
describe the global illumination problem is called the rendering equation
and was first introduced into the field of computer graphics by Kajiya
[85]. The rendering equation describes the transport of radiance through a
three-dimensional environment. It is the integral equation formulation of
the definition of the BRDF and adds the self-emittance of surface points at
light sources as an initialization function. The self-emitted energy of light
sources is necessary to provide the environment with some starting energy.

81

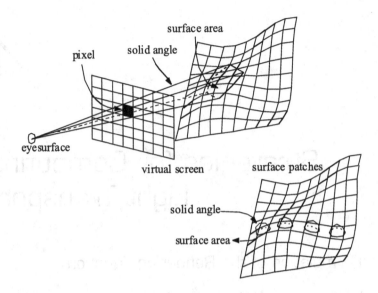

Figure 4.1. Sets of surface points and directions for ray tracing and radiosity algorithms.

The radiance leaving some point x, in direction Θ, is written as:

$$L(x \to \Theta) = L_e(x \to \Theta) + \int_{\Omega_x} f_r(x, \Psi \leftrightarrow \Theta) L(x \leftarrow \Psi) \cos(N_x, \Psi) d\omega_\Psi.$$

(4.1)

The rendering equation tells us that the exitant radiance emitted by a point x in a direction Θ equals the self-emitted exitant radiance at that point and in that direction, plus any incident radiance from the illuminating hemisphere that is reflected at x in direction Θ. This is illustrated in Figure 4.2.

Emission can result from various physical processes, e.g., heat or chemical reactions. The emission can also be time-dependent for a single surface point and direction, as is the case with phosphorescence. In the context of global illumination algorithms, one usually is not interested in the nature of the source of the self-emitted radiance of surfaces. Self-emitted radiance is merely considered as a function of position and direction.

As was shown in Chapter 2, it is possible to transform the rendering equation from an integral over the hemisphere to an integral over all surfaces in the scene. Both the hemispherical and area formulation contain exitant and incident radiance functions. We know that radiance remains unchanged along straight paths, so we can easily transform exitant radi-

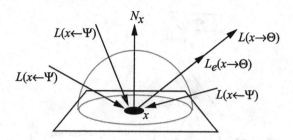

Figure 4.2. Rendering equation: incident radiance is integrated over the hemisphere.

ance to incident radiance and vice-versa, thus obtaining new versions of the rendering equation that contain exitant or incident radiance only. By combining both options with a hemispheric or surface integration, we obtain four different formulations of the rendering equation.

The formulations that integrate over surfaces or hemispheres are all mathematically equivalent. However, there can be some important differences when one develops algorithms starting from a specific formulation. For completeness, we list all possible formulations of the rendering equation.

4.1.1 Exitant Radiance, Integration over the Hemisphere

The incident radiance in the classic form of the rendering equation is replaced by the equivalent exitant radiance at the nearest visible point $y = r(x, \Psi)$, found by evaluating the ray-casting function (Figure 4.3):

$$L(x \to \Theta) = L_e(x \to \Theta) + \int_{\Omega_x} f_r(x, \Psi \leftrightarrow \Theta) L(y \to -\Psi) \cos(N_x, \Psi) d\omega_\Psi,$$

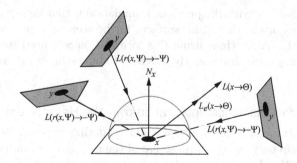

Figure 4.3. Transport of exitant radiance using hemisphere integration.

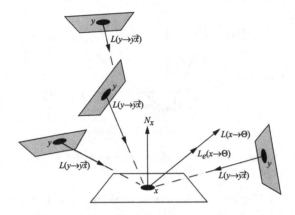

Figure 4.4. Transport of exitant radiance using surface integration.

with $y = r(x, \Psi)$. When designing an algorithm based on this formulation, one will integrate over the hemisphere, and as part of the function evaluation for each point in the integration domain, a ray will be cast and the nearest intersection point located.

4.1.2 Exitant Radiance, Integration over Surfaces

The hemispherical equation is transformed to an integral over all surface points (Figure 4.4):

$$L(x \to \Theta) = L_e(x \to \Theta) + \int_A f_r(x, \Psi \leftrightarrow \Theta) L(y \to \overrightarrow{yx}) V(x, y) G(x, y) dA_y,$$

with

$$G(x, y) = \frac{\cos(N_x, \Psi) \cos(N_y, -\Psi)}{r_{xy}^2}.$$

The main difference with the previous formulation is that incident radiance at x is seen as originating at all surfaces in the scene and not only at the hemisphere Ω_x. Algorithms using this formulation will need to check the visibility $V(x, y)$, which is slightly different than casting a ray from x in a direction Θ.

4.1.3 Incident Radiance, Integration over the Hemisphere

In order to transform the hemispherical rendering equation to incident radiance values only, we again make use of the invariance of radiance along a straight path. However, we also have to write the initial self-emitted radiance L_e as an incident measure. The concept of incident radiance

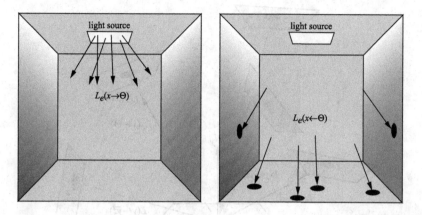

Figure 4.5. Exitant surface radiance for a light source at the ceiling and corresponding incident surface radiance.

L_e may seem odd. It is relatively easy to imagine the incident radiance at a surface point, but it is harder to imagine the incident L_e function corresponding to a certain light source (Figure 4.5).

We obtain the following equation:

$$L(x \leftarrow \Theta) = L_e(x \leftarrow \Theta) + \int_{\Omega_y} f_r(y, \Psi \leftrightarrow -\Theta) L(y \leftarrow \Psi) \cos(N_y, \Psi) d\omega_\Psi,$$

with $y = r(x, \Theta)$. This equation is graphically represented in Figure 4.6.

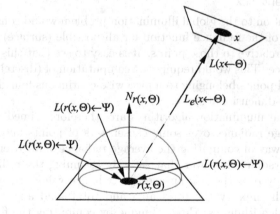

Figure 4.6. Transport of incident radiance using hemisphere integration.

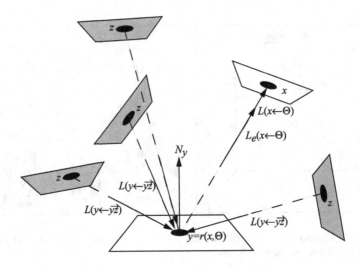

Figure 4.7. Transport of incident radiance using surface integration.

4.1.4 Incident Radiance, Integration over Surfaces

Following a similar procedure for incident radiance from surfaces, we get
the following equation (Figure 4.7):

$$L(x \leftarrow \Theta) = L_e(x \leftarrow \Theta) + \int_A f_r(y, \Psi \leftrightarrow \overrightarrow{yz}) L(y \leftarrow \overrightarrow{yz}) V(y, z) G(y, z) dA_z,$$

with $y = r(x, \Theta)$.

4.1.5 Radiant Flux

The ideal solution to the global illumination problem would consist of finding all values of the radiance function for all possible (surface) points and
all directions relative to those points. It is easy to see that this is not possible in practice. This would require the computation of (discrete) function
values over all points belonging to a piecewise-continuous four-dimensional
set in the five-dimensional space.

Most global illumination algorithms are, therefore, aimed at computing the average radiance over some chosen sets of points and directions.
One possible way of computing the average radiance value over a set is to
compute the radiant flux over that set. By assuming the radiance to be
changing slowly over the set, an average radiance value can be obtained
by dividing the flux by the total area and total solid angle of the set.
Ray tracing algorithms use this technique by computing the flux through
a pixel with regard to the aperture of the eye. Radiosity algorithms typi-

cally compute the flux, leaving a surface element or patch over the entire hemisphere.

The radiant flux can be expressed in terms of radiance by integrating the radiance distribution over all possible surface points and directions around these surface points belonging to the set for which the flux has to be computed. Let $S = A_s \times \Omega_s$ denote the set of surface points A_s and directions Ω_s we are interested in. Then the flux $\Phi(S)$ leaving S can be written using the measurement equation (see Chapter 2),

$$\Phi(S) = \int_{A_s} \int_{\Omega_s} L(x \rightarrow \Theta) \cos(N_x, \Theta) d\omega_\Theta dA_x.$$

By introducing the initial importance function $W_e(x \leftarrow \Theta)$, we can rewrite the above integral by integrating over all surfaces A in the scene, and by integrating over the complete hemisphere Ω for all surface points:

$$\Phi(S) = \int_A \int_\Omega L(x \rightarrow \Theta) W_e(x \leftarrow \Theta) \cos(N_x, \Theta) d\omega_\Theta dA_x, \qquad (4.2)$$

with

$$W_e(x \leftarrow \Theta) = \begin{cases} 1 & \text{if } (x, \Theta) \in S \\ 0 & \text{if } (x, \Theta) \notin S. \end{cases}$$

The average radiance value associated with the set is then expressed by

$$L_{average} = \frac{\int_A \int_\Omega L(x \rightarrow \Theta) W_e(x \leftarrow \Theta) \cos(N_x, \Theta) d\omega_\Theta dA_x}{\int_A \int_\Omega W_e(x \leftarrow \Theta) \cos(N_x, \Theta) d\omega_\Theta dA_x}.$$

Depending on the geometry of the set S, the denominator of this fraction can sometimes be computed analytically.

The global illumination problem can, therefore, be specified as computing the radiant fluxes for a certain number of well-defined sets. These sets are usually continuous and belong to the space $A \times \Omega$. The fluxes are computed by evaluating Equation 4.2. The integrand contains the radiance function L, which needs to be evaluated using one of four possible recursive Fredholm equations. Solving the Fredholm equations requires numerical algorithms, which are the focus of many global illumination algorithms, and which will be treated in more detail in Chapters 5 and 6.

4.2 The Importance Function

4.2.1 Definition

So far, we have thought of the global illumination problem as computing the incident or exitant radiance at a point x and in a direction Θ, given a specific distribution of light sources. Thus, a certain function L_e, defined over all points and directions belonging to $A \times \Omega$, determines a function L, also defined over $A \times \Omega$, by means of radiance transport. The relation between L_e and L is given by the rendering equation. This section looks in more detail at the importance function, which will define an adjoint transport quantity. We will first look at the importance function in an intuitive manner, and afterwards we will deal with some more complex mathematical issues. The importance function was first introduced in computer graphics by Pattanaik [139]. Some authors prefer to use the term potential function, but this function is equivalent to the importance function described here.

Suppose we are interested in the flux $\Phi(S)$ leaving a set S, consisting of points and directions around those points. Instead of starting from a fixed L_e distribution, we want to compute the possible influence of each pair (x, Θ) on $\Phi(S)$. To put it more precisely: if a single radiance value (a light source covering a differential surface area and differential solid angle) $L(x \rightarrow \Theta)$ is placed at (x, Θ), and if there are no other sources of illumination present, how large is the resulting value of $\Phi(S)$? The weight we have to attribute to $L(x \rightarrow \Theta)$ in order to obtain $\Phi(S)$ is called the importance of (x, Θ) with regard to S and is written as $W(x \leftarrow \Theta)$.

The importance value does not depend on the exact magnitude of $L(x \rightarrow \Theta)$, since any resulting flux scales linearly due to the linearity of a BRDF with regard to reflection of incident radiance. This is true regardless of the number of possible light paths between (x, Θ) and S, and regardless of the number of reflections. Thus, $W(x \leftarrow \Theta)$ depends only on the geometry of the scene and the reflective properties of the materials.

The next step is to derive an expression or equation that describes the importance $W(x \leftarrow \Theta)$. This expression can be written down by considering two ways in which contributions from the flux resulting from $L(x \rightarrow \Theta)$ can be made to $\Phi(S)$:

Self-contribution. If $(x, \Theta) \in S$, then $L(x \rightarrow \Theta)$ fully contributes to $\Phi(S)$. This is called the self-importance of the set S and is written as $W_e(x \leftarrow \Theta)$ (see also Equation 4.2):

$$W_e(x \leftarrow \Theta) = \begin{cases} 1 & \text{if } (x, \Theta) \in S \\ 0 & \text{if } (x, \Theta) \notin S. \end{cases}$$

Contribution through one or more reflections. We also have to consider all indirect contributions to the resulting flux. It is possible that some part of $L(x \rightarrow \Theta)$ contributes to $\Phi(S)$ through one or more reflections at several surfaces. We know that the radiance $L(x \rightarrow \Theta)$ travels along a straight path and reaches a surface point $r(x, \Theta)$. The energy is reflected at this surface point according to a hemispherical distribution determined by the

BRDF. Thus, we have a hemisphere of directions at $r(x, \Theta)$, each emitting a differential radiance value as a result of the reflection of the radiance $L(r(x, \Theta) \leftarrow -\Theta)$. By integrating the importance values for all these new directions, we have a new term for $W(x \leftarrow \Theta)$. By taking into account the reflection, and thus the BRDF values, we obtain the following equation for both terms combined:

$$W(x \leftarrow \Theta) = W_e(x \leftarrow \Theta)$$
$$+ \int_{\Omega_z} f_r(z, \Psi \leftrightarrow -\Theta) W(z \leftarrow \Psi) \cos(N_{r(x,\Theta)}, \Psi) d\omega_\Psi,$$

(4.3)

with $z = r(x, \Theta)$.

4.2.2 Incident and Exitant Importance

Mathematically, Equation 4.3 is identical to the transport equation of incident radiance. It is, therefore, appropriate to associate the notion of "incidence" also to importance, since importance as a transport quantity behaves in exactly the same way as an incident radiance.

The source function W_e depends on the nature of the set S. If one wants to compute individual flux values for pixels, $W_e(x \leftarrow \Theta) = 1$ if x is visible through the pixel and Θ is a direction pointing through the pixel to the aperture of the virtual camera. For a radiosity algorithm, S probably is a single patch and for each surface point, the full hemisphere of directions.

To further enhance the analogy, we can also introduce exitant importance by formally defining $W(x \rightarrow \Theta)$:

$$W(x \rightarrow \Theta) = W(r(x, \Theta) \leftarrow -\Theta).$$

This definition implies that we attribute the property of invariability along straight lines also to importance, which is in accordance with the definitions of radiance and importance. It is then easy to prove that exitant importance has exactly the same transport equation as exitant radiance:

$$W(x \rightarrow \Theta) = W_e(x \rightarrow \Theta) + \int_{\Omega_x} f_r(x, \Psi \leftrightarrow \Theta) W(x \leftarrow \Psi) \cos(N_x, \Psi) d\omega_\Psi.$$

As incident self-emitted radiance is not very intuitive to think about, so is self-emitted exitant surface importance. In the case of small sets with a narrow solid angle domain, self-emitted importance is sometimes easier to visualize by introducing a light detector. Such a detector has no influence on the propagation of light energy through the scene but detects only the flux of the set in question. Self-emitted exitant importance can then be thought of as emanating from this hypothetical detector, which acts as a source of importance. The concept of light detectors works extremely well when applied to an image generation algorithm, such as ray tracing. The eye point can then be considered as the source of exitant importance, directed towards the different pixels.

4.2.3 Flux

An expression for the flux of a set based on the importance function can now be deduced. The light sources are the only points that provide light energy in an environment. Their radiance values account for the illumination of the whole scene. Only the importance values of these points need to be considered when computing the flux. Given a certain set S,

$$\Phi(S) = \int_A \int_{\Omega_x} L_e(x \to \Theta) W(x \leftarrow \Theta) \cos(N_x, \Theta) d\omega_\Theta dA_x.$$

We can integrate over all surface points A, since L_e is suitably defined to be 0 at points and directions not belonging to light sources. This equation, together with the transport equation of the importance function, provides us with an alternative way of solving the global illumination problem.

It is also possible to write $\Phi(S)$ in the form

$$\Phi(S) = \int_A \int_{\Omega_x} L_e(x \leftarrow \Theta) W(x \to \Theta) \cos(N_x, \Theta) d\omega_\Theta dA_x,$$

and also

$$\Phi(S) = \int_A \int_{\Omega_x} L(x \to \Theta) W_e(x \leftarrow \Theta) \cos(N_x, \Theta) d\omega_\Theta dA_x,$$

$$\Phi(S) = \int_A \int_{\Omega_x} L(x \leftarrow \Theta) W_e(x \to \Theta) \cos(N_x, \Theta) d\omega_\Theta dA_x.$$

Thus, the flux of a given set can be computed by four different integral expressions, and each can be computed through double integration over all surfaces or hemispheres.

We now have two different approaches to solve the global illumination problem. The first approach starts from the definition of the set and requires the computation of the radiance values for the points and directions belonging to that set. The radiance values are computed by solving one of the transport equations describing radiance. So, we start from the set, working towards the light sources by following the recursive transport equation.

The second approach computes the flux of a given set by starting from the light sources and computes for each light source the corresponding importance value with regard to the set. The importance value also requires the use of one of the recursive integral equations. This kind of algorithm starts from the light sources and works towards the set by following the recursive transport equation for importance.

4.3 Adjoint Equations

The previous section described transport equations for incident and exitant radiance, incident and exitant importance, and also gave four different expressions for the flux. Moreover, we have a choice of integrating over a hemisphere or over all possible surfaces in the scene. This section will point out the symmetry between the two approaches more clearly. We will often refer to the complete radiance or importance functions, defined over $A \times \Omega$. We will denote them by L, $L^{\rightarrow}$ (exitant radiance), $L^{\leftarrow}$ (incident radiance), W, $W^{\rightarrow}$ (exitant importance), or $W^{\leftarrow}$ (incident importance) where appropriate.

4.3.1 Linear Transport Operators

The recursive integral equations that describe transport of radiance and importance can be written in a more concise form, using linear operators. The reflectance part of the rendering equation can actually be considered as an operator that transforms a certain radiance distribution over all surface points and directions to another distribution that gives us the reflected radiance values after one reflection. This new distribution is again a function of radiance values defined over the whole scene. We denote this operator by $\mathcal{T}$. $\mathcal{T}L$ is a new function, also defined over $A \times \Omega$.

$$L(x \rightarrow \Theta) = L_e(x \rightarrow \Theta) + \mathcal{T}L(x \rightarrow \Theta);$$

$$\mathcal{T}L(x \rightarrow \Theta) = \int_{\Omega_x} f_r(x, \Psi \leftrightarrow \Theta) L(r(x, \Theta) \rightarrow -\Psi) \cos(N_x, \Psi) d\omega_\Psi.$$

The same operator can also be written using the area integral formulation, since it is just a different parameterization.

In an analogous manner, the transport equation for the incident importance function $W^{\leftarrow}$ can also be described by use of a transport operator, which we denote by $\mathcal{Q}$:

$$W(x \leftarrow \Theta) = W_e(x \leftarrow \Theta) + \mathcal{Q}W(x \leftarrow \Theta);$$

$$\mathcal{Q}W(x \leftarrow \Theta) = \int_{\Omega_{r(x,\Theta)}} f_r(r(x, \Theta), \Psi \leftrightarrow -\Theta) W(r(x, \Theta) \leftarrow \Psi) \cdot$$
$$\cos(N_{r(x,\Theta)}, \Psi) d\omega_\Psi.$$

or the equivalent expression using area integration.

Since $L^{\leftarrow}$ and $W^{\rightarrow}$ are described with the same transport equations as $W^{\leftarrow}$ and $L^{\rightarrow}$, respectively, we have four transport equations to describe radiance and importance transport in a three-dimensional environment:

$$L^{\rightarrow} = L_e^{\rightarrow} + \mathcal{T}L^{\rightarrow}; \qquad W^{\leftarrow} = W_e^{\leftarrow} + \mathcal{Q}W^{\leftarrow};$$
$$L^{\leftarrow} = L_e^{\leftarrow} + \mathcal{Q}L^{\leftarrow}; \qquad W^{\rightarrow} = W_e^{\rightarrow} + \mathcal{T}W^{\rightarrow}.$$

These four equations clearly illustrate the symmetry between radiance and importance distributions.

4.3.2 Inner Product of Functions

In the function space defined over the five-dimensional domain $A \times \Omega$, it is possible to define an inner product of an exitant function $F^{\rightarrow}$ and an incident function $G^{\leftarrow}$ as

$$\langle F^{\rightarrow}, G^{\leftarrow} \rangle = \int_A \int_\Omega F(x \rightarrow \Theta)G(x \leftarrow \Theta)\cos(N_x, \Theta)d\omega_\Theta dA_x.$$

The same inner product can be written using area integration, and introducing the visibility function into the equation:

$$\langle F^{\rightarrow}, G^{\leftarrow} \rangle = \int_A \int_A F(x \rightarrow \overrightarrow{xy})G(x \leftarrow \overrightarrow{xy})G(x,y)V(x,y)dA_x dA_y.$$

The flux of a set S can now be seen as an inner product of a radiance function and an importance function. Based on previous transport equations, we have four different expressions available to write the flux as an inner product:

$$\Phi(S) = \langle L^{\rightarrow}, W_e^{\leftarrow} \rangle; \qquad \Phi(S) = \langle L_e^{\rightarrow}, W^{\leftarrow} \rangle;$$
$$\Phi(S) = \langle L^{\leftarrow}, W_e^{\rightarrow} \rangle; \qquad \Phi(S) = \langle L_e^{\leftarrow}, W^{\rightarrow} \rangle.$$

4.3.3 Adjoint Operators

Two operators, $\mathcal{O}_1$ and $\mathcal{O}_2$, operating on elements of the same vector-space V, are said to be adjoint with respect to an inner product $\langle F, G \rangle$ if

$$\forall F, G \in V : \langle \mathcal{O}_1 F, G \rangle = \langle F, \mathcal{O}_2 G \rangle.$$

$\mathcal{O}_2$ is called the adjoint operator of $\mathcal{O}_1$ and is written as $\mathcal{O}_1^*$.

By manipulating the area integral formulation, one can prove that the above defined operators $\mathcal{T}$ and $\mathcal{Q}$, which describe transport of radiance and importance, are adjoint to each other for the above defined inner product describing the flux $\Phi(S)$, or $Q^* = \mathcal{T}$, and thus

$$L^{\leftarrow} = L_e^{\leftarrow} + \mathcal{T}^* L^{\leftarrow} \text{ and } W^{\leftarrow} = W_e^{\leftarrow} + \mathcal{T}^* W^{\leftarrow}.$$

Due to this property of adjointness, the equivalence of the different expressions for the flux of a given set S can be written in a very compact notation. For example, the flux expressions using exitant radiance and incident importance can be transformed into each other using the properties of an inner product and the adjointness of the transport operators:

$$
\begin{aligned}
\Phi(S) &= \langle L^{\rightarrow}, W_e^{\leftarrow} \rangle \\
&= \langle L^{\rightarrow}, W^{\leftarrow} - \mathcal{T}^* W^{\leftarrow} \rangle \\
&= \langle L^{\rightarrow}, W^{\leftarrow} \rangle - \langle L^{\rightarrow}, \mathcal{T}^* W^{\leftarrow} \rangle \\
&= \langle L^{\rightarrow}, W^{\leftarrow} \rangle - \langle \mathcal{T} L^{\rightarrow}, W^{\leftarrow} \rangle \\
&= \langle L^{\rightarrow} - \mathcal{T} L^{\rightarrow}, W^{\leftarrow} \rangle \\
&= \langle L_e^{\rightarrow}, W^{\leftarrow} \rangle.
\end{aligned}
$$

The equations describing the global illumination problem, which give expressions for the flux and transport equations for radiance or importance, can thus be written in several different ways. The different choices to make are:

- Using incident or exitant functions for radiance and importance.

- Using importance-based or radiance-based transport equations.

- Integration over hemispheres or surface area integration.

We have, therefore, four possible, mathematically equivalent formulations of the global illumination problem:

$$
\begin{array}{ll}
\Phi(S) = \langle L^{\rightarrow}, W_e^{\leftarrow} \rangle & \Phi(S) = \langle L_e^{\rightarrow}, W^{\leftarrow} \rangle \\
L^{\rightarrow} = L_e^{\rightarrow} + \mathcal{T} L^{\rightarrow}; & W^{\leftarrow} = W_e^{\leftarrow} + \mathcal{T}^* W^{\leftarrow}; \\
\\
\Phi(S) = \langle L^{\leftarrow}, W_e^{\rightarrow} \rangle & \Phi(S) = \langle L_e^{\leftarrow}, W^{\rightarrow} \rangle \\
L^{\leftarrow} = L_e^{\leftarrow} + \mathcal{T}^* L^{\leftarrow}; & W^{\rightarrow} = W_e^{\rightarrow} + \mathcal{T} W^{\rightarrow}.
\end{array}
\tag{4.4}
$$

Similar descriptions for the global illumination problem, using incident and exitant functions, and operators that act in function space, have been presented by other authors [25, 26, 204]. Some of these authors introduce additional operators, such as the geometry operator, which transforms an incident function into the corresponding exitant function (or vice-versa), by making use of the invariability along straight paths. The inner product can also be defined differently, not including the cosine term. However, we feel that the symmetry in this case is not as clear as it is presented here.

4.4 Global Reflectance Distribution Function

4.4.1 Description

Given the transport equation of $L^{\rightarrow}$, it is obvious that each single radiance value in the scene is dependent on the initial distribution given by $L_e^{\rightarrow}$. For the flux of a complete set, such dependency is expressed by the importance function $W^{\leftarrow}$. We will now introduce a function that expresses the relation between a single $L(x \rightarrow \Theta)$ value at an arbitrary chosen point, and the initial $L_e^{\rightarrow}$ distribution. Such relation already exists as the transport equation for radiance. However, we want to derive a more direct function, instead of a recursive formulation. We will call this function the *global reflectance distribution function* [102, 41], or GRDF.

The GRDF is a four-dimensional transfer function that describes the entire light transport in a three-dimensional scene between two pairs (x, Θ) and (y, Ψ). It has the characteristics of both an incident and an exitant function, since the transfer can happen in both directions. We will write the GRDF as $G_r(x \leftarrow \Theta, y \rightarrow \Psi)$.

Intuitively, the $G_r(x \leftarrow \Theta, y \rightarrow \Psi)$ describes some sort of *global* transport between two point-direction pairs and can be thought of as the contribution one pair makes, if it would act as a differential source of transport quantity, to the transport quantity measured at the other pair. In other words, we want the GRDF to be such that

$$L(y \rightarrow \Psi) = \int_A \int_{\Omega_x} L_e(x \rightarrow \Theta) G_r(x \leftarrow \Theta, y \rightarrow \Psi) \cos(N_x, \Theta) d\omega_\Theta dA_x.$$

$$(4.5)$$

So, $G_r(x \leftarrow \Theta, y \rightarrow \Psi)$ expresses the influence of the total power leaving dA_x through a solid angle $d\omega_\Theta$ on the final value of the radiance measured at y in direction Ψ, through any number of reflections on intermediate surfaces. The GRDF can thus be considered as some kind of response function in the three-dimensional environment. In mathematical physics, a function like the GRDF is usually called the *Green's function* of a problem.

Since the transport is reciprocal, we want a similar equation for the importance:

$$W(x \leftarrow \Theta) = \int_A \int_{\Omega_x} W_e(y \leftarrow \Psi) G_r(x \leftarrow \Theta, y \rightarrow \Psi) \cos(N_x, \Theta) d\omega_\Theta dA_x.$$
(4.6)

Similar equations hold for incident radiance and exitant importance.

Differentiating the above equations yields

$$G_r(x \leftarrow \Theta, y \rightarrow \Psi) = \frac{d^2 L(y \rightarrow \Psi)}{L_e(x \rightarrow \Theta) \cos(N_x, \Theta) d\omega_\Theta dA_x}$$

and

$$G_r(x \leftarrow \Theta, y \rightarrow \Psi) = \frac{d^2 W(x \leftarrow \Theta)}{W_e(y \leftarrow \Psi) \cos(N_x, \Theta) d\omega_\Theta dA_x}.$$

This is very similar to the definition of the common BRDF, which describes a similar property for exitant radiance and incident irradiance at a single surface point. The GRDF extends this concept and describes the relationship between any two radiance or importance values, taking into account all possible reflections in the scene. The BRDF can be considered as a special case of the GRDF. The name global reflectance distribution function is therefore quite appropriate.

4.4.2 Properties of the GRDF

Transport Equations

The following adjoint transport equations both describe the behavior of the GRDF:

$$G_r(x \leftarrow \Theta, y \rightarrow \Psi) = \delta(x \leftarrow \Theta, y \rightarrow \Psi) + \mathcal{T} G_r(x \leftarrow \Theta, y \rightarrow \Psi),$$
$$G_r(x \leftarrow \Theta, y \rightarrow \Psi) = \delta(x \leftarrow \Theta, y \rightarrow \Psi) + \mathcal{T}^* G_r(x \leftarrow \Theta, y \rightarrow \Psi),$$

with $\delta(x \leftarrow \Theta, y \rightarrow \Psi)$ being a proper Dirac impulse defined in the four-dimensional domain. When using the $\mathcal{T}$ and $\mathcal{T}^*$ operators, we have to keep in mind that $\mathcal{T}$ operates on the exitant part of G_r, and that $\mathcal{T}^*$ operates on the incident part of G_r.

Transforming Arguments

Another useful property of G_r is that the arguments can be switched, in much the same manner as the directions of the BRDF can be reversed:

$$G_r(x \leftarrow \Theta, y \rightarrow \Psi) = G_r(r(y, \Psi) \leftarrow \Psi, r(x, \Theta) \rightarrow -\Theta).$$

This relationship is the generalization of the property of the BRDF, by
which the incident and exitant directions can switch roles, resulting in the
same BRDF value.

Flux

It is now possible to write an expression for the flux $\Phi(S)$ using the GRDF.
This expression follows from integrating Equations 4.5 and 4.6:

$$\Phi(S) = \int_A \int_{\Omega_x} \int_A \int_{\Omega_y} L_e(x \to \Theta) G_r(x \leftarrow \Theta, y \to \Psi) W_e(y \leftarrow \Psi)$$

$$\times \cos(N_x, \Theta) \cos(N_y, \Psi) d\omega_\Psi dA_y d\omega_\Theta dA_x. \quad (4.7)$$

4.4.3   Significance of the GRDF

The GRDF allows us to describe the global illumination problem in a very
short and elegant format, independent of any initial distributions for self-
emitted radiance or importance. The GRDF is only dependent on the
geometry of the scene and the reflective properties of the surfaces. No
positioning of light sources is assumed, nor is it assumed that we know
where we will place the sources of importance for which flux values need
to be computed.

Consequently, if the GRDF would be known, it is possible to compute
various fluxes for a number of light sources and importance distributions.
It suffices to evaluate Equation 4.7, which is a nonrecursive integral. In
practice, however, this may be difficult to achieve, since the GRDF has
as arguments two positions and two directions. If one wants to compute
and store the GRDF for a significant number of arguments, or if we want
to compute a discretized version of the GRDF, the required amount of
memory can easily become huge.

A Monte Carlo algorithm based on the computation of the GRDF, so-
called bi-directional path tracing, is discussed in Chapter 7.

4.5   Classification of Global Illumination Algorithms

In the previous section, it was shown that there are four possible expressions
for the flux of any given set of surface points and directions in a global
illumination environment.

When designing a global illumination algorithm, which means we want
to compute fluxes for specific sets in the scene, we can choose whether we
want to use incident radiance combined with exitant importance in the algorithm, or exitant radiance combined with incident importance. Furthermore, we can choose to consider radiance or importance as the transport

quantity which has to be computed by solving a recursive integral transport equation. This implies there are four different classes of algorithms trying to compute global illumination solutions.

4.5.1 Incident and Exitant Representations

A first option to consider is whether we want to represent radiance as an exitant or incident measure (which automatically determines importance to be incident or exitant, respectively). From a mathematical point of view, the incident and exitant functions can be transformed into each other because they remain invariant along straight lines. But the choice is important with regard to representation of the functions and storage requirements.

The previous section showed that it is easier to intuitively reason about exitant radiance and incident importance. The initial incident radiance distribution due to a light source equals zero at the surface points belonging to that light source but has a value different from zero at surface points directly visible to that light source. All points and directions belonging to a set for which we want to compute the flux have an initial incident importance value different from zero. Exitant importance is only different from zero in points that are visible to the set in question. Thus, it is a lot more convenient to think in terms of exitant radiance and incident importance.

A second issue to be considered is the nature of the incident and exitant functions with regard to continuity over the integration domains. Finite element methods make certain assumptions about the shape of the functions under consideration in order to achieve a required precision. It is, therefore, important to know whether or not features such as discontinuities are present in the function we want to compute. All of the transport quantities described above, incident and exitant, can have discontinuities in the surface area domain. It suffices to think of shadow boundaries or material boundaries for exitant radiance or directly versus indirectly lit areas for incident radiance. Analogous phenomena are present in the importance function. However, there is a difference when considering these functions in the directional domain. If the BRDF itself is a continuous function (which might not always be the case, e.g., ideal specular surfaces), then exitant radiance is continuous over the hemisphere. Incident radiance can have discontinuities, due to the angle under which light sources light a surface. The same can be said about the importance function: incident importance can have discontinuities in the directional domain, but exitant importance is continuous.

Whatever option we choose, we always have to work with a pair of functions consisting of an exitant and an incident one, so we will always have a function that has at least discontinuities in the directional domain. However, the discontinuities only matter if we construct an algorithm that uses a data representation not well suited to represent these kinds of discontinuities. For instance, in [173], spherical harmonic functions are used to represent directional distributions. They are not capable of reproducing discontinuities accurately, so it may be a bad choice to work with a combination of incident radiance and spherical harmonic functions. If we want to somehow represent discontinuities in the spatial domain, they should be integrated in the structure of the finite elements. This technique is known as discontinuity meshing [71, 111, 112].

4.5.2 Series Expansion

Once we have chosen a pair of an exitant and an incident function, the next choice to make is what transport equation to use; or more precisely, what measure will we consider to be unknown with regard to the given set, and thus needs to be computed using an appropriate recursive integral equation? For this computation, we have the following data available:

- A specific initial radiance distribution $L_e^{\rightarrow}$, thereby defining all the light sources present in the environment.

- A specific initial importance distribution $W_e^{\leftarrow}$, thereby defining the set S for which we want to compute a flux. A typical situation might be that we want to compute flux values for all areas visible through each pixel (and thus each pixel defines its own set S).

- A given scene description, thereby defining the geometric kernel function $G(x, y)$, the visibility function $V(x, y)$, and the material properties or BRDFs of all surfaces in the scene.

From a mathematical point of view, we have two different expressions, given by two inner products, from which we can start the computation for any $\Phi(S)$. We can start from the initial radiance distribution $L_e^{\rightarrow}$ and compute $W^{\leftarrow}$ by evaluating its transport equation, or we can start from the initial importance distribution $W_e^{\leftarrow}$ and compute $L^{\rightarrow}$. The first step of the computation, no matter which inner product we choose as a starting point, is the substitution of the unknown function by its appropriate transport equation. For example, if we start from $\langle L_e^{\rightarrow}, W^{\leftarrow} \rangle$, we can write down the following expansion of the inner product:

$$\Phi(S) = \langle L_e^{\rightarrow}, W^{\leftarrow} \rangle = \langle L_e^{\rightarrow}, W_e^{\leftarrow} + T^* W^{\leftarrow} \rangle = \langle L_e^{\rightarrow}, W_e^{\leftarrow} \rangle + \langle L_e^{\rightarrow}, T^* W^{\leftarrow} \rangle.$$

This first substitution gives us a first approximate term $\langle L_e^{\rightarrow}, W_e^{\leftarrow} \rangle$ (which only contains known terms) of the final solution. The second term needs to be expanded further:

$$
\begin{aligned}
\Phi(S) &= \langle L_e^{\rightarrow}, W_e^{\leftarrow} \rangle + \langle L_e^{\rightarrow}, T^* W^{\leftarrow} \rangle \\
&= \langle L_e^{\rightarrow}, W_e^{\leftarrow} \rangle + \langle L_e^{\rightarrow}, T^* W_e^{\leftarrow} \rangle + \langle L_e^{\rightarrow}, T^* T^* W^{\leftarrow} \rangle. \quad (4.8)
\end{aligned}
$$

This provides us with a second term to compute. However, we could also obtain an expression for the second term in another way, by using the property of adjoint operators. By shifting T^* in the inner product, we can express $\Phi(S)$ as

$$
\begin{aligned}
\Phi(S) &= \langle L_e^{\rightarrow}, W_e^{\leftarrow} \rangle + \langle L_e^{\rightarrow}, T^* W^{\leftarrow} \rangle \\
&= \langle L_e^{\rightarrow}, W_e^{\leftarrow} \rangle + \langle T L_e^{\rightarrow}, W^{\leftarrow} \rangle \\
&= \langle L_e^{\rightarrow}, W_e^{\leftarrow} \rangle + \langle T L_e^{\rightarrow}, W_e^{\leftarrow} + T^* W^{\leftarrow} \rangle \\
&= \langle L_e^{\rightarrow}, W_e^{\leftarrow} \rangle + \langle T L_e^{\rightarrow}, W_e^{\leftarrow} \rangle + \langle T L_e^{\rightarrow}, T^* W^{\leftarrow} \rangle. \quad (4.9)
\end{aligned}
$$

Mathematically, the second and third terms of Equation 4.8 are, of course, equal to the second and third terms of Equation 4.9 (due to adjointness of T and T^*). By further expanding the series and by using the same adjoint property, we are able to write $\Phi(S)$ in many different ways. Indeed, we have the option of using the adjoint property in any step of the expansion. All possibilities can be represented by a binary tree of possible expansions, originating from $\langle L_e^{\rightarrow}, W_e^{\leftarrow} \rangle$:

$$
\Phi(S) = \langle L_e^{\rightarrow}, W_e^{\leftarrow} \rangle +
\begin{array}{c}
\quad \langle L_e^{\rightarrow}, T^* W_e^{\leftarrow} \rangle \\
\langle T L_e^{\rightarrow}, W_e^{\leftarrow} \rangle
\end{array}
+
\begin{array}{c}
\langle L_e^{\rightarrow}, T^* T^* W_e^{\leftarrow} \rangle \\
\langle L_e^{\rightarrow}, T^* T^* W_e^{\leftarrow} \rangle \\
\langle T L_e^{\rightarrow}, T^* W_e^{\leftarrow} \rangle \\
\langle T L_e^{\rightarrow}, T^* T^* W_e^{\leftarrow} \rangle \\
\langle T T L_e^{\rightarrow}, T^* W_e^{\leftarrow} \rangle \\
\langle T T L_e^{\rightarrow}, W_e^{\leftarrow} \rangle \\
\langle T T T L_e^{\rightarrow}, W_e^{\leftarrow} \rangle
\end{array}
+ \dots
$$

$$(4.10)$$

Exactly the same tree can be constructed by expanding $\langle L^{\rightarrow}, W_e^{\leftarrow} \rangle$ and by using the same kind of substitutions. The computation of a single flux can therefore be thought of as the sum of several inner products. For each inner product, we have a choice of functions to multiply with each other, and which are equivalent to each other due to the duality of the transport operator.

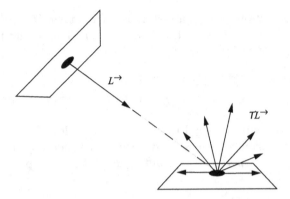

Figure 4.8. Propagation of an exitant function.

4.5.3 Physical Interpretation

The above series of inner products has, of course, a corresponding physical meaning. In order to better grasp this physical meaning, it is important to have a look at what the functional operators $\mathcal{T}$ and $\mathcal{T}^*$ actually do in a three-dimensional environment. Operator $\mathcal{T}$, operating on an exitant function, was defined as

$$\mathcal{T}L(x \to \Theta) = \int_{\Omega_x} f_r(x, \Psi \leftrightarrow \Theta)L(r(x, \Theta) \to -\Psi)\cos(N_x, \Psi)d\omega_\Psi.$$

The operator $\mathcal{T}$ transforms a function $L^\to$ int another function $\mathcal{T}L^\to$. $\mathcal{T}L^\to$ is the function we obtain when we "propagate" $L^\to$ in the environment according to the rules of the transport equation defining $\mathcal{T}$. Thus, $\mathcal{T}L^\to$ is the result of propagating $L^\to$, and evaluating this propagation in (x, Θ). The operator $\mathcal{T}$ not only implies propagating radiance along its straight path of traversal but also implies reflecting it once on a surface, in order to obtain another exitant function at the reflection point. Figure 4.8 illustrates this for a function $L^\to$ that exists only in a single point and a single direction.

$\mathcal{T}^*$, the adjoint operator of $\mathcal{T}$, was defined as

$$\mathcal{T}^*W(x \leftarrow \Theta) =$$
$$\int_{\Omega_{r(x,\Theta)}} f_r(r(x, \Theta), \Psi \leftrightarrow -\Theta)W(r(x, \Theta) \leftarrow \Psi)\cos(N_r(x, \Theta), \Psi)d\omega_\Psi.$$

The operator $\mathcal{T}^*$ behaves in a similar way as $\mathcal{T}$ but propagates incident functions through one reflection on the point on which they are incident. This is illustrated in Figure 4.9.

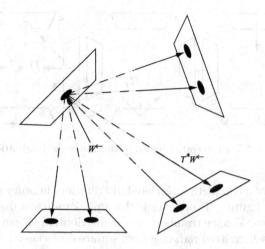

Figure 4.9. Propagation of an incident function.

One might be tempted to use the terms "shooting" and "gathering" to denote these operations. The operator T may be thought of as a shooting operation, because $TL^{\rightarrow}$ seems to be the resulting function when we "shoot" $L^{\rightarrow}$ forward. However, the terms shooting and gathering are usually applied to the way algorithms work and not to mathematical operations. It might be more convenient to think in terms of propagating the function. Whether the function is of an incident or exitant nature determines what operator (T or T^*) has to be used for the propagation.

If we look at the series of inner products that composes $\Phi(S)$, we can see that it is a succession of T and T^* operations applied to the initial radiance and importance distributions. For example, the second term in the expansion, which expresses direct illumination, can be computed by propagating $W_e^{\leftarrow}$ or by propagating $L_e^{\rightarrow}$. By successively repeating these steps, we gradually build up the flux $\Phi(S)$. At each step during the evaluation, we have a choice of evaluating the next term by applying a T or T^* operation on one of the intermediate resulting functions. For example, we might propagate the radiance distribution twice, then propagate the importance function once, propagate the radiance again, etc.

The following figures illustrate this by means of a simple example. A simple scene consisting of three surfaces is depicted in Figure 4.10. For simplicity, let us also assume that there are only three directions per surface, and that functions are only defined in one surface point. The surface labeled a is a light source, emitting radiance only in the direction of surface d (exitant radiance from surface to surface is represented by a single

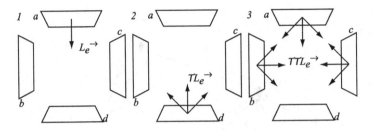

Figure 4.10. Propagation of an initial radiance distribution.

arrow, instead of a complete directional distribution, in order not to overly complicate the figure). Propagating this initial radiance distribution by applying operator $\mathcal{T}$ once results in a new distribution shown in Situation 2. Indeed, the self-emitted radiance from surface a reaches surface d, where it is reflected over the entire hemisphere (just three directions in this example), and thus emits radiance toward surfaces a, b, and c. One more propagation is shown in Situation 3. Surfaces a, b, and c emit radiance toward all other surfaces. All further propagations would result in all four surfaces emitting radiance toward all other surfaces, although the exact numerical values vary for each propagation (dependent on the values of the local BRDF, and due to absorption, each further propagation carries less total power).

Figure 4.11 shows the various propagations for the importance function by applying operator $\mathcal{T}^*$. Suppose we want to compute the flux leaving surface d. The corresponding distribution is shown in Situation 1. $W_e^{\rightarrow}$ is defined for all surface points belonging to d, and for all directions towards other surfaces. Applying the transport operator gives the results as shown in Situations 2 and 3. Further propagations result in all surfaces and all directions having an incident importance value attributed to them. As explained before, due to absorption and BRDF values, the exact numerical values would differ for each propagation.

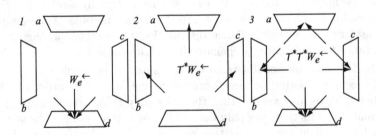

Figure 4.11. Propagation of an initial importance distribution.

In order to compute the flux, we now have to compute the various inner products, the summation of which provides us with a numerical value for the flux. This is represented in Figure 4.12. The top row shows the various propagations for the radiance distribution; the leftmost column gives the importance propagations. For each entry in the table, a thick line indicates at what surface points and for what directions a contribution to the inner product exists. Only if there are point-directions pairs that have a nonzero value for both propagations of $L_e^{\rightarrow}$ and $W_e^{\leftarrow}$ is a contribution to the inner product found.

As such, we see that the contribution to the flux due to self-emittance equals 0, which is, of course, a quite logical result, since the importance-source and radiance-source do not overlap. In order to compute the contributions as a result of direct lighting (light that reaches the set unhindered

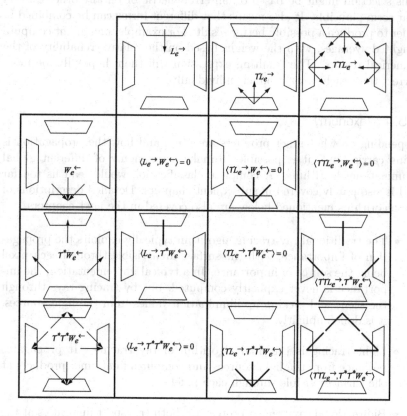

Figure 4.12. Successive propagations of exitant radiance and initial importance are shown in the top row and leftmost column, respectively. The entries in the table represent where nonzero values for the inner products can be found.

and contributes to the flux leaving that surface), we have the choice of propagating $L_e^\rightarrow$, and thus computing $\langle \mathcal{T} L_e^\rightarrow, W_e^\leftarrow \rangle$, or propagating $W_e^\leftarrow$ and thereby computing $\langle L_e^\rightarrow, \mathcal{T}^* W_e^\leftarrow \rangle$. Both inner products are equal, although the integration domain where the inner product is nonzero is different in both situations.

The next propagations compute the contributions to the flux through one or more reflections on intermediate surfaces. In this example, there are no contributions due to one intermediate reflection, but there is a contribution when the radiance is reflected at two surfaces.

The different choices available for expanding into a series of inner products are not mutually exclusive. Since all inner products at the same level of the expansion are mathematically and numerically equivalent, it is possible to compute them all and make a selection of one to use in the final result. This selection might be based on an error metric or on any other criteria that seem plausible. It also means that different terms can be combined in order to produce a possibly better result. For example, one might compute weighted averages, with the weight based on the relative reliability of the numerical results. The resulting expression will then, hopefully, be more correct than each inner product individually.

4.5.4 Taxonomy

Depending on what inner products are used, and how the propagation is being carried out, it is possible to make a taxonomy of different global illumination algorithms. A complete classification would lead us too far and is also partly covered in subsequent chapters. Detailed descriptions of the algorithms mentioned below are also covered in the next chapters.

- The traditional ray-tracing algorithm typically exploits the propagation of importance, with the surface area visible through each pixel being the source of importance. In a typical implementation, the importance is never explicitly computed, but by tracing rays through the scene and picking up illumination values from the light sources, it is done implicitly.

- Light tracing is the dual algorithm of ray tracing. It propagates radiance from the light sources and computes final inner products at the surfaces visible through each pixel.

- Bidirectional ray tracing propagates both transport quantities at the same time and, in its most advanced form, computes a weighted average of all possible inner products at all possible interactions.

- The equivalent algorithms in a radiosity context are, respectively, Gauss-Seidel radiosity, progressive radiosity, and bidirectional radiosity.

4.6 Path Formulation

The above derivation and classification of global illumination transport algorithms is based on the notion of radiance and importance. Also, the global reflection distribution function expresses the global transport between two point-direction pairs in the scene. Computing the fluxes can then be seen as computing an integral over all possible pairs of point-direction couples, evaluating the GRDF and the initial radiance and importance values. The GRDF itself is given by a recursive integral equation. By recursively evaluating the GRDF, all possible paths of different lengths in the scene are constructed.

One can also express global transport by considering path-space and computing a transport measure over each individual path. Path-space itself encompasses all possible paths of any length. Integrating a transport measure in path-space then involves generating the correct paths (e.g., random paths can be generated using an appropriate Monte Carlo sampling procedure) and evaluating the throughput of energy over each generated path. This view was developed by Spanier and Gelbard [183] and introduced into rendering by Veach [204]. The equation for the path formulation is

$$\Phi(S) = \int_{\Omega^*} f(\overline{x}) d\mu(\overline{x}),$$

in which Ω^* is the path-space, $\overline{x}$ is a path of any length, and $d\mu(\overline{x})$ is a measure in path space. $f(\overline{x})$ describes the throughput of energy and is a succession of $G(x, y)$, $V(x, y)$, and BRDF evaluations, together with a L_e and W_e evaluation at the beginning and end of the path.

An advantage of the path formulation is that paths are now considered to be the sample points for any integration procedure. Algorithms such as Metropolis light transport or bidirectional ray tracing are often better described using the path formulation.

4.7 Summary

In this chapter, we defined a mathematical framework for describing the light transport equations and the global illumination problem. This mathematical framework encompasses two sets of dual equations.

On the one hand, the radiance transport equation is based on the notion of gathering radiance values at a surface point. It assumes that the light sources are fixed and that we have several sets of interest for which we want to compute a flux. Precomputing a solution based on radiance transport and storing it in the scene would allow us to generate various images, from different camera positions.

On the other hand, the importance transport equation expresses the influence of a surface point and associated direction, if it would be a light source on the illumination of a given set. It assumes the light sources can vary, but the set of interest remains fixed. Thus, if the camera would act as a source of importance, and if an importance solution is stored in the scene, it would be possible to change the nature and characteristics of the light sources.

Both transport equations are written as recursive integral equations, known as Fredholm equations of the second kind.

Both the transport of radiance and importance can be combined by introducing the global reflectance distribution function. The GRDF describes a general transfer property from one point-direction pair in the scene to another point-direction pair. As such, it can be considered as the core function for the global illumination problem.

Computing solutions for the transport equations can be done in various ways. It is possible to distribute radiance from the light sources into the scene, and collect it at the sets for which we want to compute a flux. Or, importance can be distributed from the importance sources and collected at the light sources, upon which we would know the flux for the importance source. We can also distribute both transport quantities at once and compute their interaction at the surfaces and directions at which they meet. Based on this notion, a taxonomy of various global illumination algorithms can be constructed.

4.8 Exercises

1. Study the original formulation of the rendering equation as introduced by Kajiya [85]. It is different from the radiance formulation as mostly used today. Explain the differences. Could these differences have an influence on the final algorithms?

2. Once you have studied Chapters 5 and 6, construct a taxonomy of global illumination algorithms. Look for similarities rather than differences. Is it important whether you render pixels (as in most path-tracing variants) or patches (as in most radiosity-based algorithms)?

5

Stochastic Path-Tracing Algorithms

This chapter discusses a class of algorithms for computing global illumination pictures known as path-tracing algorithms[1]. The common aspect of these algorithms is that they generate light transport paths between light sources and the points in the scene for which we want to compute radiance values. Another, although less vital, characteristic is that they usually compute radiance values for each individual pixel directly. As such, these algorithms are pixel-driven, but many of the principles outlined here can be equally applied to other classes of light transport algorithms, such as finite element techniques (to be discussed in the next chapter).

First, we present a brief history of path-tracing algorithms in the context of global illumination algorithms (Section 5.1). Then, we discuss the camera set-up that is common to most pixel-driven rendering algorithms (Section 5.2) and introduce a simple path-tracing algorithm in Section 5.3. In Section 5.4, we introduce various methods for computing the direct illumination in a scene, followed by similar sections for the special case of environment map illumination (Section 5.5) and indirect illumination (Section 5.6). Finally, in Section 5.7, the light-tracing algorithm is discussed, which is the dual algorithm of ray tracing.

5.1 Brief History

Path-tracing algorithms for global illumination solutions started with the seminal paper on ray tracing by Whitted [194]. This paper described a novel way for extending the ray-casting algorithm to determine visible surfaces in a scene [4] to include perfect specular reflections and refractions.

---

[1]The terms ray tracing and path tracing are often used interchangeably in literature. Some prefer to use the term path tracing for a variant of ray tracing where rays do not split into multiple rays at surface points.

At the time, ray tracing was a very slow algorithm due to the number of rays that had to be traced through the scene, such that many techniques were developed for speeding up the ray-scene intersection test (see [52] for a good overview).

In 1984, Cook et al. [34] described stochastic ray tracing. Rays were distributed over several dimensions, such that glossy reflections and refractions, and other effects such as motion blur and depth of field, could be simulated in a coherent framework.

The paper of Kajiya [85] applied ray tracing to the rendering equation, which described the physical transport of light (see Chapter 2). This technique allowed full global illumination effects to be rendered, including all possible interreflections between any types of surfaces.

Other Monte Carlo sampling techniques were applied to the rendering equation, the most complete being bidirectional ray tracing, introduced by Lafortune [100] and Veach [200].

5.2   Ray-Tracing Set-Up

In order to compute a global illumination picture, we need to attribute a radiance value L_{pixel} to each pixel in the final image. This value is a weighted measure of radiance values incident on the image plane, along a ray coming from the scene, passing through the pixel, and pointing to the eye (Figure 5.1). This is best described by a weighted integral over the image plane:

$$
\begin{aligned}
L_{pixel} &= \int_{imageplane} L(p \to eye)h(p)dp \\
&= \int_{imageplane} L(x \to eye)h(p)dp,
\end{aligned}
\tag{5.1}
$$

with p being a point on the image plane, and $h(p)$ a weighting or filtering function. x is the visible point seen from the eye through p. Often, $h(p)$ equals a simple box filter such that the final radiance value is computed by uniformly averaging the incident radiance values over the area of the pixel. A more complex camera model is described in [95].

The complete ray-tracing set-up refers to the specific configuration of scene, camera, and pixels, with the specific purpose to compute radiance values for each pixel directly. We need to know the camera position and orientation, and the resolution of the target image. We assume the image is centered along the viewing axis. To evaluate $L(p \to eye)$, a ray is cast from the eye through p, in order to find x. Since $L(p \to eye) = L(x \to \overrightarrow{xp})$, we can compute this radiance value using the rendering equation.

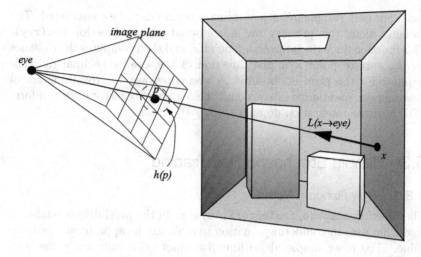

Figure 5.1. Ray-tracing set-up.

A complete pixel-driven rendering algorithm (see Figure 5.2) consists of a loop over all pixels, and for each pixel, the integral in the image (Equation 5.1) plane is computed using an appropriate integration rule. A simple Monte Carlo sampling over the image plane where $h(p) \neq 0$ can be

```
// pixel-driven rendering algorithm
computeImage(eye)
    for each pixel
        radiance = 0;
        H = integral(h(p));
        for each viewing ray
            pick uniform sample point p such that h(p) <> 0;
            construct ray at origin eye, direction p-eye;
            radiance = radiance + rad(ray)*h(p);
        radiance = radiance / (#viewingRays*H);

rad(ray)
    find closest intersection point x of ray with scene;
    computeRadiance(x, eye-x);
```

Figure 5.2. Pixel-driven rendering algorithm.

used. For each sample point p, a primary ray needs to be constructed. The
radiance along this primary ray is computed using a function rad(ray).
This function finds the intersection point x, and then computes the radiance
leaving surface point x in the direction of the eye. The final radiance
estimate for the pixel is obtained by averaging over the total number of
viewing rays, and taking into account the normalizing factor of the uniform
PDF over the integration domain $(h(p) \neq 0)$.

5.3   Simple Stochastic Ray Tracing

5.3.1   Truly Random Paths

The function compute_radiance(x, eye-x) in the pixel-driven rendering
algorithm uses the rendering equation to evaluate the appropriate radiance
value. The most simple algorithm to compute this radiance value is to
apply a basic and straightforward Monte Carlo integration scheme to the
standard form of the rendering equation. Suppose we want to evaluate the
radiance $L(x \rightarrow \Theta)$ at some surface point x (Section 2.6):

$$L(x \rightarrow \Theta) = L_e(x \rightarrow \Theta) + L_r(x \rightarrow \Theta)$$

$$= L_e(x \rightarrow \Theta) + \int_{\Omega_x} L(x \leftarrow \Psi) f_r(x, \Theta \leftrightarrow \Psi) \cos(\Psi, N_x) d\omega_\Psi.$$

The integral can be evaluated using Monte Carlo integration, by generating N random directions Ψ_i over the hemisphere Ω_x, distributed according to some probability density function $p(\Psi)$. The estimator for
$L_r(x \rightarrow \Theta)$ is then given by

$$\langle L_r(x \rightarrow \Theta) \rangle = \frac{1}{N} \sum_{i=1}^{N} \frac{L(x \leftarrow \Psi_i) f_r(x, \Theta \leftrightarrow \Psi_i) \cos(\Psi_i, N_x)}{p(\Psi_i)}.$$

The cosine and BRDF terms in the integrand can be evaluated by accessing the scene description. $L(x \leftarrow \Psi_i)$, the incident radiance at x, is
however unknown. Since

$$L(x \leftarrow \Psi_i) = L(r(x, \Psi_i) \rightarrow -\Psi_i),$$

we need to trace the ray leaving x in direction Ψ_i through the environment
to find the closest intersection point $r(x, \Psi)$. At this point, another radiance
evaluation is needed. Thus, we have a recursive procedure to evaluate
$L(x \leftarrow \Psi_i)$, and a path, or a tree of paths, is traced through the scene.

Any of these radiance evaluations will only yield a nonzero value if the
path hits a surface for which L_e is different from 0. In other words, the

recursive path needs to hit one of the light sources in the scene. Since the light sources usually are small compared to the other surfaces, this does not occur very often, and very few of the paths will yield a contribution to the radiance value to be computed. The resulting image will mostly be black. Only when a path hits a light source will the corresponding pixel be attributed a color. This is to be expected, since the algorithm generates paths in the scene, starting at the point of interest, and slowly working towards the light sources in a very uncoordinated manner.

In theory, this algorithm could be improved somewhat by choosing $p(\Psi)$ to be proportional to the cosine term or the BRDF, according to the principle of importance sampling (see Section 3.6.1). In practice, the disadvantage of picking up mostly zero-value terms is not changing the result considerably. Note, however, that this simple approach will produce an unbiased image if a sufficient number of paths per pixel are generated.

5.3.2 Russian Roulette

The recursive path generator described in the simple stochastic ray-tracing algorithm needs a stopping condition. Otherwise, the generated paths would be of infinite length and the algorithm would not come to a halt. When adding a stopping condition, one has to be careful not to introduce any bias to the final image. Theoretically, light reflects infinitely in the scene, and we cannot ignore these light paths of a long length, which might be potentially very important. Thus, we have to find a way to limit the length of the paths but still be able to obtain a correct solution.

In classic ray-tracing implementations, two techniques are often used to prevent paths from growing too long. A first technique is cutting off the recursive evaluations after a fixed number of evaluations. In other words, the paths are generated up to a certain specified length. This puts an upper bound on the number of rays that need to be traced, but important light transport might have been ignored. Thus, the image will be biased. A typical fixed path length is set at 4 or 5 but really should be dependent on the scene to be rendered. A scene with many specular surfaces will require a larger path length, while scenes with mostly diffuse surfaces can usually use a shorter path length. Another approach is to use an adaptive cut-off length. When a path hits a light source, the radiance found at the light source still needs to be multiplied by all cosine factors and BRDF evaluations (and divided by all PDF values) at all previous intersection points before it can be added to the final estimate of the radiance through the pixel. This accumulating multiplication factor can be stored along with the lengthening path. If this factor falls below a certain threshold, recursive path generation is stopped. This technique is more efficient compared to the fixed path-length, because many paths will be stopped before, and fewer errors are made, but the final image will still be biased.

Russian roulette is a technique that addresses the problem of keeping the lengths of the paths manageable but at the same time leaves room for exploring all possible paths of any length. Thus, an unbiased image can still be produced. To explain the Russian roulette principle, let us look at a simple example first. Suppose we want to compute the following one-dimensional integral:

$$I = \int_0^1 f(x)dx.$$

The standard Monte Carlo integration procedure generates random points x_i in the domain $[0, 1]$ and computes the weighted average of all function values $f(x_i)$. Assume that for some reason $f(x)$ is difficult or complex to evaluate (e.g., $f(x)$ might be expressed as another integral), and we would like to limit the number of evaluations of $f(x)$ necessary to estimate I. By scaling $f(x)$ by a factor of P horizontally and a factor of $1/P$ vertically, we can also express the quantity I as

$$I_{RR} = \int_0^P \frac{1}{P}f(\frac{x}{P})dx,$$

with $P \leq 1$. Applying Monte Carlo integration to compute the new integral, using a unform PDF $p(x) = 1$ to generate the samples over $[0, 1]$, we

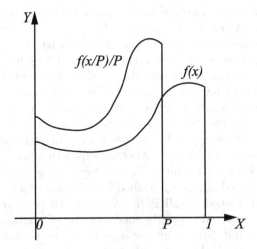

Figure 5.3. Principle of Russian roulette.

get the following estimator for I_{RR}:

$$\langle I_{RR} \rangle = \begin{cases} \frac{1}{P} f(\frac{x}{P}) & \text{if } x \le P \\ 0 & \text{if } x > P. \end{cases}$$

It is easy to verify that the expected value of $\langle I_{RR} \rangle$ equals I. If $f(x)$ would be another recursive integral (as is the case in the rendering equation), the result of applying Russian roulette is that recursion stops with a probability equal to $\alpha = 1 - P$ for each evaluation point. α is called the absorption probability. Samples generated in the interval $[P, 1]$ will generate a function value equal to 0, but this is compensated by weighting the samples in $[0, P]$ with a factor $1/P$. Thus, the overall estimator still remains unbiased.

If α is small, the recursion will continue many times, and the final estimator will be more accurate. If α is large, the recursion will stop sooner, but the estimator will have a higher variance. For our simple path-tracing algorithm, this means that either we generate accurate paths having a long length, or very short paths, which provide a less accurate estimate. However, the final estimator will be unbiased.

In principle, we can pick any value for α, and we can control the execution time of the algorithm by picking an appropriate value. In global

---

```
// simple stochastic ray tracing
computeRadiance(x, dir)
    find closest intersection point x of ray with scene;
    estimatedRadiance = simpleStochasticRT(x, dir);
    return(estimatedRadiance);

simpleStochasticRT (x, theta)
    estimatedRadiance = 0;
    if (no absorption)              // Russian roulette
        for all paths              // N rays
            sample direction psi on hemisphere;
            y = trace(x, psi);
            estimatedRadiance +=
                simpleStochasticRT(y,-psi)*BRDF
                *cos(Nx, psi)/pdf(psi);
        estimatedRadiance /= #paths;
        estimatedRadiance /= (1-absorption)
    estimatedRadiance += Le(x, theta)
    return(estimatedRadiance);
```

Figure 5.4. Simple stochastic ray-tracing algorithm.

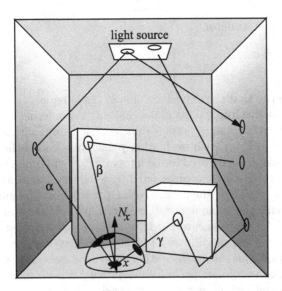

Figure 5.5. Tracing paths using simple stochastic ray tracing.

illumination algorithms, it is common for $1 - \alpha$ to be equal to the hemispherical reflectance of the material of the surface. Thus, dark surfaces will absorb the path more easily, while lighter surfaces have a higher chance of reflecting the path. This corresponds to the physical behavior of light incident on these surfaces.

The complete algorithm for simple stochastic ray tracing is given in Figure 5.4 and is illustrated in Figure 5.5. Paths are traced starting at point x. Path α contributes to the radiance estimate at x, since it reflects off the light source at the second reflection and is absorbed afterwards. Path γ also contributes, even though it is absorbed at the light source. Path β does not contribute, since it gets absorbed before reaching the light source.

5.4 Direct Illumination

The simple stochastic path tracer described in Section 5.3 is rather inefficient, since directions around each surface point are sampled without taking the position of the light sources into account. It is obvious that light sources contribute significantly to the illumination of any surface point visible to them. By sending paths to the light sources explicitly, accurate pictures are obtained much faster.

5.4.1 Direct and Indirect Illumination

As explained in Section 2.6, the reflected radiance term of the rendering equation can be split into two parts: a term that describes the direct illumination due to the light sources and one that describes the indirect illumination. We first write the reflected radiance integral using exitant radiance only:

$$L_r(x \to \Theta) = \int_{\Omega_x} L(x \leftarrow \Psi) f_r(x, \Theta \leftrightarrow \Psi) \cos(\Psi, N_x) d\omega_\Psi$$

$$= \int_{\Omega_x} L(r(x, \Psi) \to -\Psi) f_r(x, \Theta \leftrightarrow \Psi) \cos(\Psi, N_x) d\omega_\Psi.$$

Rewriting $L(r(x, \Psi) \to -\Psi)$ as a sum of self-emitted and reflected radiance at $r(x, \Psi)$ gives us

$$L_r(x \to \Theta) = \int_{\Omega_x} L_e(r(x, \Psi) \to -\Psi) f_r(x, \Theta \leftrightarrow \Psi) \cos(\Psi, N_x) d\omega_\Psi$$

$$+ \int_{\Omega_x} L_r(r(x, \Psi) \to -\Psi) f_r(x, \Theta \leftrightarrow \Psi) \cos(\Psi, N_x) d\omega_\Psi \quad (5.2)$$

$$= L_{direct}(x \to \Theta) + L_{indirect}(x \to \Theta).$$

The direct term $L_{direct}(x \to \Theta)$ expresses the contribution to $L_r(x \to \Theta)$ directly from the light sources. Since the integrand of $L_{direct}(x \to \Theta)$ contains $L_e(r(x, \Psi) \to -\Psi)$, which only differs from zero at the light sources, we can transform the hemispherical integral to an integral over the area of the light sources only (Figure 5.6),

$$L_{direct}(x \to \Theta) = \int_{A_{sources}} L_e(y \to \overrightarrow{yx}) f_r(x, \Theta \leftrightarrow \overrightarrow{xy}) G(x, y) V(x, y) dA_y,$$

$$(5.3)$$

or by explicitly summing over all N_L light sources in the scene,

$$L_{direct}(x \to \Theta) = \sum_{k=1}^{N_L} \int_{A_k} L_e(y \to \overrightarrow{yx}) f_r(x, \Theta \leftrightarrow \overrightarrow{xy}) G(x, y) V(x, y) dA_y.$$

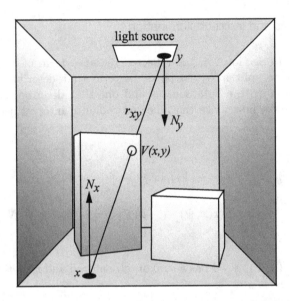

Figure 5.6. Area integration over light sources for direct illumination.

This integral over all light sources can now be computed using a very efficient sampling scheme. By generating surface points on the area of the light sources, we are sure that, if the light source is visible to the point x, a nonzero contribution is added to the Monte Carlo estimator for x. If x is in a shadow, the contribution to the estimator equals 0.

There are two options to sample surface points on the light sources: we can compute the direct illumination for each light source separately, or we can consider the combined light sources as one large light source, treating it as a single integration domain. Surface points y_i on the light sources will be generated, and for each sample y_i, the integrand $L_e(y_i \rightarrow x)$ $f_r(x, \Theta \leftrightarrow \overrightarrow{xy_i})G(x, y_i)V(x, y_i)$ has to be evaluated. Since $V(x, y_i)$ requires a visibility check and represents whether the point x is in shadow relative to y_i, the paths generated between x and y_i are often called shadow rays.

The following choices of settings will determine the accuracy of the direct illumination computation:

- Total number of shadow rays. Increasing the number of shadow rays will produce a better estimate.

- Shadow rays per light source. According to the principle of importance sampling, the number of shadow rays per light source should be proportional to the relative contribution of the light source to the illumination of x.

- Distribution of shadow rays within a light source. More shadow rays should be generated for the parts of the light source that have a greater impact on the direct illumination. For example, large area light sources will have areas that are close to the surface points to be illuminated. These areas should receive more shadow rays to obtain a more accurate estimator for direct illumination.

5.4.2 Single Light Source Illumination

To compute the direct illumination due to a single light source in the scene, i.e., a light source that consists of one continuous area, we need to define a probability density function $p(y)$ over the area of the light source, which generates the shadow rays. We assume that such a PDF can be constructed, irrespective of the geometrical nature of the light source.

Applying Monte Carlo integration (using N_S shadow rays) to Equation 5.3 yields the following estimator:

$$\langle L_{direct}(x \to \Theta) \rangle = \frac{1}{N_s} \sum_{i=1}^{N_s} \frac{L_e(y_i \to \overrightarrow{y_i x}) f_r(x, \Theta \leftrightarrow \overrightarrow{xy_i}) G(x, y_i) V(x, y_i)}{p(y_i)}.$$

For each surface point y_i sampled on the light source, the energy transfer between y_i and x needs to be computed. This requires evaluations of the

```
// direct illumination from a single light source
// for a surface point x, direction theta
directIllumination (x, theta)
    estimatedRadiance = 0;
    for all shadow rays
        generate point y on light source;
        estimatedRadiance +=
            Le(y, yx) * BRDF * radianceTransfer(x,y)/pdf(y);
    estimatedRadiance = estimatedRadiance / #shadowRays;
    return(estimatedRadiance);

// transfer between x and y
// 2 cosines, distance and visibility taken into account
radianceTransfer(x,y)
    transfer = G(x,y)*V(x,y);
    return(transfer);
```

Figure 5.7. Computing direct illumination from a single light source.

BRDF at x, a visibility check between x and y_i, the geometric coupling factor, and the emitted radiance at y_i. The whole energy transfer has to be weighted by $p(y_i)$. An overview of the sampling procedure is given in Figure 5.7.

The variance of this Monte Carlo integration, and thus the noise in the final image, is mainly determined by the choice of $p(y)$. Ideally, $p(y)$ equals the contribution each point y contributes to the final estimator, but in practice, this is almost never possible, and more pragmatic choices have to be made, mainly driven by ease of implementation. Interesting, and often used, choices for $p(y)$ are:

Uniform sampling of light source area. In this case, the points y_i are distributed uniformly over the area of the light source, and $p(y) = 1/A_{source}$. This is the easiest way of sampling a light source, and optimizations such as stratified sampling can easily be used (Figure 5.8). Using this sampling scheme, there are several sources of noise in the image. If a point x is located in the penumbra region of a shadow, some of its shadow rays will yield $V(x, y_i) = 0$, and some will not. This causes most of the noise in these soft-shadowed areas. On the other hand, if x is located outside any shadow area, all the noise is caused in variations of the cosine terms, but most importantly, variations in $1/r_{xy}^2$. This is especially noticeable if the light

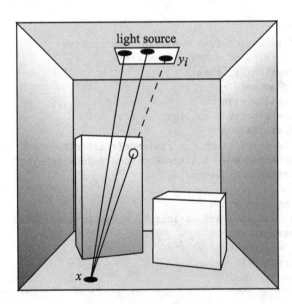

Figure 5.8. Uniform light-source sampling for direct illumination.

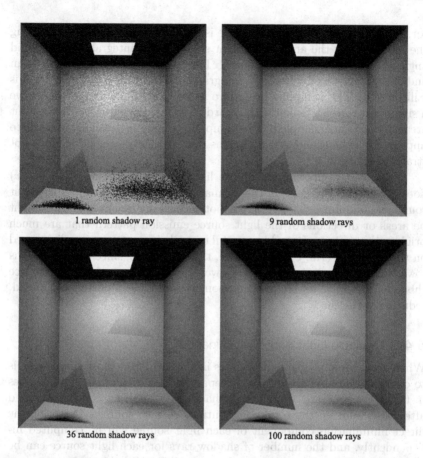

Figure 5.9. Uniform light source sampling. The images are generated with 1 viewing ray per pixel and 1, 9, 36, and 100 shadow rays. The difference in quality between soft shadows and hard shadows is noticeable.

sources are large. The pictures in Figure 5.9 show a simple scene rendered with 1, 9, 36, and 100 shadow rays, respectively. For each pixel, a single viewing ray is cast through the center of the pixel, which produces the closest intersection point x for which a radiance value needs to be computed. It is obvious that when only one shadow ray is used, surface points either lie in shadow or are visible for the light source. Some pixels in which the penumbra is visible are therefore completely black, hence, the high amount of noise in the soft shadow regions.

Uniform sampling of solid angle subtended by light source. To eliminate noise caused by either the cosine terms or the inverse distance squared factor, sampling according to solid angle is an option. This requires rewriting the integral over the area of the light source as an integral over the solid angle subtended by the light source. This would remove one cosine term and the distance factor from the integrand. However, the visibility term is still present. This sampling procedure is useful for light sources that have a significant foreshortening with regard to x, making sure these important areas are not undersampled. This sampling technique is usually difficult to implement, since generating directions over an arbitrary solid angle is not straightforward [6].

Many scenes only contain diffuse light sources, and thus $L_e(y \rightarrow \overrightarrow{yx})$ does not add to any noise in the estimation of $L_{direct}(x \rightarrow \Theta)$. If the light source is nondiffuse, $L_e(y \rightarrow \overrightarrow{yx})$ is not a constant function. There might be areas or directions of the light source emission pattern that are much brighter than others. It could be useful to apply importance sampling based on the emission term, but in practice, this is difficult, since only directions towards x need to be considered. However, a spatially variant light source thbat is diffuse in its angular component could be importance-sampled, reducing variance.

5.4.3 Multiple Light Source Illumination

When there are multiple light sources in the scene, the most simple way is to compute the direct illumination separately for each of the light sources in turn. We generate a number of shadow rays for each light source and afterwards sum up the total contributions of each source. This way, the direct illumination component of each light source will be computed independently, and the number of shadow rays for each light source can be chosen according to any criterion (e.g., equal for all light sources, proportional to the total power of the source, proportional to the inverse distance squared between the point and the point x, etc.)

However, it is often better to consider all combined light sources as a single integration domain and apply Monte Carlo integration to the combined integral. When shadow rays are generated, they can be directed to any of the light sources. It is, therefore, possible to compute the direct illumination of any number of light sources with just a single shadow ray and still obtain an unbiased picture (although, in this case, the noise in the final image will probably be very high). This approach works because we make complete abstraction of light sources as separate, disjunct surfaces and just look at the entirety of the integration domain. However, in order to have a working sampling algorithm, we still need access to any of the light sources separately, because any individual light source might require a separate sampling procedure for generating points over its surface.

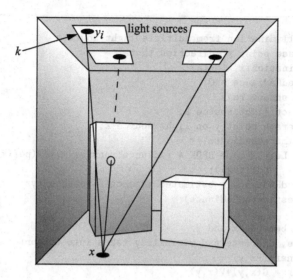

Figure 5.10. Sampling multiple light sources for direct illumination.

Generally, a two-step sampling process is used for each shadow ray (Figure 5.10):

- First, a discrete probability density function $p_L(k)$ is used to select a light sources k_i. We assign to each of N_L light source a probability value with which it will be chosen to send a shadow ray to. Typically, this probability function is the same for all shadow rays we want to cast but can be different for each different surface point x for which we want to compute a radiance value.

- During the second step, a surface point y_i on the light source k selected during the previous step is generated using a conditional PDF $p(y|k_i)$. The nature of this PDF is dependent on light source k_i. For example, some light sources might be sampled using uniform area sampling, while others might be sampled by generating shadow rays over the subtended solid angle.

The combined PDF for a sampled point y_i on the combined area of all light sources is then $p_L(k)p(y|k)$. This produces the following estimator for N shadow rays:

```
// direct illumination from multiple light sources
// for surface point x, direction theta
directIllumination(x, theta)
    estimatedRadiance = 0;
    for all shadow rays
        select light source k;
        generate point y on light source k;
        estimatedRadiance +=
            Le(y, yx) * BRDF * radianceTransfer(x,y)/(pdf(k)
                pdf(y|k));
    estimatedRadiance = estimatedRadiance / #shadowRays;
    return(estimatedRadiance);

// transfer between x and y
// 2 cosines, distance and visibility taken into account
radianceTransfer(x,y)
    transfer = G(x,y)*V(x,y);
    return(transfer);
```

Figure 5.11. Computing direct illumination from multiple light sources.

$$\langle L_{direct}(x \to \Theta) \rangle = \frac{1}{N} \sum_{i=1}^{N} \frac{L_e(y_i \to \overrightarrow{y_i x}) f_r(x, \Theta \leftrightarrow \overrightarrow{xy_i}) G(x, y_i) V(x, y_i)}{p_L(k_i) p(y_i|k_i)}.$$

$$(5.4)$$

Figure 5.11 shows the algorithm for computing the direct illumination due to multiple light sources. Note, however, that the algorithm for computing the illumination due to a single source could be used as well, repeating it for each individual light source.

Although any PDFs $p_L(k)$ and $p(y|k)$ will produce unbiased images, the specific choice for which PDFs to use will have an impact on the variance of the estimators and the noise in the final picture. Some of the more popular choices are:

Uniform source selection, uniform sampling of light source area. Both PDFs are uniform: $p_L(k) = 1/N_L$ and $p(y|k) = 1/A_{L_k}$. Every light source will receive, on average, an equal number of shadow rays, and these shadow rays are distributed uniformly over the area of each light source. This is easy to implement, but the disadvantages are that the illumination of both bright and weak light sources are computed with an equal number of shadow rays and that light sources that are far away or invisible receive an equal number of shadow rays as light sources that are close-by. Thus, the relative importance of each light source is not taken into account. Substituting the PDFs in Equation 5.4 gives the following estimator for the direct illumination:

$$\langle L_{direct}(x \rightarrow \Theta) \rangle = \frac{N_L}{N} \sum_{i=1}^{N} A_{L_k} L_e(y_i \rightarrow \overrightarrow{y_i x}) f_r(x, \Theta \leftrightarrow \overrightarrow{xy_i}) G(x, y_i) V(x, y_i).$$

Power-proportional source selection, uniform sampling of light source area.
Here, the PDF $p_L(k) = P_k / P_{total}$ with P_k the power of light source k and P_{total} the total power emitted by all light sources. Bright sources would receive more shadow rays, and very dim light sources might receive very few. This is likely to reduce variance and noise in the picture.

$$\langle L_{direct}(x \rightarrow \Theta) \rangle =$$
$$\frac{P_{total}}{N} \sum_{i=1}^{N} \frac{A_{L_k} L_e(y_i \rightarrow \overrightarrow{y_i x}) f_r(x, \Theta \leftrightarrow \overrightarrow{xy_i}) G(x, y_i) V(x, y_i)}{P_k}$$

If all light sources are diffuse, $P_k = \pi A_k L_{e,k}$, and thus

$$\langle L_{direct}(x \rightarrow \Theta) \rangle = \frac{P_{total}}{\pi N} \sum_{i=1}^{N} f_r(x, \Theta \leftrightarrow \overrightarrow{xy_i}) G(x, y_i) V(x, y_i).$$

This approach is typically superior since it gives importance to bright sources, but it could result in slower convergence at pixels where the bright lights are invisible and illumination is dominated by less bright lights at these pixels. This latter occurrence can only be solved by using sampling strategies that use some knowledge about the visibility of the light sources.

No matter what $p_L(k)$ is chosen, one has to be sure not to exclude any light sources that might contribute to $L_{direct}(x \rightarrow \Theta)$. Just dropping small, weak, or faraway light sources might result in bias, and for some portions of the image, this bias can be significant.

One of the drawbacks of the above two-step procedure is that three random numbers are needed to generate a shadow ray: one random number to select the light source k, and two random numbers to select a specific surface point y_i within the area of the light source. This makes stratified sampling more difficult to implement. In [170], a technique is described that makes it possible to use only two random numbers when generating shadow rays for a number of disjunct light sources. The two-dimensional integration domain covering all light sources is mapped on the standard two-dimensional unit square. Each light source corresponds to a small subdomain of the unit square. When a point is sampled on the unit square, we find out what subarea it is in, and then transform the location of the point to the actual light source. Sampling in a three-dimensional domain has now been reduced to sampling in a two-dimensional domain, which makes it easier to apply stratified sampling or other variance-reduction techniques.

5.4.4 Alternative Shadow Ray Sampling

Area sampling of the light sources is the most intuitive and best known algorithm for computing direct illumination in a scene. We expect the variance to be low, since knowledge is used in the sampling procedure about where light is coming from in the scene. However, some other sampling techniques can be used to compute the direct illumination, which are often less efficient, but are interesting from a theoretical point of view. These techniques offer alternative ways of constructing paths between the point of interest and the light source.

Shadow rays by hemisphere sampling. This sampling procedure is related to the simple stochastic ray-tracing algorithm, explained in Section 5.3. Directions Ψ_i are generated over the hemisphere Ω_x, after which the nearest intersection point $r(x, \Psi_i)$ is found. If $r(x, \Psi_i)$ belongs to a light source, a contribution to the direct illumination estimator is recorded. In Figure

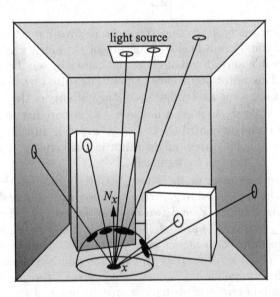

Figure 5.12. Shadow rays generated using hemisphere sampling.

5.12, only two out of seven rays reach the light source and yield a contribution different from 0. This is actually the simple stochastic ray-tracing algorithm, in which the recursion is ended after one level. Many rays will be oriented towards surfaces that are not light sources. The noise and variance are mostly caused by this fact and not by any visibility considerations, since the visibility will not be present in the final estimator. The visibility term is implicitly contained in the computation of the nearest visible point $r(x, \Psi_i)$.

Shadow rays by global area sampling. The integral describing global illumination (Equation 5.3) integrates over the area of all light sources. It is also possible to write this integral as an integration over *all* surfaces in the scene, since the self-emitted radiance equals 0 over surfaces that are not a light source (Figure 5.13). Using this formulation, surface points can be sampled over any surface in the scene. The evaluation is the same as for regular shadow rays, except that the $L_e(y_i)$ factor might be equal to 0, introducing an extra source of noise.

Although these methods do not make much sense from an efficiency point of view, they emphasize the basic principle of computing light transport: paths need to be generated between the light sources and the receiving point. The methods merely differ in how the paths are generated, but this has a drastic impact on the accuracy of their corresponding estimators.

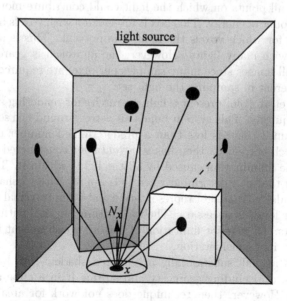

Figure 5.13. Shadow rays generated using global area sampling.

5.4.5 Further Optimizations

Many optimizations have been proposed to make the computation of direct illumination more efficient. Most of these deal with trying to make the evaluation of $V(x, y)$ more efficient, or by preselecting the light sources to which to send shadow rays.

Ward [223] accelerates the direct illumination due to multiple light sources using a user-specified threshold to eliminate lights that are less important. For each pixel in the image, the system sorts the lights according to their maximum possible contribution, assuming the lights are fully visible. Occlusion for each of the largest possible contributors at the pixel is tested, measuring their actual contribution to the pixel and stopping at a predetermined energy threshold. This approach can reduce the number of occlusion tests; however, it does not reduce the cost of occlusion tests that do have to be performed and does not do very well when illumination is uniform.

The approach of Shirley et al. [230] subdivides the scene into voxels and, for each voxel, partitions the set of lights into an important set and an unimportant set. Each light in the important set is sampled explicitly. One light is picked at random from the unimportant set as a representative of the set and sampled. The assumption is that the unimportant lights all contribute the same amount of energy. To determine the set of important lights, they construct an *influence box* around each light. An influence box contains all points on which the light could contribute more than the threshold amount of energy. This box is intersected with voxels in the scene to determine for which voxels the light is important. This is an effective way to deal with many lights. However, the approach is geared towards producing still images since many samples per pixel are required to reduce the noise inherent in sampling the light set.

Paquette et al. [136] present a light hierarchy for rendering scenes with many lights quickly. This system builds an octree around the set of lights, subdividing until there is less than a predetermined number of lights in each cell. Each octree cell then has a *virtual light* constructed for it that represents the illumination caused by all the lights within it. They derive error bounds that can determine when it is appropriate to shade a point with a particular virtual light representation and when traversal of the hierarchy to finer levels is necessary. Their algorithm can deal with thousands of point lights. One major limitation of this approach is that it does not take visibility into consideration.

Haines et al. [60] substantially accelerated shadow rays by explicitly keeping track of occluding geometry and storing it in a cube around the light source. However, their technique does not work for area lights and also does no specific acceleration for many lights.

Fernandez et al. [45] use local illumination environments. For each pixel in the image, and for each light source, a list of possible occluders is built adaptively by casting shadow rays. Their technique works well for interactive speeds. Hart et al. [65] use a similar approach, but information about what geometry causes shadows in pixels is distributed in the image using a flood-fill algorithm.

5.5 Environment Map Illumination

The techniques outlined in the previous section are applicable to almost all types of light sources. It is sufficient to choose an appropriate PDF to select one light source from amongst all light sources in the scene, and to choose a PDF to sample a random surface point on the selected light source. The total variance, and hence the stochastic noise in the image, will be highly dependent on the types of PDFs chosen.

Environment maps (sometimes also called illumination maps or reflection maps) are a type of light source that has received significant attention. An environment map encodes the total illumination present on the hemisphere of directions around a single point. Usually, environment maps are captured in natural environments using digital cameras.

An environment map can be described mathematically as a stepwise-continuous function, in which each pixel corresponds to a small solid angle $\Delta\Omega$ around the point x at which the environment map is centered. The intensity of each pixel then corresponds to an incident radiance value $L(x \leftarrow \Theta)$, with $\Theta \in \Delta\Omega$.

5.5.1 Capturing Environment Maps

Environment maps usually represent real-world illumination conditions. A light probe in conjunction with a digital camera or a digital camera equipped with a fisheye lens are the most common techniques for capturing environment maps.

Light Probe

A practical way to acquire an environment map of a real environment is the use of a light probe. A light probe is nothing more than a specular reflective ball that is positioned at the point where the incident illumination needs to be captured. The light probe is subsequently photographed using a camera equipped with an orthographic lens, or alternatively, a large zoom lens such that orthographic conditions are approximated as closely as possible.

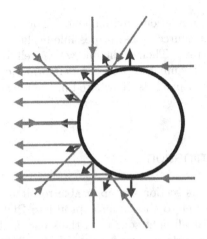 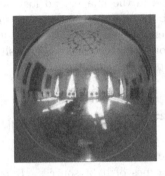

Figure 5.14. Photographing a light probe produces an environment map representing incident radiance from all directions. (Photograph courtesy of Vincent Masselus.)

The center pixel in the recorded image of the light probe corresponds with a single incident direction. This direction can be computed rather easily, since the normal vector on the light probe is known, and a mapping from pixel coordinates to incident directions can be used. A photograph of the light probe can therefore results in a set of samples $L(x \leftarrow \Theta)$ (Figure 5.14).

Although the acquisition process is straightforward, there are a number of issues to be considered:

- The camera will be reflected in the light probe and will be present in the photograph, thereby blocking light coming from directions directly behind the camera.

- The use of a light probe does not result in a uniform sampling of directions over the hemisphere. Directions opposite the camera are sampled poorly, whereas directions on the same side of the camera are sampled densely.

- All directions sampled at the edge of the image of the light probe represent illumination from the same direction. Since the light probe has a small radius, these values may differ slightly.

- Since the camera cannot capture all illumination levels due to its nonlinear response curve, a process of high dynamic range photogra-

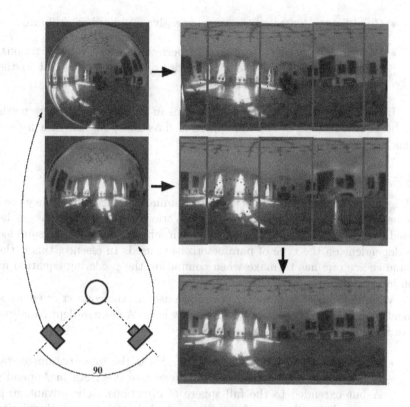

Figure 5.15. Photographing a light probe twice, 90 degrees apart. The camera positions are indicated in blue. Combining both photographs produces a well-sampled environment map without the camera being visible. (Photographs courtesy of Vincent Masselus.) (See Plate XIX.)

phy needs to be used to acquire an environment map that correctly represents radiance values.

Some of these problems can be alleviated by capturing two photographs of the light probe 90 degrees apart. The samples of both photographs can be combined into a single environment map as is shown in Figure 5.15.

Fisheye Lens

An alternative for capturing an environment map is to make use of a camera equipped with a fisheye lens. Two photographs taken from opposite view directions result in a single environment map as well. However, there are some limitations:

- Good fisheye lenses can be very expensive and hard to calibrate.

- Both images need to be taken in perfect opposite view directions, otherwise a significant set of directions will not be present in the photograph.

If the incident illumination of directions in only one hemisphere needs to be known instead of the full sphere of directions, the use of a fisheye lens can be very practical.

5.5.2 Parameterizations

When using environment maps in global illumination algorithms, they need to be expressed in some parameter space. Various parameterizations can be used, and the effectiveness of how well environments maps can be sampled is dependent on the type of parameterization used. In essence, this is the same choice one has to make when computing the rendering equation as an integral over the hemisphere.

Various types of parameterizations are used in the context of environment maps, and we provide a brief overview here. A more in-depth analysis can be found in [118].

- Latitude-longitude parameterization. This is the same parameterization as the hemispherical coordinate system describes in Appendix A but extended to the full sphere of directions. The advantage is an equal distribution of the tilt angle θ, but there is a singularity around both poles, which are represented as lines in the map. Additional problems are that the pixels in the map do not occupy equal solid angles and that the $\phi = 0$ and $\phi = 2\pi$ angles are not mapped continuously next to each other (Figure 5.16(a)).

- Projected-disk parameterization. This parameterization is also known as Nusselt embedding. The hemisphere of directions is projected on a disk of radius 1. The advantages are the continuous mapping of the azimuthal angle ϕ, and the pole being a single point in the map. However, the tilt angle θ is nonuniformly distributed over the map (Figure 5.16(b)). A variant is the paraboloid parameterization, in which the tilt angle is distributed more evenly [72] (Figure 5.16(c)).

- Concentric-map parameterization. The concentric map parameterization transforms the projected unit disk to a unit square [165]. This makes sampling of directions in the map easier and keeps the continuity of the projected-disk parameterizations (Figure 5.16(d)).

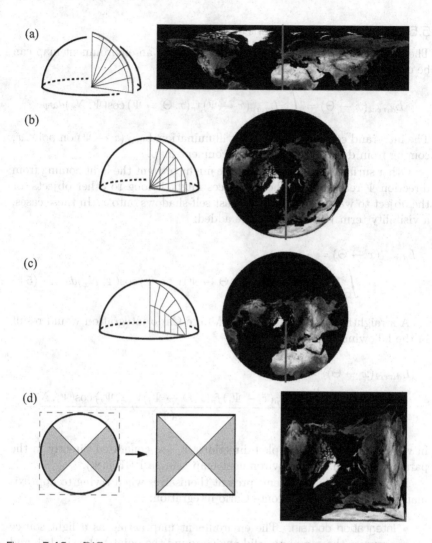

Figure 5.16. Different parameterizations for the (hemi)sphere: (a) latitude-longitude parameterization; (b) projected-disk parameterization; (c) paraboloid parameterization; (d) concentric-map parameterization. (Diagrams courtesy of Vincent Masselus.)

5.5.3　Sampling Environment Maps

The direct illumination of a surface point due to an environment map can be expressed as follows:

$$L_{direct}(x \to \Theta) = \int_{\Omega_x} L_{map}(x \leftarrow \Psi) f_r(x, \Theta \leftrightarrow \Psi) \cos(\Psi, N_x) d\omega_\Psi.$$

The integrand contains the incident illumination $L_{map}(x \leftarrow \Psi)$ on point x, coming from direction Ψ in the environment map.

Other surfaces present in the scene might prevent the light coming from direction Ψ reaching x. These surfaces might belong to other objects, or the object to which x belongs can cast self-shadows onto x. In these cases, a visibility term $V(x, \Psi)$ has to be added:

$$L_{direct}(x \to \Theta) =$$
$$\int_{\Omega_x} L_{map}(x \leftarrow \Psi) f_r(x, \Theta \leftrightarrow \Psi) V(x, \Psi) \cos(\Psi, N_x) d\omega_\Psi. \quad (5.5)$$

A straightforward application of Monte Carlo integration would result in the following estimator:

$$\langle L_{direct}(x \to \Theta) \rangle =$$
$$\frac{1}{N} \sum_{i=1}^{N} \frac{L_{map}(x \leftarrow \Psi_i) f_r(x, \Theta \leftrightarrow \Psi_i) V(x, \Psi_i) \cos(\Psi_i, N_x)}{p(\Psi_i)},$$

in which the different sampled directions Ψ_i are generated directly in the parameterization of the environment map using a PDF $p(\Psi)$.

However, various problems present themselves when trying to approximate this integral using Monte Carlo integration:

- **Integration domain.** The environment map acting as a light source occupies the complete solid angle around the point to be shaded, and thus, the integration domain of the direct illumination equation has a large extent, usually increasing variance.

- **Textured light source.** Each pixel in the environment map represents a small solid angle of incident light. The environment map can therefore be considered as a textured light source. The radiance distribution in the environment map can contain high frequencies or discontinuities, thereby again increasing variance and stochastic noise in the final image. Especially when capturing effects such as the sun or bright windows, very high peaks of illumination values can be present in the environment map.

- **Product of environment map and BRDF.** As expressed in Equation 5.5, the integrand contains the product of the incident illumination $L_{map}(x \leftarrow \Psi)$ and the BRDF $f_r(x, \Theta \leftrightarrow \Psi)$. In addition to the discontinuities and high-frequency effects present in the environment map, a glossy or specular BRDF also contains very sharp peaks. These peaks on the sphere or hemisphere of directions for both illumination values and BRDF values are usually not located at the same directions. This makes it very difficult to design a very efficient sample scheme that takes these features into account.

- **Visibility.** If the visibility term is included, additional discontinuities are present in the integrand. This is very similar to the handling of the visibility term in standard direct illumination computations but might complicate an efficient sampling process.

Practical approaches try to construct a PDF $p(\Psi)$ that addresses these problems. Roughly, these can be divided in three categories: PDFs based on the distribution of radiance values $L_{map}(x \leftarrow \Psi)$ in the illumination map only, usually taking into account $\cos(\Psi, N_x)$ that can be pre-multiplied into the illumination map; PDFs based on the BRDF $f_r(x, \Theta \leftrightarrow \Psi)$, which are especially useful if the BRDF is of a glossy or specular nature; and PDFs based on the product of both functions, but which are usually harder to construct.

- **Direct illumination map sampling.** A first approach for constructing a PDF based on the radiance values in the illumination map can be simply to transform the piecewise-constant pixel values into a PDF by computing the cumulative distribution in two dimensions and subsequently inverting it. This typically results in a 2D look-up table, and the efficiency of the method is highly dependent on how fast this look-up table can be queried.

A different approach is to simplify the environment map by transforming it to a number of well-selected point light sources. This has the advantage that there is a consistent sampling of the environment map for all surface points to be shaded, but can possibly introduce aliasing artifacts, especially when using a low number of light sources. In [97], an approach is presented in which a quadrature rule is generated automatically from a high dynamic range environment map. Visibility is taken into account in the structured importance sampling algorithm, in which the environment map is subdivided into a number of cells [1].

- BRDF sampling. The main disadvantage of constructing a PDF based only on the illumination map is that the BRDF is not included in the sampling process but is left to be evaluated after the sample directions have been chosen. This is particularly problematic for specular and glossy BRDFs, and if this is the case, a PDF based on the BRDF will produce better results.

  This of course requires that the BRDF can be sampled analytically, which is not always possible, except for a few well-constructed BRDFs (e.g., a Phong BRDF or Lafortune BRDF). Otherwise, the inverse cumulative distribution technique will have to be used for the BRDF as well.

- Sampling the product. The best approach is to construct a sampling scheme based on the product of both the illumination map and the BRDF, possibly including the cosine and some visibility information as well. In [21], *bidirectional importance sampling* is introduced, which constructs a sampling procedure based on rejection sampling. The disadvantage is that it is difficult to predict exactly how many samples will be rejected, and hence the computation time. *Resampled importance sampling* is a variant of this approach [195]. *Wavelet importance sampling* [27] constructs a PDF based on the wavelet representation of both the illumination map and the BRDF, but this implies some restrictions on what type of map and BRDF can be used.

5.6   Indirect Illumination

This section deals with the computation of indirect illumination in a scene. As opposed to direct illumination computations, this problem is usually much harder, since indirect light might reach a surface point x from all possible directions. For this reason, it is very hard to optimize the indirect illumination computations along the same lines as was done for direct illumination.

Indirect illumination consists of the light reaching a target point x after at least one reflection at an intermediate surface between the light sources and x. The indirect illumination is a very important component of the total light distribution in a scene and usually takes the largest amount of work in any global illumination algorithm. A realistic rendering of the indirect illumination is often necessary to judge any computer-generated picture as being photorealistic.

```
// indirect illumination
// for surface point x, direction theta
indirectIllumination (x, theta)
    estimatedRadiance = 0;
    if (no absorption)
        for all indirect paths
            sample direction psi on hemisphere;
            y = trace(x, psi);
            estimated radiance +=
                computeRadiance(y, -psi) * BRDF *
                cos(Nx, psi) / pdf(psi);
        estimatedRadiance = estimatedRadiance / #paths;
    return(estimatedRadiance/(1-absorption));

computeRadiance(x, dir)
    estimatedRadiance = Le(x, dir);
    estimatedRadiance += directIllumination(x, dir);
    estimatedRadiance += indirectIllumination(x, dir);
    return(estimatedRadiance);
```

Figure 5.17. Computing indirect illumination.

5.6.1 Uniform Sampling for Indirect Illumination

In Section 5.4.1, the rendering equation was split into a direct and indirect part. The indirect illumination contribution to $L(x \to \Theta)$ is expressed as

$$L_{indirect}(x \to \Theta) = \int_{\Omega_x} L_r(r(x, \Psi) \to -\Psi) f_r(x, \Theta \leftrightarrow \Psi) \cos(\Psi, N_x) d\omega_\Psi.$$

The integrand contains the reflected radiances L_r from other points in the scene, which are themselves composed of a direct and indirect illumination part (according to Equation 5.2). Unlike what was done with the direct illumination equation, we cannot reformulate this integral to a smaller integration domain. $L_r(r(x, \Psi) \to -\Psi)$ has (in a closed environment) a nonzero value for all (x, Ψ) pairs. So, the entire hemisphere needs to be considered as the integration domain and needs to be sampled accordingly.

The most general Monte Carlo procedure to evaluate the indirect illumination is to use an arbitrary, hemispherical PDF $p(\Psi)$ and to generate

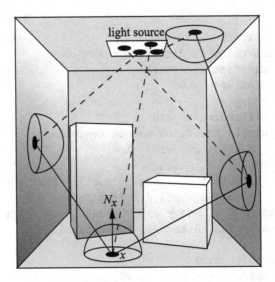

Figure 5.18. Paths generated during indirect illumination computations. Shadow rays for direct illumination are shown as dashed lines.

N random directions Ψ_i. This produces the following estimator:

$$\langle L_{indirect}(x \to \Theta) \rangle =$$
$$\frac{1}{N} \sum_{i=1}^{N} \frac{L_r(r(x, \Psi_i) \to -\Psi_i) f_r(x, \Theta \leftrightarrow \Psi_i) \cos(\Psi_i, N_x)}{p(\Psi_i)}.$$

To evaluate this estimator, for each generated direction Ψ_i, we need to evaluate the BRDF and the cosine term, trace a ray from x in the direction of Ψ_i, and evaluate the reflected radiance $L_r(r(x, \Psi_i) \to -\Psi_i)$ at the closest intersection point $r(x, \Psi_i)$. This last evaluation shows the recursive nature of indirect illumination, since this reflected radiance at $r(x, \Psi_i)$ can be split again into a direct and indirect contribution. The algorithm for evaluating the indirect illumination is given in Figure 5.17 and graphically shown in Figure 5.18.

The recursive evaluation can be stopped using Russian roulette, in the same way as was done for simple stochastic ray tracing. Generally, the local hemispherical reflectance is used as an appropriate absorption probability. This choice can be explained intuitively: we only want to spend work (i.e., tracing rays and evaluating $L_{indirect}(x)$) proportional to the amount of energy present in different parts of the scene.

5.6.2 Importance Sampling for Indirect Illumination

The simplest choice for $p(\Psi)$ is a uniform PDF $p(\Psi) = 1/2\pi$, such that directions are sampled proportional to solid angles. This is easy and straightforward to implement. Noise in the resulting picture will be caused by variations in the BRDF and cosine evaluations, and variations in the reflected radiance L_r at the distant points.

Uniform sampling over the hemisphere does not take into account any knowledge we might have about the integrand in the indirect illumination integral. In order to reduce noise, some form of importance sampling is needed. We can construct a hemispherical PDF proportional (or approximately proportional) to any of the following factors:

- The cosine factor $\cos(\Psi_i, N_x)$.

- The BRDF $f_r(x, \Theta \leftrightarrow \Psi_i)$.

- The incident radiance field $L_r(r(x, \Psi_i)$.

- A combination of any of the above.

Cosine Sampling

Sampling directions proportional to the cosine lobe around the normal N_x prevents too many directions from being sampled near the horizon of the hemisphere where $\cos(\Psi, N_x)$ equals 0. We can expect the noise to decrease, since we reduce the probability of directions being generated that contribute little to the final estimator. So

$$p(\Psi) = \cos(\Psi, N_x)/\pi.$$

If we also assume that the BRDF f_r is diffuse at x, we obtain the following estimator:

$$\langle L_{indirect}(x \to \Theta) \rangle = \frac{\pi f_r}{N} \sum_{i=1}^{N} L_r(r(x, \Psi_i) \to -\Psi_i).$$

In this estimator, the only sources of noise left are variations in the incident radiance field.

BRDF Sampling

When sampling directions Ψ over the hemisphere proportional to the cosine factor, we do not take into account that due to the nature of the BRDF at x, some directions contribute much more to the value of $L_{indirect}(x \to \Theta)$. Ideally, directions with a high BRDF value should be sampled more often.

BRDF sampling is a good noise-reducing technique when a glossy or highly specular BRDF is present. It diminishes the probability that directions are sampled where the BRDF has a low or zero value. Only for a few selected BRDF models, however, is it possible to sample exactly proportional to the BRDF.

Even better would be trying to sample proportional to the product of the BRDF and the cosine term. Analytically, this is even more difficult to do, except in a few rare cases where the BRDF model has been chosen carefully. Usually, a combination with rejection is needed to sample according to such a PDF.

A time-consuming alternative is to build a numerical table of the cumulative probability function and generate directions using this table. The PDF value will not be exactly equal to the product of BRDF and cosine factors, but a significant variance reduction can nevertheless be achieved.

A perfect specular material can be modeled using a Dirac impulse for the BRDF. In this case, sampling the BRDF simply means we only have one possible direction from which incident radiance contributes to the indirect illumination. However, such a Dirac BRDF is difficult to fit in a Monte Carlo sampling framework, and a special evaluation procedure usually needs to be written.

As an example to illustrate proportional BRDF sampling, let's consider the modified Phong BRDF,

$$f_r(x, \Theta \leftrightarrow \Psi) = k_d + k_s \cos^n(\Psi, \Theta_s),$$

where Θ_s is the perfect specular direction of Θ relative to N_x. This BRDF has a diffuse part k_d and a glossy part $k_s \cos^n(\Psi, \Theta_s)$. The indirect illumination integral can now be split into two parts, according to those terms of the BRDF:

$$L_{indirect}(x \to \Theta) = \int_{\Omega_x} L_r(r(x, \Psi) \to -\Psi) k_d \cos(\Psi, N_x) d\omega_\Psi$$

$$+ \int_{\Omega_x} L_r(r(x, \Psi) \to -\Psi) k_s \cos^n(\Psi, \Theta_s) \cos(\Psi, N_x) d\omega_\Psi.$$

Sampling this total expression proceeds as follows:

1. A discrete PDF is constructed with three events, with respective probabilities q_1, q_2, and q_3 ($q_1 + q_2 + q_3 = 1$). The three events correspond to deciding which part of the illumination integral to sample. The last event can be used as an absorption event.

2. Ψ_i is then generated using either $p_1(\Psi)$ or $p_2(\Psi)$, two PDFs that correspond, respectively, to the diffuse and glossy part of the BRDF.

3. The final estimator for a sampled direction Ψ_i is then equal to:

$$\langle L_{indirect}(x \rightarrow \Theta) \rangle = \begin{cases} \frac{L(x \leftarrow \Psi_i) k_d \cos(N_x, \Psi_i)}{q_1 p_1(\Psi_i)} & \text{if event 1} \\ \frac{L(x \leftarrow \Psi_i) k_s \cos^n(\Psi_i, \Theta_s) \cos(N_x, \Psi_i)}{q_2 p_2(\Psi_i)} & \text{if event 2} \\ 0 & \text{if event 3.} \end{cases}$$

An alternative is to consider the sampled direction as part of a single distribution and evaluate the total indirect illumination integral. The generated directions will have a subcritical distribution $q_1 p_1(\Psi) + q_2 p_2(\Psi)$, and the corresponding primary estimator is

$$\langle L_{indirect}(x \rightarrow \Theta) \rangle =$$

$$\frac{1}{N} \sum_{i=1}^{N} \frac{L_r(r(x, \Psi_i) \rightarrow -\Psi_i)(k_d + k_s \cos^n(\Psi_i, \Theta_s)) \cos(N_x, \Psi_i))}{q_1 p_1(\Psi_i) + q_2 p_2(\Psi_i)}.$$

What are good choices for these different PDFs? When the diffuse part of the BRDF is sampled with $p_1(\Psi)$, the obvious choice is to sample according to the cosine distribution. The glossy part can either be sampled according to the cosine distribution or proportional to the cosine lobe $\cos^n(\Psi, \Theta_s)$, centered around Θ_s.

The choice of q_1, q_2, and q_3 also has a significant influence on the variance of the estimator. In principle, any set of values provides an unbiased estimator, but choosing these values carefully has an impact on the final result. A good choice is to pick these values proportional to the (maximum) reflected energy in the different modes. These values can be computed by integrating the reflected energy for an incident direction along the normal N_x on the surface:

$$q_1 = \pi k_d$$

$$q_2 = \frac{2\pi}{n+2} k_s.$$

Note that the value for q_2 is actually larger than the real reflected energy in the lobe for any other incident direction than N_x, since part of the cosine lobe around Θ_s is located below the surface at x. Thus, there will be more samples generated in the specular lobe relative to the reflected energy in the lobe, but this can be adjusted by *not* resampling any directions that are located in the part of the lobe below the surface, and thus, keeping the correct balance between diffuse energy, specular energy, and absorption.

Incident Radiance Field Sampling

A last technique that can be used to reduce variance when computing the indirect illumination is to sample a direction Ψ according to the incident radiance values $L_r(x \leftarrow \Psi)$. Since this incident radiance is generally unknown when we want to compute $L_{indirect}(x \rightarrow \Theta)$, an adaptive technique needs to be used, where an approximation to $L_r(x \leftarrow \Psi)$ is built during the algorithm, and then this approximation is used to sample direction Ψ_i. Lafortune et al. [103] build a five-dimensional tree (three dimensions for position, two dimensions for direction) that does exactly this. At every leaf of the tree, an approximation $L_r^*(x \leftarrow \Psi)$ of the incident radiance resulting from earlier evaluations is used to construct a PDF. This PDF is then used to generate a random direction.

Other algorithms, such as the photon map [83], can also be used to guide the sampling of directions based on partial knowledge of the energy distribution in the scene.

5.6.3 Area Sampling

Sampling the hemisphere is the most straightforward way to compute the indirect illumination integral. For each sampled direction, a ray has to be cast to determine the closest visible point. This is a costly operation, but it also means that there will be no noise in the final image due to failed visibility checks.

As with direct illumination, there are more ways to compute indirect illumination. By writing the indirect illumination as an integral over all surfaces in the scene, we can construct an estimator by sampling surface points:

$$L_{indirect}(x \rightarrow \Theta) = \int_{A_{scene}} L_r(y \rightarrow \overrightarrow{yx}) f_r(x, \Theta \leftrightarrow \overrightarrow{xy}) G(x,y) V(x,y) dA_y.$$

The corresponding estimator when using a PDF $p(y)$ is

$$\langle L_{indirect}(x \rightarrow \Theta) \rangle = \frac{1}{N} \sum_{i=1}^{N} \frac{L_r(y_i \rightarrow \overrightarrow{y_i x}) f_r(x, \Theta \leftrightarrow \overrightarrow{xy_i}) G(x,y_i) V(x,y_i)}{p(y_i)}.$$

How is this different from the hemispherical estimator? By sampling areas, the visibility function $V(x, y_i)$ needs to be evaluated as part of the estimator. When sampling the hemisphere, the visibility is hidden in the ray-casting function for finding the closest visible point in each direction. Putting the visibility in the estimator increases the variance for an equal number of samples. This difference between area sampling and hemisphere sampling is valid, in general, for any method that has to construct paths in the scene.

5.6.4 Putting It All Together

We now have all the algorithms in place to build a full global illumination renderer using stochastic path tracing. The efficiency and accuracy of the complete algorithm will be determined by all of the following settings.

Number of viewing rays per pixel. The number of viewing rays N_p to be cast through the pixel, or more generally, the support of $h(p)$ (Equation 5.1). A higher number of viewing rays eliminates aliasing and decreases noise.

Direct illumination. For direct illumination, a number of choices are necessary that will determine the overall efficiency:

- The total number of shadow rays N_d cast from each point x.

- How a single light source is selected from among all the available light sources for each shadow ray.

- The distribution of the shadow ray over the area of a single light source.

Indirect illumination. The indirect illumination component is usually implemented using hemisphere sampling:

- Number of indirect illumination rays N_i distributed over the hemisphere Ω_x.

- Exact distribution of these rays over the hemisphere (uniform, cosine, ...).

- Absorption probabilities for Russian roulette in order to stop the recursion.

The complete algorithm for computing the global illumination for the entire image is given in schematic form in Figure 5.19.

It is obvious that the more rays we cast at each of the different choice points, the more accurate the solution will be. Also, the better we make use of importance sampling, the better the final image and the less objectionable noise there will be. The interesting question is, when given a total number of rays one can cast per pixel, how should they best be distributed to reach a maximum level of accuracy for the full global illumination solution?

This is still very much an open problem in global illumination algorithms. There are some generally accepted "default" choices, but there are no hard and fast rules. It is generally accepted that branching out too much (i.e., recursively generate multiple rays at every surface point) at all levels of the tree is less efficient. Indeed, progressively more rays will be cast at

```
// global illumination algorithm
// stochastic ray tracing
computeImage(eye)
    for each pixel
        radiance = 0;
        H = integral(h(p));
        for each sample          // Np viewing rays
            pick sample point p within support of h;
            construct ray at eye, direction p-eye;
            radiance = radiance + rad(ray)*h(p);
        radiance = radiance/(#samples*H);

rad(ray)
    find closest intersection point x of ray with scene;
    return(Le(x,eye-x) + computeRadiance(x, eye-x));

computeRadiance(x, dir)
    estimatedRadiance += directIllumination(x, dir);
    estimatedRadiance += indirectIllumination(x, dir);
    return(estimatedRadiance);

directIllumination (x, theta)
    estimatedRadiance = 0;
    for all shadow rays          // Nd shadow rays
        select light source k;
        sample point y on light source k;
        estimated radiance +=
            Le * BRDF * radianceTransfer(x,y)/(pdf(k)pdf(y|k));
    estimatedRadiance = estimatedRadiance / #paths;
    return(estimatedRadiance);

indirectIllumination (x, theta)
    estimatedRadiance = 0;
    if (no absorption)           // Russian roulette
        for all indirect paths   // Ni indirect rays
            sample direction psi on hemisphere;
            y = trace(x, psi);
            estimatedRadiance +=
                compute_radiance(y, -psi) * BRDF *
                cos(Nx, psi)/pdf(psi);
        estimatedRadiance = estimatedRadiance / #paths;
    return(estimatedRadiance/(1-absorption));

radianceTransfer(x,y)
    transfer = G(x,y)*V(x,y);
    return(transfer);
```

Figure 5.19. Total global illumination algorithm.

each deeper level, while at the same time, the contribution of each of those individual rays to the final radiance value of the pixel will diminish. For indirect illumination, a branching factor of 1 is often used after the first level. Many implementations even limit the indirect rays to one per surface point but then compensate by generating more rays through the area of the pixel. This approach is known as path tracing: Many paths, without any branching (except for direct illumination), are cast. Each path by itself is a bad approximation of the total radiance, but many paths combined are able to produce a good estimate.

5.6.5 Classic Ray Tracing

Classic ray tracing, or *Whitted-style ray tracing* [194], as it is sometimes called, is an often-used technique for computing photorealistic pictures. However, it does not compute a full solution to the rendering equation. A classic ray-tracing algorithm usually computes the following light transport components when computing an estimator for the radiance $L(x \rightarrow \Theta)$:

- Shadows. In classic ray tracing, shadows are computed in the same way as explained in this chapter for direct illumination. However, when using point light sources, care has to be taken that the correct radiometric properties are still being used.

- Reflections and refractions. This is usually the only indirect illumination component present. Instead of sampling the entire hemisphere to look for incident illumination at x, only two *interesting* directions are explicitly sampled: the perfect specular direction in case the surface is specular, and the perfect refracted ray in case the surface is transparent.

Thus, classic ray tracing only computes a small selected subset of the indirect illumination, and is not able to deal with diffuse interreflections, caustics, etc.

5.7 Light Tracing

Stochastic ray tracing, as described in the previous section, is derived from a Monte Carlo evaluation of the rendering equation. The resulting algorithm traces paths through the scene, starting at the point visible through a pixel, and through recursion or shadow rays, these paths reach the light sources, upon which a contribution to the radiance value to be computed is found.

This tracing of rays from the eye to the light sources looks unnatural, since light travels the other way: light particles originate at the light source and finally hit the film surface or the human eye where they are recorded and added to the measured intensity. This section explains the light-tracing algorithm that proceeds exactly along those lines. Light tracing is the dual algorithm of ray tracing, and many of the optimizations used in ray tracing can also be used in light tracing.

5.7.1 Light-Tracing Algorithm

The basic light-tracing algorithm evaluates the potential or importance equation for a single pixel. The importance equation, the dual of the rendering equation, is written as

$$W(x \rightarrow \Theta) = W_e(x \rightarrow \Theta) + \int_{\Omega_x} W(x \leftarrow \Psi) f_r(x, \Theta \leftrightarrow \Psi) \cos(\Psi, N_x) d\omega_\Psi,$$

(5.6)

and the accompanying measurement equation for a single pixel is

$$P = \int_{sources} W(x \rightarrow \Psi) L_e(x \rightarrow \Psi) \cos(N_x, \Psi) dA_x d\omega_\Psi.$$

(5.7)

The light-tracing algorithm then proceeds as follows (Figure 5.20):

- The measurement equation (Equation 5.7) will be evaluated using Monte Carlo integration. Points x_i and directions Θ_i on the light sources are generated (such that $L_e(x_i, \Theta_i) \neq 0$), for which the importance $W(x \rightarrow \Theta)$ will be evaluated. This will finally lead to an estimator for the flux through a pixel.

- Evaluating the importance $W(x \rightarrow \Theta)$ requires a Monte Carlo integration of the importance equation (Equation 5.6). This evaluation is very similar to the evaluation of the rendering equation in stochastic ray-tracing algorithms, and the same sampling schemes (hemisphere, area, BRDF, ...) can be used.

- In the stochastic ray-tracing algorithm, a shadow ray is generated for each surface point along the path to compute the direct illumination. The equivalent of this operation in light tracing is to send a contribution ray from each surface point along a light path to the eye of the camera and check whether it passes through the pixel under consideration. If this is the case, a contribution to the pixel is recorded.

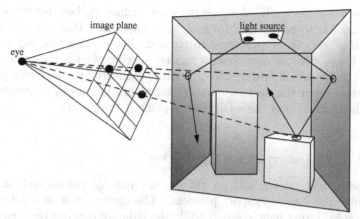

Figure 5.20. Paths traced during the light-tracing algorithm. Contribution rays to the image plane are shown as dashed lines.

Figure 5.21. Images computed using light tracing using $100,000$, $1,000,000$, $10,000,000$ and $100,000,000$ light rays, respectively.

The algorithm outlined above is rather inefficient, because the whole algorithm has to be repeated for each individual pixel. However, it is clear that all pixels can be processed in parallel: if a contribution ray passes through *any* pixel, a contribution to that specific pixel is then recorded. Thus, the image will form gradually, not by sequentially completing pixels as was the case in the stochastic ray-tracing algorithm, but by accumulating the contributions over the whole image plane (Figure 5.21).

5.7.2 Light Tracing versus Ray Tracing

Stochastic light tracing and ray tracing are dual algorithms and, in theory, solve the same transport problem. The camera acts as a source of importance during light tracing, while the light sources are the source of radiance in stochastic ray tracing. Shadow rays and contribution rays are each other's dual mechanism for optimizing the computations of final flux through a pixel.

Which algorithm performs better or is more efficient? It is generally accepted that stochastic ray tracing will perform better, but there are several factors that can contribute to the efficiency of one algorithm over the other:

Image size versus scene size. If the image only shows a very small part of the scene, it is to be expected that many particles shot from the light sources during light tracing will end up in parts of the scene that are only of marginal importance to the light transport relevant for the image. Stochastic ray tracing will perform better, because the radiance values to be computed are driven by the position of the camera and individual pixels, and so we can expect less work to be wasted on computing irrelevant transport paths.

Nature of the transport paths. The nature of transport paths also might favor one transport simulation method over the other. Shadow rays or contribution rays work best at diffuse surfaces, since the direction (towards the light sources or towards the camera) cannot be chosen. At a specular surface, there is a very high likelihood that those rays will yield a very small contribution to the final estimator. Thus, we would like to trace rays as much as possible over specular surfaces before we send out a shadow ray or contribution ray. This means that for mirrored images (where the light hits a diffuse surface before it hits a specular surface), we prefer ray tracing, and for caustics (where the light hits specular surfaces before diffuse surfaces), we would prefer light tracing. This principle is applied in building up caustic-maps with the photon-mapping algorithm [83].

Number of sources. In ray tracing, the sources for the transport we are simulating are the light sources; in light tracing, the importance sources are the individual pixels. This also has some effect on the efficiency of both algorithms, especially when sources are to be moved, in conjunction with an algorithm where partial information of the transport simulation is stored in the scene. It can be imagined that when a light-tracing algorithm is used, we could store all endpoints of all paths, and only retrace the contribution rays when the camera moves.[2] This is not as easy with ray tracing. On the other hand, if we want to apply a similar scheme to ray tracing and a moving light source, it will not be straightforward, since the number of importance sources (or pixels) is much larger, and separate information needs to be stored for all of them.

In theory, ray tracing and light tracing are dual algorithms, but in practice, they are not equivalent, since we usually want to compute a final image and not an "importance image" for each of the light sources. Only in the latter case would the algorithms be really dual and equivalent.

5.7.3 Related Techniques and Optimizations

In global illumination literature, tracing rays starting at the light sources has been used in many different forms and with different names (particle tracing, photon tracing, backwards ray tracing, etc.), and has mostly been used as part of multipass algorithms, and not so much as an algorithm to compute images by itself.

In [23], light is distributed from light sources to immediate visible diffuse surfaces, which are then classified as secondary light sources. These new secondary light sources are then treated as regular light sources in the subsequent ray-tracing pass. Complex interactions associated with caustics have been computed using backwards beam tracing [225]. Beams, generated at the light sources, are reflected through the scene at specular surfaces only, and a caustic polygon is stored at diffuse surfaces. Later, the caustic polygon is taken into account when rendering pixels in which this caustic is visible.

Two-dimensional storage maps for storing light-traced information have also been proposed in various forms and in various algorithms. These maps also result from a light-tracing pass and are used to read out illumination information during a subsequent ray-tracing pass. Examples of two-dimensional storage maps can be found in [24] and [5].

Bidirectional ray tracing combines ray tracing and light tracing. When computing the radiance value for a pixel, both a path starting at a light source and a path starting at the eye are generated in the scene. By

---

[2]This would be equivalent to a point-rendering of all end points of the light-paths.

linking up their end- and midpoints, an estimator for the radiance is found. This technique is able to combine advantages of both light tracing and ray tracing, and each of those can actually be seen as a special case of bidirectional ray tracing.

The most successful applications of light tracing, however, are in the photon-mapping and density-estimation algorithms. A more complete discussion of some of these techniques is given in Chapter 7.

The light-tracing algorithm itself has also been optimized using adaptive sampling functions. Using several iterations of light,tracing passes, adaptive PDFs are constructed, such that particles are traced more efficiently towards the camera ([41], [42]).

5.8   Summary

This chapter outlined stochastic path tracing, one of the most commonly used algorithms to compute global illumination solutions to the rendering equation. By applying Monte Carlo integration schemes to the rendering equation, various stochastic path tracing algorithms can be developed, including simple stochastic ray tracing, optimizations through the use of shadow rays, various schemes for indirect illumination, etc. An interesting variant is stochastic light tracing, the dual algorithm of stochastic ray tracing, which traces rays from the light sources towards the eye. For more details on developing ray-tracing algorithms, Shirley's book [170] is an excellent starting point.

5.9   Exercises

All exercises listed here require the rendering of various images using a ray tracer. When testing the various methods, it is usually a good idea to render the images at a low resolution. Only when one is fully convinced that the rendering computations are implemented correctly, images can be rendered at a high resolution, and the number of samples for each rendering component can gradually be increased.

1. Implement a simple stochastic ray tracer that is able to render scenes with direct illumination only. The type of geometric primitives that are included is not important; it can be limited to triangles and spheres only. Surfaces should have a diffuse BRDF, and area light sources should be included as well. This simple ray tracer can serve as a skeleton ray tracer to use in subsequent exercises.

2. Experiment with casting multiple shadow rays towards the light sources. Vary the number of samples per light source, as well as the sampling pattern (uniform, uniform stratified, etc.). Compare images with and without explicit light source sampling for computing the direct illumination. Independent of the sampling strategy used, the images should always converge to the same exact solution.

3. Experiment with multiple viewing rays cast per pixel, in order to solve aliasing problems. Again, vary the number of rays, as well as the sampling pattern. Zoom in on an area of the image containing an object-object visual discontinuity and study the results.

4. Include the Cook-Torrance shader from Chapter 3 in the skeleton ray tracer. The specular highlights should be visible especially on rounded objects such as spheres. Is the computation of the highlights affected by the sampling scheme used for direct illumination?

5. Add the computation of indirect illumination to your skeleton ray tracer. This requires the implementation of a sampling scheme over the hemisphere of directions around a surface point. As before, experiment with various sampling schemes to examine the effect on the indirect illumination component. Also change the absorption value used in the Russian roulette termination scheme.

6. Using the hemisphere sampling from the previous exercise, implement the direct illumination computation without explicitly sampling the light sources. Only when a random ray accidentally reaches the light source, a contribution for the illumination of the pixel is found.

7. Add the direct and indirect illumination components together to render the full global illumination solution of a given scene. Design a user interface such that all different sampling parameters can be adjusted by the user before the rendering computation starts.

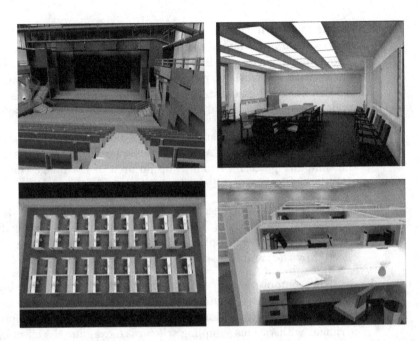

Plate I. Images computed with hierarchical Monte Carlo radiosity, with per-ray refinement (under 1 minute CPU time for up to 500,000 surface elements). (See Figure 6.28.)

Plate II. A car model rendering under real-world illumination, using a high dynamic range light probe (left images, photographs at various shutter times shown on top) and a histogram method. (See Figure 6.14.)

Plate III. Images rendered with a kernel density estimation method. (Images courtesy of F. Drago and K. Myszkowski, Max-Planck-Institute for Informatics, Saarbrücken, Germany). (See Figure 6.15.)

Plate IV. Images rendered with a kernel density estimation method. (Images courtesy of B. Walter, Ph. Hubbard, P. Shirley, and D. Greenberg, Cornell Program of Computer Graphics). (See Figure 6.19.)

Plate V. Left: Stochastic ray tracing; middle: light tracing; right: bidirectional ray tracing. (Courtesy of F. Suykens-De Laet, Dept. of Computer Science, K. U. Leuven.) (See Figure 7.5.)

Plate VI. Bidirectional ray tracing. Note the extensive caustics, an effect difficult to achieve using stochastic ray tracing. (Courtesy of F. Suykens-De Laet, Dept. of Computer Science, K. U. Leuven.) (See Figure 7.6.)

Plate VII. Metropolis Light Transport example with caustics. (Courtesy of Eric Veach.) (See Figure 7.7.)

Plate VIII. Irradiance caching example. Temple modeled by Veronica Sundstedt and Patrick Ledda. (Courtesy of Greg Ward.) (See Figure 7.8.)

Plate IX. Examples of images produced using photon mapping. Figure (a) on the left shows caustics, while Figure (b) on the right shows a scene rendered with global illumination and displacement mapping. (Courtesy of Henrik Wann Jensen.) (See Figure 7.11.)

Plate X. These images show two views of the same scene, with only direct diffuse illumination besides specular reflections (left), and including indirect diffuse illumination (right), computed with a ray-tracing version of instant radiosity. (Image courtesy of I. Wald, T. Kollig, C. Benthin, A. Keller, and Ph, Slusallek, Saarland University, Saarbrücken, and University of Kaiserslautern, Kaiserslautern, Germany.) (See Figure 7.13.)

Plate XI. Some renderings of participating media: using bi-directional path tracing (top) and volume photon mapping (bottom). (See Figure 8.6.)

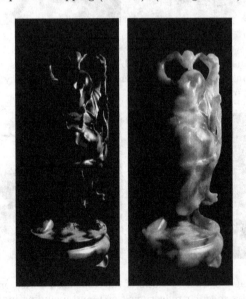

Plate XII. Two renderings of a translucent object. Left: using a standard BRDF model. Right: taking into account subsurface scattering with the dipole source model of [72]. (Image courtesy of T. Mertens, University of Limburg, Belgium.) (See Figure 8.9.)

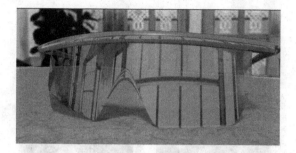

Plate XIII. Interference of light at a transparent thin film coating causes colorful reflections on these sunglasses. (Image courtesy of Jay Gondek, Gary Meyer, and John Newman, University of Oregon.) (See Figure 8.12.)

Plate XIV. The colorful reflections on this CD-ROM are caused by diffraction. (Image courtesy of Jos Stam, Alias|Wavefront.) (See Figure 8.13.)

Plate XV. These images illustrate polarization of light reflected in the glass block on the left (Fresnel reflection). The same scene is shown, but with a different filter in front of the virtual camera: a horizontal polarization filter (left), vertical polarization filter (middle); and a 50% neutral gray (nonpolarizing) filter (right). (Image courtesy of A. Wilkie, Vienna University of Technology, Austria.) (See Figure 8.14.)

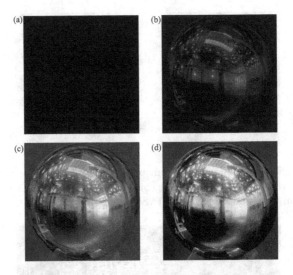

Plate XVI. Various tone-mapping operators. (a) Linear scaling; (b) gamma scaling; (c) simple model of lightness sensitivity; (d) complex model for the human visual system. (See Figure 8.15.)

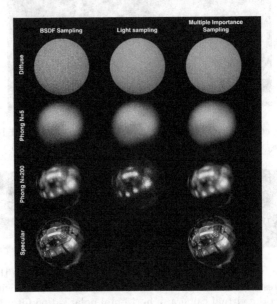

Plate XVII. Combining BSDF sampling and light sampling with multiple importance sampling is always at least as good as BSDF sampling or light sampling alone. (See Figure A.2.)

(a) Render Cache [Walter, Drettakis, Parker]

(d) Utah's interactive ray tracing [Martin et al.]

(b) Edges and Points [Bala, Walter, Greenberg]

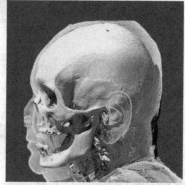

(e) Utah's rt for visualization [Parker et al.]

(c) 4D Radiance Interpolants [Bala, Dorsey, Teller]

(f) Coherent Ray Tracing [Wald, Slusallek]

Plate XVIII. Images from interactive rendering systems. On the left are systems that use sparse sampling and interpolation: (a) render cache, (b) edges and points, and (c) 4D radiance interpolants. On the right are very fast ray tracers: (d) Utah's interactive ray tracing, (e) Utah's visualization of the visible female dataset, and (f) coherent ray tracing. (See Figure 8.17.)

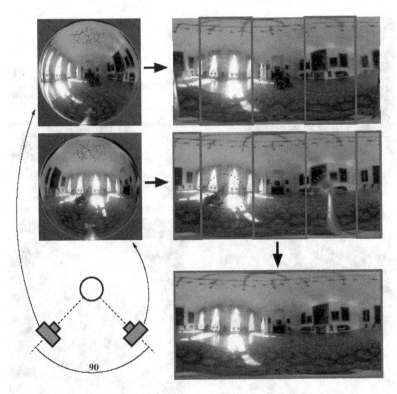

Plate XIX. Photographing a light probe twice, 90 degrees apart. The camera positions are indicated in blue. Combining both photographs produces a well-sampled environment map without the camera being visible. (Photographs courtesy of Vincent Masselus.) (See Figure 5.15.)

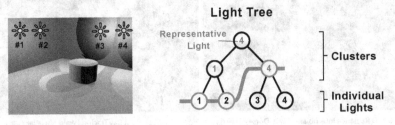

Plate XX. A simple scene with four point lights and the corresponding light tree. Each cut is a different partitioning of the lights into clusters. The cut shown in orange clusters lights three and four. The orange region in the rendered image (left) shows where the lightcut is a good approximation of the exact solution. (Image courtesy Bruce Walter.) (See Figure 7.14.)

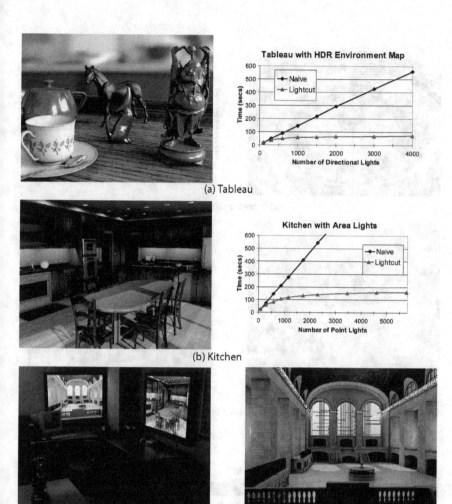

(a) Tableau

(b) Kitchen

(c) Big Screen

(d) Grand Central Station

Plate XXI. Scenes rendered using lightcuts. Tableau demonstrates glossy surfaces and HDR environment maps. The Kitchen scene includes area lights and the sun/sky model. Scalability graphs on the right show how cut size, and therefore performance, scales sublinearly with the number of lights. Big Screen includes two textured lights, the displays, each modeled with a point light source per pixel of the display. Grand Central Station includes 800 direct lights, sun/sky, and indirect illumination. (Image courtesy Bruce Walter.) (See Figure 7.15.)

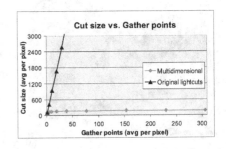

(a) Roulette Wheel, motion blur

(b) Tableau, depth of field

(c) Kitchen, participating media

Plate XXII. Scenes rendered using multidimensional lightcuts. (See Figure 7.17.)

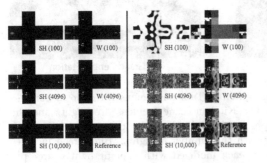

Plate XXIII. All-frequency effects. On the left, comparison of spherical harmonics (SH) and wavelets using nonlinear approximation (W) for the St. Peter's Basilica environment map. On right, the triple product integral solution for a scene. (Image courtesy Ren Ng and Ravi Ramamoorthi.) (See Figure 8.19.)

No shadows   With PRT

Plate XXIV. The Buddha model rendered with diffuse PRT using an environment map. Left: without shadows; right with PRT. (Image courtesy Peter-Pike Sloan and John Snyder.) (See Figure 8.18.)

Diffuse Buddha   Specular Buddha

Plate XXV. Diffuse and glossy Buddha rendered using PRT with separable BRDFs for high-frequency illumination. (Image courtesy Peter-Pike Sloan and John Snyder.) (See Figure 8.20.)

6

Stochastic Radiosity

The algorithms discussed in the previous chapter directly compute the intensity of light passing though the pixels of the virtual screen. In contrast, this chapter covers methods that compute a so-called *world space* representation of the illumination in a three-dimensional scene. Very often, this object space representation consists of the average diffuse illumination on triangles or convex quadrilaterals into which a three-dimensional model has been tessellated. There are, however, plenty of other possibilities, too. Since diffuse illumination is best modeled by a quantity called *radiosity* (see Section 2.3.1), such methods are usually called *radiosity methods*.

The main advantage of computing the illumination in object space is that generating new views of a model takes less work, compared to rendering from scratch. For instance, graphics hardware can be used for real-time rendering of an "illuminated" model, with colors derived from the precomputed average diffuse illumination. Also, path tracing can be augmented to exploit precomputed illumination in object space, allowing very high image quality. The combination of path tracing after a radiosity method is an example of a two-pass method. Two-pass methods, and other hybrid methods, are the topic of Chapter 7.

The most well-known algorithm for computing an object space representation of illumination is the *classic radiosity method* [56, 28, 133]. In this chapter, we will present a brief overview of the classic radiosity method (Section 6.1). More introductory or more in-depth coverage of the classic radiosity method can be found in textbooks such as [29, 172]. We will focus on a range of radiosity methods that matured only recently, since the publication of these books. In particular, we describe three classes of radiosity algorithms, based on stochastic sampling, introduced in Chapter 3.

The first class, called *stochastic relaxation* methods (Section 6.3), is based on stochastic adaptations of classic iterative solution methods for linear systems such as the Jacobi, Gauss-Seidel, or Southwell iterative methods.

The solution of linear systems, such as those that occur in the classic radiosity method, is one of the earliest applications of the Monte Carlo method [50, 224]. They are based on the notion of a *discrete random walk*. Their application to radiosity, which leads to algorithms we call *discrete random walk radiosity* methods, is discussed in Section 6.4.

The third class of Monte Carlo radiosity methods (Section 6.5) is very similar to the random walk methods for linear systems but solves the radiosity or rendering integral equation directly, rather than the radiosity linear system. The random walks of these methods are nothing but simulated photon trajectories. The density of surface hit points of such trajectories will be shown to be proportional to radiosity. Various *density estimation* methods known from statistics [175] can be used in order to estimate radiosity from the photon trajectory hit points.

These three classes of Monte Carlo radiosity methods can be made more efficient by applying *variance-reduction techniques* and *low-discrepancy sampling*, which have been discussed in general in Chapter 3. The main techniques are covered in Section 6.6.

This chapter concludes with a discussion of how adaptive meshing, hierarchical refinement, and clustering techniques can be incorporated into Monte Carlo radiosity (Section 6.7). Combined with adaptive meshing, hierarchical refinement, and clustering, Monte Carlo radiosity algorithms allow us to precompute, on a state-of-the-art PC, the illumination in three-dimensional scenes consisting of milions of polygons, such as models of large and complex buildings.

Monte Carlo radiosity methods all share one very important feature: unlike other radiosity algorithms, they do not require the computation and storage of so-called *form factors* (Section 6.1). This is possible because form factors can be interpreted as probabilities that can be sampled efficiently (Section 6.2). The photon density estimation algorithms in Section 6.5 do not even require form factors at all. Because the nasty problems of accurate form factor computation and their storage are avoided, Monte Carlo radiosity methods can handle much larger models in a reliable way. They are also significantly easier to implement and use than other radiosity methods. In addition, they provide visual feedback very early on and converge gracefully. Often, they are much faster, too.

In this chapter, we will place a large number of (at first sight) unrelated algorithms in a common perspective and compare them to each other. We will do so by analyzing the variance of the underlying Monte Carlo estimators (Section 3.4.4). The same techniques can be used to analyze other Monte Carlo rendering algorithms, but they are easier to illustrate for diffuse illumination, as is done in this chapter.

6.1 Classic Radiosity

Let's start with an overview of the classic radiosity method.

6.1.1 Outline

The basic idea of the classic radiosity method is to compute the average radiosity B_i on each surface element or patch i of a three-dimensional model (see Figure 6.1). The input consists of a list of such patches. Most often, the patches are triangles or convex quadrilaterals, although alternatives such as quadratic surface patches have been explored as well [2]. With each patch i, the self-emitted radiosity B_i^e (dimensions: [W/m^2]) and reflectivity ρ_i (dimensionless) are given. The self-emitted radiosity is the radiosity that a patch emits "on its own," even if there were no other patches in the model, or all other patches were perfectly black. The reflectivity is a number (for each considered wavelength) between 0 and 1. It indicates what fraction of the power incident on the patch gets reflected (the rest gets absorbed). These data suffice in order to compute the total emitted radiosity B_i (dimensions: [W/m^2]) by each patch, containing the radiosity received via any number of bounces from other patches in the scene, as well as the self-emitted radiosity.

The equations relating B_i with B_i^e and ρ_i on all patches are solved, and the resulting radiosities converted to display colors for the surfaces. Since only diffuse illumination is computed, the surface colors are independent

 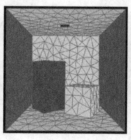 

Figure 6.1. The input of the classic radiosity method consists of a list of patches (triangles, in this example) with their average self-emitted radiosity B_i^e (left) and reflectivity ρ_i (middle) given. These data suffice in order to compute the average total radiosities B_i (right), including the effect of light bouncing around. The computed radiosities are converted to display colors for each patch. The resulting, "illuminated," model can be rendered from any viewpoint, at interactive rates using graphics hardware.

from the viewing position. Visualization from an arbitrary viewpoint can be done using graphics hardware, allowing interactive "walks" through an "illuminated" model.

The classic radiosity method is an instance of a larger class of numerical methods called *finite element methods* [69]. It is a well-known method in heat transfer, and its application to image rendering was introduced in 1984–1985—a few years after the introduction of the classical ray-tracing method [56, 28, 133]. Since these seminal papers appeared, hundreds of follow-up papers have been published, proposing significant improvements and alternatives for computation techniques. Excellent introductory and in-depth overviews of the classic radiosity method can be found in [29, 172]. Here, only a concise derivation of the underlying equations are presented, as well as the traditional way of solving the radiosity equations and a discussion of the main problems of the method.

6.1.2 Mathematical Problem Description

The problem stated above can be described mathematically in three different ways: by the general rendering equation, by a simplification of it for purely diffuse environments, and by a discretized version of the latter.

The General Rendering Equation

As explained in Chapter 2, light transport in a three-dimensional environment is described by the rendering equation. The average radiosity B_i emitted by a surface patch i with area A_i is therefore given by

$$B_i = \frac{1}{A_i} \int_{S_i} \int_{\Omega_x} L(x \to \Theta) \cos(\Theta, N_x) d\omega_\Theta dA_x, \qquad (6.1)$$

with (Section 2.6)

$$L(x \to \Theta) = L_e(x \to \Theta) + \int_{\Omega_x} f_r(x; \Theta' \leftrightarrow \Theta) L(x \leftarrow \Theta') \cos(\Theta', N_x) d\omega_{\Theta'}. \qquad (6.2)$$

The Radiosity Integral Equation

On purely diffuse surfaces (Section 2.3.4), self-emitted radiance $L_e(x)$ and the BRDF $f_r(x)$ do not depend on directions Θ and Θ'. The rendering equation then becomes

$$L(x) = L_e(x) + \int_{\Omega_x} f_r(x) L(x \leftarrow \Theta') \cos(\Theta', N_x) d\omega'_\Theta.$$

Of course, the incident radiance $L(x \leftarrow \Theta')$ still depends on incident direction. It corresponds to the exitant radiance $L(y)$ emitted towards x by the point y visible from x along the direction Θ' (see Section 2.3.3). As explained in Section 2.6.2, the integral above, over the hemisphere Ω_x, can be transformed into an integral over all surfaces S in the scene. The result is an integral equation in which no directions appear anymore:

$$L(x) = L_e(x) + \rho(x) \int_S K(x,y)L(y)dA_y.$$

In a diffuse environment (Section 2.3.4), radiosity and radiance are related as $B(x) = \pi L(x)$ and $B_e(x) = \pi L_e(x)$. Multiplication by π of the left- and right-hand sides of the above equation yields the *radiosity integral equation*:

$$B(x) = B_e(x) + \rho(x) \int_S K(x,y)B(y)dA_y. \tag{6.3}$$

The kernel of this integral equation is:

$$K(x,y) = G(x,y)V(x,y) \quad \text{with} \quad G(x,y) = \frac{\cos(\Theta_{xy}, N_x)\cos(-\Theta_{xy}, N_y)}{\pi r_{xy}^2}.$$

$$\tag{6.4}$$

Θ_{xy} is the direction pointing from x to y. r_{xy}^2 is the square distance between x and y. $V(x,y)$ is the visibility predicate (1 if x and y are mutually visible, 0 otherwise). Equation 6.1 now becomes

$$
\begin{aligned}
B_i &= \frac{1}{A_i} \int_{S_i} L(x) \int_{\Omega_x} \cos(\Theta, N_x)d\omega_\Theta dA_x \\
&= \frac{1}{A_i} \int_{S_i} L(x)\pi dA_x \\
&= \frac{1}{A_i} \int_{S_i} B(x)dA_x.
\end{aligned}
\tag{6.5}
$$

The Radiosity System of Linear Equations

Often, integral equations like Equation 6.3 are solved by reducing them to an approximate system of linear equations by means of a procedure known as Galerkin discretization [36, 98, 29, 172].

Let's assume the radiosity $B(x)$ is constant on each patch i, $B(x) = B_i'$, $x \in S_i$. Equation 6.3 can be converted into a linear system as follows:

$$B(x) = B_e(x) + \rho(x) \int_S K(x,y)B(y)dA_y$$

$$\Rightarrow \frac{1}{A_i} \int_{S_i} B(x)dA_x = \frac{1}{A_i} \int_{S_i} B_e(x)dA_x$$

$$+ \frac{1}{A_i} \int_{S_i} \int_S \rho(x)K(x,y)B(y)dA_ydA_x$$

$$\Leftrightarrow \frac{1}{A_i} \int_{S_i} B(x)dA_x = \frac{1}{A_i} \int_{S_i} B_e(x)dA_x$$

$$+ \sum_j \frac{1}{A_i} \int_{S_i} \int_{S_j} \rho(x)K(x,y)B(y)dA_ydA_x$$

$$\Leftrightarrow B_i' = B_{ei} + \sum_j B_j' \frac{1}{A_i} \int_{S_i} \int_{S_j} \rho(x)K(x,y)dA_ydA_x.$$

If we now also assume that the reflectivity is constant over each patch, $\rho(x) = \rho_i, x \in S_i$, the following classical *radiosity system of equations* results:

$$B_i' = B_{ei} + \rho_i \sum_j F_{ij}B_j'. \tag{6.6}$$

The factors F_{ij} are called *patch-to-patch form factors*:

$$F_{ij} = \frac{1}{A_i} \int_{S_i} \int_{S_j} K(x,y)dA_ydA_x. \tag{6.7}$$

The meaning and properties of these form factors are discussed in Section 6.2. For the moment, the main thing to remember is that they are nontrivial four-dimensional integrals.

Note that the radiosities B_i' that result after solving the system of linear equations (Equation 6.6) are only an *approximation* for the average radiosities (Equation 6.5). The true radiosity $B(y)$, which was replaced by B_j' in the equations above, is in practice only very rarely piecewise constant! The difference between B_i and B_i' is, however, rarely visible in practice. For this reason, we will denote both the average radiosity (Equation 6.5) and the radiosity coefficients in Equation 6.6 by B_i in the remainder of this text.

6.1.3 The Classic Radiosity Method

We are now ready to describe the steps of the classic radiosity method. They are:

1. Discretization of the input geometry into patches i. For each resulting patch i, a radiosity value (per considered wavelength) B_i will be
   computed.

2. Computation of form factors F_{ij} (Equation 6.7), for every pair of
   patches i and j.

3. Numerical solution of the radiosity system of linear equations (Equation 6.6).

4. Display of the solution, including the transformation of the resulting
   radiosity values B_i (one for each patch and considered wavelength)
   to display colors. This involves tone mapping and gamma correction
   (Section 8.2).

In practice, these steps are intertwined: for instance, form factors are
only computed when they are needed; intermediate results are displayed
during system solution; in adaptive and hierarchical radiosity [30, 64], discretization is performed during system solution, etc.

6.1.4 Problems

Each step of the classic radiosity method is nontrivial, but at first sight,
one would expect that Step 3, radiosity system solution, would be the
main problem: the size of the linear systems that need to be solved can
be very large (one equation per patch; 100,000 patches is quite common).
The radiosity system of linear equations is, in practice, very well-behaved,
so that simple iterative methods such as Jacobi or Gauss-Seidel iterations
converge after relatively few iterations.

The main problems of the radiosity method are related to the first
two steps:

Scene discretization. The patches should be small enough to capture illumination variations such as near shadow boundaries: the radiosity $B(x)$
across each patch needs to be approximately constant. Figure 6.2 shows
the image artifacts that may result from an improper discretization. On
the other hand, the number of patches shouldn't be too large, because this
would result in exaggerated storage requirements and computation times.

Form factor computation. First, even simple objects in a scene may have to
be tessellated into thousands of small patches each, on which the radiosity
can be assumed to be constant. For that reason, scenes with hundreds of
thousands of patches are quite normal. Between each pair of patches, a
form factor needs to be computed. The number of form factors can thus be
huge (billions) so that the mere storage of form factors in computer memory

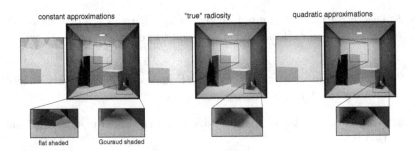

Figure 6.2. Meshing artifacts in radiosity with constant approximations (left) include undesired shading discontinuities along patch edges. Gouraud shading can be used to blur these discontinuities. Wherever the radiosity varies smoothly, a higher-order approximation of radiosity on each patch results in a more accurate image on the same mesh (a quadratic approximation was used in the right column), but artifacts remain near discontinuities such as shadow boundaries. The middle column shows the "true" radiosity solution (computed with bidirectional path tracing).

is a major problem. Second, each form factor requires the solution of a nontrivial, four-dimensional integral (Equation 6.7). The integral will be singular for abutting patches, where the distance r_{xy} in the denominator of Equation 6.4 vanishes. The integrand can also exhibit discontinuities of various degrees due to changing visibility (see Figure 6.3).

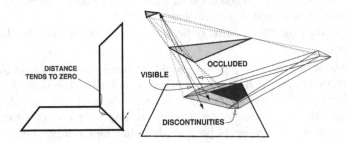

Figure 6.3. Form factor difficulties: The form factor integral (Equations 6.7 and 6.4) contains the square distance between points in the denominator. This causes a singularity for abutting patches (left). Changing visibility introduces discontinuities of various degrees in the form factor integrand (right). Due to this problem, reliable form factor integration is a difficult task.

Extensive research has been carried out in order to address these problems. Proposed solutions include custom algorithms form factor integration (hemicube algorithm, shaft culling ray-tracing acceleration, etc.), discontinuity meshing, adaptive and hierarchical subdivision, clustering, form factor caching strategies, the use of view importance, and higher-order radiosity approximations.

In the algorithms presented in this chapter, the latter problem is addressed by *avoiding* form factor computation and storage completely. This results in more reliable algorithms (no problems with form factor computational error) that require less storage (no form factors need to be stored). In addition, the presented algorithms are easier to implement and use and result in images of reasonable quality, showing multiple interreflection effects, sometimes much more rapidly than other radiosity algorithms.

The former problem, discretization artifacts, will be addressed using higher-order approximations, and—most importantly—hierarchical refinement and clustering (Section 6.7).

6.2   The Form Factors

The robust and efficient computation of the form factors F_{ij} between each pair of input patches is a major problem with the classic radiosity method. In this section, we will show that the form factors can be viewed as probabilities, and we will present an overview of algorithms for sampling according to form factor probabilities. The fact that form factors are probabilities that can be sampled efficiently leads to algorithms that allow us to solve the radiosity system of equations without the need to ever compute the value of a form factor. These algorithms will be described in Sections 6.3 and 6.4.

6.2.1   Properties of the Form Factors

Recall that the form factor F_{ij} is given by the following four-dimensional integral (Equation 6.7):

$$F_{ij} = \frac{1}{A_i} \int_{S_i} \int_{S_j} K(x,y) dA_x dA_y$$

with

$$K(x,y) = \frac{\cos(\Theta_{xy}, N_x) \cos(-\Theta_{xy}, N_y)}{\pi r_{xy}^2} V(x,y).$$

We will need the following properties of the form factors:

1. The form factors are all *positive* or *zero* in a scene consisting of closed, opaque objects: they cannot be negative because the integrand is positive or zero. They will be equal to zero for a pair of patches i and j that are mutually invisible.

2. The form factors F_{ij} between a patch i and all other patches j in a scene sum to at most one. If the scene is closed, then

$$\sum_j F_{ij} = \frac{1}{A_i} \int_{S_i} \sum_j \int_{S_j} \frac{\cos(\Theta_{xy}, N_x)\cos(-\Theta_{xy}, N_y)}{\pi r_{xy}^2} V(x,y) dA_y dA_x$$

$$= \frac{1}{A_i} \int_{S_i} \int_S \frac{\cos(\Theta_{xy}, N_x)\cos(-\Theta_{xy}, N_y)}{\pi r_{xy}^2} V(x,y) dA_y dA_x$$

$$= \frac{1}{A_i} \int_{S_i} \frac{1}{\pi} \int_{\Omega_x} \cos(\Theta_{xy}, N_x) d\omega_{\Theta_{xy}} dA_x$$

$$= \frac{1}{A_i} \int_{S_i} \frac{\pi}{\pi} dA_x$$

$$= 1.$$

If the scene is not closed, the sum of the form factors is less than 1.

3. The form factors satisfy the following *reciprocity relation*:

$$A_i F_{ij} = A_i \frac{1}{A_i} \int_{S_i} \int_{S_j} K(x,y) dA_x dA_y$$

$$= A_j \frac{1}{A_j} \int_{S_j} \int_{S_i} K(y,x) dA_y dA_x$$

$$= A_j F_{ji}.$$

Any set of positive numbers that sums up to at most one can be regarded as probabilities. For that simple reason, the form factors F_{ij} for a fixed patch i with any other patch j can always be regarded as a set of probabilities.

6.2.2 Interpretation of Form Factors

Let's recall the radiosity equation (Equation 6.6):

$$B_i = B_{ei} + \rho_i \sum_j F_{ij} B_j.$$

This equation states that the radiosity B_i at a patch i is the sum of two contributions. The first contribution consists of the self-emitted radiosity B_{ei}. The second contribution is the fraction of the irradiance (incident radiosity, Section 2.3.1) $\sum_j F_{ij} B_j$ at i that gets reflected. The form factor F_{ij} indicates what fraction of the irradiance on i originates at j.

Recall also that radiosities and fluxes are related as $P_i = A_i B_i$ and $P_{ei} = A_i B_{ei}$ (Chapter 2). By multiplying both sides of Equation 6.6 by A_i and using the reciprocity relation (Equation 6.8) for the form factors, the following system of linear equations relating the power P_i emitted by the patches in a scene is obtained:

$$B_i = B_{ei} + \rho_i \sum_j F_{ij} B_j$$

$$\Leftrightarrow \quad A_i B_i = A_i B_{ei} + \rho_i \sum_j A_i F_{ij} B_j$$

$$\Leftrightarrow \quad A_i B_i = A_i B_{ei} + \rho_i \sum_j A_j F_{ji} B_j$$

$$\Leftrightarrow \quad P_i = P_{ei} + \sum_j P_j F_{ji} \rho_i.$$

This system of equation states that the power P_i emitted by patch i also consists of two parts: the self-emitted power P_{ei} and the power received and reflected from other patches j. The form factor F_{ji} indicates the fraction of power emitted by j that lands on i, or conversely, F_{ij} indicates the fraction of power emitted by i that lands on j.

Of course, since the form factor is a ratio of positive quantities (radiosity or power), it can't be negative, giving an intuitive explanation for the first property of form factors above.

The second property (summation to 1) is also easy to see: since there is conservation of radiance, the total amount of power emitted by i and received on other patches j must equal P_i in a closed scene. In a nonclosed scene, some part of the power P_i will disappear into the background, explaining why the sum of the form factors F_{ij} will be less than 1 in that case.

6.2.3 Form Factor Sampling Using Local Lines

The interpretation of a form factor being the fraction of power emitted by a first patch i that lands on a second patch j immediately suggests that form factors can be estimated by means of a very simple and straightforward simulation (see Figure 6.4): Let i be the source of a number N_i of virtual particles that behave like photons originating on a diffuse surface. The number N_{ij} of these particles that land on the second patch j yields an estimate for the form factor: $N_{ij}/N_i \approx F_{ij}$.

Indeed, consider a particle originating at a uniformly chosen location x on S_i and being shot into a cosine-distributed direction Θ with regard to the surface normal N_x at x. The probability density $p(x, \Theta)$ associated with such a particle is

$$p(x, \Theta) = \frac{1}{A_i} \times \frac{\cos(\Theta, N_x)}{\pi}.$$

Note that this PDF is properly normalized:

$$
\begin{aligned}
\int_{S_i} \int_{\Omega_x} p(x, \Theta) dA_x d\omega_\Theta &= \int_{S_i} \frac{1}{A_i} \int_{\Omega_x} \frac{\cos(\Theta, N_x)}{\pi} d\omega_\Theta dA_x \\
&= \frac{1}{A_i} \int_{S_i} \frac{\pi}{\pi} dA_x \\
&= 1.
\end{aligned}
$$

Now, let $\chi_j(x, \Theta)$ be a predicate taking value 1 or 0 depending on whether or not the ray shot from x into Θ hits a second patch j. The probability P_{ij} that such a ray lands on a second patch j then is

$$
\begin{aligned}
P_{ij} &= \int_{S_i} \int_{\Omega_x} \chi_j(x, \Theta) p(x, \Theta) dA_x d\omega_\Theta \\
&= \int_{S_i} \int_S \chi_j(x, \Theta) \frac{1}{A_i} \frac{\cos(\Theta_{xy}, N_x) \cos(-\Theta_{xy}, N_y)}{\pi r_{xy}^2} V(x, y) dA_y dA_x \\
&= \frac{1}{A_i} \int_{S_i} \int_{S_j} \frac{\cos(\Theta_{xy}, N_x) \cos(-\Theta_{xy}, N_y)}{\pi r_{xy}^2} V(x, y) dA_y dA_x \\
&= F_{ij}.
\end{aligned}
$$

When shooting N_i such particles from i, the expected number of hits on patch j will be $N_i F_{ij}$. As usual in Monte Carlo methods, the more particles shot from i (greater N_i), the better the ratio N_{ij}/N_i will approximate F_{ij}. The variance of this binomial estimator (Section 3.3.1) is $F_{ij}(1 - F_{ij})/N_i$. This method of estimating form factors was proposed at the end of the 1980s as a ray-tracing alternative for the hemicube algorithm for form factor computation [171, 167].

As mentioned before, however, we will not need to compute form factors explicitly. The important thing for us is that the probability that a single such particle hits a patch j equals the form factor F_{ij}. In other words, if we are given a patch i, we can select a subsequent patch j among all patches in the scene, with probability equal to the form factor F_{ij}, by shooting a ray from i.

 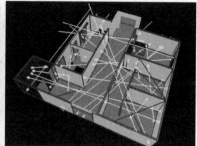

Figure 6.4. Form factor sampling: (Left) The fraction of local lines hitting a particular destination patch is an estimate for the form factor between source and destination. Global lines (right) are constructed without reference to any of the patches in the scene. Their intersection points with the surfaces in the scene are, however, also uniformly distributed. The angle between these lines and the normal on each intersected surface is cosine distributed, just like with local lines. The intersection points define spans on each line. Each global line span can be used bidirectionally for form factor computation between the connected patches.

6.2.4 Form Factor Sampling Using Global Lines

The algorithm of the previous section requires us to shoot so-called *local* lines: lines with an origin and direction selected with regard to a particular patch i in the scene. There exist, however, a number of algorithms for form factor sampling based on *uniformly distributed global* lines. The origin and direction of global lines is chosen irrespective of any particular surface in the scene, for instance, by connecting uniformly distributed sample points on a bounding sphere for the scene. It can be shown that the probability of finding an intersection of such lines at any given surface location is uniform, regardless of actual scene geometry. The construction and properties of such lines have been studied extensively in the field of *integral geometry* [155, 160, 161]. Several such sampling algorithms have been proposed for use with radiosity (see, for instance, [160, 142, 128, 161, 189]).

Lines constructed like that will, in general, cross several surfaces in the scene. The intersection points with the intersected surfaces define *spans* of mutually visible patches along the line (see Figure 6.4). Each such line span corresponds to *two* local cosine-distributed lines—one in both directions along the line—because the global uniformly distributed lines are uniformly distributed with regard to every patch in the scene. This is unlike local lines, which are uniformly distributed only with regard to the patch on which the origin was sampled.

It can be shown that the probability that a global uniform line, generated with the aforementioned algorithms, intersects a given patch i is proportional to the surface area A_i [161]. If N global lines are generated, the number N_i of lines crossing a patch i will be

$$N_i \approx N \frac{A_i}{A_T}. \tag{6.8}$$

It can also be shown that if N_{ij} is the number of lines that have successive intersections with the surfaces in the scene on patch i and j, then again

$$\frac{N_{ij}}{N_i} \approx F_{ij}.$$

The main advantage of global lines over local lines is that geometric scene coherence can be exploited in order to generate global lines more efficiently; that is, for the same computation cost, more global line spans can be generated than local lines.

The main limitation of global lines with regard to local lines is that their construction cannot easily be adapted in order to increase or decrease the line density on a given patch. In particular, when used for form factor calculation, it can be shown that the form factor variance is approximately inversely proportional to the area A_i of the source patch i. The variance will be high on small patches.

6.3   Stochastic Relaxation Radiosity

This section and the next one (Section 6.4) cover radiosity algorithms that solve the radiosity system of equations (Equation 6.6) using form factor sampling as discussed in the previous section. We shall see that by doing so, the form factor will appear in the numerator and denominator of the mathematical expressions to be evaluated, so that their numerical value will never be needed. Because of this, the difficult problems of accurately computing form factors and their storage are simply avoided. These algorithms therefore allow much larger models to be rendered with a fraction of the storage cost of other radiosity algorithms. In addition, Monte Carlo radiosity algorithms have a much better time complexity: roughly log-linear in the number of patches rather than quadratic like their deterministic counterparts. In short, they do not only require less storage, but for all but the simplest models, they also finish in less computation time.

There are basically two approaches to solve the radiosity system of linear equations (Equation 6.6) by means of Monte Carlo methods. This section covers the first approach: *stochastic relaxation methods*; the next section covers the second approach: *discrete random walk methods*.

The main idea of stochastic relaxation methods is that the radiosity system is solved using an iterative solution method such as Jacobi, Gauss-Seidel, or Southwell iterations [29, 172]. Each iteration of such a relaxation method consists of sums: dot products of a row of the form factor matrix with the radiosity or power vector. When these sums are estimated using a Monte Carlo method, as explained in Section 3.4.2, a stochastic relaxation method results.

6.3.1 The Jacobi Iterative Method for Radiosity

The Basic Idea

The Jacobi iterative method is a method to solve systems of linear equations $\mathbf{x} = \mathbf{e} + \mathbf{A}\mathbf{x}$ using a very simple iteration scheme. Suppose a system with n equations and n unknowns is to be solved. $\mathbf{e}$, $\mathbf{x}$, and any approximation for $\mathbf{x}$ are n-dimensional vectors, or points in an n-dimensional Euclidean space. The idea of the Jacobi iterative method is to start with an arbitrary point $\mathbf{x}^{(0)}$ in this space. During each iteration, a current point, say $\mathbf{x}^{(k)}$, is transformed into a next point $\mathbf{x}^{(k+1)}$ by filling in $\mathbf{x}^{(k)}$ into the right-hand side of the equations: $\mathbf{x}^{(k+1)} = \mathbf{e} + \mathbf{A}\mathbf{x}^{(k)}$. It can be shown that if $\mathbf{A}$ is a *contraction*, then the sequence of points $\mathbf{x}^{(k)}$ will always converge to the same point $\mathbf{x}$, the solution of the system. The point $\mathbf{x}$ is also called the *fixed point* of the iteration scheme. $\mathbf{A}$ is a contraction if its matrix norm is strictly less than 1, meaning that repeated application of $\mathbf{A}$ will eventually always reduce the distance between transformed points (see Figure 6.5).

The coefficient matrix in the radiosity or power system of equations (Equation 6.6 or 6.8) fulfills this requirement. In the context of radiosity, vectors like $\mathbf{x}$ and $\mathbf{e}$ correspond to a distribution of light power over the surfaces of a scene. L. Neumann [128] suggested viewing the distribution of light power in a scene as a point in such an n-dimensional space and applying the iteration scheme sketched above. The radiosity or power system matrix models a single bounce of light interreflection in the scene. For instance, multiplication with the self-emitted radiosity or power vector results in direct illumination. When applied to direct illumination, one-bounce indirect illumination is obtained. Each Jacobi iteration consists of computing a single bounce of light interreflection, followed by re-adding self-emitted power. The equilibrium illumination distribution in a scene is the fixed point of this process.

Neumann and others suggested numerous statistical techniques for simulating single-bounce light interreflection. The main advantage of these methods over others to be discussed, based on random walks, lies in the fact that simulating a single bounce of light interreflection is an easier problem than simulating any number of bounces at once.

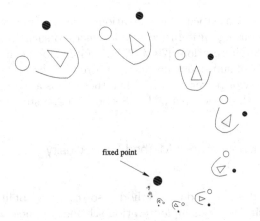

fixed point

Figure 6.5. The basic idea of the Jacobi iterative method in two dimensions. The figure in the upper left has been repeatedly scaled down and rotated. As one continues doing so, all points in the plane, including the figure, will be moved towards the dot in the middle. The combination of a rotation and down-scaling transform is a contractive transform. Eventually, all points in the plane are moved closer to each other. The dot in the middle is the fixed point of the transformation, applied repeatedly. In the same way, the right-hand side of the radiosity or power system of equations contains a contractive transformation in n-dimensional space, n being the number of patches. By repeatedly applying this transformation to an arbitrary initial radiosity or power distribution vector, the radiosity problem can be solved.

We will now make these statements concrete. First, we show three slightly different ways that repeated single-bounce light interreflection steps can be used in order to solve the radiosity problem. Then, we will focus on the statistical simulation of single-bounce light interreflection.

Regular Gathering of Radiosity

Let's first apply the above idea to the radiosity system of equations (Equation 6.6). As the starting radiosity distribution $B_i^{(0)} = B_{ei}$, self-emitted radiosity can be taken. A next approximation $B_i^{(k+1)}$ is then obtained by filling in the previous approximation $B^{(k)}$ in the right-hand side of Equation 6.6:

$$B_i^{(0)} = B_{ei}$$
$$B_i^{(k+1)} = B_{ei} + \rho_i \sum_j F_{ij} B_j^{(k)}. \qquad (6.9)$$

A hemicube algorithm, for instance [28], allows us to compute all form factors F_{ij} for fixed patch i simultaneously. Doing so, iteration steps according to the above scheme can be interpreted as *gathering* steps: in each step, the previous radiosity approximations $B_j^{(k)}$ for all patches j are "gathered" in order to obtain a new approximation for the radiosity $B^{(k+1)}$ at i.

Regular Shooting of Power

When applied to the power system, a shooting variant of the above iteration algorithm follows:

$$
\begin{aligned}
P_i^{(0)} &= P_{ei} \\
P_i^{(k+1)} &= P_{ei} + \sum_j P_j^{(k)} F_{ji} \rho_i.
\end{aligned} \tag{6.10}
$$

Using a hemicube-like algorithm again [28], one can compute all form factors F_{ji} for fixed j and variable i at a time. In each step of the resulting algorithm, the power estimate $P_i^{(k+1)}$ of all patches i, visible from j, will be updated based on $P_j^{(k)}$: j "shoots" its power towards all other patches i.

Incremental Shooting of Power

Each regular power-shooting iteration above *replaces* the previous approximation of power $P^{(k)}$ by a new approximation $P^{(k+1)}$. Similar to progressive refinement radiosity [31], it is possible to construct iterations in which *unshot* power is propagated rather than total power. An approximation for the total power is then obtained as the sum of *increments* $\Delta P^{(k)}$ computed in each iteration step:

$$
\begin{aligned}
\Delta P_i^{(0)} &= P_{ei} \\
\Delta P_i^{(k+1)} &= \sum_j \Delta P_j^{(k)} F_{ji} \rho_i \\
P_i^{(k)} &= \sum_{l=0}^{k} \Delta P_i^{(l)}.
\end{aligned}
$$

Discussion

With deterministic summation, there is no difference between the results after complete iterations with the above three iteration schemes. We will see below, however, that they lead to quite different algorithms when the sums are estimated stochastically.

Note that the computation cost of each iteration is quadratic in the number of patches.

6.3.2 Stochastic Jacobi Radiosity

We now discuss what happens if the sums in the above iteration formulae are estimated using a Monte Carlo method. It was explained in Section 3.4.2 that sums can be estimated stochastically by randomly picking terms from the sum according to some probability. The average ratio of the value of the picked terms, over the probability by which they have been picked, yields an unbiased estimate for the sum.

When applied to the above iteration formulae for radiosity, this procedure corresponds to a straightforward simulation of single bounce light interreflection by tracing one-bounce photon paths (see Figure 6.6).

Stochastic Incremental Shooting of Power

Consider the incremental power shooting iterations above. For purely technical reasons, we write the sum $\sum_j \Delta P_j^{(k)} F_{ji} \rho_i$ above as a double sum, by introducing Kronecker's delta function $\delta_{li} = 1$ if $l = i$ and 0 if $l \neq i$:

$$\Delta P_i^{(k+1)} = \sum_{j,l} \Delta P_j^{(k)} F_{jl} \rho_l \delta_{li}. \qquad (6.11)$$

This double sum can be estimated stochastically using any of the form factor sampling algorithms discussed in the previous section:

1. Pick terms (pairs of patches) (j, l) in either of the following ways:

   (a) By local line sampling:

       • Select a "source" patch j with probability p_j proportional to its unshot power:

       $$p_j = \Delta P_j^{(k)} / \Delta P_T^{(k)} \quad \text{with:} \quad \Delta P_T^{(k)} = \sum_j \Delta P_j^{(k)}.$$

       • Select a "destination" patch l with conditional probability $p_{l|j} = F_{jl}$ by tracing a local line as explained in Section 6.2.3.

   The combined probability of picking a pair of patches (j, l) is

   $$p_{jl} = p_j p_{l|j} = \Delta P_j^{(k)} F_{jl} / \Delta P_T^{(k)}. \qquad (6.12)$$

Algorithm 1 Incremental stochastic Jacobi iterative method.

1. Initialize total power $P_i \leftarrow P_{ei}$, unshot power $\Delta P_i \leftarrow P_{ei}$, and received power $\delta P_i \leftarrow 0$ for all patches i and compute total unshot power $\Delta P_T = \sum_i \Delta P_i$.

2. Until $\|\Delta P_i\| \leq \varepsilon$ or number of steps exceeds maximum, do

 (a) Choose number of samples N.

 (b) Generate a random number $\xi \in (0, 1)$.

 (c) Initialize $N_{prev} \leftarrow 0$; $q \leftarrow 0$.

 (d) Iterate over all patches i, for each i, do

  i. $q_i \leftarrow \Delta P_i / \Delta P_T$.

  ii. $q \leftarrow q + q_i$.

  iii. $N_i \leftarrow \lfloor Nq + \xi \rfloor - N_{prev}$.

  iv. Do N_i times:

   A. Sample random point x on S_i.

   B. Sample cosine-distributed direction Θ at x.

   C. Determine patch j containing the nearest intersection point of the ray originating at x and with direction Θ, with the surfaces of the scene.

   D. Increment $\delta P_j \leftarrow \delta P_j + \frac{1}{N} \rho_j \Delta P_T$.

  v. $N_{prev} \leftarrow N_{prev} + N_i$.

 (e) Iterate over all patches i, increment total power $P_i \leftarrow P_i + \delta P_i$, replace unshot power $\Delta P_i \leftarrow \delta P_i$, and clear received power $\delta P_i \leftarrow 0$. Compute new total unshot power ΔP_T on the fly.

 (f) Display image using P_i.

(b) By global line sampling (transillumination method [128, 191]), the intersections of each global line (Section 6.2.4) with the surfaces in the scene define spans of mutually visible pairs of points along the line. Each such pair corresponds to a term (j, l) in the sum. The associated probability is

$$p_{jl} = A_j F_{jl} / A_T.$$

2. Each picked term yields a score equal to the value of that term divided by its probability p_{jl}. The average score is an unbiased estimate for $\Delta P_i^{(k+1)}$. Estimation with N local lines, for instance, yields

$$\frac{1}{N} \sum_{s=1}^{N} \frac{\Delta P_{j_s}^{(k)} F_{j_s, l_s} \rho_{l_s} \delta_{l_s, i}}{\Delta P_{j_s}^{(k)} F_{j_s, l_s} / \Delta P_T^{(k)}} = \rho_i \Delta P_T^{(k)} \frac{N_i}{N} \approx \Delta P_i^{(k+1)}. \quad (6.13)$$

$N_i = \sum_{s=1}^{N} \delta_{l_s, i}$ is the number of local lines that land on i.

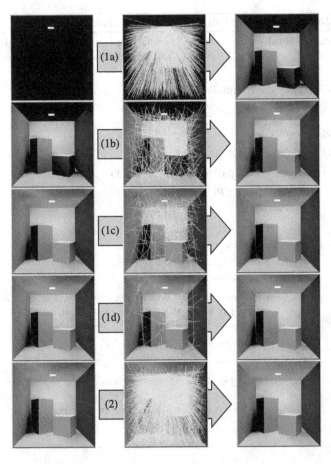

Figure 6.6. Stochastic Jacobi radiosity in action. (Top left) The initial approximation: self-emitted illumination; (top middle) propagation of self-emitted power
by shooting cosine-distributed rays from the light source; (top right) this step results in a first approximation of direct illumination. The next rows (1b)–(1d)
illustrate subsequent incremental shooting steps. In each step, the illumination
received during the previous step is propagated by shooting cosine-distributed
rays. The number of rays is chosen proportional to the amount of power to be
propagated so that all rays carry the same amount. After a while, the power to
be distributed, and the number of rays, drops below a small threshold. When
this happens ((1d), right), a first "complete" radiosity solution is available. This
initial solution shows the effect of all relevant higher-order interreflections of light
but can be noisy. From that point on, the total power is propagated in so-called
regular shooting steps (bottom row). Regular shooting iterations result in new
complete solutions, which are, to very good approximation, independent of the
input. Noise is reduced by averaging these complete solutions.

The procedure above can be used to estimate $\Delta P_i^{(k+1)}$ for all patches i simultaneously. The same samples (rays or photons) (j_s, l_s) can be used. The difference is only in the scores (Equation 6.13), which basically requires us to count the number of rays hitting each patch. With stratified local line sampling, Algorithm 1 results.

Stochastic Regular Shooting of Power

The sums in regular power-shooting iterations (Equation 6.10) can be estimated using a very similar Monte Carlo method as described above for incremental power shooting. The first stochastic Jacobi radiosity algorithms, proposed by L. and A. Neumann et al. [123], consisted entirely of such iterations. Unlike its deterministic counterpart, the resulting radiosity solutions of each iteration are averaged, rather than having the result of a new iteration replace the previous solution. The main disadvantage of using only regular iterations is that higher-order interreflections appeared in the result only at a slow pace, especially in bright environments. This problem has been called the *warming-up* or *burn-in* problem [123, 128, 124, 127].

The warming-up problem can be avoided by first performing a sequence of incremental power-shooting iterations until convergence is obtained, as explained above. This results in a first *complete* radiosity solution, including higher-order interreflections. Especially when the number of samples N is rather low, this first complete solution will exhibit noisy artifacts. Stochastic regular power-shooting iterations can then be used in order to reduce these artifacts. A regular power-shooting iteration can be viewed as a transformation, transforming a first complete radiosity solution into a new complete one. It can be shown that the output is largely independent of the input. The average of the two radiosity distributions obtained subsequently is to good approximation the same as the result of one iteration with twice the number of samples. Figure 6.6 illustrates this process.

Stochastic Regular Gathering of Radiosity

Regular radiosity gathering iterations (Equation 6.9) can be converted into a stochastic variant using the procedure outlined above. The main difference with power-shooting iterations is that now, a new radiosity estimate is obtained as the average score associated with rays that are *shot from* each patch i, rather than from rays that land on i. Gathering iterations are mainly useful to clean up noisy artifacts from small patches, which have a small chance of being hit by rays in a shooting iteration and therefore exhibit a high variance.

6.3.3 Discussion

Several questions remain to be answered: how shall the number of samples N be chosen; when will the presented algorithms perform well and when will they be suboptimal; and how do they compare? A variance analysis allows us to answer these questions.

The most expensive operation in the algorithms above is ray shooting. The number of rays that needs to be shot in order to compute the radiosities in the scene to given accuracy with given confidence is determined by the variance of the involved estimators.

Incremental Shooting

A detailed analysis of the stochastic incremental shooting algorithm is presented in Appendix C. The results of this analysis can be summarized as follows:

- The variance on the resulting radiosity estimates $\tilde{B}_i$ for each patch i is, to good approximation, given by

$$V[\hat{B}_i] \approx \frac{P_T}{N} \frac{\rho_i(B_i - B_{ei})}{A_i}. \tag{6.14}$$

  In particular, it is inversely proportional to the surface area A_i, meaning that incremental shooting will not be the optimal solution for small patches. Regular gathering does not have this drawback and can be used in order to clean up noisy artifacts on small patches.

- The number of samples N in Step 2 (a) of Algorithm 1 shall be chosen proportional to the amount of power $\Delta P_T^{(k)}$ to be propagated in each iteration, so that rays always carry the same amount of power. A heuristic for the total number of rays in a sequence of iterations until convergence is

$$N \approx 9 \cdot \max_i \frac{\rho_i A_T}{A_i}. \tag{6.15}$$

  In practice, it makes a lot of sense to skip, for instance, the 10% of patches in a scene with the largest ratio ρ_i/A_i. Note that a rough heuristic for N suffices: a higher accuracy can always be obtained by averaging the result of several independent runs of the algorithm.

- The time complexity of the stochastic Jacobi iterative algorithms for radiosity is roughly log-linear. This is much lower than the quadratic time complexity of deterministic Jacobi iterations.

Figure 6.7 illustrates that stochastic relaxation can yield useful images faster than corresponding deterministic relaxation algorithms.

Figure 6.7. Stochastic relaxation methods can yield useful images much faster than their deterministic counterparts. The environment shown consists of slightly more than 30,000 patches. The top image was obtained with incremental stochastic power-shooting iterations in about 10 seconds on a 2GHz Pentium-4 PC, using about 10^6 rays. Even if only 1 ray were used for each form factor, $9 \cdot 10^8$ rays would be required with a deterministic method. Noisy artifacts are still visible but are progressively reduced using regular stochastic power-shooting iterations. After about 3 minutes, they are not visible anymore.

This progressive variance reduction is illustrated in the bottom images, shown without Gouraud shading to make noisy artifacts more visible. The shown images have been obtained after 1, 4, 16, 64, and 252 (right-to-left, top-to-bottom) iterations of about 10 seconds each. The model shown is an edited part of the Soda Hall VRML model made available at the University of California at Berkeley.

Regular Shooting

A similar analysis of the variance of regular shooting iterations shows that the variance of a regular shooting iteration, when used with a "complete" radiosity solution as its input, is the same as for a whole sequence of incremental iterations to convergence when the total number of rays being shot is the same. The variance is also given by Equation 6.14. For this reason, the "complete" radiosity results obtained by a sequence of incremental iterations to convergence, and of subsequent regular iterations, are optimally combined by simple averaging.

Regular Gathering

The variance of regular gathering is in practice most often higher than that of shooting, but it does not depend on the patch area. Gathering can therefore be useful in order to "clean" noisy artifacts from small patches, which have a small chance of being hit by shooting rays from elsewhere and can suffer from a large variance with shooting.

Other Stochastic Relaxation Methods for Radiosity

It is possible to design stochastic adaptations of other relaxation methods in the same spirit. Shirley has investigated algorithms that can be viewed as stochastic incremental Gauss-Seidel and Southwell algorithms [167, 169, 168]. Bekaert has studied stochastic adaptations of over-relaxation, Chebyshev's iterative method, and the conjugate gradient method (suggested by L. Neumann). These relaxation methods have been developed in the hope of reducing the number of iterations to convergence. Since the deterministic iterations have a fixed computation cost, strongly related to the size of a linear system, reducing the number of iterations clearly reduces the total computation cost to convergence. This is, however, not so with the stochastic variants. The computation cost of stochastic relaxation methods is dominated by the number of samples to be taken. The number of samples is only loosely related to the size of the system. In the radiosity case, it turns out that the simple stochastic Jacobi iterations described above are at least as good as other stochastic relaxation methods.

6.4 Discrete Random Walk Methods for Radiosity

In the previous section, a first class of stochastic methods was described for solving the radiosity system of equations (Equation 6.6) or the equivalent power system (Equation 6.8) by means of stochastic variants of well-known iterative solution methods for linear systems, such as the Jacobi iterative method. It was shown that form factor computation and storage is effectively avoided, allowing us to compute radiosity in large models with less computer storage and less computing time than their deterministic counterparts.

This section covers a second class of methods with identical properties. The methods discussed here are based on the concept of a random walk in a so-called *discrete state space*, explained in Section 6.4.1. Unlike stochastic relaxation methods, random walk methods for linear systems are well covered in Monte Carlo literature [62, 183, 61, 43, 153]. They have been proposed for solving linear systems similar to the radiosity system since the beginning of the 1950s [50, 224]. Their application to radiosity has been proposed in [161, 162].

It turns out that these algorithms are not better than the stochastic Jacobi algorithm of the previous section. We will, however, introduce a number of fundamental concepts that are needed in later sections and chapters, but that are easier to understand first in this context.

6.4.1 Random Walks in a Discrete State Space

Consider the following experiment, involving a set of n urns, labeled i, $i = 1, \ldots, n$. One of the urns contains a ball, subject to the following "game of chance":

- The ball is initially inserted in a randomly chosen urn. The probability that the ball is stored in urn $i, i = 1, \ldots, n$, is π_i. These probabilities are, of course, properly normalized: $\sum_{i=1}^{n} \pi_i = 1$. They are called *source* or *birth probabilities*.

- The ball is randomly moved from one urn to another. The probability p_{ij} of moving the ball from urn i to urn j is called the *transition probability*. The transition probabilities from a fixed urn i need not sum to one. If the ball is in urn i, then the game will be terminated with probability $\alpha_i = 1 - \sum_{j=1}^{n} p_{ij}$. α_i is called the *termination* or *absorption* probability at urn i. The sum of the transition probabilities and the termination probability for any given urn is equal to unity.

- The previous step is repeated until termination is sampled.

Suppose the game is played N times. During the games, a tally is kept of how many times each urn i is "visited" by the ball. It is then interesting to study the expected number of times C_i that the ball will be observed in each urn i. It turns out that

$$C_i = N\pi_i + \sum_{j=1}^{n} C_j p_{ji}.$$

The first term on the right-hand side of this equation indicates the expected number of times that a ball is initially inserted in urn i. The second term indicates the expected number of times that a ball is moved to urn i from another urn j.

Usually, the urns are called *states* and the ball is called a *particle*. The game of chance outlined above is an example of a *discrete random walk process*. The process is called *discrete* because the set of states is countable. In Section 6.5, we will encounter random walks in a continuous state space. The expected number of visits C_i per random walk is called the *collision density* χ_i . The collision density of a discrete random walk process with source probabilities π_i and transition probabilities p_{ij} is the solution of a linear system of equations:

$$\chi_i = \pi_i + \sum_{j=1}^{n} \chi_j p_{ji}. \tag{6.16}$$

Note that χ_i can be larger than unity. For this reason, χ_i is called the collision *density* rather than a *probability*. In summary, we have shown that at least a certain class of linear systems of equations, like the one above, can be solved by simulating random walks and keeping count of how often each state is being visited. The states of the random walk correspond to the unknowns of the system.

6.4.2 Shooting Random Walk Methods for Radiosity

The system of equations in Equation 6.16 is similar to the power system (Equation 6.8):

$$P_i = P_{ei} + \sum_{j} P_j F_{ji} \rho_i.$$

However, the source terms P_{ei} in the power system do not sum to one. Of course, the remedy is very easy: divide both sides of the equations by the total self-emitted power $P_{eT} = \sum_i P_{ei}$:

$$\frac{P_i}{P_{eT}} = \frac{P_{ei}}{P_{eT}} + \sum_{j} \frac{P_j}{P_{eT}} F_{ji} \rho_i.$$

This system of equations suggests a discrete random walk process with:

- Birth probabilities $\pi_i = P_{ei}/P_{eT}$: particles are generated randomly on light sources, with a probability proportional to the self-emitted power of each light source.

- Transition probabilities $p_{ij} = F_{ij}\rho_j$: first, a candidate transition is sampled by tracing, for instance, a local line (Section 6.2.3).[1] After candidate transition, the particle is subjected to an acceptance/rejection test with *survival probability* equal to the reflectivity ρ_j. If the particle does not survive the test, it is said to be *absorbed*.

By simulating N random walks in this way, and keeping a count C_i of random walk visits to each patch i, the light power P_i can be estimated as

$$\frac{C_i}{N} \approx \frac{P_i}{P_{eT}}. \tag{6.17}$$

Because the simulated particles originate at the light sources, this random walk method for radiosity is called a *shooting* random walk method. It is called a *survival* random walk estimator because particles are only counted if they survive the rejection test (see Figure 6.8).

Usually, particles at the light source are not counted, because they estimate the self-emitted light distribution, which is known. We call this *source term estimation suppression*.

Collision Estimation

Transition sampling as described above is suboptimal. Candidate transition sampling involves an expensive ray-shooting operation. If the candidate transition is not accepted, this expensive operation has been performed in vain. This will often be the case if a dark surface is hit. It will always be more efficient to count the particles visiting a patch, whether they survive or not. The estimates (Equation 6.17) then, of course, need to be reduced in order to compensate for the fact that too many particles are counted. The resulting *collision random walk estimates* are

$$\rho_i \frac{C_i'}{N} \approx \frac{P_i}{P_{eT}}. \tag{6.18}$$

C_i' denotes the total number of particles hitting patch i. The expected number of particles that survive on i is $\rho_i C_i' \approx C_i$.

---

[1]Similar algorithms based on global line sampling have been proposed as well [157, 161].

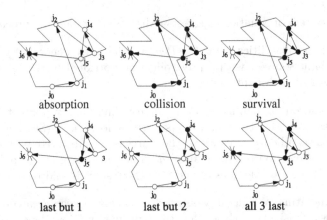

Figure 6.8. Absorption, collision, and survival random walk estimators differ by
when particle hits are counted: only when they are absorbed, only when they
survive impact with a surface, or always. The black dots indicate when a particle
is counted; a white dot indicates hits at which it is not counted. The score,
recorded when a particle is counted, reflects this choice. Absorption, collision,
and survival estimation are not the only possibilities. The bottom row shows
some alternatives described in the literature.

Absorption Estimation

A third, related, random walk estimator only counts particles if they are
absorbed. The resulting *absorption random walks estimates* are

$$\frac{\rho_i}{1 - \rho_i} \frac{C_i''}{N} \approx \frac{P_i}{P_{e_T}}. \tag{6.19}$$

C_i'' denotes the number of particles that are absorbed on i. It fulfills
$C_i' = C_i + C_i''$. The expected number of particles being absorbed on i
is $(1 - \rho_i)C_i' \approx C_i''$. The collision estimator is usually, but not always,
more efficient than the absorption estimator. A detailed comparison can
be made by computing the variance of the random walk methods (Section
6.4.4).

6.4.3 Adjoint Systems, Importance or Potential, and Gathering Random Walk Methods for Radiosity

The estimators above are called *shooting* estimators, because they simulate the trajectory of imaginary particles that originate at a light source.
The particles are counted whenever they hit a patch of which we want
to estimate the light power. Alternatively, it is also possible to estimate

the radiosity on a given patch i, by means of particles that originate at i and that are counted when they hit a light source. Such *gathering* random walk estimators can be derived in a brute force manner, analogous to the development of the path-tracing algorithm in Chapter 5. There is, however, also a more elegant, although slightly more abstract, interpretation of gathering random walk estimators: *a gathering random walk estimator corresponds to a shooting random walk estimator for solving an adjoint system of equations.*

Adjoint systems of equations. Consider a linear system of equations $\mathbf{Cx} = \mathbf{e}$, where $\mathbf{C}$ is the coefficient matrix of the system, with elements c_{ij}; $\mathbf{e}$ is the source vector; and $\mathbf{x}$ is the vector of unknowns. A well-known result from algebra states that each scalar product $\langle \mathbf{x}, \mathbf{w} \rangle = \sum_{i=1}^{n} x_i w_i$ of the solution $\mathbf{x}$ of the linear system, with an arbitrary *weight vector* $\mathbf{w}$, can also be obtained as a scalar product $\langle \mathbf{e}, \mathbf{y} \rangle$ of the source term $\mathbf{e}$ with the solution of the *adjoint* system of linear equations $\mathbf{C}^\mathsf{T} \mathbf{y} = \mathbf{w}$:

$$\langle \mathbf{w}, \mathbf{x} \rangle = \langle \mathbf{C}^\mathsf{T} \mathbf{y}, \mathbf{x} \rangle = \langle \mathbf{y}, \mathbf{Cx} \rangle = \langle \mathbf{y}, \mathbf{e} \rangle.$$

$\mathbf{C}^\mathsf{T}$ denotes the transpose of the matrix $\mathbf{C}$: if $\mathbf{C} = \{c_{ij}\}$, then $\mathbf{C}^\mathsf{T} = \{c_{ji}\}$. The second equality in the derivation above is a fundamental property of scalar products, which is extremely easy to verify yourself.

Adjoints of the radiosity system, and the concept of importance or potential. Adjoint systems corresponding to the radiosity system of equations (Equation 6.6) look like:

$$Y_i = W_i + \sum_j Y_j \rho_j F_{ji}. \tag{6.20}$$

These adjoint systems and the statement above can be interpreted as follows (see Figure 6.9): Consider the power P_k emitted by a patch k. P_k can be written as a scalar product $P_k = A_k B_k = \langle B, W \rangle$ with $W_i = A_i \delta_{ik}$: all components of the *direct importance* vector W are 0, except the kth component, which is equal to $W_k = A_k$. The statement above implies that P_k can also be obtained as $P_k = \langle Y, E \rangle = \sum_i Y_i B_{ei}$, which is a weighted sum of the self-emitted radiosities at the light sources in the scene. The solution Y of the adjoint system (Equation 6.20) indicates to what extent each light source contributes to the radiosity at k. Y is called the *importance* or *potential* in the literature [181, 140, 25]; see also Section 2.7.

Gathering random walk estimators for radiosity. The adjoints (Equation 6.20) of the radiosity system also have the indices of the form factors in the

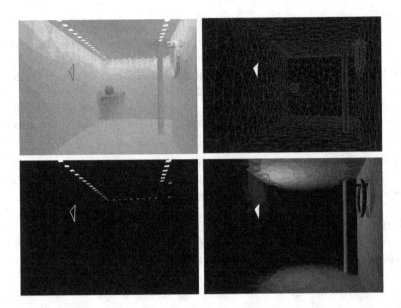

Figure 6.9. Duality between gathering and shooting in radiosity. The light flux emitted by the patch shown in bright in the top right image can be obtained in two ways: 1) as the scalar product of radiosity B (top left) and the response or measurement function W (top right), and 2) as the scalar product of the self-emitted radiosity E (bottom left) with importance Y (bottom right).

right order, so they can be solved using a random walk simulation with transitions sampled with local or global lines. The particles are now, however, shot from the patch of interest ($\pi_i = \delta_{ki}$), instead of from the light sources. The transition probabilities are $p_{ji} = \rho_j F_{ji}$: First, an absorption/survival test is performed. If the particle survives, it is propagated to a new patch, with probabilities corresponding to the form factors. A nonzero contribution to the radiosity of patch k results whenever the imaginary particle hits a light source. Its physical interpretation is that of *gathering*.

The gathering random walk estimator described here is a collision estimator. It is possible to construct a survival or absorption gathering estimator as well. A survival gathering random walk estimator will only count particles that survive on a hit light source, for instance.

6.4.4 Discussion

Discrete random walk estimators for radiosity thus can be classified according to the following criteria:

- Whether they are *shooting* or *gathering*.

estimator	score $\tilde{s}(j_0,\ldots,j_\tau)$	variance $V[\tilde{s}]$
absorption	$\frac{\rho_k}{A_k}\frac{P_{eT}}{1-\rho_k}\delta_{j_\tau k}$	$\frac{\rho_k}{A_k}\frac{P_{eT}}{1-\rho_k}b_k - b_k^2$
collision	$\frac{\rho_k}{A_k}P_{eT}\sum_{t=1}^{\tau}\delta_{j_t k}$	$\frac{\rho_k}{A_k}P_{eT}(1+2\zeta_k)b_k - b_k^2$
survival	$\frac{1}{A_k}P_{eT}\sum_{t=1}^{\tau-1}\delta_{j_t k}$	$\frac{1}{A_k}P_{eT}(1+2\zeta_k)b_k - b_k^2$

Table 6.1. Score and variance of discrete shooting random walk estimators for radiosity.

- According to where they generate a contribution: at absorption, survival, at every collision.

In order to make statements about how these variants compare with each other and with the stochastic Jacobi method discussed in the previous section, the variance of these methods needs to be computed. Except for the variance of the absorption estimators, which are simple hit-or-miss estimators, the calculation of random walk variances is fairly complicated and lengthy. The results are summarized in Tables 6.1 and 6.2. The derivation of these results can be found in [161, 162, 15].

In Table 6.1, j_0 is the patch at which a random walk originates. It is a patch on a light source in the scene, chosen with probability proportional to its self-emitted power. $j_1,\ldots,j_\tau$ are the patches subsequently visited by the random walk. Transitions are sampled by first doing a survival/absorption test, with survival probability equal to the reflectivity. After survival, the next visited patch is selected with probability equal to the form factor, by tracing local or global lines. τ is the length of the random walk: The random walk is absorbed after hitting the patch j_τ. The expectation of all these estimators is equal to the non-self-emitted radiosity $b_k = B_k - B_{ek}$ at a patch k (source term estimation is suppressed). ζ_k is the recurrent radiosity at k: If k is the only source of radiosity, with unit strength, the total radiosity on k would be larger than 1, say I_k, because other patches in the scene reflect part of the light emitted by k back to k. The recurrent radiosity then would be $\zeta_k = I_k - 1$. The recurrent radiosity also indicates the probability that a random walk visiting a patch k will return to k. Usually, this probability is very small, and the terms containing ζ_k can be ignored.

Table 6.2 shows the score and variance of discrete gathering random walks. The expectation is $b_k = B_k - B_{ek}$, as well, but this time k refers to the patch on which the random walk originates: $k = j_0$. Transitions are sampled exactly as for shooting random walks. b_{ks} is the radiosity at k

estimator	score $\tilde{s}(j_0 = k, \ldots, j_\tau)$	variance $V[\tilde{s}_k]$
absorption	$\rho_k \frac{B_{ej_\tau}}{1-\rho_{j_\tau}}$	$\rho_k \sum_s \frac{B_{es}}{1-\rho_s} b_{ks} - b_k^2$
collision	$\rho_k \sum_{t=1}^{\tau} B_{ejt}$	$\rho_k \sum_s (B_{es} + 2b_s) b_{ks} - b_k^2$
survival	$\rho_k \sum_{t=1}^{\tau-1} \frac{B_{ejt}}{\rho_{jt}}$	$\rho_k \sum_s \frac{B_{es}+2b_s}{\rho_s} b_{ks} - b_k^2$

Table 6.2. Score and variance of discrete gathering random walk estimators for radiosity.

due to the light source s, received directly or via interreflections from other patches: $b_k = \sum_s b_{ks}$.

Shooting versus Gathering

The variance expressions in Tables 6.1 and 6.2 allow us to make a detailed theoretical comparison of discrete shooting and gathering random walks. The shooting estimators have lower variance, except on small patches, which have low probability of being hit by rays shot from light sources. Unlike shooting estimators, the variance of gathering estimators does not depend on the patch area A_k. For sufficiently small patches, gathering will be more efficient. Gathering could, like in the case of stochastic relaxation methods, be used in order to "clean" noisy artifacts on small patches after shooting.

Absorption, Survival, or Collision?

The variance results in Tables 6.1 and 6.2 also indicate that the survival estimators are always worse than the corresponding collision estimators, because the reflectivity ρ_k (shooting) or ρ_s (gathering) is always smaller than 1.

As a rule, the collision estimators also have lower variance than the absorption estimators:

- Shooting estimators: the recurrent radiosity ζ_k is, in general, negligible and $1 - \rho_k < 1$.

- Gathering estimators: as a rule, self-emitted radiosity B_{es} of a light source is much larger than the non-self-emitted radiosity b_s, and again, $1 - \rho_s < 1$.

These results hold when transitions are sampled according to the form factors. When the transition probabilities are modulated, for instance, to shoot more rays into important directions (Section 6.6.1), an absorption estimation can sometimes be better than a collision estimator. In particular, it can be shown that a collision estimator can never be perfect, because random walks can contribute a variable number of scores. An absorption estimator always yields a single score, so it does not suffer from this source of variance. For this reason, absorption estimators can be made perfect, at least in theory.

Discrete Collision Shooting Random Walks versus Stochastic Jacobi Relaxation

According to Table 6.1, the variance of N^{RW} discrete collision shooting random walks is approximately

$$\frac{V^{RW}}{N^{RW}} \approx \frac{1}{N^{RW}} \frac{\rho_k}{A_k} P_{eT}(B_k - B_{ek}).$$

The variance of incremental power shooting (Equation 6.14) with N^{SR} rays is approximately

$$\frac{V^{SR}}{N^{SR}} \approx \frac{1}{N^{SR}} \frac{\rho_k}{A_k} P_T(B_k - B_{ek}).$$

It can be shown that N^{RW} random walks result on the average in $N^{RW} P_T/P_{eT}$ rays to be shot. Filling in $N^{SR} = N^{RW} P_T/P_{eT}$ in the expression above thus indicates that *for the same number of rays, discrete collision shooting random walks and incremental power-shooting Jacobi iterations are approximately equally efficient.* This observation has been confirmed in experiments [11].

This rather unexpected result can be understood as follows. Both algorithms have an intuitive interpretation in the sense of particles being shot from patches. The particles have a uniform starting position on the patches, and they have cosine-distributed directions with regard to the normal on the patches. The number of particles shot from each patch is proportional to the power propagated from the patch. Since the two methods compute the same result, the same number of particles will be shot from each of the patches. If the same random numbers are also used to shoot particles from each patch, the particles themselves can also be expected to be the same. The main difference is the order in which the particles are shot: they are shot in "breadth-first" order in stochastic relaxation and in "depth-first" order with random walks (see Figure 6.10). For the variance, this makes no difference.

There are, however, other, more subtle differences between the algorithms, in particular in the survival sampling: In the random walk algorithm, the decision whether a particle will survive on a patch or not is

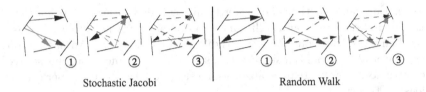

Stochastic Jacobi   Random Walk

Figure 6.10. This figure illustrates the difference in order in which particles are shot in stochastic Jacobi iterations ("breadth-first" order) and in collision shooting random walk radiosity ("depth-first" order). Eventually, the shot particles are very similar.

made independently for all particles. In stochastic relaxation radiosity, the decision is made once for a group of particles that landed on a patch during a previous iteration step. For instance, if 10 particles land on a patch with reflectivity 0.45, in the random walk method, any number of particles, ranging from 0 to 10, might survive on the patch. In the stochastic relaxation algorithm, the number of surviving particles will be 4 or 5. In both cases, the average will be 4.5. Experiments with very simple scenes, such as an empty cube, where recurrent radiosity ζ_k is important, do reveal a different performance [11].

The conclusion that stochastic Jacobi iterations and random walks are equally efficient is also no longer true when higher-order approximations are used, or with low-discrepancy sampling, or in combination with variance reduction techniques. Many variance-reduction techniques and low-discrepancy samplings are easier to implement and appear more effective for stochastic relaxation than with random walks (see Section 6.6).

6.5 Photon Density Estimation Methods

The algorithms discussed in Sections 6.3 and 6.4 solved the radiosity system of linear equations (Equation 6.6) stochastically. By sampling according to the form factors, the numerical value for the form factors was never needed. In this section, we will discuss a number of random walk methods that are highly related to those of Section 6.4, but that solve the radiosity integral equation (Equation 6.3), or the general rendering equation (Equation 6.2), rather than the radiosity system of equations. Indeed, just like discrete random walks are used to solve linear systems, random walks in a *continuous state space* can be used to solve integral equations like the radiosity or rendering integral equation. They are, therefore, sometimes also called *continuous random walk radiosity methods*.

The random walks that are introduced in this section are nothing but simulated trajectories of photons emitted by light sources and bouncing throughout a scene, as dictated by the laws of light emission and scattering described in Chapter 2. The surface hit points of these photons are recorded in a data structure, for later use. An essential property of such particle hit points is that their density at any given location (the number of hits per unit of area) is proportional to the radiosity at that location (Section 6.5.1). This density can be estimated at any surface location where this needs to be done, by means of density estimation methods known from statistics [175]. The basic density estimation methods that have been used for global illumination are covered in Sections 6.5.2 through 6.5.5. In addition, the instant radiosity algorithm by Keller [91] fits in this class (Section 6.5.6).

The main benefit of this approach is that nondiffuse light emission and scattering can be taken into account to a certain extent. Just like the methods of the previous sections, the methods described here do not allow us to solve the rendering equation exactly at every surface point. Still, some world-space representation of the illumination on the surfaces in the scene needs to be chosen, with corresponding approximation errors like blurred shadow boundaries or light leaks. However, photon density estimation methods open the way to more sophisticated and pleasing representations of the illumination than the average radiosity on surface patches. For this reason, they have gained considerable importance and attention in the last years. In the photon-mapping method, for instance, [83], the representation of illumination is independent of scene geometry. This allows us to use nonpolygonized geometry representations, procedural geometry such as fractals, and object instantiation in a straightforward manner.

6.5.1 Photon Transport Simulation and Radiosity

Photon trajectory simulation, according to the laws of physics as outlined in Chapter 2, is called *analog* photon trajectory simulation. We start by explaining how analog photon trajectory simulation works and how it can be used for computing radiosity. Figure 6.11 illustrates this process.

We start out (1a) by selecting an initial particle location x_0 on a light source. We do that with a (properly normalized) probability proportional to the self-emitted radiosity:

$$S(x_0) = \frac{B_e(x_0)}{P_{eT}}. \tag{6.21}$$

x_0 is the starting point for a random walk. $S(x_0)$ is called the *birth* or *source* density.

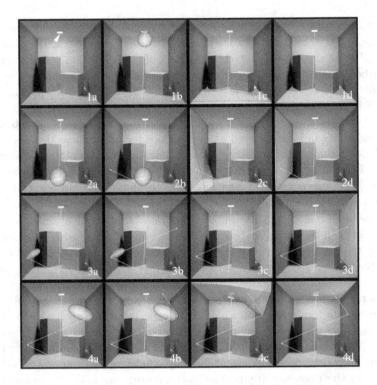

Figure 6.11. Analog photon transport simulation, from the selection of an initial particle location to absorption.

Next, an initial particle direction Θ_0 is selected using the directional light emission distribution of the light source at x_0, times the outgoing cosine. For a diffuse light source (1b),

$$T(\Theta_0|x_0) = \frac{\cos(\Theta_0, N_{x_0})}{\pi}.$$

Consider now a ray shot from the sampled location x_0 into the selected direction Θ_0. The density of hit points x_1 of such rays with object surfaces depends on surface orientation, distance, and visibility with regard to x_0:

$$T(x_1|x_0, \Theta_0) = \frac{\cos(-\Theta_0, N_{x_1})}{r_{x_0 x_1}^2} V(x_0, x_1).$$

The transparent surface in (1c) shows this density on the bottom surface of the shown model. In (1d), the density of incoming hits is shown, taking into account these geometric factors as well as the (diffuse) light emission characteristics at x_0:

$$T^{in}(x_1|x_0) = T(\Theta_0|x_0)T(x_1|x_0, \Theta_0)$$

$$= \frac{\cos(\Theta_0, N_{x_0})\cos(-\Theta_0, N_{x_1})}{\pi r_{x_0 x_1}^2} \quad V(x_0, x_1) = K(x_0, x_1).$$

Next, (2a), a survival test is carried out at the obtained surface hit point x_1: A random decision is made whether or not to sample absorption (and path termination) or reflection. We take the probability $\sigma(x_1)$ of sampling reflection equal to the albedo $\rho(x_1, -\Theta_0)$, the fraction of power coming in from x_0 that gets reflected at x_1. For a diffuse surface, the albedo is the same as the reflectivity $\rho(x_1)$. The full *transition density* from x_0 to x_1 is thus

$$T(x_1|x_0) = T^{in}(x_1|x_0)\sigma(x_1) = K(x_0, x_1)\rho(x_1). \qquad (6.22)$$

If survival is sampled, a reflected particle direction is chosen according to the BRDF times the outgoing cosine. For a diffuse surface, again only the outgoing cosine remains (2b).

Subsequent transitions are sampled in the same way, by shooting a ray, performing a survival test, and sampling reflection if the particle is not absorbed. Image (2c) shows the influence of surface orientation, distance, and visibility on the left surface of the scene with regard to x_1. (2d) shows the combined effect of the cosine distribution at x_1 and the former. The third and fourth rows of Figure 6.11 illustrate the process twice more, this time for nondiffuse reflection.

Now, consider the expected number $\chi(x)$ of particle hits resulting from such a simulation, per unit of area near a surface location x. This particle hit density consists of two contributions: the density of particles being born near x, as given by $S(x)$, and the density of particles visiting x after visiting some other surface location y. The density of particles coming from elsewhere depends on the density $\chi(y)$ elsewhere and the transition density $T(x|y)$ to x:

$$\chi(x) = S(x) + \int_S \chi(y)T(x|y)dA_y.$$

For a diffuse environment, the birth and transition density are given by Equations 6.21 and 6.22:

$$\chi(x) = \frac{B_e(x)}{P_{eT}} + \int_S \chi(y)K(y, x)\rho(x)dA_y \quad \Rightarrow \quad \chi(x) = \frac{B(x)}{P_{eT}}. \qquad (6.23)$$

In other words, *the number of particle hits per unit area expected near a surface location x is proportional to the radiosity $B(x)$*. We have derived

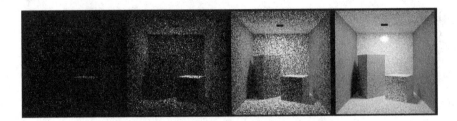

Figure 6.12. The density of particle hits after a photon transport simulation according to the physics of light emission and scattering, is proportional to the radiosity function. These images show the particle hits of 1,000, 10,000, 100,000, and 1,000,000 paths, respectively.

this result for diffuse environments here, but also with nondiffuse light emission and scattering, the particle hit density after analog simulation will be proportional to the radiosity. This is illustrated in Figure 6.12. This is, of course, not a surprise: it is our mental model of how nature works, and which we simulate in a straightforward manner on the computer.

The problem of computing radiosity has thus been reduced to the problem of estimating particle hit densities: to estimating the number of particle hits per unit area at a given surface location. The problem of estimating a density like that, given nothing more than a set of sample point locations, has been studied intensively in statistics [175]. The next sections cover the main density estimation methods that have been applied in the context of rendering: histogram methods, orthogonal series estimation, kernel methods, and nearest neighbor methods.

An alternative, equivalent point of view is to regard the problem at hand as a Monte Carlo integration problem: we want to compute integrals of the unknown radiosity function $B(x)$ with a given measurement, or response, function $M(x)$ (see also Section 2.8):

$$B_M = \int_S M(x)B(x)dA_x.$$

The radiosity $B(x)$, and thus the integrand, cannot be evaluated a priori, but since analog simulation yields surface points x_s with density $\chi(x_s) = B(x_s)/P_{eT}$, M can be estimated as

$$B_M \approx \frac{1}{N} \sum_{s=1}^{\text{nr of hits}} \frac{M(x_s)B(x_s)}{B(x_s)/P_{eT}} = \frac{P_{eT}}{N} \sum_{s=1}^{\text{nr of hits}} M(x_s).$$

Basically, all we have to do is simulate a number of photon trajectories and accumulate the value of measurement function $M(x_s)$ at the photon surface hit points x_s.[2] The measurement functions corresponding to histogram methods, orthogonal series estimation, and kernel methods are described below.

Note that the procedure explained here corresponds closely with the survival estimator in Section 6.4.1: Particles are only taken into account after surviving impact on a surface. Just like before, absorption and collision estimators can be defined, and source term estimation can be suppressed. In practice, collision estimation, that is, counting *all* particles that land on a surface, is preferred. Like before, this "over-counting" shall be compensated by multiplying all resulting expressions by the reflectivity.

6.5.2 Histogram Methods

The easiest, and probably most often used, way of estimating density functions is by subdividing the domain of the samples into bins—surface patches in our case—and to count the number of samples N_i in each bin (Figure 6.13). The ratio N_i/A_i yields an approximation for the particle density in each bin.

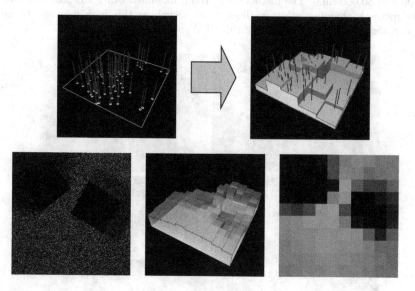

Figure 6.13. The histogram method, illustrated for the particle hits on the bottom side of the cube shown in Figure 6.12.

---

[2]Note that the sum is over the sample points, while division is by the number of photon trajectories!

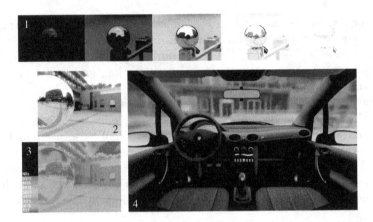

Figure 6.14. Image 4 shows the result of a real-world lighting simulation in a car model. A histogram method (Section 6.5.2) was used. Real-world lighting was captured by photographing a mirror sphere at various shutter speeds (1), and combining these images into a single high dynamic range environment map. Image 2 shows a mirror sphere, ray traced using this environment map. Image 3 shows the color-coded illumination levels from Image 2, which vary between 200 and 30,000 nits. The histogram method, like most other stochastic radiosity methods, handles arbitrary light sources such as this high dynamic range environment map with ease. (See Plate II.)

Figure 6.15. These images have been rendered using a histogram method [206] taking into account measured BRDFs. Specular effects have been added by ray tracing in a second pass. (Images courtesy of F. Drago and K. Myszkowski, Max-Planck-Institute for Informatics, Saarbrücken, Germany.) (See Plate III.)

An alternative explanation is as follows: Recall that the average radiosity on a patch i is by definition given by the following integral of $B(x)$:

$$B_i = \frac{1}{A_i} \int_{S_i} B(x) dA_x.$$

A random walk constructed as outlined is a technique to sample points x with density $\chi(x) = B(x)/P_{eT}$. With N random walks, B_i can be estimated as

$$\frac{P_{eT} N_i}{N A_i} \approx B_i,$$

where N_i is the number of visits to the patch i. The measurement functions $M^{hist}(x)$ of histogram methods are the so-called *characteristic functions* of the surface patches: functions taking value 1 for points on the surface patch, and 0 for other points.

Histogram methods for radiosity computations have been proposed in [5, 70, 138] and by others later on. This form of density estimation is very popular because of its simplicity.

6.5.3 Orthogonal Series Estimation

Histogram methods yield a single average radiosity value for each surface patch. It is possible to obtain linear, quadratic, cubic, or other higher-order approximations for the radiosity function $B(x)$, too. The problem of computing such higher-order approximations comes down to computing the coefficients $B_{i,\alpha}$ in the following decomposition of $B(x)$:

$$\tilde{B}_i(x) = \sum_{\alpha} B_{i,\alpha} \psi_{i,\alpha}(x).$$

The functions $\psi_{i,\alpha}(x)$ are called *basis functions*. The sum is over all basis functions defined on patch i. A constant approximation is obtained when using just one basis function $\psi_i(x)$ per patch, which is 1 on the patch and 0 outside. In that case, we will again obtain the histogram method of the previous section. Figure 6.16 illustrates higher-order basis functions that can be used on quadrilaterals. The idea is to approximate $B(x)$ as a linear combination of such functions.

The coefficients $B_{i,\alpha}$ can be obtained as scalar products with so-called *dual* basis functions $\tilde{\psi}_{i,\alpha}$:

$$B_{i,\alpha} = \int_S B(x) \tilde{\psi}_{i,\alpha}(x) dA_x. \tag{6.24}$$

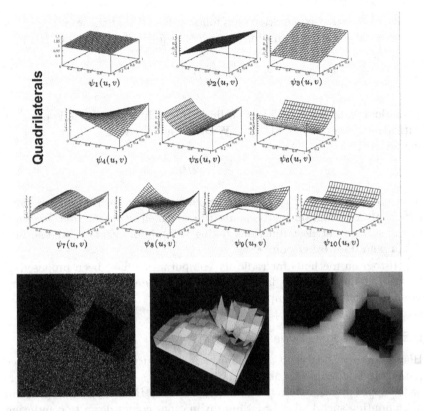

Figure 6.16. The top image shows a set of orthogonal functions, usable for orthogonal series estimation on quadrilaterals. The bottom image shows a linear approximation for the density of the particle hits on the bottom side of the cube shown in Figure 6.12.

Each dual basis function $\tilde{\psi}_{i,\alpha}$ is the unique linear combination of the original basis functions $\psi_{i,\beta}$ that fulfills the relations (fixed α, variable β)

$$\int_{S_i} \tilde{\psi}_{i,\alpha}(x)\psi_{i,\beta}(x)dA_x = \delta_{\alpha,\beta}.$$

In the case of a constant approximation, the dual basis function is $\tilde{\psi}_i(x) = 1/A_i$ if $x \in S_i$ and 0 elsewhere.

With N photon trajectories, Equation 6.24 can be estimated as

$$\frac{P_{eT}}{N} \sum_s \tilde{\psi}_{i,\alpha}(x_s) \approx B_{i,\alpha}.$$

Figure 6.17. Two images generated from the same converged cubic approximation solution. Once the solution has been obtained, a new image for a new viewpoint can be generated in fractions of a second. These images illustrate that orthogonal series estimation (as well as stochastic relaxation methods for higher-order approximations) can result in very high image quality in regions where illumination varies smoothly. In the neighborhood of discontinuities, however, image artifacts may remain. Discontinuity meshing would eliminate these artifacts.

The sum is over all points x_s visited by the random walks. The measurement functions of orthogonal series estimation are the dual basis functions $\tilde{\psi}_{i,\alpha}$.

Radiosity computation by *orthogonal series estimation*, as such methods are called, has been proposed by Bouatouch et al. [18] and Feda [44].

The main advantage of orthogonal series estimation over the histogram method is that a smoother approximation of radiosity is possible on a fixed mesh. Its main disadvantage is the cost. One can show [44, 13] that the cost of computing a higher-order approximation with K basis functions to fixed statistical error is about K times the cost of computing a constant approximation. The increase in computation time for higher-order approximations is larger than in deterministic methods [69, 228], but the resulting algorithms are significantly easier to implement, still require no form factor storage, and are much less sensitive to computational errors (see Figure 6.17).

6.5.4 Kernel Methods

The radiosity $B(z)$ at a point z could also be written as an integral involving a Dirac impulse function:

$$B(z) = \int_S B(x)\delta(x - z)dA_x.$$

Estimating the latter integral with random walks wouldn't work, because the Dirac pulse function is zero everywhere, except when its argument is zero. The chance of finding a particle hitting exactly the point z is zero in theory.[3] Even if we could find a particle hitting exactly at z, the value of the Dirac pulse is not determinate. It can't be finite because the Dirac function is zero everywhere except at one point and its integral is equal to 1. An approximation for the radiosity at z can, however, be obtained by using a different, normalized *density kernel* or *footprint* function $F(x, z)$ with nonzero width centered around z:

$$B_F(z) = \int_S B(x)F(x,z)dA_x \approx B(z). \tag{6.25}$$

Usually, a symmetric kernel is chosen, which depends only on the distance between x and z: $F(x, z) = F(z, x) = F(r_{xz})$. Examples include a cylindrical kernel ($F(r) = 1/2\pi R$ if $r < R$ and 0 otherwise) or a Gaussian bell.

With N photon trajectories, the integral in Equation 6.25 can be estimated as

$$\frac{P_{eT}}{N} \sum_s F(x_s, z) \approx B_F(z).$$

The sum is again over all points x_s visited by the random walks. The measurement functions this time are the kernels $F(x, z)$, centered at the query locations z.

For symmetric kernels, one can also interpret this result as follows: A kernel $F_s(z) = F(x_s, z)$ is placed at every particle hit point x_s. The radiosity estimate at a surface point z is then obtained by summing the value of these kernels at z.

This form of *kernel density estimation* has been used by Chen [24], Collins [32], and Shirley and Walter et al. [166, 210].

The main advantage of kernel methods is that they allow a representation of illumination that is not necessarily mesh-based, or that allows a suitable mesh to be constructed a posteriori. This allows us to get rid of edge discontinuities (see Figure 6.2). On the other hand, the choice of the kernel *bandwidth* is a difficult problem, and a lot of effort is required in order to avoid underestimation at surface edges, called *boundary bias* (see Figure 6.18). The cost of kernel evaluation can be considerable too, for instance, for a Gaussian kernel.

---

[3] In practice, the chance is not zero because of finite-precision arithmetic.

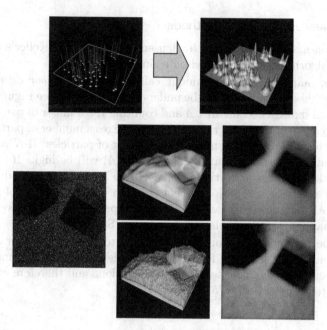

Figure 6.18. Kernel methods can be viewed as follows: A normalized kernel function is placed centered at each particle hit point. Radiosity is estimated by summing these kernels. The bottom rows of this figure show the result with a cylindrical kernel (middle row) and a Gaussian kernel (bottom row). The kernels have the same bandwidth. A Gaussian kernel results in a smoother result but at a higher computation cost than a cylindrical kernel. Note that the resulting radiosity estimates at the edges are only half of what they should be. This effect, due to the fact that the area on which particles are found around a query location is constrained (no particles beyond the edge), is called boundary bias.

Figure 6.19. Images obtained with the kernel density estimation method from [210]. Kernel density estimation allows for a posteriori meshing: A mesh capturing the illumination variations in the scene accurately is constructed after particle tracing and density estimation. The resulting mesh can be rendered in real time using graphics hardware. (Images courtesy of B. Walter, Ph. Hubbard, P. Shirley, and D. Greenberg, Cornell Program of Computer Graphics.) (See Plate IV.)

6.5.5 Nearest Neighbor Methods

The photon-mapping algorithm by Jensen et al. [81] and Keller's instant radiosity algorithm [91] are based on a similar principle.

Photon mapping uses a technique called *nearest neighbor estimation*. Nearest neighbor estimation can be understood as follows (see Figure 6.20): Rather than fixing a certain area A and counting the number of particles N on that area like in the histogram method, one fixes a number of particles N and looks for an area that contains this number of particles. If N particles can be found on a small area, the density (N/A) will be high. If they are only found on a large area, the density will be low. The main advantage of nearest neighbor estimation is that one can entirely get rid of surface meshes. All one needs to store is the set of particle hit-point locations. Photon mapping will be explained in detail in Section 7.6.

The measurement functions corresponding to nearest neighbor estimation are more complex than for the previous density estimation methods. They depend on the whole set of sample locations and therefore can only be evaluated a posteriori [175, Chapter 1].

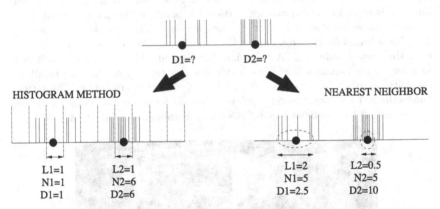

Figure 6.20. Two ways to estimate the density of samples D_1 and D_2 near the indicated locations (top row): 1) histogram methods (bottom left) first subdivide the domain into bins (the size of the bins here is $L = 1$) and count the number of samples N_1 and N_2 in the bins where density needs to be estimated; and 2) nearest neighbor estimation methods (bottom right) fix a number of samples N (here: $N = 5$) and find regions at the query locations that contain this number of samples (size L_1 and L_2). In both cases, density is estimated as the number of samples N over the size L of the considered regions. In the limit for a large number of samples and small bins, these methods will yield identical results.

6.5.6 Instant Radiosity

Instant radiosity [91] is based on the following observation: The right-hand side of the radiosity integral equation (Equation 6.3) is also an integral containing the radiosity function

$$B(z) = B_e(z) + \rho(z) \int_S K(z,x)B(x)dA_x.$$

Here too, this integral can be estimated by tracing a number of photon trajectories. This results in estimates for $B(z)$ of the following form:

$$B(z) \approx B_e(z) + \rho(z)\frac{P_{eT}}{N}\sum_s K(z,x_s).$$

The sum in the right-hand side can be interpreted as the direct illumination at z due to point light sources with strength P_{eT}/N placed at every photon hit point x_s. Instant radiosity will be explained in more detail in Section 7.7.

6.5.7 Discussion

We now discuss gathering variants and compare the algorithms with each other and with discrete random walk methods for radiosity.

Continuous Gathering Random Walks

The algorithms explained in this section are shooting algorithms. Just like with discrete random walk methods (Section 6.4.3), gathering variants can be obtained by introducing adjoints of an integral equation. Adjoints of the radiosity integral equation, for instance, look like

$$I(x) = M(x) + \int_S I(y)\rho(y)K(y,x)dA_y. \tag{6.26}$$

Their interpretation is exactly the same as explained in Section 6.4.3. Continuous gathering random walks are the basis of path-tracing algorithms discussed in Chapter 5. They have received little attention for the computation of world-space illumination representations. They may, however, help to "clean up" noisy artifacts on small patches in the histogram method, or when orthogonal series estimation is used. They might also be valuable in the context of bidirectional algorithms for object-space illumination computation, complementing shooting random walks.

Variance

A detailed comparison of various continuous random walk estimators among each other, or continuous versus discrete random walks, requires that the variance of the continuous random walk estimators be calculated. The calculation of continuous random walk variances can be done in exactly the same way as for a discrete random walk. A compact derivation, based on Green's function for the radiosity integral equation, can be found in [11]. The result for a continuous collision shooting random walk method with source term estimation suppression and using measurement function $M(x)$ is

$$V[\hat{b}_M] = P_{eT} \int_S \rho(x)\left[M(x) + 2\zeta(x)\right]M(x)b(x)dA_x - \left(\int_S M(x)b(x)dA_x\right)^2.$$
(6.27)

In this equation, $\zeta(x) = I(x) - M(x)$, with $I(x)$ the solution of the adjoint integral equation (Equation 6.26) with source term $M(x)$. Most often, $\zeta(x)$ is much smaller than 1, so it can be ignored. The expected value is $b_M = \int M(x)b(x)dA_x$ with $b(x) = B(x) - B_e(x)$, the non-self-emitted radiosity. By filling in the appropriate response functions $M(x)$, the variance can be computed for any of the aforementioned density estimation methods.

Bias

All density estimation algorithms described here compute a kind of convolution of the radiosity function:

$$B_M(z) = \int_S M(z,x)B(x)dA_x \neq B(z).$$

The approximations are visible in the images in the form of artifacts such as blurred shadow boundaries, edge discontinuities and light or shadow leaks, and boundary bias artifacts. For this reason, the density estimates are often not directly visualized, but a final gathering step is performed in order to avoid artifacts. Final gathering, and other hybrid methods, are the topic of Chapter 7.

It can be shown that all density estimation methods discussed here share a similar bias versus variance trade-off (see Figures 6.21 and 6.22): A response function with a large support, for instance, a histogram method on large patches, or a kernel method with wide kernels, will yield a lower variance. On the down side, however, a large support in general also means worse blurring of the radiosity function. The converse is true as well: narrow response functions reduce blurring and therefore result in, for instance, sharper shadow boundaries, but at the cost of a higher variance.

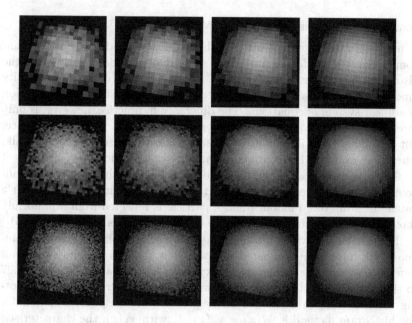

Figure 6.21. Variance versus bias trade-off of density estimation algorithms: The same scene is shown in all images, with increasingly fine discretization top-to-bottom and increasing number of samples left-to-right. The number of patches is 256 in the top row, 1024 in the middle row, and 4096 in the bottom row. The number of samples has been taken proportional to the number of patches: 10 times the number of patches (left), 40 times, 160 times, and 640 times (right). These images illustrate that the variance of the histogram method is inversely proportional to the patch area: images in the same column have the same variance. All other photon density estimation algorithms exhibit a similar variance versus bias trade-off as well.

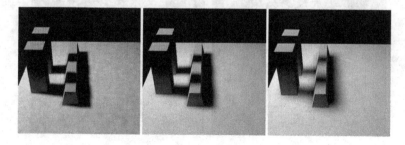

Figure 6.22. Variance versus bias trade-off in a kernel density estimation method: The number of particles is kept the same. The kernel bandwidth has been increased from left to right. A large bandwidth (right) yields low noise but blurred radiosity results. (Image courtesy of B. Walter, Ph. Hubbard, P. Shirley, and D. Greenberg, Cornell Program of Computer Graphics).

Continuous versus Discrete Random Walks

Continuous random walks with the histogram method and discrete random walks solve different problems. Continuous random walks with the histogram method estimate the area average of the continuous radiosity function $B(x)$ over a patch. Discrete random walks estimate the solution of a linear system of equations. The difference in practice, however, is only rarely noticeable: both methods can suffer from light leaks, for instance, but leaked light will illuminate other surfaces with a discrete random walk, whereas it won't with a continuous random walk method.

The algorithmic difference is quite small, also, with a continuous random walk; a particle is always reflected from its point of incidence on a patch. In a discrete random walk, a particle is reflected from a uniformly chosen different location on the patch on which it lands (see Figure 6.23).

Experiments in which a continuous and discrete collision shooting random walk have been compared indicate that there is also no significant difference in variance. This can be explained by comparing Equation 6.27 to the histogram method with the variance of the discrete collision shooting random walk in Table 6.1 on page 181. The response function for the histogram method is $M(x) = \chi_k(x)/A_k$ with $\chi_k(x)$, the characteristic function of a patch k.

Low-discrepancy sampling, however, appears to be significantly more effective with the discrete random walk than with the continuous random walk [15].

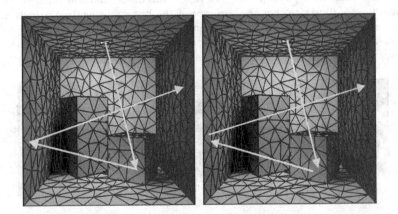

Figure 6.23. Continuous (left) versus discrete (right) random walks differ slightly in the way particles are reflected: Particles reflect off their point of incidence in continuous random walks. In discrete random walks, they emerge from a uniformly chosen new location on the patch they hit.

6.5.8 Stochastic Iteration Variants of Density Estimation Algorithms

The stochastic Jacobi method of Section 6.3 only allows us to compute the average radiosity on surface patches. The continuous random walk methods in this section allow for more advanced radiosity representations. In this paragraph, we show how to extend the stochastic Jacobi method to compute more advanced radiosity representations as well. By doing so, low-discrepancy sampling becomes more effective, and variance reduction is easier to obtain.

A general recipe for designing stochastic Jacobi methods based on the radiosity measurement equation,

$$B_M(z) = \int_S M(z,x)B(x)dA_x,$$

is as follows. We first replace $B(x)$ by the right-hand side of the radiosity equation,

$$B(x) = B_e(x) + \rho(x)\int_S K(x,y)B(y)dA_y.$$

This yields

$$B_M(z) = \int_S M(z,x)B_e(x)dA_x + \int_S \int_S M(z,x)\rho(x)K(x,y)B(y)dA_ydA_x.$$

Now suppose that some approximation $B_M^{(k)}(y)$ for $B(y)$ is available. We substitute this approximation in the right-hand side of the expression above. What comes out on the left-hand side then becomes the next approximation $B_M^{(k+1)}(z)$:

$$B_M^{(k+1)}(z) = \int_S M(z,x)B_e(x)dA_x$$
$$+ \int_S \int_S M(z,x)\rho(x)K(x,y)B_M^{(k)}(y)dA_ydA_x.$$

This iteration formula can be used in order to construct stochastic iterative algorithms in the same way as explained in Section 6.3. In particular, the double integral on the right-hand side suggests the following sampling approach:

1. Sample points y on the surfaces of the scene with a probability density proportional to $B_M^{(k)}(y)$.

2. Sample a point x conditional on y according to the conditional probability density $K(y,x) = K(x,y)$. This can be done by shooting a cosine-distributed ray from y. The first surface point hit by this ray is x.

3. The score contributed by each sample is essentially $M(z,x)\rho(x)$. There's a nonzero score to every z for which $M(z,x)$ is nonzero.

This approach has been shown to work very well for computing higher-order radiosity approximations [13]. Similar stochastic iterative methods have also been proposed for nondiffuse illumination [193].

6.6   Variance Reduction and Low-Discrepancy Sampling

The basic algorithms in the previous sections can be made more effective by using variance reduction techniques and low-discrepancy sampling. In this section, we will discuss variance reduction by view-importance sampling, by control variates, by combining gathering and shooting estimators using the same random walks or rays, and by weighted importance sampling. The material covered in this section is of a great practical importance and also serves as an illustration of the variance reduction techniques discussed in Chapter 3.

6.6.1   View-Importance–Driven Shooting

View Importance

In the basic algorithms in the previous sections, transitions are sampled using probabilities that reflect the laws of physics. The quality of the computed result mainly depends on the area and reflectivity of the patches but is furthermore uniform in the whole scene. Sometimes, however, one would like to save computation time by having high quality only in a part of the scene, for instance, the part of the scene that is visible in a view, while compromising on the quality in unimportant parts of the scene (see Figure 6.24). For example, when computing an image inside a single room in a large building with several floors, each containing many rooms, the basic estimators would spend a lot of work in computing the illumination in all rooms on all floors to similar quality. One might prefer to concentrate the computation work on the room one is in, at the expense of a lower quality of the radiosity solution in other rooms and other floors of the building. With view-importance sampling, the sampling probabilities in our Monte Carlo radiosity algorithms are modulated in such a way that more samples are taken in important regions of a scene and fewer in less important regions.

This requires a measure for the importance of the illumination across the surfaces in the scene. As explained in Section 6.4.3, the adjoints of the

Figure 6.24. View-importance–driven stochastic Jacobi radiosity. The top images have been obtained using approximately the same total amount of work (3.3 10^6 rays, under 1 minute of computation time). The top left image, computed with view importance, is significantly less noisy than the top right image, which has been obtained without computing and taking advantage of view importance. The bottom left image shows an overview of the scene in which the view was taken. The scene was subdivided into 162,000 patches. The bottom-right image shows the importance distribution for the view. High intensity indicates high view importance. The model shown is an edited part of the Soda Hall VRML model, available from the University of California at Berkeley.

radiosity system of equations yield such a measure. Here, it will be more convenient to use adjoints of the power system of equations (Equation (6.8):

$$I_i = V_i + \sum_j F_{ij} \rho_j I_j .^4 \qquad (6.28)$$

The importance I_i is always defined with regard to some direct importance distribution V_i. When choosing $V_i = 1$ for the patches i that are visible in a view and $V_i = 0$ for patches that are not visible in a view, I_i is called *view importance* and indicates what fraction of the radiosity B_i will

---

[4]Adjoint radiosity systems (Equation 6.20) are obtained by multiplying the left- and right-hand side of Equation 6.28 with the patch area A_i. Y_i and W_i in Equation 6.20 are related to I_i and V_i here as $Y_i = A_i I_i$ and $W_i = A_i V_i$.

be contributed to the patches visible in a view, directly or via interreflections.

A continuous view-importance function $I(x)$ on the surfaces of the scene can be defined in a very similar way by means of adjoints of the radiosity integral equation (Equation 6.3):

$$I(x) = V(x) + \int_S I(y)\rho(y)K(y,x)dA_y. \qquad (6.29)$$

The equations from which importance is to be solved are of the same form as the equations that describe light transport, and therefore the same algorithms as for light transport can be used for computing importance in a scene. This can happen either in separate phases or at the same time. Moreover, the computation of importance can possibly be sped up by taking advantage of the adjoint of importance: the radiosity. In practice, one should take care that importance is only used for computing radiosity (and vice versa) if the importance solution is sufficiently stable.

View-Importance–Driven Shooting Random Walks

View importance I_i can be used in various ways during random walk sampling:

- For modulating the transition probabilities, so that random walks are scattered preferentially towards regions of high importance. Unfortunately, this can no longer be done using uniformly distributed local or global lines and requires that incoming importance at every patch is stored or can be queried efficiently in some way [103, 192].

- For modulating the survival probabilities only, so particles near important regions get a higher chance of survival. In regions of low importance, particles will be killed off with a higher probability than according to the reflectivity (*Russian roulette*). In interesting regions, it is even possible to split a particle into two or more new particles of which the scores are appropriately combined (*splitting*).

- For modulating the birth probabilities, so that more random walks are started from important light sources and fewer from unimportant sources. This can be combined with importance-modulated transition sampling or can be done with analog transition sampling. In the latter case, the best results are obtained by modulating the analog birth probabilities at light sources (proportional to self-emitted power) by the *square root* of view importance [163].

In order to keep the estimation unbiased, scores shall be decreased when probabilities are increased and vice versa. If the survival chance of a particle is reduced in Russian roulette, for instance, the contribution of a particle that survives the test shall be increased in order to compensate. View-importance–based sampling has been studied for continuous as well as discrete random walks [140, 42, 163, 158, 15].

View-Importance–Driven Stochastic Relaxation Radiosity

In the context of incremental and regular power shooting (Section 6.3.2), view importance can be used to:

- Aim particles preferentially towards interesting regions. The problem is the same as with random walks: local or global line sampling is no longer helpful, and incoming importance needs to be stored with each patch.

- Increase or decrease the probability of shooting a ray from a given patch: this yields the same effect as Russian roulette, splitting and modulating birth probabilities together in random walks. It is very easy to implement with local line sampling.

In general, view-importance–driven stochastic relaxation methods can be derived in exactly the same way as analog stochastic relaxation methods by considering the power system of equations (Equation 6.8) modified as

$$P_i I_i = P_{ei} I_i + \sum_j P_j (I_j - V_j) F_{ji} \frac{\rho_i I_i}{I_j - V_j}.$$

Non–view-importance–driven stochastic relaxation radiosity corresponds with the choices $I_i = 1/\rho_i$ and $V_i = 1/\rho_i - 1$ (these choices are always a valid solution of Equation 6.28 in closed environments). Figure 6.24 shows some results, obtained with algorithms developed by Neumann and Bekaert [126, 15].

6.6.2 Control Variates

Recall that the main idea of control variate variance reduction (Section 3.6.6) is as follows. Suppose a function $f(x)$ is to be numerically integrated and that we know the integral G of a similar function $g(x)$. If the difference $f(x) - g(x)$ is to good approximation constant, it will be more efficient to use a Monte Carlo method for integrating the difference $f(x) - g(x)$ and add G afterwards. The function $g(x)$ is called a control variate. Control variates have been proposed for variance reduction in stochastic ray tracing by Lafortune [101]. We discuss here the application to discrete random walks and stochastic relaxation.

Control Variates for Linear Systems

This idea can be applied to the solution of linear systems (and integral equations) in the following way: Suppose we know an approximation $\tilde{x}$ for the solution x of $x = e + Ax$. The correction $\Delta x = x - \tilde{x}$ then fulfills

$$\Delta x = (e + A\tilde{x} - \tilde{x}) + A \cdot \Delta x. \tag{6.30}$$

Proof:

$$\Delta x = (I - A) \cdot \Delta x + A \cdot \Delta x \; ; \; (I - A) \cdot \Delta x = x - Ax + A\tilde{x} - \tilde{x} = e + A\tilde{x} - \tilde{x}.$$

This is true regardless of the error in the approximation $\tilde{x}$. Now suppose Δx is computed using, for instance, a random walk method. The resulting estimate $\Delta \tilde{x}$ for the correction Δx will not be exact, so that $\tilde{\tilde{x}} = \tilde{x} + \Delta \tilde{x}$ will not be exactly equal to the solution x of the system to be solved, either. However, regardless of the error on the first approximation $\tilde{x}$, the error on the new approximation $\tilde{\tilde{x}}$ is only determined by the error on the computed correction $\Delta \tilde{x}$! Sometimes, the correction $\Delta \tilde{x}$ can be estimated more efficiently than x itself.

Constant Control Variates in Random Walk Radiosity

The only choice for $\tilde{x}$ that allows $A\tilde{x}$ to be calculated analytically in the case of radiosity is the constant choice $\tilde{B}_i = \beta$. With this choice, we get

$$\begin{aligned}
\Delta B_i &= \left(B_{ei} + \sum_j \rho_i F_{ij} \beta - \beta \right) + \sum_j \rho_i F_{ij} \Delta B_j \\
&= (B_{ei} - (1 - \rho_i)\beta) + \sum_j \rho_i F_{ij} \Delta B_j.
\end{aligned}$$

The question now is how to determine an optimal value for β. Heuristics for choosing β can be derived by minimizing the expected mean square error of random walk estimators. Several crude approximations need to be made, however, and the benefits are not very significant in practice.

Constant Control Variates in Stochastic Relaxation Radiosity

In stochastic Jacobi relaxation, however, constant control variate variance reduction is easier to obtain and more effective. Monte Carlo summation shall be applied to the following modified power equation:

$$P'_i = P_{ei} + A_i \rho_i \beta + \sum_i \sum_j A_j (B_j - \beta) F_{ji} \rho_i \delta_{ik}.$$

A good value for the control radiosity β can be obtained by numerical optimization of $F(\beta) = \sum_s A_s \,|B_s - \beta|$ [15, 125].

One disadvantage of constant control variates in radiosity is that the scene being rendered needs to fulfill certain requirements:

- It needs to be closed, because otherwise $\sum_j F_{ij}\beta \neq \beta$ for some patches i in the scene.

- There cannot be closed "holes" in a scene that do not receive any light, e.g., the interior of a box.

The speed-up that can be obtained with a constant control variate typically is in the range of 5–50%.

6.6.3 Gathering for Free

If more than one Monte Carlo estimator is at hand for a given quantity, their combination can also reduce variance considerably. In Monte Carlo radiosity in particular, one will always find a gathering estimator corresponding with each shooting estimator. Gathering is, in general, less efficient than shooting except on small patches, but by combining gathering and shooting over random walks and rays sampled for shooting, variance reduction is possible at negligible additional cost.

Recall that there are basically two ways to combine estimators (see Section 3.6.5).

The classic way. The classic way of combining two estimators $\hat{S}_1$ and $\hat{S}_2$ for a quantity S is based on the observation that any linear combination $w_1\hat{S}_1 + w_2\hat{S}_2$ with constant weights $w_1 + w_2 = 1$ will also be an unbiased estimator for S. For independent estimators, the optimal combination weights can be shown to be inversely proportional to the variance:

$$\frac{w_1}{w_2} = \frac{V[\hat{S}_2]}{V[\hat{S}_1]}.$$

In practice, the weights can be obtained in two different ways:

- Using analytical expressions for the variance of the involved estimators (such as presented in this text).

- Using a posteriori estimates for the variances based on the samples in an experiment themselves (Section 3.4.5). By doing so, a slight bias is introduced. As the number of samples is increased, the bias vanishes: the combination is asymptotically unbiased or *consistent*.

In general, the combination of M estimators, with N_m samples each, looks like

$$\sum_{m=1}^{M} w_m \frac{1}{N_m} \sum_{k=1}^{N_m} \tilde{S}_m^k \approx S.$$

Multiple importance sampling. It is neither necessary, nor optimal, to take the combination weights w_m the same for all samples. By using potentially different sets of weights w_m^k for each sample k, more robust combination will often be possible:

$$\sum_{m=1}^{M} \frac{1}{N_m} \sum_{k=1}^{N_m} w_m^k \tilde{S}_m^k \approx S.$$

The result is unbiased as long as $\sum_{m=1}^{M} w_m^k = 1$ for every sample.

An often-used heuristic for choosing the combination weights is the *balance heuristic*. With this heuristic, the weights w_m^k are chosen proportional to the probability that the sample k would be generated with the mth technique $\hat{S}_m$ times N_m.

Combining Gathering and Shooting in Discrete Random Walk Radiosity

Combining gathering and shooting over a single set of random walks can be done in several ways:

Using multiple importance sampling. The basic observation is that gathering radiosity over a path segment $j_t, j_{t+1}, \ldots, j_s$ is identical to shooting power over the reverse segment $j_s, j_{s-1}, \ldots, j_t$. Multiple importance sampling can be applied if the probability of having a subpath originating at the endpoints j_t and j_s are both known. In practice, combined gathering and shooting based on multiple importance sampling is useful only with global lines, in global multipath algorithms [157, 161]. With local lines, the required probabilities are unfortunately not known in advance.

Using a posteriori variance estimates. Such estimates can be obtained by approximating analytical expressions [159]. Alternatively, sample-based variance estimation is also possible [15]. Sample-based variance estimation yields very good weights eventually, but the weights are unreliable in the beginning of the computations, when only few random walks have been visiting a patch. A posteriori variance estimation allows us to combine shooting and gathering also with local line sampling. Figure 6.25 shows the shooting and gathering contributions associated with a single path.

Combining gathering and shooting in random walk radiosity yields moderate variance reduction, again 5–50%, but the additional computation cost is negligible.

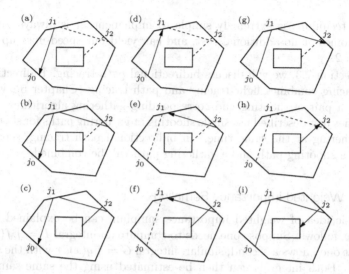

Figure 6.25. The main idea of "gathering for free." A single random walk j_0, j_1, j_2, j_3 yields multiple scores, which are combined in a provable good way, yielding lower variance at a negligible additional computation cost: (a, b, c) gathering at j_0; (d) shooting at j_1; (e, f) gathering at j_1; (g) shooting at j_2; (h) gathering at j_2; and (i) shooting at j_3.

Combining Gathering and Shooting in Stochastic Jacobi Radiosity

Combining gathering and shooting in stochastic Jacobi iterations is again very simple [15]. Each line shot in power-shooting iterations (Section 6.3.2) yields a contribution to the patch that it hits, while in gathering iterations, the line yields a contribution to the patch from where it was shot. Also here, gathering corresponds with shooting over the reverse line. Unlike with random walks, the probability of shooting a line from every patch is known, so multiple importance sampling can be used. The result is that a score can be recorded at both ends of each shot line. For a line connecting the patches i and j, the scores at both endpoints are

$$w_{ij} S_{ij}^{\leftarrow} = \frac{\rho_i P_j}{p_i A_j + p_j A_i} \quad \text{on } i$$

$$w_{ij} S_{ij}^{\rightarrow} = \frac{\rho_j P_i}{p_i A_j + p_j A_i} \quad \text{on } j.$$

As before, p_i and p_j indicate the probability of shooting a line from i and j. With local lines, we can choose p_i proportional to the power to be shot from i. With global lines, p_i is proportional to the patch area A_i.

The technique is extremely simple to implement, it is always safe to use, it comes at no additional cost, and can yield fair speed-ups: up to a factor of 2.

In Section 7.3, we will discuss bidirectional path tracing. Bidirectional path tracing combines light tracing and path tracing (Chapter 5), which are also a pair of shooting and corresponding gathering algorithms. The techniques just described use single shooting or gathering paths for shooting and gathering at the same time. In bidirectional path tracing, separate pairs of a shooting path and a gathering path will be combined.

6.6.4 Weighted Importance Sampling

The basic idea of weighted importance sampling can be explained intuitively as follows: Suppose one needs to compute an integral $F = \int f(x)dx$ and that one knows a second, similar, integral $G = \int g(x)dx$ with the same domain. Both integrals can then be estimated using the same samples. The resulting Monte Carlo estimate $\tilde{G}$ for G can then be compared with the true, known value of G. Due to its random nature, the estimate $\tilde{G}$ will sometimes be larger than G and sometimes be smaller. Suppose that one knows that the corresponding estimate $\tilde{F}$ for F will also be larger than F in case $\tilde{G}$ is larger than G, a more accurate estimate for F than may be $\tilde{F}G/\tilde{G}$: $\tilde{F}$ is decreased if $\tilde{G} > G$ and it is increased if $\tilde{G} < G$. In short, weighted importance sampling is a *multiplicative* rather than an additive control variate variance reduction technique.

Unlike the variance reduction techniques described before, weighted importance sampling is biased, but it is consistent if f and g fulfill certain requirements. The bias vanishes as $1/N$ (N is the number of samples). This is much faster than the statistical error, which vanishes as $1/\sqrt{N}$. A more elaborate exposition of this idea, with application to form factor integration and stochastic relaxation radiosity, can be found in [14].

6.6.5 Low-Discrepancy Sampling

As discussed in Section 3.6.7, it is often possible to obtain convergence rates considerably faster than $\mathcal{O}(1/\sqrt{N})$ by using low-discrepancy sampling [132]. The main idea of low-discrepancy sampling is to use sample number sequences that are more uniform than random numbers.[5] Integration using low-discrepancy number sequences is also called *quasi–Monte Carlo*

---

[5]Numbers generated with so-called random number algorithms are not truly random. They merely pass a certain set of statistical tests that truly random numbers would pass as well. Truly random numbers can only be generated with specialized electronic devices (or on certain defective computer equipment).

integration. Unlike Monte Carlo integration, which is based on statistics, quasi–Monte Carlo methods have a very different origin, in number theory.

In practice, however, improved convergence rates are often obtained by little more than replacing the random number generator by a low-discrepancy number sequence. Local line sampling (Section 6.2.3), for instance, requires four-dimensional random vectors: two random numbers are needed for choosing a ray origin and two more for sampling a cosine-distributed direction. Keller [89] showed that using four-dimensional low-discrepancy vectors instead yields speed-ups of about an order of magnitude when computing form factors with local lines. Neumann et al. observed a similar speed-up when using quasi-random numbers instead of random numbers in stochastic relaxation radiosity [127]. The speed-up obtained with quasi-random sampling in continuous shooting random walk radiosity [90] is much smaller. In discrete shooting random walk radiosity, it is of the same magnitude as in stochastic relaxation radiosity, and often much higher than in continuous random walks [15]. A theoretical study of the convergence rate of quasi-random sampling in radiosity has been carried out by Szirmay-Kalos [190].

There are several important differences between random and quasi-random sampling. The main difference in practice is that quasi-random samples are not statistically independent. They can even be very strongly correlated, leading to disturbing aliasing patterns. Fortunately, there exist very simple and effective techniques to break these correlations, while still maintaining fast convergence [96, 127].

6.7 Hierarchical Refinement and Clustering

All mesh-based algorithms covered so far in this chapter share a common drawback, illustrated in Figure 6.26. If patches are chosen too small, variance will be high. If they are chosen too large, however, disturbing discretization artifacts, such as too smooth illumination and blurred shadow boundaries, result. We discuss here how hierarchical refinement [30, 64, 164] and clustering [182, 174] can be incorporated in stochastic radiosity algorithms. Doing so significantly reduces these problems and considerably boosts the performance of stochastic radiosity algorithms.

Hierarchical refinement and clustering have been introduced in radiosity with two goals in mind: automatic, adaptive meshing and a reduction of the number of form factors. First, it splits up large patches into smaller ones so that a more accurate radiosity solution is obtained where necessary. Collections of small patches, on the other hand, can also be grouped

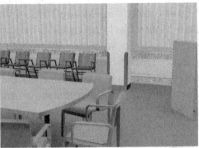

Figure 6.26. The left image illustrates meshing difficulties with stochastic radiosity. On the one hand, high variance on small patches leads to disturbing noisy artifacts: some of these patches will receive no rays, so that they will be rendered black, while other small patches appear overly bright. Large patches, such as the walls and floor in this image, for instance, appear too smooth as only a single radiosity value is computed for the whole patch. Adaptive meshing, hierarchical refinement, and clustering reduce these problems (right image). (The conference room model shown is by Anat Grynberg and Greg Ward, Lawrence Berkeley Laboratory, Berkeley, California).

into single *cluster elements* behaving like a larger patch. The second key idea is to compute a multiresolution representation of radiosity. A so-called *oracle function* predicts whether or not light transport can be computed accurately enough between a given pair of elements (patches or clusters) in this multiresolution representation. It ensures that light transport will always be computed at the right level of detail. Doing so leads to significant reduction of the number of form factors to be computed compared to

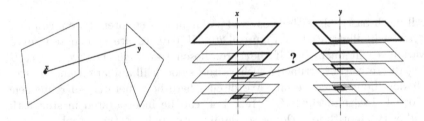

Figure 6.27. Per-ray hierarchical refinement in stochastic Jacobi radiosity. For each ray shot, connecting two points x and y, the algorithm will determine which level of the element hierarchies at x and y is appropriate for computing light transport from x to y. The element hierarchies are lazily constructed. In non-hierarchical Monte Carlo radiosity, light transport would always be computed between the top-level patches containing the endpoints x and y of the ray.

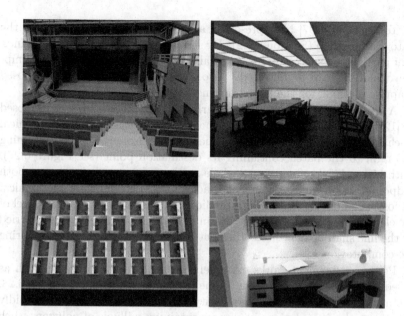

Figure 6.28. Images rendered with hierarchical Monte Carlo radiosity [12]. The number of elements in the shown images varies from 88,000 (theater) to more than 500,000 (cubicle office space). The radiosity computations for these images took less than 1 minute on a 2GHz Pentium-4 PC with 256MB of RAM. Once computed, the illuminated model can be rendered from new viewpoints in real time, using a low-cost PC three-dimensional graphics accelerator.

Model credits: Candlestick Theater. Design: Mark Mack Architects. Three-dimensional model: Charles Ehrlich and Greg Ward (work conducted as a research project during the Architecture 239X course taught by Kevin Matthews formerly at UC Berkeley, College of Environmental Design). Conference room and cubicle space models by Anat Grynberg and Greg Ward. (Courtesy of Lawrence Berkeley Laboratory, Berkeley, California.) (See Plate I.)

the classic radiosity method: $\mathcal{O}(N \log N)$ rather than $\mathcal{O}(N^2)$, with N the number of patches.

Adaptive meshing has been integrated with local line form factor computation (Section 6.2.3) by several authors [106, 94, 92]. The basic idea in these three proposals is identical: A large number of rays is shot from the source patch. The surrounding scene is subdivided into receiver elements so that each receiver element (a surface or cluster) receives the same number of rays. The disadvantage is that these techniques will only work if a large number of rays is shot simultaneously from the shooting patch. This is not the case in more recent stochastic relaxation algorithms.

Tobler et al. [197] have presented an adaptive meshing scheme for the histogram method (Section 6.5.2). By simultaneously keeping track of incident particles on successive hierarchical element levels, smoothness assumption violations can be detected. Also, Myszkowski et al. have proposed adaptive meshing for the histogram method [121].

A truly multiresolution Monte Carlo radiosity algorithm was proposed in [12]. The basic observation is that each line cast in nonhierarchical stochastic Jacobi radiosity carries some light flux from the patch containing its origin to the patch containing its destination point (see Figure 6.27). With hierarchical refinement, a whole stack of elements is located at both endpoints. The same refinement oracles as in deterministic hierarchical radiosity can be used in order to predict for each cast line, at what level of the element stack containing the destination point of a line, the flux carried by the line shall be deposited. Elements are refined lazily, on the fly during the computations.

Per-ray refinement works extremely well with a cheap oracle, such as based on transported power [64]. Some results are presented in Figure 6.28. Hierarchical stochastic Jacobi radiosity has been used in order to rapidly compute radiosity solutions in scenes containing millions of polygons, such as entire building and car models, on commodity PCs.

6.8 Exercises

1. Compute the form factor for the following configuration. Two identical rectangular plates are positioned parallel to each other (Figure 6.29). Compute the form factor using Monte Carlo integration and compare with the analytical solution. Make a plot of absolute

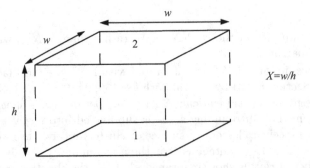

Figure 6.29. Two parallel rectangular plates.

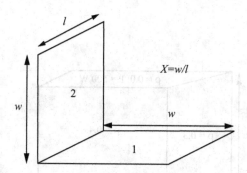

Figure 6.30. Two perpendicular rectangular plates.

error as a function of the number of sample lines used. Compare empirically stratified, non-stratified, and low-discrepancy sampling (e.g., Halton or Niederreiter; see Section 3.6.7).

$$F_{12} = \frac{2}{\pi X^2} \left(\ln \left(\frac{1 + X^2}{\sqrt{1 + 2X^2}} \right) \right.$$
$$\left. + 2X\sqrt{1 + X^2} \tan^{-1} \frac{X}{\sqrt{1 + X^2}} - 2X \tan^{-1} X \right).$$

2. Repeat the Exercise 1, but now the plates are perpendicular to each other (Figure 6.30).

$$F_{12} = \frac{1}{\pi X} \left(2X \tan^{-1} \frac{1}{X} - X\sqrt{2} \tan^{-1} \frac{1}{X\sqrt{2}} \right.$$
$$\left. + \frac{1}{4} \ln \left(\frac{(1 + X^2)^2}{1 + 2X^2} \left(\frac{1 + 2X^2}{2(1 + X^2)} \right)^{2X^2} \right) \right).$$

3. When comparing the Monte Carlo results of the configurations in Exercises 1 and 2, is there a difference in the convergence speed for the two cases? If there is, explain this difference. If there is no difference in convergence speed, why not?

4. Given is the scene in Figure 6.31 containing 3 diffuse polygons with diffuse reflectivity values of 0.3, 0.4 and 0.5; and 1 diffuse light source emitting 500 watts, covering the complete ceiling.

   Compute the relevant form factors using the analytic expressions given above, and compute the radiosity solution for this scene. You

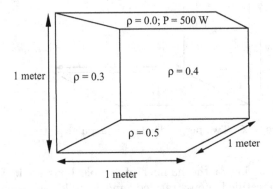

Figure 6.31. Four diffuse square plates.

can solve the linear system by hand or use a mathematical software tool.

5. Increase the diffuse reflectivity for all surfaces in the scene by 10%. What is the result on the new radiosity values? Do the new radiosity values increase by more or less than 10%.? Why?

6. Compare the radiosity solution for the scene given above to a solution that only computes direct illumination (assume all form factors are zero except the ones encoding transport starting at the light source).

7. Instead of using analytic form factors, insert the form factors computed with Monte Carlo integration. If the Monte Carlo evaluation of form factors in a general scene results in overestimates for the form factors, what could the resulting effect be for the radiosity algorithm?

8. Consider a closed environment (there is no loss of radiative energy), for which the average reflectivity $\rho_{average}$ over all surfaces is known. Find a general expression for the total amount of emitted and reflected power over all surfaces in the scene.

9. Write a basic radiosity program, using deterministic shooting Jacobi iterations for system solution, as explained in Section 6.3.1. Use the local lines approach described in Section 6.2.3 for computing the form factors. Compare with pairwise form factor Monte Carlo integration as in the previous exercises. (Hint: since most of the work in this

exercise is in writing the code for reading in a 3D model, for tracing rays, and for displaying images, it is a good idea to start with a simple ray-tracing program and extend that.)

10. Adapt the basic radiosity program of the previous exercise to compute radiosity in other ways discussed in the radiosity chapter, for instance:

- Implement stochastic regular shooting, incremental shooting, and regular gathering by means of local lines. Compare empirically.

- Implement and compare local and global line sampling.

- Implement discrete random walk radiosity: compare shooting and gathering, absorption versus survival versus collision sampling.

- Implement photon density estimation algorithms. Compare the histogram method with discrete random walk radiosity. In orthogonal series estimation, compare image quality and computation times with constant, linear, quadratic, and cubic approximation. (Hint: display the resulting images either through ray casting or by means of a fragment shader on a GPU). Experiment with the kernel method comparing a cylindrical, Gaussian, Epanechnikov, and other kernels you find in cited literature.

- Try out view-importance–driven sampling in its variants, control variates, and gathering for free in discrete random walk radiosity and stochastic Jacobi.

11. For the math-inclined: Familiarize yourself with variance calculation by starting with some simple cases. For instance, derive the variance of:

- regular gathering stochastic Jacobi radiosity;

- absorption random walk radiosity: compare shooting versus gathering, discrete versus continuous.

12. Give an intuitive explanation of why collision random walks are generally more efficient than absorption or survival random walks.

13. Give an intuitive explanation of why shooting is generally more efficient than gathering.

7

Hybrid Algorithms

Chapters 5 and 6 described two of the most popular global illumination algorithms: ray tracing and radiosity. These algorithms have evolved significantly since they were first introduced, but mainly, the core ideas for both are still the same: a ray-tracing algorithm computes radiance values for every pixel in the final image by generating paths between the pixel and the light sources; a radiosity algorithm computes a radiance value for every mesh element in the scene, after which this solution is displayed using any method that can project polygons to the screen.

This chapter focuses on algorithms that try to combine the best of both worlds. These algorithms often use various elements from the previously mentioned approaches, and therefore we call them hybrid algorithms.

7.1 Final Gathering

Once a radiosity solution is computed and an image of the scene is generated, Gouraud shading is often used to interpolate between radiance values at vertices of the mesh, thus obtaining a smoothly shaded image. This technique can miss significant shading features. It is often difficult to generate accurate shadows; shadows may creep under surfaces (shadow leaks and light leaks), Mach-band effects may occur, and other secondary illumination effects containing features with a frequency higher than that which the mesh can represent are also possible.

One way of solving this is to consider the radiosity solution to be a coarse precomputed solution of the light distribution in the scene. During a second phase, when the image is actually generated, a more accurate per-pixel illumination value is computed, which is based on the ray-tracing algorithm.

As was explained in Chapter 5, the ray-tracing set-up for computing the radiance for a pixel is given by

$$L_{pixel} = \int_{imageplane} L(p \to eye)h(p)dp.$$

$L(p \to eye)$ equals $L(x \to \Theta)$ with x being the visible point in the scene and Θ the direction from x towards the eye. Suppose we have a precomputed radiance solution in a diffuse scene, given by $\tilde{L}(y)$ for every surface point y. We can then acquire the value of $L(x \to \Theta)$ by writing the rendering equation, approximating the radiance distribution in the kernel of the transport equation by $\tilde{L}(y)$:

$$L(x \to \Theta) = L(x) = L_e(x) + f_r(x) \int_A \tilde{L}(y)G(x,y)V(x,y)dA_y \qquad (7.1)$$

or equivalently, using integration over the hemisphere,

$$L(x) = L_e(x) + f_r(x) \int_{\Omega_x} \tilde{L}(r(x, \Psi)) \cos(N_x, \Psi)d\omega_\Psi. \qquad (7.2)$$

This integral can now be evaluated using Monte Carlo integration. The main difference with the stochastic ray-tracing algorithm is that there is no recursive evaluation of the radiance distribution, since it is substituted by the precomputed radiosity solution. Thus, one gains the advantage of using an accurate per-pixel method, using a fast precomputed finite element method.

Various sampling strategies can now be used to evaluate either Equation 7.1 or 7.2. In a diffuse scene, with a constant radiance value $\tilde{L}_j$ for each surface element j, the above equation can also be rewritten as

$$L(x) = L_e(x) + f_r(x) \sum_j \tilde{L}_j \int_{A_j} G(x,y)V(x,y)dA_y. \qquad (7.3)$$

7.1.1 Simple Hemisphere Sampling

The most straightforward approach is to sample random directions over the hemisphere and evaluate $\tilde{L}$ at the nearest intersection point. This strategy is very similar to simple stochastic ray tracing (Section 5.3) and will result in a lot of noise in the final image. The reason is the same as with stochastic ray tracing: light sources will be missed by just randomly sampling the hemisphere. Therefore, splitting the integral into a direct and indirect term is a good approach for increasing the accuracy.

To save time, only the direct illumination can be computed using a per-pixel gathering step [167], and the indirect illumination can be read out directly from the interpolated radiosity solution. However, the distinction between primary and secondary light sources is rather arbitrary. Therefore, illumination from the most important secondary light sources can be directly re-evaluated as well [93].

7.1.2 Importance Sampling

Importance sampling can be used to evaluate Equation 7.3 or its equivalent. We want to construct a probability density function that matches the kernel of the integral as closely as possible. Generally, since we have a precomputed solution, it can be used to sample surface elements and directions to bright areas in the scene. Depending on the radiosity algorithm used, the following data may be available to construct a PDF:

- The average radiance value for each surface element j,

$$\widetilde{L}_j = \frac{1}{A_j} \int_{A_k} \widetilde{L}(y) dA_y.$$

- The form factors $F_{i \to j}$ between surface elements i and j. This is only the case in classic radiosity, in which links between surface elements are stored explicitly.

An importance sampling procedure can then be constructed by first selecting a surface element, and then sampling a surface point within that surface element.

1. The probability of picking surface element j should be proportional to

$$\int_{A_j} \widetilde{L}(y) G(x, y) V(x, y) dA_y \approx \pi F_{i \to j} \widetilde{L}_j,$$

with surface element i containing point x.

Thus, each surface element j is assigned a probability

$$P_j = \frac{F_{i \to j} \widetilde{L}_j}{\sum_j F_{i \to j} \widetilde{L}_j}.$$

2. The second step then involves the evaluation of

$$\frac{1}{P_j} \int_{A_j} \widetilde{L}(y) G(x, y) V(x, y) dA_y \qquad (7.4)$$

for the surface element j selected in Step 1. Several methods for evaluating this integral are possible. We list just a few possibilities:

(a) Choosing a sample point y with uniform probability $1/A_j$ on surface element j. The total estimator for Equation 7.4 is then given by

$$\frac{A_j \widetilde{L}(y) G(x,y) V(x,y)}{P_j}.$$

(b) In [6], an algorithm is presented to sample a random direction with uniform probability $1/\Omega_j$ on a spherical triangle Ω_j. This sampling procedure can be used to sample a surface point y by first selecting a direction $\Theta_x \in \Omega_j$; y is the point on surface element j along Θ_x. The total estimator is then

$$\frac{\Omega_j \widetilde{L}(y) \cos(N_x, \Theta_x) V(x,y)}{P_j}.$$

(c) The cosine factor $\cos(N_x, \Theta_x)$ can be taken into account as well by using rejection sampling. A direction is sampled on a bounding region $\overline{\Omega}_j$ for Ω_j on the hemisphere. The bounding region needs to be chosen such that sampling according to a cosine distribution is possible. If the sampled direction falls outside Ω_j, the estimator evaluates to 0. Alternatively, one can also generate samples until a nonrejected sample is generated. In both cases, care has to be taken to use the correct sampling densities.

(d) When surface element j is fully visible from point x, the point-to-surface form factor can be computed analytically, and thus no Monte Carlo sampling is needed.

Figure 7.1. Final gathering: radiosity solution on the left, final gathering on the right. (Courtesy of Frank Suykens-De Laet, Dept. of Computer Science, K. U. Leuven.)

7.1.3 Results

Figure 7.1 shows the result of applying final gathering to a precomputed radiosity solution. The scene on the left shows the precomputed radiosity solution. Meshing artifacts in the shading and shadows are clearly visible. The image on the right is computed using final gathering. All illumination features are much more smooth.

Final gathering techniques can also be extended for scenes with nondiffuse surfaces. In that case, the nondiffuse BRDF should be included in the integral evaluations.

7.2 Multipass Methods

The final gathering algorithm is an example of a broader class of methods, called multipass methods. A multipass method uses various algorithms (finite-element–based, image-based) and combines them into a single image-generation algorithm. Care has to be taken that light transport components are not counted twice, since this would introduce errors in the image. At the same time, all possible light transport modes need to be covered by at least one pass. A good multipass algorithm tries to exploit the various advantages of the different individual passes.

In this section, we follow the explanation of multipass algorithms as given in [99].

7.2.1 Regular Expressions

Regular expressions are often used to express which light transport modes are covered by which pass. One can introduce the following notations:

- L: One of the light sources in the scene.

- D: A diffuse reflection component of the BRDF.

- G: A semidiffuse or glossy reflection component of the BRDF.

- S: A perfect specular component of the BRDF.

- E: The eye or virtual camera.

A light transport path between a light source and the camera, only reflecting at diffuse surfaces, can then formally be written as being of type

LD^+E. D^+ indicates the path bounces off of at least one diffuse surface. A diffuse surface, reflected in a visible specular material, would be described by the path of type $LDSE$. All possible paths in the scene are described by $L(D|G|S)^*E$, with * indicating zero or more reflections.

Algorithms can now be characterized by describing what light transport paths they cover. Radiosity algorithms cover all paths of type LD^*E, or all diffuse bounces. A classic ray-tracing algorithm, stopping the recursion of reflected rays at nonspecular surfaces, covers all paths of type $LD^{0\cdots1}(G|S)E$, with $D^{0\cdots1}$ indicating 0 to 1 reflections at a diffuse surface.

7.2.2   Construction of a Multipass Algorithm

A multipass algorithm usually starts with one or more object-space methods, which store a partial approximation of the light transport in the scene. For example, a radiosity method might only store the diffuse light interactions and might ignore all other types of light transport. More sophisticated algorithms might include some nondiffuse reflections as well.

The image-space algorithms compute radiance values per pixel, but they rely on the partially computed and stored light transport approximations of the previous passes. To access these stored solutions, they need a read-out strategy. This read-out strategy might itself include some computations or interpolations, and this is determined by the nature of the stored partial solution. The read-out strategy also determines the nature of the paths that are covered by the image-space pass.

Some typical read-out strategies include:

- **Direct visualization of the stored solution.** For each pixel, the stored light transport solution is accessed directly and the resulting value attributed to the pixel. Radiosity solutions are often displayed this way. The covered light transport paths are exactly the same as those covered by the object-space pass.

- **Final gathering.** The final gathering method reconstructs the incoming radiance values over the hemisphere for each point visible through the pixel. These radiance values are read from the stored radiance solution. Suppose the stored radiance solution only covers paths of type LD^*. Because the final gathering takes into account the full BRDF at the visible point through the pixel, the paths covered by this multipass algorithm are of type $LD^*(D|G|S)E$, and LE when the light sources are directly visible.

- Recursive stochastic ray tracing. A recursive ray-tracing algorithm is used as a read-out strategy, but paths are only reflected at those surfaces; use only those reflection components that are not covered by the object-space pass. For example, if the first pass stores a radiosity solution, covering all paths of type LD^*, then the recursive ray-tracing pass would only reflect rays at G or S surfaces. At each D surface, the stored value in the precomputed solution is read out and incorporated in the estimator at that reflection point. Thus, the covered paths are of type $LD^*(G|S)^*E$.

7.2.3 Weighted Multipass Algorithms

Most multipass strategies make sure that the light transport paths covered in the different passes do not overlap. Otherwise, some light transport might be counted twice, and the resulting image will look too bright in some parts of the scene. Every pass of the multipass algorithm covers distinct, separate types of light transport.

An alternative approach is to have some overlap between the different passes, but weigh them appropriately, such that the correct image is still obtained. The problem is now to find the right weighting heuristics, such that the strengths of each individual pass are used in the optimal way. A very good strategy assigns weights to the different types of paths in each pass, based on the respective probability density functions for generating these paths. Thus, caustic effects might predominantly use their results from a bidirectional ray-tracing pass, while direct illumination effects might originate mostly from a ray-tracing or radiosity pass. A very detailed discussion and good overview of this technique can be found in [99].

An example is given in Figure 7.2. A total of three passes are used. First, a radiosity solution is computed, which is subsequently enhanced by a stochastic ray tracer (image in upper left). This specific example covers only paths of type $LD(G|S)(D|G|S)^*E$. A third pass involves a bidirectional ray tracer (image in upper right), which generates paths of the same type but with different probabilities due to the nature of the sampling process.

When applying the weighting heuristic, one can see that the caustic on the floor (due to refraction through the glass sphere) is mostly assigned to bidirectional path tracing, while the direct illumination is mostly assigned to the radiosity and stochastic ray-tracing solution. Some difficult effects, which are not well covered by either method, are weighted more equally, such as the reflection in the right wall of the white panel above the light source.

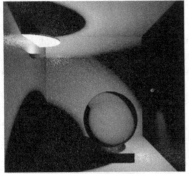
Bidirectional Path Tracing

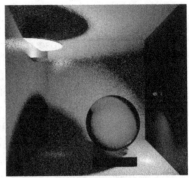
Radiosity + Stochastic Ray Tracing

Weighted Bidirectional Path Tracing

Weighted Radiosity + Stochastic Ray Tracing

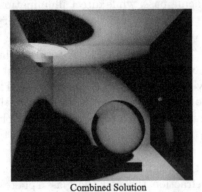
Combined Solution

Figure 7.2. Radiosity and stochastic ray tracing is shown in the right column; bidirectional path tracing is shown in the left column. The resulting image, which is the sum of the two weighted images, is shown at the bottom. (Courtesy of Frank Suykens-De Laet, Dept. of Computer Science, K. U. Leuven.)

7.3 Bidirectional Tracing

In Chapter 5, path-tracing algorithms are described in detail. Ray tracing traces paths through the scene starting at the surface points, which eventually end at the light sources (whether or not explicit light source sampling is used). Light tracing, another path-tracing algorithm, does the opposite: paths start at the light sources and end up in any relevant pixels.

Bidirectional ray tracing combines both approaches in a single algorithm and can be viewed as a two-pass algorithm in which both passes are tightly intertwined. Bidirectional ray tracing generates paths starting at the light sources and at the surface point simultaneously and connects both paths in the middle to find a contribution to the light transport between the light source and the point for which a radiance value needs to be computed. Thus, it combines the specific advantages of ray tracing as well as light tracing. Bidirectional ray tracing was developed independently by both Lafortune [102] and Veach [200].

Bidirectional path tracing is one of the few algorithms that start from the formulation of the global reflection distribution function (GRDF) as described in Chapter 4. The flux $\Phi(S)$ (consider S to be defined by the surface points visible through a pixel) is given by Equation 4.7:

$$\Phi(S) = \int_A \int_{\Omega_x} \int_A \int_{\Omega_y} L_e(x \to \Theta) G_r(x \leftarrow \Theta, y \to \Psi) W_e(y \leftarrow \Psi)$$
$$\times \cos(N_x, \Theta) \cos(N_y, \Psi) d\omega_\Psi dA_y d\omega_\Theta dA_x.$$

The core idea of the algorithm is that one has the availability of two different path generators when computing a Monte Carlo estimate for the flux through a certain pixel:

- An eye path is traced starting at a sampled surface point y_0 visible through the pixel. By generating a path of length k, the path consists of a series of surface points $y_0, y_1, \ldots, y_k$. The length of the path is controlled by Russian roulette. The probability of generating this path can be composed of the individual PDF values of generating each successive point along the path.

- Similarly, a light path of length l is generated starting at the light source. This path, $x_0, x_1, \ldots, x_l$, also has its own probability density distribution.

By connecting the endpoint y_k of the eye path with the endpoint x_l of the light path, a total path of length $k + l + 1$ between the importance source S and the light sources is obtained. The probability density function for this path is the product of the individual PDFs of the light and eye paths.

Thus, an estimator for the $\Phi(S)$ using this single path is given by

$$\Phi(S) = \frac{K}{pdf(y_0, y_1, \ldots, y_k, x_l, \ldots, x_1, x_0)},$$

with

$$K = L_e(x_0 \rightarrow \overrightarrow{x_0 x_1})G(x_0, x_1)V(x_0, x_1)f_r(x_1, \overrightarrow{x_1 x_0} \leftrightarrow \overrightarrow{x_1 x_2})\ldots$$
$$G(x_l, y_k)V(x_l, y_k)f_r(y_k, \overrightarrow{y_k x_l} \leftrightarrow \overrightarrow{y_k y_{k-1}})\ldots$$
$$f_r(y_1, \overrightarrow{y_1 y_0} \leftrightarrow \overrightarrow{y_1 y_2})G(y_1, y_0)V(y_1, y_0)W_e(y_0 \leftarrow \overrightarrow{y_0 y_1}).$$

Paths of a certain length can now be generated by using different combinations. For example, a path of length 3 could be generated by a light path of length 2 and an eye path of length 0 (this is a single point y_0); or by a light path of length 1 and an eye path of length 1; or by a light path of length 0 (a single point at the light source) and an eye path of length 2. As such, stochastic ray tracing and light tracing are special cases of bidirectional ray tracing. When tracing a shadow ray in stochastic ray tracing, we actually generate a light path of length 0, which is connected to an eye path. These different combinations of generating a path of given length are shown in Figure 7.3.

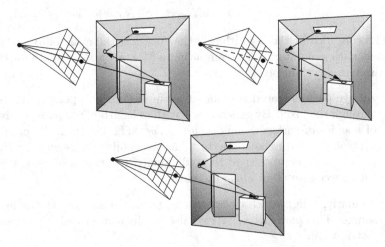

Figure 7.3. Different combinations for a path of length 3: eye path is of length 2, light path of length 1 (upper left), both of length 1 (middle), eye path is of length 0, light path of length 2 (upper right).

Depending on the light transport mode, and the sequence of G, V, and f_r functions, some light distribution effects are better generated using either light paths or eye paths. For example, when rendering a specular reflection that is visible in the image, it is better to generate those specular bounces in the eye path. Similarly, the specular reflections in caustics are better generated in the light path. Generally, it is better to use the BRDF f_r to sample the next point or direction if f_r has sharp peaks. If f_r is mainly diffuse, the energy transport along the connection between the two paths will not be influenced by the value of the BRDF and thus will not possibly yield a low contribution to the overall estimator. Another advantage is that if light sources are concealed, it might be easier to generate light paths to distribute the light, rather than count on shadow rays to be able to reach the light source.

When implementing bidirectional path tracing, an eye or light path of length $k - 1$ can be extended to a path of length k. Thus, we use the same subpath more than once. Intuitively, this means that if we have a light path and an eye path, we not only connect the endpoints, but also all possible subpaths to each other (Figure 7.4). Care has to be taken that the Monte Carlo estimators are still correct. This can be achieved by optimally combining the sampling methods of each of the individual subpaths. More details and an extensive discussion can be found in [204].

Figure 7.5 shows a simple scene, with a comparison of images generated by stochastic ray tracing, light tracing, and bidirectional ray tracing. In both images, the total number of paths is the same, so each image took an

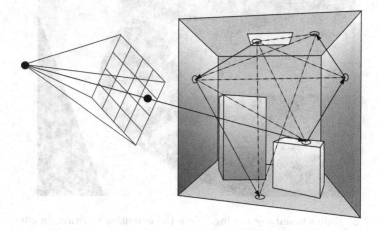

Figure 7.4. Reuse of all subpaths of both the eye path and the light path in a bidirectional ray-tracing algorithm.

Figure 7.5. Left: stochastic ray tracing; middle: light tracing; right: bidirectional ray tracing. (Courtesy of F. Suykens-DeLaet, Dept. of Computer Science, K. U. Leuven.) (See Plate V.)

equal time to compute. Figure 7.6 shows a picture generated by bidirectional ray tracing, with a significant amount of caustics, which would have taken a long time to generate using stochastic ray tracing only.

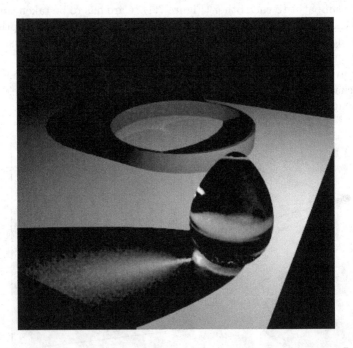

Figure 7.6. Bidirectional ray tracing. Note the extensive caustics, an effect difficult to achieve using stochastic ray tracing. (Courtesy of F. Suykens-De Laet, Dept. of Computer Science, K. U. Leuven.) (See Plate VI.)

7.4   Metropolis Light Transport

Metropolis light transport (MLT) [202] aims for robust global illumination that can handle light transport paths that are difficult to capture. MLT demonstrates the application of Metropolis sampling [119] to image generation by sampling the extremely high-dimensional (infinite dimensions!) space of all possible paths.

The Metropolis sampling technique, first introduced in 1953, can generate a sequence of samples from a non-negative function f such that the samples are distributed according to f, i.e., there are more samples where f is large and vice-versa. This important property of Metropolis sampling is achieved without any knowledge of f or its PDF; the only requirement is that it should be possible to evaluate the function f at each generated sample.

MLT applies this sampling technique to the infinite-dimensional space of paths. The key idea of MLT is that paths are sampled according to the contribution they make to the final image. The algorithm generates a sequence of light transport paths by applying random mutations to the previous path. Example mutations are adding a vertex in the path, deleting an existing vertex, etc. Each proposed mutation could be accepted or rejected; the probabilities that determine acceptance/rejection are chosen so that paths are sampled according to their contribution to the image plane. The image is computed by sampling many paths and recording their contributions to the image plane.

The main advantage of the MLT algorithm is that it is an unbiased algorithm that can handle hard-to-compute illumination situations. For example, MLT is efficient in computing images for scenes with strong indirect illumination that only arises through a small set of paths. The reason for this is that once the algorithm finds an important, but hard to find, light transport path, it explores other paths "near" that path through mutations. The assumption is that exploring that part of the path space will find other important light transport paths. This *local exploration* of the space of paths can result in faster convergence in scenes as compared to other approaches such as bidirectional path tracing. Additionally, the fundamental framework of Metropolis sampling ensures that this faster convergence is achieved while still maintaining an unbiased technique.

Another (relatively minor) benefit of this approach is that the contribution of a new path can be computed relatively inexpensively. This is because only a small part of the entire path is changed by the mutation, and the visibility information for the unchanged segments of the path do not need to be recomputed.

Detailed Balance

Stated more formally, given a state space Ω, a non-negative function $f\colon \Omega \to R^+$, and an initial seed $x_0 \in \Omega$, the Metropolis sampling algorithm generates a random walk $x_0, x_1, \ldots$, such that the x_i are eventually distributed according to f, irrespective of the choice of x_0. To achieve this steady-state distribution of samples, mutations have to be accepted or rejected carefully. The acceptance probability $a(x \to y)$ gives the probability that a mutation from x to y is accepted. A transition function $T(x \to y)$ gives the probability density that a mutation technique would propose a mutation from state x to y. For a random walk in steady-state, the transition density between two states must be equal:

$$f(x)T(x \to y)a(x \to y) \;=\; f(y)T(y \to x)a(y \to x).$$

This condition is known as *detailed balance*. Since f and T are given, the following choice of a results in equilibrium being achieved the fastest:

$$a(x \to y) \;=\; min(1, \frac{f(y)T(y \to x)}{f(x)T(x \to y)}).$$

The Algorithm

The MLT algorithm starts with a set of n random paths, constructed using bidirectional path tracing, from the lights to the image plane.[1] These paths are then mutated using mutation strategies described below. When a path x is mutated to produce a path y, the mutation is accepted based on the probability a given above. In particular, if the new path y does not contribute to the image (e.g., $f(y) = 0$ because two adjacent vertices of the path are not mutually visible), then the acceptance probability will be zero and the mutation will be rejected.

Veach defined several ways in which paths can be mutated; each of these mutation strategies optimizes for finding some set of of light transport paths.

- Bidirectional mutation. This mutation deletes a subpath of the path, extends the ends of the two remaining subpaths with one or more vertices, and then connects these ends together. The paths are accepted based on the acceptance probability a.

- Perturbations. Perturbations try to make small changes to a path, say by moving one or more vertices of the path, while leaving most of

---

[1] There are some important details to eliminate start-up bias that must be considered; we refer the reader to Veach's thesis [204] for a description.

Figure 7.7. Metropolis light transport example with caustics. (Courtesy of Eric Veach.) (See Plate VII.)

the path the same. Veach defined caustic perturbations, lens perturbations, and multichain perturbations to capture different light paths more efficiently. For example, the caustic perturbation might change the outgoing light direction in the path to try to mutate all the paths that focus light to form a caustic.

The basic MLT algorithm is:

```
MLT () {
  clear pixels in image to 0;
  x = initialSeedPath(); // actually n such paths are chosen
  for i = 1 to N {
    y = mutate (x);
    a = acceptanceProbability (x,y);
    if (random() < a) x = y; // accept mutation
    recordSample (image, x);
  }
}
```

Discussion

MLT is an unbiased technique to compute light transport that is efficient at computing images of scenes that include hard-to-find light transport paths. This is because once a hard-to-find path is found, mutations explore that part of the path space thoroughly before going to another part of the space. However, the implementation of MLT is quite complicated, and care must be taken to get several important details of the algorithm right [204, 79] for it to work. Additionally, it is unclear how MLT performs for scenes that include multiple important paths; it is possible that the mutations will result in slower convergence by exploring only a few of the many important paths thoroughly.

7.5 Irradiance Caching

Monte Carlo rendering can take a long time to converge to images of reasonable quality. Irradiance caching, introduced by Ward [219], is an effective technique for accelerating the computation of indirect illumination in diffuse scenes. Using pure Monte Carlo sampling to compute irradiance (incoming radiosity) at a point could require hundreds of ray-tracing operations. Each of these operations, in turn, could result in more rays being traced in the scene. Thus, this computation could be extremely slow. Irradiance caching exploits the insight that the irradiance at diffuse surfaces, while expensive to compute, varies smoothly in most scenes. In this technique, irradiance is cached in a data structure, and when possible, these cached values are interpolated to approximate irradiance at nearby surfaces.

Interpolation

Irradiance gradients [217] are used to determine when cached values can be interpolated to produce reasonably accurate results. The translation and rotation gradient estimate how irradiance changes with position and direction. An error estimate, based on the *split-sphere model* (see [107] for details), is used to determine which samples can be used for interpolation without (hopefully) introducing visible artifacts. Using this model, the error at a point P due to a cached sample i at location P_i is given as

$$\epsilon_i(P) \quad = \quad \frac{||P - P_i||}{R_i} + \sqrt{1 - N_P \cdot N_{P_i}},$$

where R_i is the mean harmonic distance of objects visible from the cached sample i, and N_P and N_{P_i} are the normals at P and the sample at P_i, respectively. Note that this error term penalizes samples whose normals differ significantly from the normal of the point whose irradiance is being approximated. Similarly, samples that are far away are penalized. Also, samples that are close to other surfaces, i.e., their mean harmonic distance is small, are penalized.

Irradiance at the point P is interpolated using the cached irradiance values of nearby samples using the weight w_i for the ith sample:

$$w_i(P) = \frac{1}{\epsilon_i(P)}.$$

If a point has a large error, its weight is small, and vice-versa. A user-specified parameter a is further used to eliminate samples whose weights are too small.

The interpolated irradiance at point P is then

$$E(P) = \frac{\sum_{i=1}^{N} w_i(P) E_i(P)}{\sum_{i=1}^{N} w_i(P)},$$

where $E_i(P)$ is the computed illuminance at P_i extrapolated to P; the extrapolation is computed using the rotation and translation gradients of the cached values. For a detailed description of these terms, refer to [107].

The Irradiance Cache

The cached samples are stored in an octree constructed over the scene. This data structure permits the decoupling of geometry from illumination values. When the irradiance at a point must be computed, the octree is searched to find "nearby" cached samples that are accurate enough to be used to approximate irradiance; the user-specified weight cutoff a specifies a

Figure 7.8. Temple scene rendered with irradiance caching. Temple modeled by Veronica Sundstedt and Patrick Ledda. (Courtesy of Greg Ward.) (See Plate VIII.)

radius over which the samples are searched. If such samples are found, they are used to interpolate irradiance using the weighting algorithm described above. If such samples do not exist, a sample is computed for the current point. This sample is then stored in the irradiance cache to be reused for interpolation later, if possible.

This algorithm is extremely effective at accelerating rendering for diffuse scenes. See Figure 7.8 for results.

7.6 Photon Mapping

Photon mapping, introduced by Jensen [77, 82, 81], is a practical two-pass algorithm that, like bidirectional path tracing, traces illumination paths both from the lights and from the viewpoint. However, unlike bidirectional path tracing, this approach caches and reuses illumination values in a scene for efficiency. In the first pass, "photons" are traced from the light sources into the scene. These photons, which carry flux information, are cached in a data structure, called the *photon map*. In the second pass, an image is rendered using the information stored in the photon map. A detailed description of the photon mapping technique can be found in [83].

Photon mapping decouples photon storage from surface parameterization. This representation enables it to handle arbitrary geometry, including procedural geometry, thus increasing the practical utility of the algorithm. It is also not prone to meshing artifacts.

By tracing or storing only particular types of photons (i.e., those that follow specific types of light paths), it is possible to make specialized photon maps, just for that purpose. The best example of this is the caustic map, which is designed to capture photons that interact with one or more specular surfaces before reaching a diffuse surface. These light paths cause caustics. Traditional Monte Carlo sampling can be very slow at correctly producing good caustics. By explicitly capturing caustic paths in a caustic map, the photon mapping technique can find caustics efficiently.

One point to note is that photon mapping is a biased technique. Recall that in a biased technique, the bias is the potentially nonzero difference between the expected value of the estimator and the actual value of the integral being computed. However, since photon maps are typically not used directly, but are used to compute indirect illumination, increasing the photons eliminates most artifacts.

Tracing Photons: Pass 1

The use of compact, point-based "photons" to propagate flux through the scene is key in making photon mapping efficient. In the first pass, photons

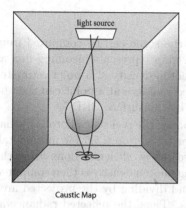
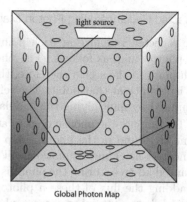

Figure 7.9. Caustic map and global photon map. The caustic map captures photons that traverse the paths LS^+D, while the global photon map represents all paths.

are traced from the light sources and propagated through the scene just as rays are in ray tracing; i.e., they are reflected, transmitted, or absorbed. Russian roulette and the standard Monte Carlo sampling techniques described earlier are used to propagate photons.[2]

When the photons hit nonspecular surfaces, they are stored in a global data structure called the photon map. To facilitate efficient searches for photons, a balanced kd-tree is used to implement this data structure.

As mentioned before, photon mapping can be efficient for computing caustics. A caustic is formed when light is reflected or transmitted through one or more specular surface before reaching a diffuse surface. To improve the rendering of scenes that include caustics, the algorithm separates out the computation of caustics from global illumination. Thus, two photon maps, a caustic photon map and a global photon map, are computed for each scene. The caustic map includes photons that traverse the paths LS^+D, while the global photon map represents all paths $L(S|D)^*D$, as shown in Figure 7.9.

Caustic photon maps can be computed efficiently because caustics occur when light is focused; therefore, not too many photons are needed to get a good estimate of caustics. Additionally, the number of surfaces resulting in caustics in typical scenes is often very small. Efficiency is achieved by shooting photons only towards this small set of specular surfaces.

---

[2]There are some differences between tracing photons and tracing rays. The main difference is that when a photon undergoes refraction, the power carried by the photon does not change. In contrast, the radiance of a ray must be weighted by the square of the relative indices of refraction (see Chapter 2 and [204]).

Reflected Radiance using Photon Maps

The reflected radiance at each point in the scene can be computed from the photon map as follows. The photon map represents incoming flux at each point in the scene; therefore, the photon density at a point estimates the irradiance at that point. The reflected radiance at a point can then be computed by multiplying the irradiance by the surface BRDF.

To compute the photon density at a point, the n closest photons to that point are found in the photon map (refer to Section 6.5.5 for more detail on nearest-neighbor estimation.). This search is efficiently done using the balanced kd-tree storing the photons. The photon density is then computed by adding the flux of these n photons and dividing by the projected area of the sphere containing these n photons. Thus, the reflected radiance at the point x in the direction ω is

$$L(x \to \omega) \quad = \quad \sum_{i=1}^{n} f_r(x, \omega \leftrightarrow \omega_i) \frac{\Delta \Phi_i(x \leftarrow \omega_i)}{\pi r^2}. \tag{7.5}$$

Computing Images: Pass 2

The simplest use of the photon map would be to display the reflected radiance values computed above for each visible point in an image. However, unless the number of photons used is extremely large, this display approach can cause significant blurring of radiance, thus resulting in poor image quality. Instead, photon maps are more effective when integrated with a ray tracer that computes direct illumination and queries the photon map only after one diffuse or glossy bounce from the viewpoint is traced through the scene.

Thus, the final rendering of images could be done as follows. Rays are traced through each pixel to find the closest visible surface. The radiance for a visible point is split into direct illumination, specular or glossy illumination, illumination due to caustics, and the remaining indirect illumination. Each of these components is computed as follows:

- Direct illumination for visible surfaces is computed using regular Monte Carlo sampling as described in Chapter 4.

- Specular reflections and transmissions are ray traced.

- Caustics are computed using the caustic photon map. Since caustics occur only in a few parts of the scene, they are computed at a higher resolution to permit direct high-quality display.

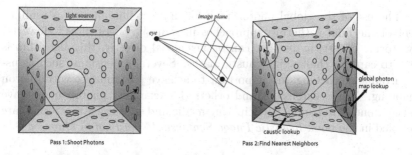

Figure 7.10. Two passes of photon mapping in a Cornell box with a glass sphere. In Pass 1, photons are traced and deposited on nonspecular surfaces. In Pass 2, global illumination is indirectly computed using the global photon map (as shown). For each indirect ray, the N closest photons in the global photon map are found. Caustics are also found by doing a similar look-up in the caustic map at the visible point. Direct illumination, specular, and glossy reflections (not shown) are computed using ray tracing.

- The remaining indirect illumination is computed by sampling the hemisphere; the global photon map is used to compute radiance at the surfaces that are not directly visible using Equation 7.5. This extra level of indirection decreases visual artifacts.

Figure 7.10 shows a visualization of both passes of the photon-mapping algorithm. See Figure 7.11 for results.

(a)   (b)

Figure 7.11. Examples of images produced using photon mapping. Figure (a) shows caustics, while Figure (b) shows a scene rendered with global illumination and displacement mapping. (Courtesy of Henrik Wann Jensen.) (See Plate IX.)

The use of the global photon map for indirect illumination is reminiscent of the final gathering approaches in radiosity algorithms. However, by storing caustic maps that can be visualized directly, this algorithm is able to capture challenging caustic paths. Several extensions, such as using irradiance caching, are important to achieve performance with photon mapping. These extensions and others (for example, photon maps have been extended to handle participating media and subsurface scattering) are detailed in the book *Realistic Image Synthesis Using Photon Mapping* [83].

7.7 Instant Radiosity

Instant radiosity is the name of another interesting hybrid algorithm, related to bidirectional path tracing and two-pass methods [91]. The key idea of instant radiosity is to replace indirect diffuse illumination in a scene by direct diffuse illumination from a set of point sources. The point sources are placed at the locations where a number of simulated photon trajectories hit the surfaces of objects. Figure 7.12 illustrates this approach.

We showed in Section 6.5.6 that this approach can be viewed as a kind of kernel method for density estimation, using the kernel of the radiosity integral equation (Equation 6.3) as a footprint function. Instant radiosity can also be viewed as a kind of bidirectional path tracing. The eye paths are only one segment long, or are allowed to scatter specularly only. On the other hand, more than one light path is combined with each eye-path vertex. The same set of light paths is used for all eye paths.

The main advantage of instant radiosity is in the so-called *positively correlated sampling* for all pixels. Because the same light paths are used for all pixels, images computed with instant radiosity look smoother and lack the typical noisy artifacts of (bidirectional) path tracing. An example is shown in Figure 7.13.

In addition, the shadow rays traced between eye-path vertices and the light-path vertices are highly coherent, similar to eye rays traced in ray casting. They can be traced significantly faster than in (bidirectional) path tracing. With an efficient ray-casting engine, high-quality results can be obtained in seconds on a single processor.

One potential problem with this approach is in the singularity of the kernel of the radiosity equation, which needs to be evaluated between each light-path and eye-path vertex:

$$G(x, y) = \frac{\cos(\Theta_{xy}, N_x) \cos(\Theta_{yx}, N_y)}{\pi r_{xy}^2}.$$

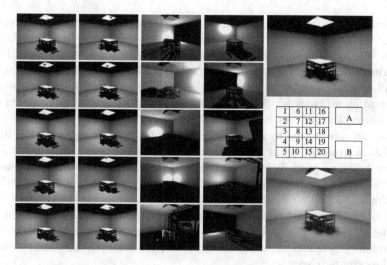

Figure 7.12. The basic idea of Keller's instant radiosity algorithm. First, a small number of photon trajectories is traced. Point light sources are placed at the locations where these trajectories hit object surfaces. The direct illumination due to these point light sources (Images 1 to 20) is accumulated. Image A shows the result of accumulating the Images 1 to 10, with light source points at the origin of the simulated trajectories, on the extended light source. This results in direct illumination due to the extended light source. Accumulating Images 11 to 20, corresponding to the other places visited by the photon trajectories, adds indirect diffuse illumination (Image B). (Images courtesy of A. Keller, University of Kaiserslautern, Germany.)

Figure 7.13. These images show two views of the same scene, with only direct diffuse illumination besides specular reflections (left), and including indirect diffuse illumination (right). The right image shows that indirect diffuse illumination can be a very important effect. The indirect diffuse illumination in this image was computed with a ray-tracing version of instant radiosity. (Image courtesy of I. Wald, T. Kollig, C. Benthin, A. Keller, and Ph, Slusallek, Saarland University, Saarbrücken, and University of Kaiserslautern, Kaiserslautern, Germany.) (See Plate X.)

When the distance r_{xy} tends to zero (x and y move closer to each other, as shown in Figure 6.3), $G(x,y)$ becomes very large. In bidirectional path tracing, this singularity is avoided by multiplying with appropriate weight factors favoring alternative path combinations. As a solution, a small constant can be added to the denominator, similar to certain classic integration schemes for point-to-patch form factors in radiosity. Doing so introduces a small, but hardly noticeable, bias.

As an alternative to ray tracing, Keller proposed computing the illumination from the point sources using graphics hardware [91]. Typically, a few hundred point lights are used, which is much more than hardware typically can handle in a single pass. Therefore, an accumulation buffer or similar technique needs to be used in order to combine the results from several rendering passes. Implementation using graphics hardware is interesting in view of the rapidly increasing processing power and accuracy of commodity graphics accelerators. Interactive rendering rates are possible for less complex scenes.

7.8 Lightcuts and Multidimensional Lightcuts

Even with all the advances in Monte Carlo sampling, rendering complex scenes that include a large number of light sources, and effects such as motion blur, depth of field, and participating media, remains challenging. Most existing techniques are too slow (and noisy) in the face of such complexity. Lightcuts [213] and multidimensional lightcuts [214] are scalable rendering algorithms for high complexity scenes.

7.8.1 Lightcuts

Rendering scenes with a large number of complex light sources is a challenge. Convergence of Monte Carlo sampling for direct illumination, even with the optimizations from Section 5.4.5, is often too slow for such scenes. Furthermore, hybrid algorithms like instant radiosity convert indirect illumination into direct illumination from a set of indirect lights. The performance of such algorithms depends linearly on the number of lights created; this linear performance often limits the complexity of scenes and illumination that these approaches can handle.

Lightcuts [213] introduce a scalable solution for computing illumination from many point lights. Their rendering cost is sublinear in the number of point lights, thus enabling rendering from an extremely large number of light sources. This sublinear performance can be exploited to

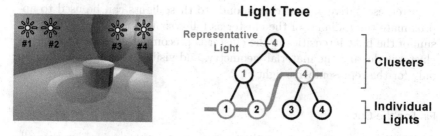

Figure 7.14. A simple scene with four point lights and the corresponding light tree. Leaves are individual lights while upper nodes are progressively larger light clusters. Each cut is a different partitioning of the lights into clusters. The cut shown in orange clusters lights three and four. The orange region in the rendered image (left) shows where the lightcut is a good approximation of the exact solution. (Image courtesy Bruce Walter.) (See Plate XX.)

render difficult illumination problems simulated as illumination from many point lights. For example, area lights, sun/sky models, high dynamic range (HDR) environment maps, and indirect illumination using instant radiosity, and of course, point lights, can be unified into one common framework. Apart from quality, this unification allows performance gains because bright illumination from one source can mask errors in approximating other illumination.

Lightcuts achieve scalability by constructing a *light tree* over all light sources. The light tree clusters lights in a binary tree where the leaves are individual lights and the interior nodes are light clusters containing the lights below them in the tree. Each tree node has a representative light that approximates the contribution of all the lights in the node's cluster.

Lightcuts achieve sublinear performance by using tree nodes when possible to approximate the contribution of a group of lights without having to evaluate each light individually. When rendering the image, for each eye ray, a *cut* through the light tree is found. A cut is a set of nodes such that every path from the root of the tree to a leaf contains exactly one node from the cut. Only representatives on the cut are evaluated to shade the eye ray. The cut corresponds to a valid partitioning of the lights into clusters, such that evaluation of the cut approximates the shading of the eye ray. A simple example scene with four lights is shown in Figure 7.14.

Using the Cut

Given a set of point light sources, the radiance caused by their illumination at a surface point is a product of each light's material, geometry, visibility, and intensity terms, summed over all the lights: $\sum_i M_i G_i V_i I_i$. The cluster, with representative j, that corresponds to these lights can be used to approximate the radiance of the cluster as follows: $M_j G_j V_j \sum_i I_i$, where the sum of the light intensities in the cluster is precomputed and stored in the cluster node, and the material, geometry, and visibility term are evaluated only for the representative light j.

Finding the Cut

The goal is to compute a cut that approximates the original image well. Cuts that use nodes higher up in the tree are more efficient because they use more clustering; however, they could also introduce more error. Lightcuts use conservative error bounds to determine the error introduced by approximating a cluster by using its representative. Upper bounds for the material, geometry, and visibility terms for the entire cluster are analytically computed and used to bound the approximation error (see [213] for details). A cluster is selected only when the approximation error introduced by the cluster is provably below a perceptual visibility threshold (2%) determined by Weber's Law.

The cut selection algorithm starts at the root for each eye ray; the cut is progressively refined to meet the error criterion. The algorithm uses both the cluster's approximate contribution and error bound to determine when refinement is necessary. An additional optimization, reconstruction cuts, exploits spatial coherence in lightcuts to further reduce light evaluations.

Figure 7.15 demonstrates scenes with a large number of point lights (13,000–600,000) used to simulate area lights, HDR environment maps, sun/sky model, and indirect illumination. The most complex scene is the Big Screen scene (Figure 7.15(c)), which includes two textured lights (the HDR displays on the walls) that are modeled as a point light per pixel of the displays. Using lightcuts for these scenes, each shaded point on average only evaluates 150–500 lights, which is further reduced to 10–90 lights for reconstruction cuts. The figure also shows graphs that demonstrate the scalability of lightcuts for the Tableau and Kitchen scenes (Figures 7.15(a) and (b)); performance varies *sublinearly* with increasing number of lights.

7.8.2 Multidimensional Lightcuts

Monte Carlo rendering is powerful enough to handle a wide range of effects, including motion blur, depth of field, and participating media. These effects can all be cast into the rendering equation as integrals over different domains. For example, motion blur is an integration of radiance over time, participating media is an integration along the ray in the medium, depth

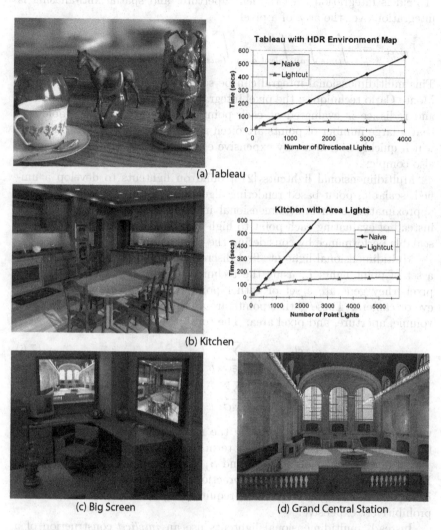

(a) Tableau

(b) Kitchen

(c) Big Screen

(d) Grand Central Station

Figure 7.15. Scenes rendered using lightcuts. Tableau demonstrates glossy surfaces and HDR environment maps. The Kitchen scene includes area lights and the sun/sky model. Scalability graphs on the right show how cut size, and therefore performance, scales sublinearly with the number of lights. Big Screen includes two textured lights, the displays, each modeled with a point light source per pixel of the display. Grand Central Station includes 800 direct lights, sun/sky, and indirect illumination. (Image courtesy Bruce Walter.) (See Plate XXI.)

of field is integration over the lens aperture, and spatial anti-aliasing is integration over the area of a pixel:

$$L_{pixel} = \int_{time} \int_{ray} \int_{pixel\ area} \int_{lens\ aperture} \int_{hemisphere} L(x \leftarrow \omega).$$

This multidimensional integral can be solved by sampling using standard Monte Carlo techniques; the pixel integral is converted into a set of points, and radiance is evaluated at each point and averaged. The problem is that a large number of points are often required for good approximations, which quickly becomes very expensive especially when the illumination is also complex.

Multidimensional lightcuts [214] build on lightcuts to develop a unified, scalable, point-based rendering algorithm for rapidly and accurately approximating such multidimensional integrals. The key insight is that instead of evaluating each point to high accuracy, it is possible to achieve scalable performance by considering the pixel as a whole.

Multidimensional lightcuts first discretize the illumination sources into a set of point lights L, using the techniques of lightcuts. Then for each pixel, they generate a set of gather points G, by tracing rays from the eye or camera. These gather points are appropriately distributed in time, volume, aperture, and pixel area. The total pixel value is then:

$$pixel = \sum_{(j,i)\in G\times L} L_{ji} \tag{7.6}$$

$$= \sum_{(j,i)\in G\times L} S_j M_{ji} G_{ji} V_{ji} I_i \tag{7.7}$$

where the M, G, and I terms are the material, geometry, and intensity terms as before, V_{ji} is the visibility term that also checks that points i and j exist at the same time instant, and S_j is the strength of a gather point. Directly evaluating all pairwise interactions (g, l), where g is a gather point in G, and l is a light point in L, requires $|G||L|$ computations, which is prohibitively expensive.

Instead, multidimensional lightcuts use an *implicit* construction of a hierarchy over the space of gather-light pairs. Separate hierarchies over the gather points and the light points are constructed: the gather tree and light tree, respectively. The Cartesian *product graph* of the gather tree and light tree is then an implicit hierarchy on the set of all gather-light pairs, as illustrated in Figure 7.16. The root node of the product graph corresponds to the set of all gather-light pairs (pairing of the gather and light tree roots) while leaf nodes correspond to individual gather-light pairs (pairing of leaf nodes from the gather and light trees). This implicit construction allows

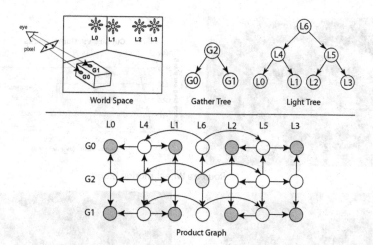

Figure 7.16. Product graph. Top left: scene with two gather points and four light points. Top right: gather and light cluster trees. Bottom: product graph of gather tree and light tree. Each product graph node corresponds to the pairing of a gather and light node and represents all pairwise interactions between points in their respective clusters.

computation using a hierarchy of gather-light pairs without actually having to explicitly construct the full hierarchy.

A cut partitions the set of gather-light pairs into clusters, and the goal is to adaptively select a cut that will result in an accurate approximation of the pixel. In analogy with lightcuts, a cut in the product graph is a set of nodes such that the set of all paths from the root to a leaf will always contain exactly one node from the cut. This condition guarantees that the cut corresponds to a valid partitioning of gather-light pairs.

This algorithm discretizes time into a fixed set of T time instants for any frame. The strengths S and intensities I of the gather and light points are then time vectors. A representative (g, l) approximates shading as follows:

$$L_C = M_{gl} G_{gl} V_{gl} (\vec{S}_C \cdot \vec{I}_C), \qquad (7.8)$$

where the material, geometry, and visibility terms are evaluated at the representative (g, l), g and l are required to exist at the same time instant, and $\vec{S}_C$ and $\vec{I}_C$ are the sum of the strength and intensity vectors for all the gather and light points in the corresponding gather and light clusters.

The rendering algorithm then starts at the root of both the gather and light trees and refines the cut based on the error of nodes on the cut. As in lightcuts, finding the cut in the product graph requires bounding the

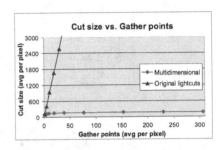

(a) Roulette Wheel, motion blur

(b) Tableau, depth of field   (c) Kitchen, participating media

Figure 7.17. Multidimensional lightcuts results. The Roulette Wheel demonstrates motion blur. The split image shows the static wheel on the left and the wheel spinning on the right. The scalability graph (right) shows how cut size, and therefore performance, scales sublinearly with the number of gather points. Tableau demonstrates depth of field, and the Kitchen demonstrates participating media. (Image courtesy Bruce Walter.) (See Plate XXII.)

error introduced by the representatives on the cut. However, bounding the error for materials and geometry is more complicated (see [214] for details). Again, a perceptual threshold based on Weber's Law is used to determine when an approximation on the cut is good enough.

Figure 7.17 demonstrates scenes with various effects, including motion blur, depth of field, participating media, and spatial anti-aliasing. Using multidimensional lightcuts for these scenes, each shaded *pixel* on average only evaluates 200–950 point-light interactions for these scenes that include hundreds of gather points and up to 600,000 lights. The figure also shows a graph that demonstrates the scalability of multidimensional lightcuts for the Roulette Wheel scene (Figure 7.17(a)) as the gather point cloud increases in size.

Summary

Rendering complex scenes with the wide range of geometric, material, and lighting complexity and effects that arise in the real world remains hard. Scalable rendering algorithms that can handle such complexity are an interesting area of future research.

7.9 Exercises

In the following exercises, some specific scenes are given, with at first sight not too uncommon geometry or lighting configurations. Suppose we want to use straightforward Monte Carlo ray tracing (including explicit sampling of the light sources) to compute the images of these scenes from the given camera positions.

We know that Monte Carlo path tracing will always produce the correct image, given enough samples. However, this might result in unacceptably long rendering times.

For each of the scenes, what problems will occur if we use standard Monte Carlo path tracing? Can you think of any algorithmic improvements or other optimization schemes that might solve these problems? Explain why your proposed improvements will work. Note that there are no "correct" solutions to these problems. In most cases, several different strategies might be used.

1. A glass sphere is resting on a diffuse surface (Figure 7.18). The transparent BRDF of the sphere is almost perfectly specular. A so-called caustic is formed on the diffuse floor, due to the focusing effect

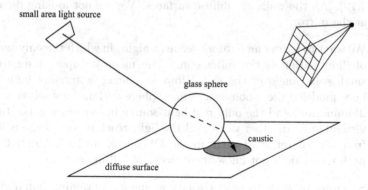

Figure 7.18. Glass sphere forming a caustic on a diffuse floor.

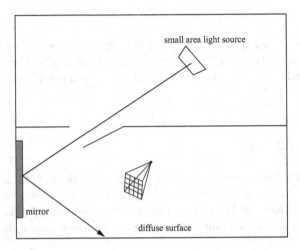

Figure 7.19. Light reaching the room through a half-open door, and reflected off a mirror (top view).

of the glass sphere. An example light ray, causing this caustic, is shown. What problems will occur when rendering the caustic?

A very similar problem occurs when we want to render indoor scenes, where the only source of illumination is the light from the sun shining through the glass windows (in case they are correctly modeled as double-sided glass panes).

2. The only light reaching the room containing the camera is coming from an adjacent room through a half-open door and is then being reflected by a flat perfect mirror positioned at one of the walls (Figure 7.19). All the walls are diffuse surfaces. We are not looking directly at the mirror.

3. We want to render an outdoor scene at night, in which the only source of illumination is the full moon. The moon occupies a relatively small solid angle in the sky. However, being astronomy buffs, we have modeled the moon as a diffuse sphere without any self-emissive illumination, and the only real light source in our scene is the (non-visible) sun. In other words, all the light reaching our scene is light from the sun reflected at the moon. Of course, our basic Monte Carlo path tracer does not know the concept of full moon.

4. Suppose we want to render a city at night, containing hundreds of different modeled light sources (street lights, neon signs, lit windows,

Figure 7.20. Light patterns at the bottom of a stream of water.

etc.). Shooting a shadow ray to each of these light sources would mean a large amount of inefficient work, since clearly not every light source contributes significantly to the illumination of every visible surface point. What optimization techniques would you use such that scenes like this can be rendered in a reasonable amount of time?

A very similar problem can occur if the light source is textured (e.g., a stained-glass window), effectively subdividing the light source into many different smaller light sources, each with uniform color and intensity.

5. We look at the same city, but from across the river next to the city. Now we see the entire city scene reflected in the water, including all different light sources. The water is modeled as a surface with many different little waves (e.g., using bump mapping) and behaves as a perfect mirror-like surface with respect to reflection. For any given ray, the direction in which the ray will be reflected on the water can therefore not be predicted unless the intersection point and hence the surface normal is already known.

   The shimmering waves one can see at the bottom of a swimming pool or stream of water (Figure 7.20) pose the same problem.

6. A large area light source is partly hidden behind a number of smaller objects, which altogether block a fair amount of light coming for the light source (e.g., a number of slats between two rooms, or Venetian

Figure 7.21. Venetian blinds casting shadows on a desk-surface.

blinds in a window; see Figure 7.21). Most of the shadow rays will be blocked by these small intervening objects, but a significant part of the light source is still visible and contributing to the illumination. How can we make sure we do not waste any shadow rays?

8

The Quest for Ultimate Realism and Speed

In this last chapter, we cover a number of topics that are the subject of ongoing research. Indeed, the quest for realism and speed has not yet come to an end.

While deriving the rendering equation in Chapter 2, several restrictions were imposed on light transport. We assumed that wave effects could be ignored and that radiance is conserved along its path between mutually visible surfaces. We also assumed that light scattering happens instantaneously; that scattered light has the same wavelength as the incident beam; and that it scatters from the same location where it hits a surface. This is not always true. We start this chapter with a discussion of how to deal with participating media, translucent objects, and phenomena such as polarization, diffraction, interference, fluorescence, and phosphorescence, which do not fall within our assumptions. We need to refine our light transport model in order to obtain high realism when these phenomena come into play. Fortunately, most of the algorithms previously covered in this book can be extended rather easily to handle these phenomena, although some new and specific approaches exist as well.

Radiometry is, however, only part of the story, albeit an important part. Most often, computer graphics images are consumed by human observers, looking at a printed picture or a computer screen, or watching a computer graphics movie in a movie theater. Unfortunately, current display systems are not nearly capable of reproducing the wide range of light intensities that occurs in nature and that results from our accurate light transport simulations. These radiometric values need to be transformed in some way to display colors. For good realism, this transformation should take into account the response of the human vision system, which is known to be sophisticated and highly nonlinear. Human visual perception can also be exploited to avoid computing detail that one wouldn't notice anyway, thus saving computation time.

The last part of this chapter deals with rendering speed. We cover how frame-to-frame coherence can be exploited in order to more rapidly render computer animation movies or walk-throughs of nondiffuse static environments. Very recently, a number of approaches have appeared that go even further on this track and achieve interactive global illumination, without predefined animation script or camera path.

8.1 Beyond the Rendering Equation

8.1.1 Participating Media

We assumed in Chapter 2 that radiance is conserved along its path between unoccluded surfaces. The underlying idea was that all photons leaving the first surface needed to land on the second one because nothing could happen to them along their path of flight. As everyone who has ever been outside in mist or foggy weather conditions knows, this is not always true. Photons reflected or emitted by a car in front of us on the road for instance, will often not reach us. They will rather be absorbed or scattered by billions of tiny water or fog droplets immersed in the air. At the same time, light coming from the sky above will be scattered towards us. The net effect is that distant objects fade away in gray. Even clear air itself causes photons to be scattered or absorbed. This is evident when looking at a distant mountain range, and it causes an effect known as *aerial perspective*. Clouds in the sky scatter and absorb sunlight strongly, although they don't have a real surface boundary separating them from the air around. Surfaces are also not needed for light emission, as in the example of a candle flame.

Our assumption of radiance conservation between surfaces is only true in a vacuum. In that case, the relation between emitted radiance and incident radiance at mutually visible surface points x and y along direction Θ is given by the simple relation

$$L(x \rightarrow \Theta) = L(y \leftarrow -\Theta). \tag{8.1}$$

If a vacuum is not filling the space between object surfaces, this will cause photons to change direction and to transform into other forms of energy. In the case of the candle flame, other forms of energy are also transformed into visible light photons. We now discuss how these phenomena can be integrated into our light transport framework. We start by studying how they affect the relation (Equation 8.1) between emitted radiance and incident radiance at mutually visible surface points x and y.

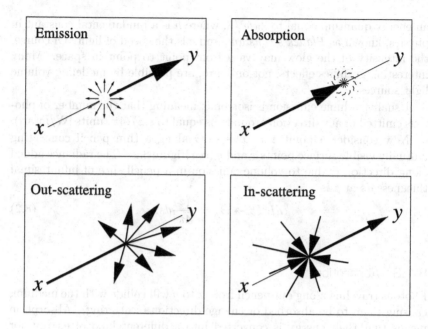

Figure 8.1. A participating medium affects radiance transfer along the line from
x to y through four processes: absorption (top right) and out-scattering (bottom
left) remove radiance; volume emission (top left) and in-scattering (bottom right)
add radiance. These processes are explained in more detail in the following
sections.

We distinguish four processes: volume emission (Section 8.1.2), absorption
(Section 8.1.3), out-scattering (Section 8.1.4), and in-scattering (Section
8.1.5). Figure 8.1 illustrates these processes. This will allow us to generalize the rendering equation of Chapter 2 (Section 8.1.6). Once a good
basic understanding of the physics of the problem has been gained, it is
quite easy to extend most of the global illumination algorithms previously
described in this book to handle participating media (Section 8.1.7).

8.1.2   Volume Emission

The intensity by which a medium, like fire, glows can be characterized by a
volume emittance function $\epsilon(z)$ (units [W/m^3]). A good way to think about
the volume emittance function is as follows: it tells us basically how many
photons per unit of volume and per unit of time are emitted at a point z in
three-dimensional space. Indeed, there is a close relationship between the
number of photons and energy: each photon of a fixed wavelength λ carries

an energy quantum equal to $2\pi\hbar c/\lambda$, where $\hbar$ is a fundamental constant in physics, known as *Planck's constant*, and c is the speed of light. Of course, the intensity of the glow may vary from point to point in space. Many interesting graphics effects, not only fire, are possible by modeling volume light sources.

Usually, volume emission is isotropic, meaning that the number of photons emitted in any direction around z is equal to $\epsilon(z)/4\pi$ (units $[\text{W/m}^3\text{sr}]$).

Now consider a point $z = x + s \cdot \Theta$ along a thin pencil connecting mutually visible surface points x and y (see Figure 8.2). The radiance added along direction Θ due to volume emission in a pencil slice of infinitesimal thickness ds at z is

$$dL^e(z \to \Theta) = \frac{e(z)}{4\pi}ds. \qquad (8.2)$$

8.1.3 Absorption

Photons traveling along our pencil from x to y will collide with the medium, causing them to be absorbed or change direction (scattering). Absorption means that their energy is converted into a different kind of energy, for instance, kinetic energy of the particles in the medium. Transformation into kinetic energy is observed at a macroscopic level as the medium heating up by radiation. Strong absorption of microwave radiation by water allows you to boil water in a microwave oven.

The probability that a photon gets absorbed in a volume, per unit of distance along its direction of propagation, is called the *absorption coefficient* $\sigma_a(z)$ (units $[1/\text{m}]$). This means that a photon traveling a distance Δs in a medium has a chance $\sigma_a \cdot \Delta s$ of being absorbed. Just like the emission density, the absorption coefficient can also vary from place to place. In cigarette smoke, for example, absorption varies because the number of smoke particles per unit volume varies from place to place. In addition, absorption is usually isotropic: a photon has the same chance of being absorbed regardless of its direction of flight. This is rarely true for absorption by a single particle, but in most media, particles are randomly oriented so that their average directional absorption (and also scattering) characteristics are observed.

Absorption causes the radiance along the thin pencil from x to y to decrease exponentially with distance. Consider a pencil slice of thickness Δs at $z = x + s\Theta$ (see Figure 8.2). The number of photons entering the slice at z is proportional to the radiance $L(z \to \Theta)$ along the pencil. Assuming that the absorption coefficient is equal everywhere in the slice, a fraction $\sigma_a(z)\Delta s$ of these photons will be absorbed. The radiance coming out on

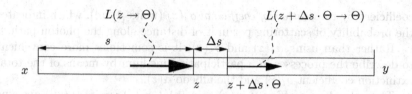

Figure 8.2. Pencil slice geometry.

the other side of the slice at $z + \Delta s\Theta$ will be

$$L(z + \Delta s \cdot \Theta \to \Theta) = L(z \to \Theta) - L(z \to \Theta)\sigma_a(z)\Delta s,$$

or equivalently,

$$\frac{L(z + \Delta s \cdot \Theta \to \Theta) - L(z \to \Theta)}{\Delta s} = -\sigma_a(z)L(z \to \Theta).$$

Taking the limit for $\Delta s \to 0$ yields the following differential equation[1]:

$$\frac{dL(z \to \Theta)}{ds} = -\sigma_a(z)L(z \to \Theta) \quad \text{with} \quad z = x + s\Theta.$$

In a homogeneous nonscattering and nonemissive medium, the reduced radiance at z along the pencil will be

$$L(z \to \Theta) = L(x \to \Theta)e^{-\sigma_a s}.$$

This exponential decrease of radiance with distance is sometimes called *Beer's Law*. It is a good model for colored glass, for instance, and has been used for many years in classic ray tracing [170]. If the absorption varies along the considered photon path, Beer's Law looks like this:

$$L(z \to \Theta) = L(x \to \Theta) \exp\left(-\int_0^s \sigma_a(x + t\Theta)dt\right).$$

8.1.4 Out-Scattering, Extinction Coefficient, and Albedo

The radiance along the pencil will, in general, not only reduce because of absorption, but also because photons will be scattered into other directions by the particles along their path. The effect of *out-scattering* is almost identical to that of absorption—one just needs to replace the absorption

---

[1] The derivative of a function $f(x)$ is, by definition, the limit of $(f(x+\Delta x) - f(x))/\Delta x$ for $\Delta x \to 0$.

coefficient by the *scattering coefficient* $\sigma_s(z)$ (units [1/m]), which indicates the probability of scattering per unit of distance along the photon path.

Rather than using $\sigma_a(z)$ and $\sigma_s(z)$, it is sometimes more convenient to describe the processes in a participating medium by means of the total extinction coefficient $\sigma_t(z)$ and the albedo $\alpha(z)$.

The *extinction coefficient* $\sigma_t(z) = \sigma_a(z) + \sigma_s(z)$ (units [1/m]) gives us the probability per unit distance along the path of flight that a photon *collides* (absorbs or scatters) with the medium. It allows us to write the reduced radiance at z as

$$L^r(z \to \Theta) = L(x \to \Theta)\tau(x, z) \text{ with } \tau(x, z) = \exp\left(-\int_0^{r_{xz}} \sigma_t(x + t\Theta)dt\right).$$
(8.3)

In a homogeneous medium, the average distance between two subsequent collisions can be shown to be $1/\sigma_t$ (units [m]). The average distance between subsequent collisions is called the *mean free path*.

The *albedo* $\alpha(z) = \sigma_s(z)/\sigma_t(z)$ (dimensionless) describes the relative importance of scattering versus absorption. It gives us the probability that a photon will be scattered rather than absorbed when colliding with the medium at z.

The albedo is the volume equivalent of the reflectivity ρ at surfaces. Note that the extinction coefficient was not needed for describing surface scattering since all photons hitting a surface are supposed to scatter or to be absorbed. In the absence of participating media, one could model the extinction coefficient by means of a Dirac delta function along the photon path: it is zero everywhere, except at the first surface boundary met, where scattering or absorption happens for sure.

8.1.5 In-Scattering, Field- and Volume-Radiance, and the Phase Function

The out-scattered photons change direction and enter different pencils between surface points. In the same way, photons out-scattered from other pencils will enter the pencil between the x and y we are considering. This entry of photons due to scattering is called *in-scattering*.

Similar to volume emission, the intensity of in-scattering is described by a volume density $L^{vi}(z \to \Theta)$ (units [W/m^{3}sr]). The amount of in-scattered radiance in a pencil slice of thickness ds will be

$$dL^i(z \to \Theta) = L^{vi}(z \to \Theta)ds.$$

A first condition for in-scattering at a location z is that there is scattering at z at all, in other words, that $\sigma_s(z) = \alpha(z)\sigma_t(z) \neq 0$. The amount of in-scattered radiance further depends on the *field radiance* $L(z, \Psi)$ along other directions Ψ at z, and the *phase function* $p(z, \Psi \leftrightarrow \Theta)$.

Field radiance is our usual concept of radiance. It describes the amount of light energy flux in a given direction per unit of solid angle and per unit area perpendicular to that direction. The product of field radiance with the extinction coefficient $L^v(z, \Psi) = L(z, \Psi)\sigma_t(z)$ describes the number of photons entering collisions with the medium at z per unit of time. Being a volume density, it is sometimes called the *volume radiance* (units $[1/m^3sr]$).

Note that the volume radiance will be zero in empty space. The field radiance, however, does not need to be zero and fulfills the law of radiance conservation in empty space.

Note also that for surface scattering, no distinction is needed between field radiance and *surface radiance*, since all photons interact at a surface.

Of these photons entering collision with the medium at z, a fraction $\alpha(z)$ will be scattered. Unlike emission and absorption, scattering is usually not isotropic. Photons may scatter with higher intensity in certain directions than in others. The *phase function* $p(z, \Psi \leftrightarrow \Theta)$ at z (units $[1/sr]$) describes the probability of scattering from direction Ψ into Θ. Usually, the phase function only depends on the angle between the two directions Ψ and Θ. Some examples of phase functions are given below.

The product $\alpha(z)p(z, \Psi \leftrightarrow \Theta)$ plays the role of the BSDF for volume scattering. Just like BSDFs, it is reciprocal, and energy conservation must be satisfied. It is convenient to normalize the phase function so that its integral over all possible directions is one:

$$\int_\Omega p(z, \Psi \leftrightarrow \Theta)d\omega_\Psi = 1.$$

Energy conservation is then clearly satisfied, since $\alpha(z) < 1$.

Putting this together, we arrive at the following *volume scattering equation*:

$$
\begin{aligned}
L^{vi}(z \to \Theta) &= \int_\Omega \alpha(z)p(z, \Psi \leftrightarrow \Theta) \cdot L^v(z \to \Psi)d\omega_\Psi \\
&= \sigma_s(z) \int_\Omega p(z, \Psi \leftrightarrow \Theta)L(z \to \Psi)d\omega_\Psi.
\end{aligned}
\tag{8.4}
$$

The volume scattering equation is the volume equivalent of the surface scattering equation introduced in Section 2.5.1. It describes how scattered volume radiance is the integral over all directions of the volume radiance $L^v(z \to \Psi)$, weighted with $\alpha(z)p(z, \Psi \leftrightarrow \Theta)$. The former is the volume equivalent of surface radiance, and the latter is the equivalent of the BSDF.

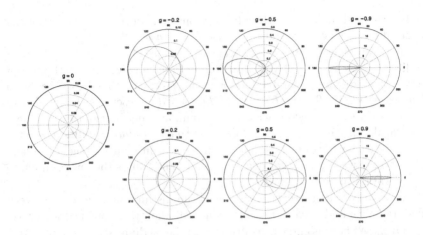

Figure 8.3. Polar plots of the Henyey-Greenstein phase function for anisotropy parameter value $g = 0.0$ (isotropic, left), $g = -0.2, -0.5, -0.9$ (dominant backward
scattering, top row), and $g = +0.2, +0.5, +0.9$ (dominant forward scattering,
bottom row). These plots show the intensity of scattering as a function of the
angle between forward and scattered direction.

Examples of Phase Functions

The equivalent of diffuse reflection is called isotropic scattering. The phase
function for isotropic scattering is constant and equal to

$$p(z, \Psi \leftrightarrow \Theta) = \frac{1}{4\pi}. \tag{8.5}$$

An often used nonisotropic phase function is the following *Henyey-
Greenstein* phase function, which was introduced to model light scattering
in clouds:

$$p(z, \Psi \leftrightarrow \Theta) = \frac{1}{4\pi} \frac{1 - g^2}{1 + g^2 - 2g\cos(\Psi, \Theta)^{3/2}}. \tag{8.6}$$

The parameter g allows us to control the anisotropy of the model: it is
the average cosine of the scattering angle. With $g > 0$, particles are scattered with preference in forward directions. With $g < 0$, they are scattered
mainly backward. $g = 0$ models isotropic scattering (see Figure 8.3).

Other common nonisotropic phase functions are due to Lord Rayleigh
and Blasi et al. Rayleigh's phase function [22, Chapter 1] describes light
scattering at very small particles, such as air molecules. It explains why a
clear sky is blue above and more yellow-reddish towards the horizon.

Blasi et al. have proposed a simple-to-use, intuitive, and efficient-to-
evaluate phase function for use in computer graphics [17].

8.1.6   The Rendering Equation in the Presence of Participating Media

We are now ready to describe how the radiance $L(x \to \Theta)$ gets modified along its way to y. Equations 8.2 and 8.4 model how volume emission and in-scattering add radiance along a ray from x to y. Equation 8.3, on the other hand, describes how radiance is reduced due to absorption and out-scattering. Not only the surface radiance $L(x \to \Theta)$ inserted into the pencil at x is reduced in this way, but also all radiance inserted along the pencil due to in-scattering and volume emission is reduced. The combined effect is

$$L(y \leftarrow -\Theta) = L(x \to \Theta)\tau(x, y) + \int_0^{r_{xy}} L^+(z \to \Theta)\tau(z, y)dr. \qquad (8.7)$$

For compactness, we let $z = x + r\Theta$ and

$$L^+(z \to \Theta) = \epsilon(z)/4\pi + L^{vi}(z \to \Theta) \qquad \text{(units } [\text{W}/\text{m}^3\text{sr}]).$$

The *transmittance* $\tau(z, y)$ indicates how radiance is attenuated between z and y:

$$\tau(z, y) = \exp\left(-\int_0^{r_{zy}} \sigma_t(z + s\Theta)ds\right). \qquad (8.8)$$

Equation 8.7 replaces the law of radiance conservation (Equation 8.1) in the presence of participating media.

Recall that the rendering equation in Chapter 2 was obtained by using the law of radiance conservation in order to replace the incoming radiance $L(x \leftarrow \Psi)$ in

$$L(x \to \Theta) = L_e(x \to \Theta) + \int_\Omega f_r(x, \Theta \leftrightarrow \Psi)L(x \leftarrow \Psi)\cos(\Psi, N_x)d\omega_\Psi$$

by the outgoing radiance $L(y \to -\Psi)$ at the first surface point y seen from x in the direction Ψ. Doing a similar substitution here, using Equation 8.7 instead, yields the following rendering equation in the presence of participating media (see Figure 8.4):

$$L(x \to \Theta) = L_e(x \to \Theta) \qquad (8.9)$$
$$+ \int_\Omega L(y \to -\Psi)\tau(x, y)f_r(x, \Theta \leftrightarrow \Psi)\cos(\Psi, N_x)d\omega_\Psi$$
$$+ \int_\Omega \left(\int_0^{r_{xy}} L^+(z \to -\Psi)\tau(z, y)dr\right) f_r(x, \Theta \leftrightarrow \Psi)\cos(\Psi, N_x)d\omega_\Psi.$$

The in-scattered radiance L^{vi} in $L^+(z \to -\Psi) = \epsilon(z)/4\pi + L^{vi}(z \to -\Psi)$ is expressed in terms of field radiance by Equation 8.4. In turn, field

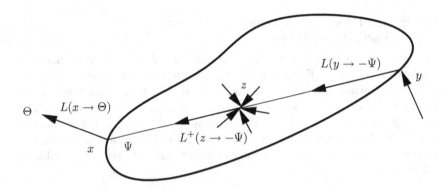

Figure 8.4. Symbols used in Equation 8.9.

radiance is expressed in terms of surface radiance and volume emitted and in-scattered radiance elsewhere in the volume by Equation 8.7.

These expressions look much more frightening than they actually are. The important thing to remember is that participating media can be handled by extending the rendering equation in two ways:

- Attenuation of radiance received from other surfaces: the factor $\tau(x, y)$ given by Equation 8.8 in the former integral.

- A volume contribution: the latter (double) integral in Equation 8.9.

Spatial Formulation

In order to better understand how to trace photon trajectories in the presence of participating media, it is instructive to transform the integrals above to a surface and volume integral, respectively. The relation $r_{xy}^2 d\omega_\Psi = V(x, y) \cos(-\Psi, N_y) dA_y$ between differential solid angle and surface was derived in Section 2.6.2. A similar relationship exists between $dr d\omega_\Psi$ and differential volume: $r_{xz}^2 dr d\omega_\Psi = V(x, z) dV_z$. This results in

$$
\begin{aligned}
L(x \to \Theta) = {} & L_e(x \to \Theta) \\
& + \int_S f_r(x, \Theta \leftrightarrow \Psi) L(y \to -\Psi) \tau(x, y) V(x, y) \frac{\cos(\Psi, N_x) \cos(-\Psi, N_y)}{r_{xy}^2} dA_y \\
& + \int_V f_r(x, \Theta \leftrightarrow \Psi) L^+(z \to -\Psi) \tau(x, y) V(x, z) \frac{\cos(\Psi, N_x)}{r_{xz}^2} dV_z. \quad (8.10)
\end{aligned}
$$

The two integrands are very similar: the volume integral contains $L^+(z \to -\Psi)$ [W/m^{3}sr] rather than surface radiance $L(y \to -\Psi)$ [W/m^{2}sr], but also, surface points always come with a cosine factor, while volume points don't.

Volumes	Surfaces
Volume emittance $\epsilon(z)$ $[W/m^3]$	Surface emittance $B^e(x)$ $[W/m^2]$
Scattering albedo $\alpha(z) = \sigma_s(z)/\sigma_t(z)$	Surface reflectance/transmittance $\rho(x)$
Phase function $\alpha(z)p(z, \Theta \leftrightarrow \Psi)$	BSDF $f_r(x, \Theta \leftrightarrow \Psi) \cos(N_x, \Theta)$
Extinction coefficient $\sigma_t(z)$	No equivalent (Dirac δ function)
Volume radiance $L^v(z \to \Theta) = \sigma_t(z)L(z \to \Theta)$	Surface radiance = field radiance $L(x \to \Theta)$
Attenuation factor $0 \le \tau(x, z) \le 1$	$\tau(x, y) = 1$ (no attenuation in vacuum)
Volume integral of $L^+(z \to -\Psi)$ in Equation 8.9	Surface integral of $L(y \to -\Psi)$ in Equation 8.9

Figure 8.5. This table summarizes the main correspondences and differences in volume and surface scattering and emission.

The correspondences and differences between volume and surface scattering quantities and concepts are summarized in Figure 8.5.

8.1.7 Global Illumination Algorithms for Participating Media

Rendering participating media has received quite some attention since the end of the 1980s. Proposed approaches include deterministic methods and stochastic methods. Classic and hierarchical radiosity methods have been extended to handle participating media by discretizing the volume integral above into volume elements and assuming that the radiance in each volume element is isotropic [154, 174]. Many other deterministic approaches have been proposed as well, based on spherical harmonics (P_N methods) and discrete ordinates methods. An overview is given in [143]. Deterministic approaches are valuable in relatively "easy" settings, for instance, homogeneous media with isotropic scattering, or simple geometries.

Various authors, including Rushmeier, Hanrahan, and Pattanaik, have proposed extensions to path tracing to handle participating media. These extensions have been used for some time in other fields such as neutron transport [183, 86]. They are summarized in Section 8.1.8. The extension of bidirectional path tracing to handle participating media has been proposed in [104]. As usual, these path-tracing approaches are flexible and accurate, but they become enormously costly in optically thick media, where photons suffer many collisions and trajectories are long.

A good compromise between accuracy and speed is offered by *volume photon density estimation* methods. In particular, the extension of photon

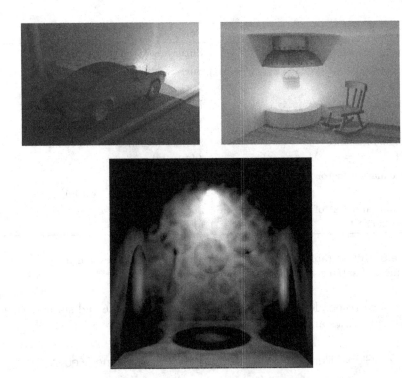

Figure 8.6. Some renderings of participating media. The top images have been rendered with bidirectional path tracing. (Courtesy of Eric Lafortune, Katholieke Universiteit Leuven, Belgium.) The bottom image was rendered with volume photon mapping. Note the volume caustics cast on this inhomogeneous medium behind the colored spheres. (Courtesy of Frederik Anrys and Karl Vom Berge, Katholieke Universiteit Leuven, Belgium.) (See Plate XI.)

mapping to participating media [78] is a reliable and affordable method capable of rendering highly advanced effects such as volume caustics. Volume photon density estimation is described in more detail in Section 8.1.9.

Monte Carlo and volume photon density estimation are methods of choice for optically thin media, in which photons undergo only relatively few collisions. For optically thick media, they become intractable. Highly scattering optically thick media can be handled with the *diffusion approximation*, covered concisely in Section 8.1.10.

For the special case of light scattering and attenuation in the Earth's atmosphere, an analytical model has been proposed [148]. It plausibly reproduces the color variations of the sky as a function of sun position and adds great realism to outdoor scenes without costly simulations.

Figure 8.6 shows some example renderings of participating media using techniques covered here.

8.1.8 Tracing Photon Trajectories in Participating Media

Most algorithms discussed so far in this book are based on the simulation of the trajectory of photons or *potons*, potential particles originating at the eye rather than at light sources. We discuss here how to extend photon- or poton-trajectory tracing to deal with participating media.

Sampling volume emission. Light particles may not only be emitted at surfaces, but also in midspace. First, a decision needs to be made whether to sample surface emission or volume emission. This decision can be a random decision based on the relative amount of self-emitted power by surfaces and volumes, for instance. If volume emission is to be sampled, a location somewhere in midspace needs to be selected, based on the volume emission density $\epsilon(z)$: bright spots in the participating media shall give birth to more photons than dim regions. Finally, a direction needs to be sampled at the chosen location. Since volume emission is usually isotropic, a direction can be sampled with uniform probability across a sphere. Just like with surface emission sampling, this is a spatial position and a direction result.

Sampling a next collision location. In the absence of participating media, a photon emitted from point x into direction Θ always collides on the first surface seen from x along the direction Θ. With participating media, however, scattering and absorption may also happen at every location in the volume along a line to the first surface hit. Note that both surface and volume collisions may take place, regardless of whether x is a surface or a volume point. A good way to handle this problem is to sample a distance along the ray from x into Θ, based on the transmittance factor (Equation 8.8). For instance, one draws a uniformly distributed random number $\zeta \in [0, 1)$ (including 0, excluding 1) and finds the distance r corresponding to

$$\exp\left(-\int_0^r \sigma_t(x + s\Theta)ds\right) = 1 - \zeta \quad \Leftrightarrow \quad \int_0^r \sigma_t(x + s\Theta)ds = -\log(1 - \zeta).$$

In a homogeneous medium, $r = -\log(1 - \zeta)/\sigma_t$. In a heterogeneous medium, however, sampling such a distance is less trivial. It can be done exactly if the extinction coefficient is given as a voxel grid, by extending ray-grid traversal algorithms. For procedurally generated media, one can step along the ray in small, possibly adaptively chosen, intervals [78]. If the selected distance becomes greater than or equal to the distance to the

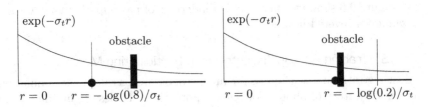

Figure 8.7. Sampling a next photon collision location along a ray. First, a distance r is sampled using the attenuation $\tau(x, z)$ as a PDF ($\tau(x, z) = \exp(-\sigma_t r_{xz})$ in a homogeneous medium). If this distance is less than the distance to the nearest surface (left), then volume scattering or absorption is chosen as the next event. If r is further than the nearest surface (right), surface absorption or scattering is selected at the nearest surface.

first surface hit point of the ray, surface scattering shall be selected as the next event. If the sampled distance is nearer, volume scattering is chosen (see Figure 8.7).

Sampling scattering or absorption.   Sampling scattering or absorption in a volume is pretty much the same as for surfaces. The decision whether to scatter or absorb will be based on the albedo $\alpha(z)$ for volumes just like the reflectivity $\rho(z)$ is used for surfaces. Sampling a scattered direction is done by sampling the phase function $p(z, \Theta \leftrightarrow \Psi)$ for volumes. For surfaces, one ideally uses $f_r(z, \Theta \leftrightarrow \Psi) \cos(N_x, \Psi)/\rho(z)$.

Connecting path vertices.   Algorithms such as path tracing and bidirectional path tracing require us to connect path vertices, for instance, a surface or volume hit with a light source position for a shadow ray. Without participating media, the contribution associated with such a connection between points x and y is

$$V(x, y) \frac{\cos(N_x, \Theta) \cos(N_y, -\Theta)}{r_{xy}^2}.$$

In the presence of participating media, the contribution shall be

$$\tau(x, y) \frac{V(x, y)}{r_{xy}^2} C_x(\Theta) C_y(-\Theta),$$

with $C_x(\Theta) = \cos(N_x, \Theta)$ if x is a surface point or 1 if it is a volume point (similarly for $C_y(-\Theta)$).

8.1.9 Volume Photon Density Estimation

The photon density estimation algorithms of Section 6.5 computed radiosity on surfaces by estimating the density of photon hit points on surfaces. In order to render participating media, it is also necessary to estimate the volume density of photons colliding with the medium in midspace. Any of the techniques described in Section 6.5 can be extended for this purpose in a straightforward manner. A histogram method, for instance, would discretize the space into volume bins and count photon collisions in each bin. The ratio of the number of photon hits over the volume of the bin is an estimate for the volume radiance in the bin. Photon mapping has been extended with a volume photon map, a third kd-tree for storing photon hit points, in the same spirit as the caustic and global photon map discussed in Section 7.6 [78]. The volume photon map contains the photons that collide with the medium in midspace. Rather than finding the smallest disc containing a given number N of photon hit points, as was done on surfaces, one will search for the smallest sphere containing volume photons around a query location. Again, the ratio of the number of photons and the volume of the sphere yields an estimate for the volume radiance.

Viewing Precomputed Illumination in Participating Media

Due to the law of conservation of radiance, viewing precomputed illumination using ray tracing in the absence of participating media takes nothing

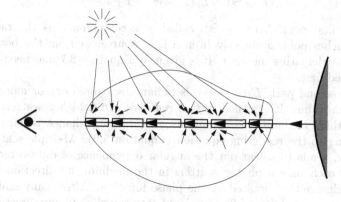

Figure 8.8. Using precomputed volume radiance for rendering a view can best be done with a technique called ray marching. One marches over an eye ray, with fixed or adaptive step size. At every step, precomputed volume radiance is queried. Self-emitted and single scattered ("direct") volume radiance is calculated on the spot. Finally, the surface radiance at the first hit surface is taken into account. All gathered radiance is properly attenuated.

more than finding what surface point y is visible through each pixel on the virtual screen and querying the illumination at that point.

In the presence of participating media, conservation of radiance does not hold, and the radiance coming in at the observer through each pixel will be an integral over an eye ray, according to Equation 8.7. A good way to evaluate this integral is by ray marching [78]: by stepping over the ray in small, potentially adaptively chosen, intervals (see Figure 8.8). At every visited location along the ray, precomputed volume radiance is queried, and volume emission and single scattered radiance evaluated. Of course, the surface radiance at the first hit object should not be overlooked. All radiance contributions are appropriately attenuated towards the eye.

8.1.10 Light Transport as a Diffusion Process

The rendering equation (Equation 8.9) is not the only way light transport can be described mathematically. An interesting alternative is to consider the flow of light energy as a diffusion process [75, Chapter 9]. This point of view has been shown to result in efficient algorithms for dealing with highly scattering optically thick participating media, such as clouds [185]. The diffusion approximation is also at the basis of recently proposed models for subsurface scattering [80]; see Section 8.1.11. We present it briefly here.

The idea is to split field radiance in a participating media into two contributions, which are computed separately:

$$L(x \to \Theta) = L_r(x \to \Theta) + L_d(x \to \Theta).$$

The first part, $L_r(x \to \Theta)$, called *reduced radiance*, is the radiance that reaches point x directly from a light source, or from the boundary of the participating medium. It is given by Equation 8.7 and needs to be computed first.

The second part, $L_d(x \to \Theta)$, is radiance scattered one or more times in the medium. It is called *diffuse radiance*. In a highly scattering optically thick medium, the computation of diffuse radiance is hard to do according to the rendering equation (Equation 8.9). Multiple scattering, however, tends to smear out the angular dependence of diffuse radiance. Indeed, each time a photon scatters in the medium, its direction is randomly changed as dictated by the phase function. After many scattering events, the probability of finding the photon traveling in any direction will be nearly uniform.

For this reason, one approximates diffuse radiance by the following function, which varies only a little with direction:

$$L_d(x \to \Theta) = U^d(x) + \frac{3}{4\pi} \left(\vec{F}^d(x) \cdot \Theta \right).$$

$U^d(x)$ represents the average diffuse radiance at x:

$$U^d(x) = \frac{1}{4\pi} \int_\Omega L_d(x, \Theta) d\omega_\Theta.$$

The vector $\vec{F}^d(x)$, called the *diffuse flux vector*, models the direction and magnitude of the multiple-scattered light energy flow through x. It is defined by taking Θ equal to the unit vector in X, Y, and Z directions in the following equation:

$$\left(\vec{F}^d(x) \cdot \Theta\right) = \int_\Omega L(x \to \Psi) \cos(\Psi, \Theta) d\omega_\Psi.$$

In this approximation, it can be shown that the average diffuse radiance U^d fulfills a so-called steady-state diffusion equation:

$$\nabla^2 U^d(x) - \sigma_{tr}^2 U^d(x) = -Q(x). \tag{8.11}$$

The driving term $Q(x)$ can be computed from reduced radiance [185, 80, 75, Chapter 9]. The diffusion constant equals $\sigma_{tr}^2 = 3\sigma_a \sigma_t'$ with $\sigma_t' = \sigma_s' + \sigma_a$ and $\sigma_s' = \sigma_s(1 - g)$. g is the average scattering cosine (see Section 8.1.5) and models the anisotropy of scattering in the medium.

Once the diffusion equation has been solved, the reduced radiance and the gradient of $U^d(x)$ allow us to compute the flux vector $\vec{F}^d(x)$ wherever it is needed. The flux vector, in turn, yields the radiosity flowing through any given real or imaginary surface boundary.

For simple cases, such as a point source in an infinite homogeneous medium, the diffusion equation can be solved analytically [80, 75, Chapter 9]. In general, however, solution is only possible via numerical methods. Stam proposed a multigrid finite difference method and a finite element method based on blobs [185]. In any case, proper boundary conditions need to be taken into account, enforcing that the net influx of diffuse radiance at the boundary is zero (because there is no volume scattering outside the medium).

A different alternative for the rendering equation, based on principles of invariance [22], has been described in [145]. It is, however, significantly more involved.

8.1.11 Subsurface Scattering

In the derivation of the rendering equation (Chapter 2), it was also assumed that light hitting an object surface is reflected or refracted from the spot of incidence. This assumption is not always true. Consider, for instance, the small marble horse sculpture in Figure 8.9. Marble, but also other

Figure 8.9. Two renderings of a small marble horse sculpture (5 cm head-to-tail). Left: using a BRDF model; right: taking into account subsurface scattering. A BRDF does not capture the distinct, soft appearance of materials such as marble. The right figure has been computed using the model and the path-tracing extension proposed in [80]. These images also illustrate that translucency is an important visual cue for estimating the size of objects. (See Plate XII.)

materials including fruits, leaves, candle wax, milk, human skin, etc., are *translucent materials*. Photons hitting such materials will enter the object, scatter below the surface, and emerge at a different place (see Figure 8.10). Because of this, such materials have a distinct, soft appearance. Figure 8.9 illustrates that a BRDF, which models only local light reflection, cannot capture this soft appearance.

In principle, translucency can be handled using any of the previously discussed algorithms for participating media. Materials such as marble and milk are, however, highly scattering and optically thick. A photon entering a marble object for instance, will scatter hundreds of times before being absorbed or reappearing at the surface. Algorithms based on photon trajectory tracing are very inefficient in this case. The diffusion approximation, however, can be used.

Translucency can also be treated in a more macroscopic way, by extending the model for light reflection introduced in Section 2.5.1, so that light can reflect off a different location than where it entered the material:

$$L(y \to \Theta) = \int_S \int_{\Omega_x^+} L(x \leftarrow \Psi) S(x, \Psi \leftrightarrow y, \Theta) \cos(N_x, \Psi) d\omega_\Psi dA_x. \quad (8.12)$$

The function $S(x, \Psi \leftrightarrow y, \Theta)$ is called the *bidirectional surface scattering reflectance distribution function* (BSSRDF, units $[1/m^2 sr]$). It depends on

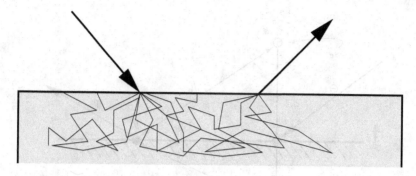

Figure 8.10. Subsurface scattering. Photons entering a translucent material will undergo a potentially very large number of scattering events before they reappear at a different location on the surface.

two surface positions rather than one, but other than that it plays exactly the same role, and has a similar meaning as the BRDF.

Practical models for the BSSRDF have been proposed by Hanrahan et al. [63] and Jensen et al. [80]. The former model is based on an analytic solution of the rendering equation (Equation 8.9) in a planar slab of a homogeneous medium, taking into account only single scattering. The latter model is based on an approximate analytic solution of the diffusion equation (Equation 8.11) in an infinitely thick planar slab filled with a homogeneous medium. It looks like this:

$$S(x, \Theta \leftrightarrow y, \Psi) = \frac{1}{\pi} F_t(\eta, \Theta) R_d(x, y) F_t(\eta, \Psi) \qquad (8.13)$$

$$R_d(x, y) = \frac{\alpha'}{4\pi} \left[z_r(1 + \sigma_{tr}d_r) \frac{e^{-\sigma_{tr}d_r}}{d_r^3} + z_v(1 + \sigma_{tr}d_v) \frac{e^{-\sigma_{tr}d_v}}{d_v^3} \right].$$

$F_t(\eta, \Theta)$ and $F_t(\eta, \Psi)$ denote the Fresnel transmittance for incident/outgoing directions Θ at x and ψ at y (see Section 2.8). The parameters η (relative index of refraction), $\alpha' = \sigma_s'/\sigma_t'$, and $\sigma_{tr} = \sqrt{3\sigma_a\sigma_t'}$ are material properties (σ_s', σ_t', and σ_{tr} were introduced in Section 8.1.10). z_r and z_v are the distance a pair of imaginary point sources are placed above and below x (see Figure 8.11). d_r and d_v are the distance between y and these source points. z_r and z_v are to be calculated from the material parameters [80]. Jensen et al. also proposed practical methods for determining the material constants σ_a and σ_s', and they give values for several interesting materials like marble and human skin [80, 76].

Several algorithms have been proposed for rendering images with this BSSRDF model. In path-tracing and similar algorithms, computing direct

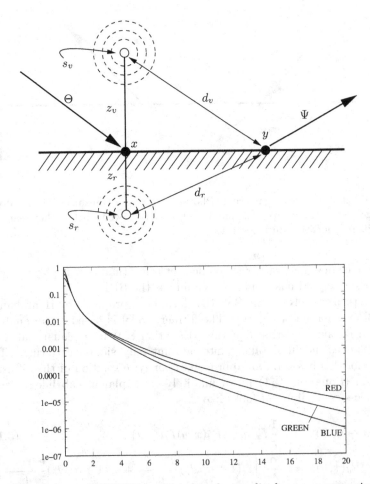

Figure 8.11. Jensen BSSRDF model is based on a dipole source approximation: A pair of imaginary point sources s_r and s_v are placed one above and one below the surface point x. The distance z_r and z_v at which these sources are placed with regard to x are calculated from the reduced scattering coefficient σ_s' and the absorption coefficient σ_a of the medium inside the object (see [80]). The BSSRDF model further depends on the distance d_r and d_v between a surface point y and these point sources.

The graphs at the bottom show the diffuse reflectance due to subsurface scattering R_d for a measured sample of marble using parameters from [80]. $R_d(r)$ indicates the radiosity at a distance r [mm] in a plane, due to unit incident power at the origin. The graphs illustrate that subsurface scattering is significant up to a distance of several millimeters in marble. The graphs also explain the strong color filtering effects observed at larger distances. The right image in Figure 8.9 was computed using this model.

illumination at a point x on a translucent object takes tracing a shadow ray at a randomly sampled other location y on the object surface, rather than at x [80]. The factor $R_d(x, y) = R_d(r)$ in Equation 8.13 at the heart of Jensen's model depends only on the distance r between points x and y. $R_d(r)$ can be used as a PDF for sampling a distance r. The point y is then chosen on the object surface, at this distance r from x. The right image in Figure 8.9 was rendered in this way.

The extension to full global illumination with algorithms such as photon mapping has been proposed in [76]. In [109], a radiosity-like approach can be found, which allows us to interactively change viewing and lighting conditions after some preprocessing.

8.1.12 Polarization, Interference, Diffraction, Fluorescence, Phosphorescence and Nonconstant Media

So far in this chapter, we have discussed how to extend the rendering equation in order to deal with participating media and nonlocal light reflection. Here, we cover how some more approximations made in Chapter 2 can be overcome.

Nonconstant Media: Mirages and Twinkling Stars and Such

The assumption that light travels along straight lines is not always true. Gradual changes in the index of refraction of the medium cause light rays to bend. Temperature changes in the earth's atmosphere, for instance, affect the index of refraction and cause midair reflections such as mirages. Another example is the twinkling of stars in a clear, but turbulent, night sky. Several efficient techniques to trace rays in such nonconstant media can be found in [184].

Fluorescence and Phosphorescence: Reflection at a Different Wavelength and a Different Time

We assumed that reflected light has the same wavelength as incident light and that scattering is instantaneous. This allows us to solve the rendering equation independently and in parallel for different wavelengths, and at different time instances.

Some materials, however, absorb electromagnetic radiation to reradiate it at a different wavelength. For instance, ultraviolet or infrared radiation can be reradiated as visible light. If reradiation happens (almost) immediately, such materials are called *fluorescent* materials. Examples of fluorescent objects include fluorescent light bulbs, Post-It notes, and certain detergents that "wash whiter than white."

Other materials reradiate only at a significantly later time. Such materials are called *phosphorescent* materials. Phosphorescent materials sometimes store light energy for hours. Some examples are the dials of certain wrist watches and small figures, such as decorations for children's bedrooms, that reradiate at night the illumination captured during the day.

Fluorescence and phosphorescence can be dealt with by extending the BRDF to a matrix, describing cross-over between different wavelengths in scattering. Delay effects in phosphorescence can be modeled adequately by extending the notion of self-emitted radiation, keeping track of incident illumination in the past [53, 226].

Interference: Soap Bubbles and Such

When two waves of the same frequency meet at some place, they will cancel or amplify each other depending on their phase difference. This effect is called interference and can be observed, for instance, in water surface waves in a (not too crowded) swimming pool. Electromagnetic radiation, and thus light, also has wave properties (see Section 2.1) and may suffer from interference. Interference of radio waves, for instance, due to two radio stations broadcasting at the same shortwave frequency, is very well known to radio amateurs and causes an effect sometimes called the *Mexican dog*. Interference of light waves can be observed in reflections at transparent thin films, and causes a colorful effect called *Newton rings*. This happens, for instance, in soap bubbles or gas spills on the road.

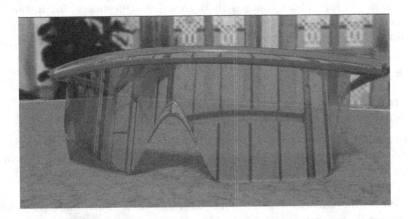

Figure 8.12. Interference of light at a transparent thin film coating causes colorful reflections on these sunglasses. The BRDF model used for rendering this image has been calculated using a wave-phase–aware ray tracer. (Image courtesy of Jay Gondek, Gary Meyer, and John Newman, University of Oregon.) (See Plate XIII.)

Interference is explained by addition of wave amplitudes, taking into account wave phase correctly. The transport theory of electromagnetic radiation, which leads to the rendering equation, is based on the addition of power, rather than amplitudes, and ignores phase effects. It is, however, possible to extend ray tracing to take phase effects into account. Gondek et al. [55] have used such a ray tracer as a virtual gonio-reflectometer to calculate BRDFs that are capable of reproducing interference effects (see Figure 8.12).

Diffraction: Compact Discs and Brushed Metals

Diffraction is the cause of other colorful light-scattering effects, such as at the surface of a compact disc or brushed metals. Diffraction can be viewed as interference of coherent secondary spherical waves originating at nearby locations. It is observed when light is scattered at surface features with size comparable to the wavelength of light (around 0.5 micrometers). The holes on a CD-ROM surface, for instance, are of this size. They are also regularly

Figure 8.13. The colorful reflections on this CD-ROM are caused by diffraction. Like other effects due to the wave nature of light, diffraction is not accounted for in the transport theory of light. Diffraction in reflections at certain rough surfaces can, however, be incorporated in a BRDF model. (Image courtesy of Jos Stam, Alias|Wavefront.) (See Plate XIV.)

spaced so that they form a so-called *diffraction grating*. Since diffraction is a wave effect as well, it is not accounted for in the transport theory of light. Diffraction observed in reflections at certain rough surfaces can be modeled by means of an appropriate BRDF [186]. Figure 8.13 shows an image rendered with such a diffraction shader.

Polarization

Polarization of light is an effect well known to outdoor photographers, who use polarization filters to make the sky appear more pure in their pictures. It can play an important role whenever multiple specular reflections and refractions occur at smooth surfaces. Examples are optical instruments, multifaceted crystal objects, and gemstones.

Polarization can be explained by considering electromagnetic radiation as a superposition of two transverse waves, which oscillate in directions perpendicular to each other and to the direction of propagation.

Often, there is no correlation between the phases of these waves, so that average properties are observed. Such light is called unpolarized or *natural light*. Most light sources emit natural light. Light usually becomes polarized due to scattering. The Fresnel equations (Section 2.8), for instance, demonstrate how the two components reflect and refract with different intensities at smooth surface boundaries. Rayleigh's phase function [22, Chapter 1] models how light scattered at air molecules gets polarized. Outdoor photographers take advantage of the latter.

In order to describe the polarization state of light completely, four parameters are needed. Often in optics literature, amplitude and phase correlation functions of the two component waves are used. In transport theory,

Figure 8.14. These images illustrate polarization of light reflected in the glass block on the left (Fresnel reflection). The same scene is shown, but with a different filter in front of the virtual camera: a horizontal polarization filter (left), vertical polarization filter (middle); and a 50% neutral gray (nonpolarizing) filter (right). (Image courtesy of A. Wilkie, Vienna University of Technology, Austria.) (See Plate XV.)

it is more convenient to use a different parametrization, due to Stokes (see, for instance, [75, Chapter 7] and [22, Chapter 1]).

From the point of view of a global illumination practitioner, the main issue is that polarized light is characterized by four radiance functions, rather than just one. Surface and volume scattering is described by a 4×4 matrix of BSDF or phase functions that model the cross-over between any of the four radiance components before and after scattering. Wilkie et al. [226] have implemented this in a stochastic ray tracer. Some of their renderings are reproduced in Figure 8.14.

8.2 Image Display and Human Perception

Most of the discussion in this book so far has focused on computing the correct radiometric values for each pixel in the final image. These values are measured in radiance, which expresses the amount of energy per surface area per solid angle that can be measured at a specific point in space and in a specific direction. However, these physically based radiance values do not adequately express how brightly the human eye perceives different illumination levels. The human visual system does not respond linearly to changing levels of illumination. By knowing how the human visual system reacts to light incident on the eye's receptors, aspects such as the display of images or the computation of the light transport distribution can be improved.

A global illumination solution for a typical scene might contain many different levels of illumination. The most typical example is a scene in which the sun is present. This very bright light source has a radiance level much higher than any other surface in the scene (except for perhaps other artificial, unnatural light sources that might be present). For some scenes, the ratio between the lowest and highest radiance levels could be as high as 10^5. Figure 8.16 shows a logarithmic plot of the environment map shown in Figure 8.15, and 5 orders of magnitude are present in this picture. The same scene rendered by daylight, artificial light, or lit by a night sky might also yield very different levels of illumination. Typical luminance levels vary from 10^{-3} candela per square meter for starlight to 10^5 candela per square meter for bright sunlight. It is therefore important to design procedures that can map these different intensity ranges on the desired output device, while preserving the perceived realism of the high intensity ratios present in the radiometrically accurate image.

As we all experience every day, the human eye can quickly adapt to such varied levels of illumination. For example, we might be in a dark room and see the features of the room, and at the same time see the brightly lit scene outdoors when looking through the window. Car drivers can adapt quickly from darkness to sunlight when exiting a tunnel or vice versa. This process is known as visual adaptation. Different mechanism are responsible for the visual adaption of the human eye:

- Receptor types. There are two types of receptors in the human retina, named after their respective shapes: cones and rods. The cone receptors are mostly sensitive to color and bright illumination; the rods are sensitive to vision in the lower illumination ranges. By having two types of receptors being sensitive to different illumination conditions, the human visual system is able to adapt between various levels of illumination.

- Photopigment bleaching. When a receptor reacts to incident light, bright light might make the receptor less sensitive. However, this loss of sensitivity is restored after a short period of time, when the receptor has adapted to the new illumination level.

- Neural mechanisms. Most visual neurons respond linearly within only a very narrow band of the entire range of incoming illumination.

Visual adaptation is also highly dependent on the background illumination intensity. When exposed to a high background illumination, the photoreceptors become saturated and lose their sensitivity to any further increments of the intensity. However, after some time, the response gradually returns to its former levels, and the sensitivity returns to its previous levels. As such, the level of background illumination, or the adaptation luminance, is an important factor in defining the state of the visual adaption.

All these factors have been acquired by experimental data. There is a large amount of psychophysical data available, quantifying the performance of the human visual system under different conditions.

8.2.1 Tone Mapping

Tone-mapping operators solve the problem of how to display a high dynamic range picture on a display device that has a much lower range of available displayable intensities. For example, a typical monitor can display only luminance values from 0.1 up to 200 cd/m^2. Depending on the type of monitor, the dynamic range (the ratio between the highest and lowest possible emitted intensities) can be 1 : 1000 to 1 : 2000; although with the introduction of new high-dynamic range display technology, this ratio is steadily growing. Mapping the vast range of luminance values that can be present in high dynamic range images to this very limited display range therefore has to be carried out accurately in order to maintain the perceptual characteristics of the image, such that a human observer receives the same visual stimuli when looking at the original image or at the displayed image.

A very simple solution for displaying the different illumination ranges in the image is by linearly scaling the intensity range of the image into the intensity range of the display device. This is equivalent to setting the exposure of a camera by adjusting the aperture or shutter speed, and results in the image being shown as if it would have been photographed with these particular settings. This, however, is not a viable solution, since either bright areas will be visible and dark areas will be underexposed, or dark areas will be visible and the bright areas will be overexposed. Even if the dynamic range of the image falls within the limits of the display, two images that only differ in their illumination levels by a single scale factor will still map to the same display image due to the simple linear scaling. It is therefore possible that a virtual scene illuminated by bright sunlight will produce the same image on the display compared to the same scene illuminated by moonlight or starlight. Rather, effects such as differences in color perception and visual acuity, which change with various levels of illumination, should be maintained.

A tone-mapping operator has to work in a more optimal way than just a linear scaling, by exploiting the limitations of the human visual system in order to display a high dynamic range image. Generally, tone-mapping operators create a scale factor for each pixel in the image. This scale factor is based on the local adaptation luminance of the pixel, together with the high dynamic range value of the pixel. The result is typically an RGB value that can be displayed on the output device. Different tone-reproduction operators differ in how they compute this local adaptation luminance for each pixel. Usually, an average value is computed in a window around each pixel, but some algorithms translate these computations to the vertices present in the scene.

Different operators can be classified in various categories [74]:

- Tone-mapping operators can be global or local. A global operator uses the same mapping function for all pixels in an image, as opposed to a local operator, where the mapping function can be different for each pixel or group of pixels in the image. Global operators are usually inexpensive to compute but do not always handle large dynamic range ratios very well. Local operators allow for better contrast reduction and therefore a better compression of the dynamic range, but they can introduce artifacts in the final image such as contrast reversal, resulting in halos near high contrast edges.

- A second distinction can be made between empirical and perceptually based operators. Empirical operators try to strive for effects such as detail preservation, avoidance of artifacts, or compression of the dynamic range. Perceptually based operators try to generate images that look perceptually the same as the real scene when observed by the human visual system. These operators take into account effects such as the loss of visual acuity or color sensitivity under different illumination levels.

- A last distinction can be made between static or dynamic operators, depending on whether one wants to map still images only or a video sequence of moving images. Time-coherency obviously is an important part of a dynamic operator. Effects such as sudden changes from dim to bright environments (the classic example being a car driver entering or leaving a tunnel) can be modeled with these dynamic operators.

Commonly used tone-mapping operators include the following:

- The Tumblin-Rushmeier tone-mapping operator [199] was the first to be used in computer graphics. This operator preserves the perceived brightness in the scene by trying to match the *perceived* brightness of a certain area in the image to the brightness of the same area on the output display. It behaves well when brightness changes are large and well above the threshold at which differences in brightness can be perceived.

- The tone-mapping operator developed by Ward [222] preserves threshold visibility and contrast, rather than brightness, as is the case in the Tumblin-Rushmeier operator. This technique preserves the visibility at the threshold of perception (see also the TVI function below). A similar operator was developed by Ferwerda et al. [47] that also preserves contrast and threshold visibility but at the same time tries to reproduce the perceived changes in colors and visual acuity under different illumination conditions.

- Ward [51] also has developed a histogram-based technique that works by redistributing local adaptation values such that a monotonic mapping utilizing the whole range of display luminance is achieved. This technique is somewhat different from previous approaches, in that the adaptation luminance is not directly used to compute a scale factor.

Rather, all adaptation and luminance values are used to construct a mapping function from scene luminance to display luminance values.

- Several time-dependent tone operators [141] that take into account the time-dependency of the visual adaptation have also been developed, such that effects such as experiencing a bright flash when walking from a dark room into the bright sunlight can be simulated. These operators explicitly model the process of bleaching, which is mainly responsible for these changing effects due to the time-dependency of the visual adaptation level.

Figure 8.15 shows the result of applying some tone-mapping operators on a high dynamic range picture of an environment reflected in a sphere, of which the actual luminance values are plotted in Figure 8.16. Figure 8.15(a) shows the resulting image when the original high dynamic range picture is scaled linearly to fit into the luminance range of the display device. Fig-

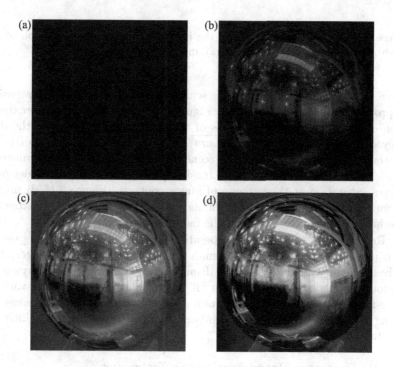

Figure 8.15. Various tone-mapping operators. (a) Linear scaling; (b) gamma scaling; (c) simple model of lightness sensitivity; (d) complex model for the human visual system. (See Plate XVI.)

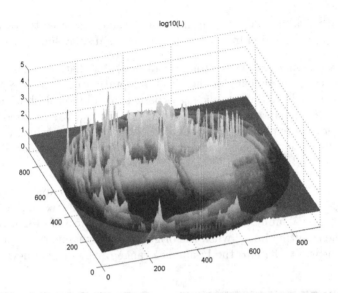

Figure 8.16. Luminance values for the high dynamic range photograph of an environment reflected in a scene shown in Figure 8.15.

ure 8.15(b) applies a simple gamma scaling, in which the displayed intensity is proportional to $Luminance^{1/\gamma}$. Figure 8.15(c) uses a simple approximation of the sensitivity to lightness of the human eye, by making the displayed values proportional to $\sqrt[3]{Lum/Lum_{ref}}$, with Lum_{ref} proportional to the average luminance in the scene, such that the average luminance would be displayed at half the intensity of the display. This model preserves saturation at the expense of image contrast. Figure 8.15(d) uses a more complicated model of the human visual system (Ward's histogram method), incorporating some of the factors described above.

Research into tone-mapping operators is still continuing, making use of new understanding of how the human visual system perceives images, and driven by the availability of new display technology. A good overview of various operators can be found in [37]. In [108], an evaluation of various tone-mapping operators using a high dynamic range display is presented, using user studies to determine what operators operate best under different conditions.

8.2.2 Perception-Based Acceleration Techniques

Knowledge of the human visual system cannot only be used to design tone-mapping operators but can also help to accelerate the global illumination

computations themselves. As an example, consider that the ability to detect changes in illumination drops with increasing spatial frequency and
speed of movement. Thus, if these factors are known, it is possible to
compute a margin within which errors in the computed illumination values
can be tolerated without producing a noticeable effect in the final images.
From a physical point of view, these are errors tolerated in the radiometric
values, but from a perception point of view, the human visual system will
not be able to detect them. Thus, the improvements in speed originate in
calculating only what the human visual system will be able to see.

Several acceleration algorithms have been proposed in literature, each
trying to take advantage of a specific aspect, or combination of aspects, of
the human visual system. The main limitations of human vision can be
characterized by several functions, which are described below.

- **Threshold versus intensity function (TVI).** The threshold versus intensity function describes the sensitivity of the human visual system with
  regard to changes in illumination. Given a certain level of background
  illumination, the TVI value describes the smallest change in illumination that can still be detected by the human eye. The brighter
  the background illumination, the less sensitive the eye becomes to
  intensity differences.

- **Contrast sensitivity function (CSF).** The TVI function is a good predictor for the sensitivity of uniform illumination fields. However, in most
  situations, the luminance distribution is not uniform but is changing
  spatially within the visual field of view. The contrast sensitivity
  function describes the sensitivity of the human eye versus the spatial
  frequency of the illumination. The contrast sensitivity is highest for
  values around 5 cycles per degree within the visual field of view and
  decreases when the spatial frequency increases or decreases.

- **Other mechanisms.** There are other mechanisms that describe the
  workings of the human visual system, such as contrast masking,
  spatio-temporal contrast sensitivity, chromatic contrast sensitivity,
  visual acuity, etc. For a more complete overview, we refer to the
  appropriate literature. [47] provides a good understanding of these
  various mechanisms.

Visual Difference Predictor

In order to design perceptually based acceleration techniques, it is necessary to be able to compare two images and predict how differently a human

observer will experience them. The best-known visual difference predictor is the one proposed by Daly [35]. Given the two images that have to be compared, various computations are carried out that result in a measure of how differently the images will be perceived. These computations take into account the TVI sensitivity, the CSF, and various masking and psychometric functions. The result is an image map that predicts local visible differences between the two images.

Maximum Likelihood Difference Scaling

A different methodology of comparing images is based on perceptual tests by observers to obtain a quality scale for a number of stimuli. The maximum likelihood difference scaling method (MLDS) presented in [117] can be used for such measurements.

When one wants to rank images on a quality scale (e.g., these could be images with various levels of accuracy for computed illumination effects such as shadows), each observer will be presented with all possible combinations of 2 pairs of images. The observer then has to indicate which pair has the largest perceived difference according to the criterion requested. This method has several advantages over previous approaches, which required the observer to sort or make pairwise comparisons between the stimuli themselves [135]. This class of methods, introduced by [114], relies on the fact that observers behave stochastically in their choices between stimuli; thus it follows that the stimuli may only differ by a few just noticeable differences. By using the perceived distance between two images itself as stimulus, this restriction is overcome, and a larger perceptual range can be studied.

Typically, two pairs of images are presented simultaneously on a monitor in a slightly darkened environment. The observers might be unaware of the goal of the tests, and all should receive the same instructions. From the resulting measurements, it is possible to compute a ranking and hence a quality scale of images. Each image will be ranked, and a quality increase or decrease can be computed. Such rankings can then be used to design rendering algorithms.

Perceptually Based Global Illumination Algorithms

Various approaches for translating the limitations of the human visual system into workable global illumination algorithms have been described in literature. Most of the work has been focused on two different goals:

- **Stopping criteria.** Most global illumination algorithms compute the radiance visible through a pixel by sampling the area of the pixel using a proper filter. Each sample typically spawns a random walk in the scene. Monte Carlo integration tells us that the higher the number of samples, the lower the variance, and hence less stochastic noise will be visible in the image. In practice, the number of samples is usually set "high enough" to avoid any noise, but it would be better to have the algorithm decide how much samples are enough. Perceptual metric offer criteria to decide, depending on the context of the pixel, when one can stop drawing additional samples without noticeably affecting the final image.

- Allocating resources. A second use of perceptual metrics in rendering algorithms can be introduced at a different level. A full global illumination algorithm usually employs different, often independent, strategies for computing various components of the light transport, e.g., the number of shadow rays used when computing direct illumination; or the number of indirect illumination rays are often chosen independently from each other. One can expect that in an optimal global illumination algorithm, the allocation of number of samples for each rendering component can be chosen dependent on the perceptual importance this specific lighting component has in the final image.

The first global illumination algorithms that were using perceptual error metrics were proposed by Myszkowski [122] and Bolin and Meyer [115]. These algorithms make use of TVI sensitivity, contrast sensitivity, and contrast masking. Myszkowksi employs the Daly visual difference predictor to accelerate two different algorithms: a stochastic ray tracer and a hierarchical radiosity algorithm. Both types of algorithms compute different iterations of the light transport in the scene in order to produce the final image. After each iteration, the computed image so far is compared with the image of a previous iteration. If the visual difference predictor indicates no visual differences, those areas of the image are considered to have converged, and no further work is necessary.

The approach followed by Bolin and Meyer also accelerated a stochastic ray tracer. Again, after each iteration (in which a number of samples are distributed over the pixels), a visual difference predictor produces a map that indicates at which location of the image more radiance samples are needed in order to reduce the visual difference as much as possible during the next iteration. Thus, the algorithm steers the sampling function in the image plane. The disadvantage of both these algorithms is that they require very frequent evaluations of their respective visual difference predictors and thus are very expensive, almost up to the point that the achieved perceptual acceleration was lost.

A very promising approach has been proposed by Ramasubramanian et al. [116] to solve this problem of having to carry out very expensive visual difference predictor evaluations during the global illumination computations. Instead of evaluating a visual difference predictor after various iterations during the algorithm and comparing images so far, a physically based radiometric error metric is constructed. This error metric is used only during the radiometric light transport simulation. There is no longer a conversion necessary to the perceptual domain by means of a visual difference predictor. The algorithm computes for a given intermediate image during the light transport simulation a *threshold map*, which indicates for each pixel what difference in radiance values will not be detectable by a human viewer. This error metric is based on the TVI function, the contrast sensitivity, and spatial masking. After each iteration, only the components that are cheap to evaluate are recomputed, in order to achieve a new threshold map. The expensive spatial-frequency effects are only computed at the start of the algorithm, by using sensible guesses of the overall ambient lighting, and by using information of the texture maps present in the scene. If the radiometric differences between the last two iterations fall within the limits of the current threshold map, the iterative light transport algorithm is stopped.

Some work has also been done in the context of moving images. An *Animation Quality Metric* is developed by Myszkowski in [84], in which it is assumed that the eye follows all moving objects in the scene, and thus the moving scene can be reduced to a static scene. Yee et al. [227] explicitly use temporal information. Spatiotemporal contrast sensitivity and approximations of movements and visual attention result in a saliency map. This map is computed only once and is used as an oracle to guide the image computations for each frame, avoiding the use of a very expensive visual difference predictor several times during each frame of the animation.

A perceptually driven decision theory for interactive realistic rendering is described by Dumont et al. [40]. Different rendering operations are ordered according to their perceptual importance, thereby producing images of high quality within the system constraints. The system uses map-based methods in graphics hardware to simulate global illumination effects and is capable of producing interactive walk-throughs of scenes with complex geometry, lighting, and material properties.

A new approach to high-quality global illumination rendering using perceptual metrics was introduced by Stokes et al. [187]. The global illumination for a scene is split into direct and indirect components, also based on the type of surface interaction (diffuse or glossy). For each of these components, a perceptual importance is determined, such that computation time can be allocated optimally for the different illumination components. The goal is to achieve interactive rendering and produce an image of maximum quality within a given time frame. In order to determine the perceptual importance of each illumination component, tests similar to the maximum likelihood difference scaling are carried out. A hypothetical perceptual component renderer is also presented, in which the user can allocate the resources according to the application and desired quality of the image.

In the future, we can expect to see more clever uses of perceptual criteria in rendering algorithms, not only to compute images of high quality faster, but also to render images that might not necessarily contain all possible illumination effects. For example, very soft shadows are not always necessary to correctly perceive the realism of a scene, yet they might require large computational efforts to be computed correctly. In such cases, a rendering algorithm could insert a rough approximation for this shadow, without a human observer noticing that something "is missing." Such rendering algorithms, which take a step in the direction of rendering only those features of *what-the-brain-can-see*, instead of rendering *what-the-eye-can-see*, will definitely be investigated more rigourously in the future. The works of Sattler et al. [156] for shadow generation, Ferwerda et al. [48] for shape perception, or Rademacher et al. [150] for the influence of scene complexity on perceived realism have taken initial steps in this direction.

8.3 Fast Global Illumination

Ray tracing is a flexible, powerful paradigm to produce high-quality images. However, in the past, its performance has typically been too slow for interactive applications as compared to hardware rendering. With recent growth in processor speeds and advances in programmable graphics processors, there has been increasing interest in using ray tracing for interactive applications.

There are two types of recent approaches to accelerating ray tracing: sparse sampling and reconstruction, and fast ray-tracing systems. The first approach bridges the performance gap between processors and rendering speed by sparsely sampling shading values and reusing these shading values to reconstruct images at interactive rates when possible. These systems exploit spatial coherence (in an image) and temporal coherence (from frame to frame) to reduce the number of rays that must be traced to produce an image. The fast ray-tracing systems use highly optimized ray tracers to decrease the cost of tracing any given ray. These systems are often termed *brute-force*, because their focus is on tracing all rays that are needed as fast as possible. We describe recent research in both these approaches below. (See Figure 8.17 for results.)

(a) Render Cache [Walter, Drettakis, Parker]

(d) Utah's interactive ray tracing [Martin et al.]

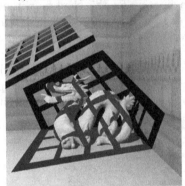

(b) Edges and Points [Bala, Walter, Greenberg]

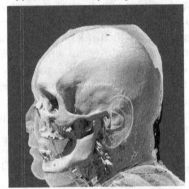

(e) Utah's rt for visualization [Parker et al.]

(c) 4D Radiance Interpolants [Bala, Dorsey, Teller]

(f) Coherent Ray Tracing [Wald, Slusallek]

Figure 8.17. Images from interactive rendering systems. On the left are systems that use sparse sampling and interpolation: (a) render cache, (b) edges and points, and (c) 4D radiance interpolants. On the right are very fast ray tracers: (d) Utah's interactive ray tracing, (e) Utah's visualization of the visible female dataset, and (f) coherent ray tracing. (See Plate XVIII.)

8.3.1 Sparse Sampling: Exploiting Coherence

Sparse sampling approaches try to decrease the huge gap in processor performance and rendering speeds by exploiting spatial and temporal coherence. These techniques sparsely sample shading values and cache these values. Images are then generated at interactive rates by interpolating these cached values when possible. Because they sparsely sample shading, and sometimes even visibility, they can substantially decrease the number of rays that must be traced per frame.

We briefly review several of these approaches. One major feature that differentiates between these approaches is how they cache and reuse samples. We categorize these algorithms as being image space, world space, or line space approaches based on how sampling and reconstruction is done.

Image Space

The render cache [211, 212] is an image-space algorithm that bridges the performance gap between processor performance and rendering speed by decoupling the display of images from the computation of shading. The display process runs synchronously and receives shading updates from a shading process that runs asynchronously. A fixed-size cache, the render cache, of shading samples (represented as three-dimensional points with color and position) is updated with the values returned by the shading process. As the user walks through a scene, the samples in the render cache are reprojected from frame to frame to the new viewpoint (similar to image-based reprojection techniques [16]). The algorithm uses heuristics to deal with disocclusions and other artifacts that arise from reprojection. The image at the new viewpoint is then reconstructed by interpolating samples in a 3×3 neighborhood of pixels. This interpolation filter smooths out artifacts and eliminates holes that might arise due to the inadequate availability of samples. A priority map is also computed at each frame to determine where new samples are needed. Aging samples are replaced by new samples.

The render cache produces images at interactive rates while sampling only a fraction of the pixels each frame. By decoupling the shader from the display process, the performance of the render cache depends on reprojection and interpolation and is essentially independent of the speed of the shader. This means the render cache can be used for interactive rendering with a slow (high-quality) renderer such as a path tracer. One disadvantage of the render cache is that the images could have visually objectionable artifacts because interpolation could blur sharp features in the image or reprojection could compute incorrect view-dependent effects.

The edge-and-point rendering system [9] addresses the problem of poor image quality in a sparse sampling and reconstruction algorithm by combining analytically computed discontinuities and sparse samples to reconstruct high-quality images at interactive rates. This approach introduces an efficient representation, called the edge and point image, to combine perceptually important discontinuities (edges), such as silhouettes and shadows, with sparse shading samples (points). The invariant maintained is that shading samples are never interpolated if they are separated by an edge. A render-cache–based approach is used to cache, reproject, and interpolate shading values while satisfying this edge-respecting invariant. The availability of discontinuity information further permits fast antialiasing. The edge-and-point renderer is able to produce high-quality, antialiased images at interactive rates using very low sampling densities at each frame. The edge-and-point image and the image filtering operations are well-matched for GPU acceleration [205], thus achieving greater performance.

World Space

The following techniques cache shading samples in object or world space and use the ubiquitous rasterization hardware to interpolate shading values to compute images in real time.

Tapestry [176] computes a three-dimensional world-space mesh of samples, where the samples are computed using a slow, high-quality renderer [107]. A Delaunay condition is maintained on the projection of the mesh relative to a viewpoint for robustness and image quality. A priority image is used to determine where more sampling is required. As the viewpoint changes, the mesh is updated with new samples while maintaining the Delaunay condition.

Tole et al. [198] introduce the shading cache, an object-space hierarchical subdivision mesh where shading at vertices is also computed lazily. The mesh is progressively refined with shading values that, like the render cache and Tapestry, can be computed by a slow, high-quality, asynchronous shading process. The mesh is refined either to improve image quality or to handle dynamic objects. A priority image with flood filling is used to ensure that patches that require refining are given higher priority to be updated. A perceptual metric is used to age samples to account for view-dependent changes. This approach renders images in real time even with extremely slow asynchronous shaders (path tracers) and dynamic scenes.

Both these approaches use the graphics hardware to rasterize their meshes and interpolate the mesh samples to compute new images. In both techniques, visual artifacts arise while samples are accumulated and added to the meshes. However, these artifacts typically disappear as the meshes get progressively refined.

Line Space

Radiance is a function over the space of rays; this space is a five-dimensional space. However, in the absence of participating media and occluding objects, radiance does not vary along a ray. Thus, in free space, each radiance sample can be represented using four parameters; this space is called line space [57, 110]. We now discuss algorithms that cache samples in four-dimensional line space.

The radiance interpolants system [10, 8, 196] computes radiance samples lazily and caches these samples in four-dimensional line trees. Each leaf of the tree stores a *radiance interpolant*, a set of 16 radiance samples that can be interpolated to reconstruct radiance for any ray that lies in that leaf of the tree. One important contribution of this approach is the use of sophisticated interval-based techniques to bound the error that could arise by using interpolation to approximate shading. As the user walks around the scene, for each pixel in an image, the system uses a valid interpolant (if available) from the visible object's line tree to approximate the pixel's radiance. If no interpolant is available, the pixel is rendered using the ray tracer. This system achieves an order of magnitude speed-up in walk-throughs and successfully interpolates radiance for most pixels in each frame. The use of ray segment trees [7] (described below) further extends the radiance interpolant system to support dynamic scenes. While the error guarantees ensure that pixels are never incorrectly interpolated, since pixels are ray traced when a valid interpolant is not available, this system could be noninteractive for complex scenes.

The Holodeck [218] also caches samples in four-dimensional line space. These beams are stored on disk and recovered as needed to reconstruct images. Different reconstruction techniques are used based on Voronoi diagrams and Tapestry-like Delaunay triangulation of the samples.

8.3.2 Dynamic Scenes

One major challenge with caching shading values is dealing with dynamic scenes. When objects or lights move in a scene, the cached shading values could become invalid and must be updated accordingly. There are two reasons this update should be done incrementally. First, all these algorithms, to varying extents, assume the cached values accumulate over time. Recomputing all cached values from scratch would be too slow for interactive use. The second reason is that in typical interactive applications, the effect of an update (for example, an object being moved) can be quite localized.[2] In such cases, updating all cached points unnecessarily is inefficient.

---

[2]There are cases when this localized effect is not true, for example, when a light is moved.

Some of the interactive rendering techniques, for example, the render cache and shading cache, age samples and eliminate outdated samples to ensure that all samples are recomputed from time to time. This ensures that images will eventually be correct once the moved objects are stationary for some number of frames. However, since these approaches do not explicitly find the effect of a scene change (for example, a moving shadow) and invalidate samples, they do not directly handle fully dynamic scenes.

Many techniques have been proposed to address this problem of invalidating samples in dynamic scenes. We briefly describe a few of them.

Drettakis and Sillion [39] introduce a four-dimensional line space hierarchy in the context of hierarchical radiosity to support dynamic scenes. When an object moves, this hierarchy of four-dimensional shafts is traversed at interactive rates to find the radiosity links that are affected by the object move.

Bala et al. [7] introduce a five-dimensional ray space hierarchy for updating radiance interpolants [8] in a ray-tracing context. A five-dimensional tree, called the ray segment tree, is used to rapidly find and invalidate all bundles of rays that are affected by an object movement. Their system starts to address updates in ray-traced applications but does not deal with full global illumination solutions. Selective photon tracing [38] uses the periodicity properties of quasi–Monte Carlo sampling sequences to rapidly identify and update the photons that are affected by changes in a scene. They progressively refine the global illumination solution to compute images in dynamic scenes.

All these techniques try to address the important problem of efficiently updating cached shading values in dynamic scenes. These approaches must satisfy two conflicting goals: correctness and efficiency. On the one hand, they must find all shading values that are affected by a change in the scene. On the other hand, they should avoid unnecessarily invalidating samples that remain accurate in spite of the change to the scene. While these approaches are promising, this is still an open area of research.

8.3.3 Fast Ray Tracing

The availability of increasingly fast processors and programmable GPUs is fueling research in systems for interactive ray tracing. These systems explore ray tracing as an alternative to hardware rendering because of ray tracing's asymptotically superior performance in rendering complex scenes. When a ray tracer is supported by an acceleration structure (for example, octrees, kd-trees, or hierarchical bounding volumes), the cost of determining visibility for a single ray is typically logarithmic in scene complexity. In contrast, hardware, z-buffer algorithms render the entire scene each frame, achieving linear performance.[3]   Furthermore, ray tracers are extremely flexible and can support with full generality high-quality rendering effects. Thus, ray tracers are being considered as plausible alternatives for rendering complex scenes.

Parker et al. [137] implemented a highly optimized, parallel ray tracer to demonstrate the efficacy of ray tracing in interactive applications for complex scenes. They carefully tuned a shared-memory ray tracer on a 64-processor SGI Origin 2000 and exploited the fast synchronization capabilities and interconnect of the SGI Origin to achieve interactive performance. Load balancing was used to achieve linear speed-ups on the Origin. Their ray tracer was demonstrated rendering large scenes and visualizing extremely large data sets for scientific visualization, such as the visible female data set and crack propagation data sets.

Wald et al. [207, 208] have implemented interactive ray tracing in a cluster of PCs while paying careful attention to the performance of memory caches. Ray tracers, which traditionally do a depth-first traversal of rays, have poor memory access patterns. Their ray tracer exploits coherence by restructuring the order in which rays are traced to be a partial breadth-first evaluation.[4] They avoid data replication over multiple processors by caching scene geometry on processors when needed. These performance optimizations give an order of magnitude speed-up and permit them to ray trace extremely large scenes at interactive rates. Subsequently, Reshetov et al. [152] introduce optimizations such as hierarchical beam tracing, to accelerate ray tracing performance in their multi level ray tracer.

8.3.4 Graphics Hardware and Precomputed Radiance Transfer

Modern graphics processing units (GPUs) are programmable parallel processors that provide flexibility by supporting vertex and pixel programmability. Apart from exploiting parallelism, GPUs also derive their power from their support for texturing, which requires very high memory bandwidth. In fact, the power and flexibility of GPUs has resulted in interest in GPUs as general computing systems. A branch of research called GPGPUs, for *general purpose GPUs*, treats GPUs as general stream processors and develops techniques to map general-purpose algorithms, for example, for sorting and linear algebra, on the GPU. On the graphics side, there has been increased interest in using the graphics hardware to integrate richer shading models and global illumination effects in rendered images.

---

[3]If hardware rendering is supported by sophisticated hierarchical data structures, its performance is logarithmic. However, these data structures require significant support from the application.

[4]In a noninteractive setting, Pharr et al. [146] also use restructuring of ray traversals to optimize memory access.

A description of these approaches is beyond the scope of this book, and the interested reader is referred to the books *Real-Time Rendering* [120] and *Real-Time Shading* [134] and the GPU Gems books [46, 144].

One deterrent to the practical application of global illumination in interactive applications is the significant time required to compute a full global illumination solution. While the advent of GPUs has decreased the cost of local pixel shading, the cost of determining visibility between two arbitrary points remains expensive. This is because this computation requires nonlocal access of data that is not cheap in the GPU model. Here, we discuss a few approaches that precompute visibility to achieve interactive rendering of high-quality illumination.

8.3.5 Ambient Occlusion

Ambient occlusion is a popular technique to "simulate" global effects in interactive applications. This approach precomputes and approximates the visibility between a point and the incoming hemisphere so that shading can be computed on the fly using this precomputed visibility term. While this technique is not accurate, it is fast and adds realism at a relatively low price. Ambient occlusion assumes rigid geometry and diffuse materials, though recent work attempts to relax the assumption of rigid geometry [20].

Ambient occlusion precomputes the visibility of the hemisphere at each point of the scene. This precomputation can be per-vertex or per-pixel, where the per-pixel information is encoded as textures. At each point (vertex or pixel), the algorithm samples the hemisphere to approximate visibility. This is where the assumption of view-independent diffuse materials comes into play. Using either uniform sampling or cosine-weighted sampling, the following integral is estimated as the ambient occlusion factor:

$$AO = \frac{1}{\pi} \int_{\Omega} V(\omega)(N \cdot \omega)d\omega. \tag{8.14}$$

This precomputation is quite expensive. In the early days of the technique, several hardware-based approaches were developed to decrease the cost of this hemisphere sampling. However, with the availability of powerful ray tracers, ray tracing using Monte Carlo sampling is now the most popular and robust approach to compute the ambient occlusion.

Once the ambient occlusion values are computed, they are then used to render each point as follows. The simplest use is to modulate ambient lighting, just as its name suggests. In this case the precomputed ambient occlusion term is multiplied with a constant ambient term to achieve greater realism in the ambient shading term.

Ambient occlusion is also used, less accurately, to modulate more complex lighting environments, such as prefiltered environment maps. This is done by computing an additional value in the precomputation, the *bent normal*. The bent normal is the average unoccluded normal; i.e., it is the average normal of all unoccluded samples over the hemisphere. This bent normal approximates the main direction of illumination and is used when rendering the point instead of the surface normal. There are clear cases where the bent normal is inaccurate, but this approximation produces reasonable values for applications, such as movies and games, where accuracy is of less importance.

A generalization of ambient occlusion that is principled and accurate is discussed next: precomputed radiance transfer.

8.3.6 Precomputed Radiance Transfer

Precomputed radiance transfer (PRT) is a family of techniques that supports complex illumination effects by precomputing light transport and computing shading on the fly using the precomputed transport. This ability to support interactive performance with expensive shading has had a big impact on both research and practical applications such as games. We briefly introduce PRT concepts in this section and refer the reader to the original papers for details.

PRT uses precomputation to support expensive illumination effects such as interreflections, caustics, and subsurface scattering. However, to achieve interactive performance, some restrictions are imposed. PRT algorithms typically assume that the scene is static, and that lighting of the scene is from light sources that are infinitely far away, i.e., environment maps. In this section, we describe the basic PRT framework for diffuse materials lit by environment maps. We then describe the generalization of PRT concepts to support non-diffuse materials.

Diffuse PRT

The original PRT paper [177] illuminates diffuse and glossy objects lit by infinitely far away environment maps. For simplicity, let us first only consider direct illumination. The direct illumination at a point x, denoted as L_0, is

$$L_0(x \rightarrow \Theta) \quad = \quad \int_{\Omega_x} L_{env}(x \leftarrow \Psi) f_r(x, \Theta \leftrightarrow \Psi) \cos(\Psi, N_x) d\omega_\Psi.$$

Since lighting is from a distant environment map, L_{env} does not depend on position and only depends on direction. We further restrict ourselves to diffuse surfaces for now; thus, the BRDF is a constant and can be moved out of the integral:

$$L_0(x) = \frac{\rho}{\pi} \int_{\Omega_x} L_{env}(\Psi) V(x, \Psi) \cos(\Psi, N_x) d\omega_\Psi.$$

The visibility V and cosine term are often combined together into a cosine-weighted visibility term.

The main insight of PRT is that this integral can be split into a precomputed transfer function that includes the effects of self-shadowing and interreflections, and a runtime computation that efficiently combines the transfer function with the dynamically changing environment map.

To achieve this goal, PRT projects the lighting onto a set of basis functions over the sphere. The original formulation used spherical harmonics (SH). Thus, $L_{env}(\Psi) = \sum_i l_i y_i(\Psi)$, where the y_i are the spherical harmonic basis functions and l_i are the lighting coefficients. Each l_i term is computed by projecting the environment map on the basis functions as follows: $l_i = \int L_{env}(\Psi) y_i(\Psi) d\omega_\Psi$. Ramamoorthi [151] demonstrated that nine basis functions suffice to represent the appearance of diffuse surfaces lit by typical environment maps. For high-frequency shadowing, a potentially large set of basis functions are required. Since PRT aims at supporting shadows from relatively large area lights, the original PRT system used 25 basis functions.

Substituting the SH lighting coefficients, we get:

$$L_0(x) = \frac{\rho}{\pi} \int_{\Omega_x} \sum_i l_i y_i(\Psi) V(x, \Psi) \cos(\Psi, N_x) d\omega_\Psi$$

$$= \frac{\rho}{\pi} \sum_i l_i \int_{\Omega_x} y_i(\Psi) V(x, \Psi) \cos(\Psi, N_x) d\omega_\Psi$$

$$= \sum_i l_i t_{x,i}^0,$$

$$t_{x,i}^0 = \frac{\rho}{\pi} \int_{\Omega_x} y_i(\Psi) V(x, \Psi) \cos(\Psi, N_x) d\omega_\Psi,$$

where the transfer function, represented as vector t, captures how an object casts shadows on itself (self-shadowing). The $t_{x,i}^0$ are evaluated using Monte Carlo sampling.

The same derivation can be generalized to handle multiple reflections. We derive the generalization for the first bounce of illumination; the other bounces can straighwardly be derived in a similar manner. We first simplify some of the notation: we denote the diffuse reflectivity at point x as ρ_x and point y as ρ_y, and the point $y = r(x, \Psi)$ is the surface visible from x in direction Ψ. The first-bounce radiance L_1 arriving at x through y is given as

$$L_1(x) = \int_{\Omega_x} \frac{\rho_x}{\pi} \cos(\Psi, N_x) L_0(y \to -\Psi) d\omega_\Psi$$

$$L_0(y \to -\Psi) = \int_{\Omega_y} \frac{\rho_y}{\pi} \cos(\Psi', N_y) L_{env}(\Psi') d\omega_{\Psi'}$$

$$= \sum_i l_i t_{y,i}^0$$

$$L_1(x) = \int_{\Omega_x} \frac{\rho_x}{\pi} \cos(\Psi, N_x) \sum_i l_i t_{y,i}^0 d\omega_\Psi$$

$$t_{x,i}^1 = \frac{\rho_x}{\pi} \int_{\Omega_x} t_{y,i}^0 \cos(\Psi, N_x) d\omega_\Psi.$$

This approach can be generalized to more bounces. The corresponding terms for all bounces are added together to compute the total transfer function for each spherical harmonic basis function for the point x: $t_{x,i} = \sum_b t_{x,i}^b$. In these equations, the reflectivity has been folded into the transfer function for all bounces, direct and indirect. However, in fact, the reflectivity is often separated out for the direct bounce to permit denser BRDF sampling for directly visible surfaces.

A frame is rendered as follows. The environment map is projected into the spherical harmonic basis functions taking into account the object's rotation with respect to the environment map. Rendering a vertex or

No shadows   With PRT

Figure 8.18. The Buddha model rendered with diffuse PRT using an environment map. Left: without shadows; right: with PRT. (Image courtesy Peter-Pike Sloan and John Snyder.) (See Plate XXIV.)

pixel x then involves computing the dot product of the two vectors: the environment map coefficient vector l and the transfer function vector t for the point x. This dot product is easily supported on the GPU achieving interactive performance. Figure 8.18 shows results using diffuse PRT.

The original PRT paper [177] introduced a powerful new technique for using precomputation to achieve interactive display of global illumination. Applications such as games for which interactive performance is crucial have adopted this basic approach. Some fairly major assumptions are made in the original formulation: static scenes, low-frequency environment maps, and diffuse and Phong-like materials. Subsequent research has tried to address these limitations. Kautz et al. [87] extends the SH transfer function vectors to handle arbitrary BRDFs; PCA clustering [178] further enables real-time performance.

All-Frequency PRT

High-frequency illumination effects, such as sharp shadows, cannot be represented with great fidelity using a small number of coefficients in the spherical harmonics basis functions. The next major set of innovations in PRT aim at supporting both all-frequency illumination effects and generalized BRDFs.

Ng et al. [129] introduce the use of wavelets for high-frequency illumination. Wavelet coefficients are selected on-the-fly to achieve a nonlinear approximation of high quality. This system demonstrates interactive performance for fixed viewing of nondiffuse scenes and arbitrary viewing of diffuse scenes. Figure 8.19 compares spherical harmonics with wavelets.

Liu et al. [113] and Wang et al. [215] approximate arbitrary, nondiffuse BRDFs by factoring them into components that are dependent on the viewing direction only and lighting direction only, respectively. Essentially, the 4D BRDF is split into two 2D functions that are separately approximated. Each separable function is represented using Haar wavelets, which are further clustered using PCA [113]. In this approach, the BRDF (and the cosine factor) are factored as: $f_r(x, \Theta \leftrightarrow \Psi) \cos(\Psi, N_x) = G(\Theta)F(\Psi)$, where G and F are vector functions that depend entirely on the view direction Θ and the light direction Ψ, respectively. The final shading result is then $G^T M_x L$, where M_x is the linear transfer matrix at x, and L is the vector of lighting coefficients. It should be noted that BRDF separability is an approximation to the original BRDF, and it might not be valid and accurate for all BRDFs. Figure 8.20 shows results using this approach.

The *triple product integral* [130] takes a general approach to all-frequency lighting for *direct illumination* with nondiffuse materials. Radiance at x, where the BRDF term includes the cosine term and any rotation of the

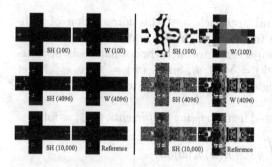

Figure 8.19. All-frequency effects. On the left, comparison of spherical harmonics (SH) and wavelets using nonlinear approximation (W) for the St. Peter's Basilica environment map. On right, the triple product integral solution for a scene. (Image courtesy Ren Ng and Ravi Ramamoorthi.) (See Plate XXIII.)

BRDF to align with the global coordinate frame, is:

$$L(x \to \Theta) = \int_{\Omega_x} L(x \leftarrow \Psi) f_r(x, \Theta \leftrightarrow \Psi) \cos(\Psi, N_x) d\omega_\Psi$$

$$= \int_{\Omega_x} L(\Psi) f(\Theta \leftrightarrow \Psi) V(x, \Psi) d\omega_\Psi.$$

Diffuse Buddha   Specular Buddha

Figure 8.20. Diffuse and glossy Buddha rendered using PRT with separable BRDFs for high-frequency illumination. (Image courtesy Peter-Pike Sloan and John Snyder.) (See Plate XXV.)

The triple product integral approach uses this formulation of radiance as the product of three functions: lighting, material, and visibility. Each of these functions is projected into an orthonormal basis of functions: $L_{env}(\Psi) = \sum_i l_i y_i$, $f(\Psi) = \sum_j f_j y_j$, and $V(\Psi) = \sum_k v_k y_k$. Ng et al. [130] developed efficient algorithms to use Haar wavelet basis functions for high-frequency effects.

The integral is then expressed using *tripling coefficients*, C_{ijk}, as follows:

$$C_{ijk} = \int y_i(\omega) y_j(\omega) y_k(\omega) d\omega.$$

The radiance at vertex or pixel x using the tripling coefficients is computed as

$$L = \sum_i \sum_j \sum_k C_{ijk} l_i f_j v_k.$$

Figure 8.19 shows a scene rendered using triple product integrals encoded in Haar wavelets. The scene includes high-frequency shadows, glossy materials, and dynamic lighting from environment maps.

Summary of PRT

PRT remains an active area of research with several approaches that seek to generalize its applicability to support dynamics and a wide range of materials and illumination. Most PRT techniques assume the geometry is static: zonal harmonics are used to support deformable geometry in [180]; Kautz et al. [88] use hemispherical rasterization to recompute visibility for self-shadowing of dynamic objects; and Zhou et al. [229] precompute shadow fields for dynamic shadows from low-frequency illuminants. Support for subsurface scattering [178, 216] and bi-scale rendering [179] expands the range of materials and effects supported. Illumination from environment maps does not capture local lighting effects: Hasan et al. [66] extend fixed-viewpoint PRT for cinematic relighting, which requires support for arbitrary direct lighting, including high-frequency lighting shaders, with indirect illumination; Annen et al. [3] introduce spherical harmonic gradients to capture midrange illumination.

9

Conclusion

9.1 Achievements of Photorealistic Rendering

Photorealistic rendering and global illumination algorithms have come a long way since the publication of the first recursive ray-tracing algorithm in 1979. There has been a gradual evolution from simple algorithms, some of them deemed to be hacks by today's standards, to very advanced, fully physically based rendering algorithms.

It is now possible, within a reasonable amount of time, to generate an image that is indistinguishable from a photograph of a real scene. This has been achieved by carefully researching the physical processes that form the basis of photorealistic rendering: light-material interaction, light transport, and the psychophysical aspects of the human visual system. In each of these domains, extensive research literature is available. In this book, we have tried to give an overview of some of these aspects, mostly focusing on the light transport mechanism. As in most modern algorithms, we strongly believe that a good understanding of all fundamental issues is the key to well-designed global illumination light transport algorithms.

Global illumination has not yet found its way to many mainstream applications, but some use has already been made in feature-animation films and to a limited extent in some computer games. High-quality rendering of architectural designs has become more common (although still unusual), and car manufacturers have become more aware of the possibilities of rendering cars in real virtual environments for glossy advertisements. Moreover, recent advances have indicated that full interactive ray tracing is already a possibility for specialist applications and machinery.

As such, photorealistic rendering has certainly propelled forward the development of high-quality visualization techniques.

9.2 Unresolved Issues in Photorealistic Rendering

Research in photorealistic rendering is still alive and well, with a large number of publications devoted to the topic every year. There are still a number of unresolved issues, which will undoubtedly form the topic of future research. We have tried to compile a few topics we think will become heavily researched in the near future:

Acquisition and modeling of BRDFs. There has been quite some effort to measure the BRDF of real materials and to design usable models for use in computer graphics, but this whole field still needs a lot of research to provide us with reliable, accurate, and cheap ways to evaluate BRDF models. Measuring devices such as gonio-reflectometers should be made adaptive, such that they can measure more samples in those areas of the BRDF where more accuracy is needed. Image-based acquisition techniques will be used much more often, driven by cheaper digital cameras.

Acquisition of geometry and surface appearance. Computer vision has developed several techniques for acquiring the geometry of real objects from camera images, but it is still a major problem when the surface of the object is nondiffuse or when the nature of the illumination on the object is unknown. Surface appearance, such as textures and local BRDFs, has recently been captured based on photographs as well. Combining these two fields in order to build an integrated scanner seems a very promising research area. Also, emphasis should be placed on in-hand scanning, where the user manipulates an object in front of a camera and all relevant characteristics are captured.

Self-adaptive light transport. The light transport simulation algorithms outlined in this book come in many different flavors and varieties. Some algorithms perform better in specific situations than others (e.g., radiosity-like algorithms behave better in pure diffuse environments, ray tracing works well in highly specular scenes, etc.) Little effort has been made so far to try to make an overall global illumination algorithm that behaves in an adaptive way in these various situations. Such an algorithm would pick the right mode of simulating the light transport, depending on the nature of the surfaces, the frequency of the geometry, the influence on the final image, etc. Also, partially computed illumination results should always be stored and available for future use by different light transport modes.

Scalable and robust rendering. Scenes that include very high complexity in illumination, materials, and geometry remain challenging. Better and cheaper acquisition technology is driving the demand for rendering such complex scenes in the future. Currently, a user has to manually pick approximations, rendering algorithms, and levels of detail to achieve reasonable quality and performance for such scenes. But this manual approach is clearly not desirable, particularly when we get to the realm of applications such as games where players interact with dynamically varying scenes while generating content on the fly. Robust algorithms that can scale to complex scenes and can automatically handle scene complexity without user intervention will be critical in the future.

Geometry-independent rendering. Current light transport algorithms assume that the geometry of the scene is known and explicitly compute a huge number of ray-object intersections in order to know where light gets reflected off surfaces. In the future, it is likely that primitives, whose geometry is not explicitly known, will be used in scenes to be rendered. Such primitives might be described by a light field, or another implicit description of how light interacts with the object (e.g., a series of photographs). Incorporating such objects in a global illumination algorithm will pose new problems and challenges. Also, storing partial illumination solutions independent of the underlying geometry (e.g., photon mapping) should be researched further.

Psychoperceptual rendering. Radiometric accuracy has been the main driving force for global illumination algorithms, but since most images are to be viewed by human observers, it is usually not necessary to compute up to this level of accuracy. New rendering paradigms should be focused around rendering perceptually correct images. A perceptually correct image does not necessarily have all the radiometric details, but a viewer might still judge the image to be realistic. It might be possible not to render certain shadows, or to drop certain highlights, or even simplify geometry, if this would not harm the human observer judging the image as being realistic. Radiometric accuracy is best judged by comparing a rendered image with a reference photograph and measuring the amount of error. Psychoperceptual accuracy is probably best judged by having a human look at the rendered picture and asking whether the picture looks "realistic." However, at this point, very little research is available about how this could be done.

Integration with real elements. It is likely that more integration between real and virtual environments will become an integral part of many applications. This does not only entail putting real objects in virtual scenes, but also putting virtual elements in real scenes, e.g., by using projectors or holography. A perfect blend between the real and virtual elements becomes a major concern. This blend includes geometric alignment of real and virtual elements, but also consistent illumination. For example, a virtual element could throw shadows on real objects and vice versa. Developing a good framework for achieving such an integrated rendering system will probably evolve into a major research field during subsequent years.

As a major theme covering all these issues, one can think, or dream, about what the ultimate photorealistic rendering would look like in the future. It is very hard to make any predictions about any specific algorithmic techniques, but it is nevertheless possible to list a few of the requirements or features such a rendering tool should possess:

Interactivity. Any rendering algorithm of the future should be able to render scenes at interactive speeds, irrespective of scene or illumination complexity.

Any material, any geometry. All possible materials, from pure diffuse to pure specular, should be handled efficiently and accurately. Moreover, any type of geometry should be handled as well, whether it is a low-complexity polygon model or a scanned model containing millions of sample points.

Many different input models. It should be possible to take any form of input, whether it is a virtual model or a model based on acquisition from the real world. This probably means leaving the classic polygon model and texture maps for describing geometry and surface appearance and adapting other forms of geometry representation.

Realism slider. Depending on the application, one might settle for different styles of realism: for example, realistic lighting as one would experience in real life; studio-realism with lots of artificial lighting designed to eliminate unwanted shadows; lighting designed for optimally presenting products and prototypes, etc. This should be possible without necessarily altering the scene input or configuration of the light sources.

9.3 Concluding Remarks

Computer graphics is a very exciting field in which to work and is probably one of the most challenging research areas in computer science because it has links with many other disciplines, many of them outside the traditional computer science community. It is exactly this mix with disciplines such as art, psychology, filmmaking, biology, etc. that makes computer graphics very attractive to many students and enthusiasts.

The authors have an accumulated experience of more than 40 years in this field, but we still have the ability to be amazed and surprised by many of the new exciting ideas that are being developed each year. By writing this book, we hope to have made a small contribution in keeping people motivated and enthusiastic about computer graphics, and we can only hope that someday in the future, an exciting new computer graphics technique will develop from some of the ideas presented here.

A

A Class Library for Global Illumination

Global illumination is all about generating paths connecting a virtual camera with a light source. In this appendix, we propose a library of software classes that will facilitate generating such paths in a computer program, by hiding the details of geometry and materials representation and ray casting from a higher-level algorithm implementation.

The library offers the following building blocks:

- Classes for representing **path nodes**, such as a point on a light source, a surface scattering point, the viewing position, etc. (Section A.1).

- Classes for **light source sampling**. These classes generate path nodes that serve as the head of light paths (Section A.2).

- **Support classes**, representing a virtual screen buffer, classes for doing tone mapping, etc. (Section A.3).

The relationship between the classes is depicted in Figure A.1. Some example code fragments, illustrating the use of these classes, are presented in Section A.4.

The interface we describe here does not include a representation of geometry or materials itself. Such a representation is, of course, required in an actual implementation. Our implementation, on top of a VRML-based scene graph management library, is available from this book's website (http://www.advancedglobalillumination.com). In our experience, it is easy to port the class library to other global illumination platforms. Algorithms implemented on top of this interface may be portable to other global illumination systems supporting this interface almost without modifications. Our

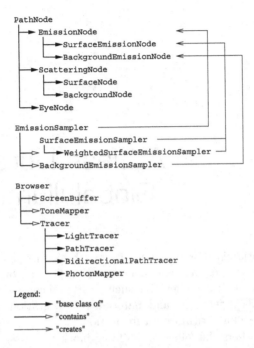

Figure A.1. Graphical overview of the classes contained in the library described here.

experiments have indicated that the additional computation cost caused by the interface is relatively small: on the order of 10% to 20% of the rendering time at most, even if the underlying scene graph management, shader implementation, and ray-tracing kernel are highly optimized. The programming language we used in our implementation is C++. The same interface can obviously also be realized using a different object-oriented programming language.

A.1 Path Node Classes

A.1.1 Overview

All the algorithms described in this book require that light paths or eye paths are generated stochastically. These paths have an associated value and a probability density (PDF). In order to form an image, average ratios are computed of path values over their PDFs.

The value associated with a path is always the product of values associated with the nodes in the path and transition factors such as $\text{vis}(x, y)$ $\cos\theta_y/r_{xy}^2$ between subsequent nodes x and y. The value associated with a path node depends on the type of node. For instance, for a surface scattering event, it is the BSDF times the outgoing cosine; for a light source node, it is the self-emitted radiance, etc.

The PDF indicates the chance that a particular path is being generated. It is also the product of PDFs associated with each node in the path and transition factors. The PDF associated with a surface scattering node, for instance, is the probability by which a scattered light direction is sampled; for a light source node, it is the probability of sampling a light emission direction on a light source.

We call every event at which a path is generated, or its trajectory changed, a path node. The library contains a representation for a variety of path nodes corresponding to:

- Emission of an eye ray through a virtual screen pixel, that is, emission of potential: see EyeNode class (Section A.1.3).

- Emission of light, at a surface or from the background (for instance, a model for sky illumination or a high dynamic range environment map): see EmissionNode class (Section A.1.4).

- Scattering of light or potential at a surface, or light/potential disappearing into the background: see ScatteringNode class (Section A.1.5).

A full path corresponds to a list of such path nodes.

A.1.2 Common Interface: The PathNode Base Class

All path node classes inherit from a single PathNode base class. The PathNode class encapsulates the common properties of all path nodes and provides a uniform interface, so that complete algorithms can be implemented without having to know what types of path nodes may be generated. The main members of the PathNode class are:

- The cumulative *probability density* by which a path up to a given node has been generated.

- The cumulative *value* associated with the path up to a given node.

- An eval() member function for querying the value (BSDF, EDF, etc.), path survival PDF, the PDF of sampling a given outgoing direction, and the outgoing cosine factor (if applicable) associated with the path node.

- A `sample()` function that calculates from two random numbers whether or not a path at a node shall be expanded and, if so, in what direction.

- A `trace()` function that returns a new path node resulting from tracing a ray into a given direction. The resulting node is always a scattering node (see Section A.1.5). Its precise type depends on the event that occurs next: If the ray hits a surface, a `SurfaceNode` is returned. If the ray disappears to the background, a `BackgroundNode` is returned. The `trace()` function also computes geometric factors associated with the transition to the new path node and properly initializes the cumulative PDF and value of the resulting path node.

`eval()`, `sample()`, and `trace()` are virtual member functions, implemented in children classes of `PathNode`. We choose to provide a single `eval()` function, for evaluating everything related to a path node, in order to minimize the number of virtual function calls and in order to make it easier to share the calculation of certain partial results between the value and the PDF. The latter can result in significant time savings. For instance, PDFs are quite often very similar to values. Results are filled in objects pointed to by pointers passed as parameters to the `eval()` function. If null pointers are passed, corresponding quantities (value, survival or direction sampling PDF, outgoing cosine) are not computed if not needed for other results. In the same spirit, the `sample()` and `trace()` functions can also return values and PDFs that are computed on the fly if nonnull pointer arguments are passed for filling in such side results. The `trace()` function optionally accepts a set of pointers to path node objects of each type that can be returned, in order to avoid dynamic storage allocation and to allow easy type checking afterwards. This will be illustrated in Section A.4.

Besides the above members, the `PathNode` base class also maintains and offers:

- The depth of the path node in its path: 0 for the head of a path, depth of the parent node plus 1 for nonhead path nodes.

- The light emission and scattering modes to take into account for evaluation and sampling (diffuse/glossy/specular emission/reflection/refraction);

- A pointer to the parent node in the path.

- Various flags: whether the path node belongs to a light path or eye path (required for making certain corrections due to nonsymmetric light scattering [203]), whether the path node is at the end of a subpath, whether it has a finite position in space, or whether it is located "at infinity" (for instance: background emission nodes).

- Member functions for accessing the position of a path node in space, or the geometry at that location, or for obtaining the head of the path, or direction and distance (taken to be 1 for background nodes) to another path node, or for computing visibility with regard to another node.

- Static member variables indicating the minimum and maximum path depth for generating paths. These values affect survival probabilities computed in the `sample()` and `eval()` functions.

- Some more member functions for convenience: `scatter()` computes the radiance or potential accumulated along a path and scattered into a given direction. The `expand()` member function combines `sample()` and `trace()` in a single function.

A.1.3 Pixel Filtering and Sampling: The `EyeNode` Class

The `EyeNode` class represents the head of eye paths. The position of an `EyeNode` object is the position of the pinhole camera used to view a scene. `EyeNode` objects are associated with a virtual screen pixel. They encapsulate pixel filtering and sampling. The value returned by `EyeNode::eval()` is the pixel measurement function of a given direction (see Section 5.7.1). `EyeNode::sample()` will select a direction through the associated virtual screen pixel for shooting an eye ray. Currently, a simple box pixel filter is implemented.

A.1.4 Light Emission: The `EmissionNode` Classes

An `EmissionNode` object represents the head of a light path. It corresponds with a point on a surface light source (`SurfaceEmissionNode` sub-class) or a direction towards the background for background illumination such as sky illumination or a high dynamic range environment map (`BackgroundEmissionNode` subclass). The value associated with an emission node is the self-emitted radiance into a given direction. The `sample()` member function will sample a direction according to the directional emission distribution at a surface emission location. For background emission nodes, where the emission direction is encoded in the node, `sample()` will select a point on the projection of the scene bounding box perpendicular to the emission direction. In both cases, `sample()` results in a point and a direction, enough for constructing a ray to shoot self-emitted radiance along.

Emission nodes can be generated by means of the `EmissionSampler` classes described in Section A.2.

A.1.5 Light and Potential Scattering: The ScatteringNode Classes

The trace() function of any path node usually results in a new ScatteringNode object representing surface scattering (SurfaceNode) or light or potential that disappears into the background (BackgroundNode).

Surface Scattering: SurfaceNode Class

The position of a SurfaceNode object is the position on the surface of an object in the scene at which a light path or eye path can be reflected, refracted, or absorbed. The value associated with such a node is the BSDF for a given direction. By default, the survival probability is computed based on the fraction of incident illumination or potential that will be scattered rather than absorbed. It depends on the direction of incidence and is, of course, affected by the currently required minimum and maximum path length. The "outgoing cosine" computed by SurfaceNode::eval() is the absolute value of the cosine between a given outgoing direction and the shading normal at the scattering location. The sample() member function samples an outgoing direction ideally according to the BSDF times the outgoing cosine. SurfaceNode objects know whether they belong to a light path or eye path, and appropriate correction factors for nonsymmetric scattering due to bump mapping or normal interpolation are applied on the BSDF [203]. There is also a version of SurfaceNode::eval() that allows us to specify incident directions other than the one for which the path node was constructed.

Occasionally, a path will hit a surface light source. In order to evaluate self-emitted radiance at a scattering location, and to compute the probability of obtaining the surface location by means of surface emission sampling (with a SurfaceEmissionSampler object, see Section A.2), appropriate source_radiance() and source_pdf() member functions are provided. Some algorithms, like bidirectional path tracing, require more complex operations if a path hits a light source. A conversion from the SurfaceNode class to the SurfaceEmissionNode class is provided in order to meet such requirements. An on_light_source() member function returns whether or not a SurfaceNode lays on a light source.

Paths Disappearing into the Background: BackgroundNode Class

If a path doesn't hit a surface, it's said to disappear into the background. A special BackgroundNode marks the end of such paths. The BackgroundNode class inherits from the ScatteringNode base class, but of course, no scattering happens: A path that disappears into the background is always terminated. The value and PDFs returned by BackgroundNode::eval()

are always zero, and the BackgroundNode::sample() member function will always result in an error. The trace() function returns a null result.

If background illumination has been modeled in a scene to be rendered, however, the BackgroundNode::source_radiance() and BackgroundNode ::source_pdf() member functions will compute the self-emitted radiance received from the background along the path direction, as well as the probability of sampling that direction using a BackgroundEmissionSampler object. Also for background "scattering," a conversion from the class BackgroundNode to the class BackgroundEmissionNode is provided so all queries for self-emitted illumination can be performed at a background "scattering" node.

A.2   Light Source Sampling Classes

A scene can contain both a number of surfaces that emit light spontaneously, as well as a model for background illumination such as sky light or a high dynamic range environment map. A second set of classes provided by the library will select either a position on a light source surface (SurfaceEmissionSampler class) or a direction for background illumination (BackgroundEmissionSampler class). Unlike path node objects, which are very frequently created and destroyed during the global illumination computations, there is normally only a single surface and background emission sampler active while rendering a frame.

A.2.1   Surface Emission Sampling: The SurfaceEmissionSampler and WeightedSurfaceEmissionSampler Classes

A SurfaceEmissionSampler class object maintains a list (or better, an array) of light source surfaces in the scene. Our current implementation assumes scenes modeled out of triangles, so our SurfaceEmissionSamplers will contain a list of pointers to light-emitting triangles. It is straightforward to extend the interface to handle curved light sources, too. Besides member functions for building up such a list, the main member functions are:

- A sample() function that will select a triangle from the list and return a point on the selected triangle as a SurfaceEmissionNode. Triangles are selected with a probability proportional to their self-emitted power. Points are selected uniformly on a triangle.

- A pdf() member function returns the probability density of sampling a given point on a given triangle using sample().

The pdf() member function assumes an index mechanism for quickly locating a given triangle in the list of light source triangles. Our SurfaceEmissionNodes and SurfaceNodes contain a pointer to the surface triangle on which they are located. This allows us to find out easily whether a SurfaceNode is located on a light source, or to calculate all relevant light source quantities.

Weighted Surface Emission Sampling

Sometimes, surface emission sampling according to emitted power is not optimal, and other probabilities for selecting light source triangles are required. One example of such a case is view-importance–driven light source sampling (Section 5.4.5), when a light source needs to be selected according to its estimated impact on a particular view. A powerful, but distant or occluded light source for instance, receives a lower probability of being selected than a less powerful, but nearby, light source. The WeightedSurfaceEmissionSampler subclass of SurfaceEmissionSampler allows us to enable/disable light source triangles from a list and to attach weights to light source triangles in a very general way. For convenience, a member function is provided that will assign weights according to light source distance and orientation with regard to a specified point and normal. Our implementation also contains an adapted version of a light-path tracer that estimates the light flux each light source contributes to the current view and that assigns light source weights proportional to these fluxes eventually.

A.2.2 Background Emission Sampling: The BackgroundEmissionSampler Class

The BackgroundEmissionSampler class works in a very similar way to the SurfaceEmissionSampler class, except that usually, the number of background light sources is small, and it returns a sampled direction to the background in the form of a BackgroundEmissionNode. Background directions are selected with a probability that reflects the intensity of self-emitted radiance received from the direction. It is much harder to take into account surface orientation here so there is no class for weighted background emission sampling.

A.2.3 The EmissionSampler Wrapper Class

The library provides an EmissionSampler wrapper class that contains a pointer to a WeightedSurfaceEmissionSampler and to a BackgroundEmissionSampler for the scene. By default, surface emission sampling and background emission sampling receive a weight proportional to the total emitted power from surfaces and the background, respectively. In order to calculate these weights, it is necessary to know in what length units a scene has been modeled. The default weights can, of course, be modified in a program. Our adapted light tracer, described above, does so after measuring the light flux contributed to the current view by surfaces and background.

The public implementation provides only triangle light sources and background emission. Other light sources, such as spherical or disc light sources, can easily be added in the form of additional emission sampler classes. The `EmissionSampler` wrapper class shall contain a reference to all light source samplers, with proper weights, so that it can hide the variety of light sources in a scene from the implementation of global illumination algorithms by providing a single `sample()` function for any kind of light emission.

A.3   Support Classes

The path node and sampler class interfaces are pretty much self-contained, but they need to be embedded in a suitable working environment, of course. For convenience, the library also contains a number of additional classes providing such an environment. Unlike the path node class interface, it is likely that some tuning will be needed in order to integrate these support classes into your global illumination application.

A.3.1   A Pinhole Camera Virtual Screen Abstraction: The ScreenBuffer Class

`EyeNode` class objects correspond to pixels on a virtual screen. Their implementation requires an abstraction of a virtual screen buffer. The library provides a `ScreenBuffer` class for this purpose. The `ScreenBuffer` class represents the virtual screen of a pinhole camera. It offers member functions `getDirection()` and `getPixelCoord()` for mapping pixel coordinates to the corresponding primary ray direction and vice versa. A member function `setView()` initializes the current view point, focus point, direction point upwards, and field of view angle in the same way as the `gluLookAt()` function in OpenGL. The `getPixelCoord()` function returns whether or not a primary ray direction points towards the screen. It is used in light tracing and bidirectional path tracing in order to splat path contributions to the screen, as shown in the examples (Section A.4.1).

The `ScreenBuffer` class also maintains two arrays of pixel color values: one usual set of low dynamic range RGB triplets plus transparency that can be displayed efficiently using, for instance, the `glDrawPixels()` OpenGL function; and one set that contains high dynamic range color values in 32-bit packed RGBE format [220]. The `ScreenBuffer` class offers member functions `clear()`, `clearRGBA()`, `clearHDR()`, `setPixel()`, `getRGBAPixel()`, `getHDRPixel()`, `addPixel()`, etc., for clearing, querying, and modifying low and high dynamic range pixel color values.

A.3.2 Converting High to Low Dynamic Range Color Values: The ToneMapper Classes

A global illumination algorithm computes and stores high dynamic range pixel color values in the `ScreenBuffer`. A `ToneMapper` object will map the high dynamic range pixels to RGB color triplets for display as explained in Section 8.2. Different tone mapping algorithms are implemented in subclasses of a base `ToneMapper` class. Such classes maintain their own set of required parameters, such as the world adaptation luminance in the current view. The `ScreenBuffer` class provides a member function `adaptation_luminance()` for computing the world adaptation luminance as the exponentiated mean logarithmic luminance of the virtual screen high dynamic range pixel color values. The main member function provided by the `ToneMapper` classes is a `map()` function that does everything to convert the high dynamic range color values in a given `ScreenBuffer` object into low dynamic range color values for display.

A.3.3 Integration into an Application: The Browser and Tracer Classes

The library described here comes with an application in which several global illumination algorithms have been implemented. We describe here two additional classes that integrate the path node and sampler classes into this application.

The Browser Classes

We implemented a `Browser` base class to group and maintain the whole software environment in which the `PathNode` and `EmissionSampler` classes operate:

- **The scene graph.** In our implementation, the scene graph is a VRML97 scene graph with numerous extension nodes for representing physically based appearance and high dynamic range backgrounds as well as color calibration parameters of the computer monitor on which a model has been designed.

- The interface to a *ray-tracing engine* needed for finding ray-object intersections and for performing visibility queries.

- One instance of an EmissionSampler, containing a WeightedSurface-EmissionSampler and a BackgroundEmissionSampler, as well as a reference unweighted SurfaceEmissionSampler.

- A ScreenBuffer and a ToneMapper object.

The Browser base class does not support a graphical user interface, and neither does it perform any global illumination computations itself. It needs to be augmented with such capabilities by means of inheritance. The Browser base class provides a virtual trace() member function, which needs to be implemented in a child class in order to:

- Initialize the ScreenBuffer for the current view.

- Perform the real global illumination computations for the view.

- Call the ToneMapper in order to map computed high dynamic range pixel colors into low dynamic range RGB color triplets for display.

- Display the results on a computer screen, or save them into a file.

The Tracer Classes

Rather than implementing each global illumination algorithm as a separate Browser subclass, we introduced yet another class, called Tracer, providing a common software interface for global illumination algorithms. Algorithms such as path tracing and light tracing (Chapter 5), bidirectional path tracing (Section 7.3), a ray-traced version of the instant radiosity algorithm (Section 7.7), and photon mapping (Sectoin 7.6) are implemented in PathTracer, LightTracer, BiDirTracer, InstantRadiosity, and PhotonMapper child classes of the Tracer base class. The main functions implemented by these classes are:

- An init() function performs initializations such as storage allocation of large arrays for each frame to be rendered.

- A trace() function computes an image for the current view.

- A tonemap() function properly rescales ScreenBuffer high dynamic range pixels and uses the current Browser's ToneMapper object in order to convert to displayable RGB color triplets.

Our **Browser** subclass object creates an appropriate **Tracer** object according to the desires of a user and calls the above listed **Tracer** functions in its **Browser::trace()** handler.

In addition to the above functions, our **Tracer** classes also provide member function for distributed computations, for instance, indicating how to separate an image into several subimages to be computed on different network clients, and how to merge the resulting pixel values computed by each client afterwards.

A.4 Example Code Fragments

In this section, we provide some example code fragments, illustrating how global illumination algorithms can be implemented on top of the path node and sampler classes described previously.

A.4.1 A Light Tracer

We first present the core part of our **LightTracer** class, implementing light particle tracing (see Section 5.7):

```
// scrn is pointer to the current ScreenBuffer object
// class Vec3 and class Spectrum represent 3D vectors and spectra
// lightsampler is pointer to current EmissionSampler object
int nrparticles;   // nr of particles to trace

// splats particle on the screen
inline void LightTracer::splat(class PathNode *n)
{
    float dist;                     // distance between eye and n
    const Vec3 eyedir = scrn->eye.dirto(n->pos(), &dist);  // direction
    if (n->at_infinity()) dist = 1.; // don't divide by square distance

    float i, j;                     // compute pixel coordinates (i,j)
    if (scrn->getPixelCoord(eyedir, &i, &j)) {
        class EyeNode e(i, j);          // eye node corresponding to pixel
        if (visible(&e, n)) {           // n is not occluded from the eye
            float ncos, ecos;           // cosine factors at the eye
                            // and at n
        scrn->addPixel(i, j, e.scatter(eyedir, &ecos)
                    * n->scatter(-eyedir, &ncos)
                    * (ncos * ecos / (dist*dist * (float)nrparticles)));
        }
    }
}

inline void LightTracer::traceparticle(class PathNode *l)
{
```

```
    splat(l);                            // splat particle on screen
    class PathNode *n = l->expand();     // expand path
    if (n) traceparticle(n);             // recurse
    delete n;
}

void LightTracer::trace(void)
{
    for (int i=0; i<nrparticles; i++) {
        class EmissionNode *l = lightsampler->sample(); // sample lights
        if (l) traceparticle(l);                        // trace light path
        delete l;
    }
}
```

In order to implement photon mapping, the `splat()` function shall be modified in order to store `SurfaceNode` hit points `n->pos()`, incident direction `n->indir`, and flux `n->value/n->pdf` in a photon map data structure. A ready-to-use implementation of a photon map data structure can be found in Jensen's book [83].

A.4.2 A Path Tracer

The implementation of a path tracer below is only slightly more complicated, in order to avoid dynamic storage allocation and to obtain easy checking of path node types returned by the `PathNode::expand()` and `EmissionSampler::sample()` functions.

```
// Again, scrn and lightsampler are the current ScreenBuffer
// and EmissionSampler.

// Array of SurfaceNodes in order to avoid the need for
// dynamic storage allocation in PathNode::expand().
// Storage is allocated in setup(), and freed in cleanup().
class SurfaceNode* PathTracer::sbuf =0;

// nr of light samples (shadow rays) at each path surface hit
int PathTracer::nrlightsamples = 1;

// Compute score associated with path landing on a light source.
inline const Spectrum PathTracer::source(class ScatteringNode* s)
{
    class Spectrum score(0.);
    if (s->depth() <= 1 || nrlightsamples == 0) {
        // Source contribution computed exclusively by means of
        // scattering.
        score = s->source_radiance() * s->value / s->pdf;
    } else {
        // Source contribution computed exclusively by means of
        // light source sampling.
```

```
    }
    return score;
}

// Light source sampling for computing direct illumination at
// the SurfaceNode s.
inline const Spectrum PathTracer::tracelight(class SurfaceNode* s)
{
    // Avoid dynamic storage allocation
    static class SurfaceEmissionNode sl;
    static class BackgroundEmissionNode bl;
    class EmissionNode *l = lightsampler->sample(&sl, &bl);
    if (l) {
        // cosine/distance at the light and at the surface
        float lcos, scos, dist;
        // dir/dist surface to light
        const Vec3 dir = s->dirto(l, &dist);
        // compute cosine at the light
        l->eval(-dir, 0, 0, 0, &lcos);
        // surface behind light or occluded
        if (lcos <= 0 || !visible(s, l))
            return Spectrum(0.);
        else
            return s->scatter(dir, &scos) * l->scatter(-dir)
                   * (scos * lcos / (dist * dist));
    }
    return Spectrum(0.);
}

// Light source sampling at surface scattering node s.
inline const Spectrum PathTracer::tracelights(class SurfaceNode* s)
{
    class Spectrum score(0.);
    if (nrlightsamples > 0) {
        for (int i=0; i<nrlightsamples; i++) {  // shoot shadow rays
            score += tracelight(s);
        }
        score /= (float)nrlightsamples;
    }
    return score;
}

// Traces a path through the pixel represented by the EyeNode e
inline const Spectrum PathTracer::tracepixel(class EyeNode* e)
{
    static class BackgroundNode b;  // avoid dynamic storage allocation
    class SurfaceNode *s = sbuf;
    // sample + shoot eye ray
    class ScatteringNode *n = e->expand(s, &b);
    class Spectrum score(0.);
    while (n) {
        score += source(n);         // self-emitted illumination
```

```
      if (n == s)                    // direct illumination: only surface nodes
        score += tracelights(s);
      n = n->expand(++s, &b);  // indirect illumination: expand path
   }

   return score;
}


void PathTracer::setup(void)
{
   sbuf = new SurfaceNode [PathNode::max_eye_path_depth];
}

void PathTracer::cleanup(void)
{
   delete [] sbuf;
}


// computes image for current view
void PathTracer::trace(void)
{
   setup();
   for (int j=0; j<scrn->height; j++) {
     for (int i=0; i<scrn->width; i++) {
       class EyeNode e(i, j);
       scrn->addPixel(i, j, tracepixel(&e));
     }
   }
   cleanup();
}
```

A.4.3 Multiple Importance Light Source Sampling

When light reflection at a surface hit by a path is highly specular, it is usually much better to compute direct illumination by means of a scattered
ray rather than by light source sampling. We show here the modifications
to the path tracer implementation above, in order to calculate direct illumination at path nodes by means of multiple importance sampling [201].
These modifications illustrate the use of the PathNode::eval() functions
in cases where the higher-level PathNode::scatter() functions fall short.
Some example results are shown in Figure A.2 on page 332.

```
// flag indicating whether or not to use bidirectional weighting
// for source contributions.
bool PathTracer::bidir_weighting = true;

// Compute score associated with path landing on a light source.
inline const Spectrum PathTracer::source(class ScatteringNode* s)
{
```

```
  class Spectrum score(0.);
  if (s->depth() <= 1 || nrlightsamples == 0) {
    // Source contributions computed exclusively by means of
    // scattering.
    score = s->source_radiance() * s->value / s->pdf;
  } else if (bidir_weighting) {
    // Source contributions computed by means of both scattering
    // and light source sampling.
    // Attenuate source radiance taking into account the probability
    // that s would have been obtained by light source sampling
    // rather than scattering.
    float w_scattering = s->pdf / s->parent()->pdf;
    float w_lsampling  = s->source_pdf() * (float)nrlightsamples;
    float w = w_scattering / (w_scattering + w_lsampling);
    score = s->source_radiance() * s->value * (w / s->pdf);
  } else {
    // Source contributions computed exclusively by means of
    // light source sampling.
  }
  return score;
}

// Light source sampling for computing direct illumination at
// the SurfaceNode s.
inline const Spectrum PathTracer::tracelight(class SurfaceNode* s)
{
  // Avoid dynamic storage allocation
  static class SurfaceEmissionNode sl;
  static class BackgroundEmissionNode bl;
  class EmissionNode *l = lightsampler->sample(&sl, &bl);
  if (l) {
    // cosine/distance at the light and at the surface
    float lcos, scos, dist;
    const Vec3 dir = s->dirto(l, &dist);
    // compute cosine at the light
    l->eval(-dir, 0, 0, 0, &lcos);
    // surface behind light or occluded
    if (lcos <= 0 || !visible(s, l))
      return Spectrum(0.);

    if (!bidir_weighting) {
      // source() doesn't pick up source radiance at hit surfaces
      return s->scatter(dir, &scos) * l->scatter(-dir)
             * (scos * lcos / (dist * dist));
    }

    else {
      // Attenuate direct illumination taking into account the
      // probability that the light source could have been hit
      // by a scattered ray.
      float survpdf, scatpdf;   // survival and scattering pdf
      class Spectrum fr, Le;    // BRDF at s and EDF at l
```

```
        s->eval( dir, &fr, &survpdf, &scatpdf, &scos);
        l->eval(-dir, &Le, 0, 0, 0);
        float g = lcos / (dist*dist);  // transition factor
        float w_scattering = survpdf * scatpdf * g; // scatt. weight
        float w_lsampling = l->pdf * (float)nrlightsamples;
        float w = w_lsampling / (w_lsampling + w_scattering);
        float G = scos * g;
        return (s->value * fr * Le) * (G * w / (s->pdf * l->pdf));
    }
  }
  return Spectrum(0.);
}


// The tracelights(), tracepixel() and trace() functions
// are the same as in the previous section.
```

A.4.4 A Bidirectional Path Tracer

Here is our code for a bidirectional path tracer:

```
// The purpose of the following arrays is to prevent dynamic
// storage allocation in PathNode::expand() and to allow
// efficient PathNode child class checking by comparing pointers.
class EyeNode eyenode;            // head of eye path
class SurfaceEmissionNode senode;      // surface emisison node
class BackgroundEmissionNode benode;// background emission node
// head of light path: pointer to senode or benode:
class EmissionNode *lightnode;
// surface scattering nodes
class SurfaceNode *eyesurfnodes, *lightsurfnodes;
class BackgroundNode eyebkgnode, lightbkgnode; // background nodes
// pointers surface or background scattering nodes:
class ScatteringNode **eyescatnodes, **lightscatnodes;

int eyepathlen, lightpathlen;            // eye/light path length
class PathNode **eyepath, **lightpath; // pointers to path nodes
float *erdpdf, *lrdpdf;  // reverse dir. selection  probabilities
float *erspdf, *lrspdf;  // survival prob. in reverse path direction
float *erhpdf, *lrhpdf;  // hit densities in reverse path direction
float nrparticles;       // nr of light particles traced

// for avoiding dynamic storage allocation when converting
// scattering nodes to emission nodes.
class BackgroundEmissionNode eeb;
class SurfaceEmissionNode ees;

// minimum and maximum light/eye/combined path length
static int min_light_path_length=2,
    max_light_path_length=7,
    min_eye_path_length=2,
```

```
        max_eye_path_length=7,
        max_combined_path_length=7;

// trace an eye path by expanding the eye node e.
// . a pointer to the eye node goes into eyepath[0]
// . the surface scattering nodes come into eyesurfnodes[1] etc... and
// a pointer to them in eyepath[1] and eyescatnode[1], etc...
// . the final background node goes into eyebkgnode and a pointer to
// it in eyepath[.] and eyescatnode[.] as well.
// Returns length of the eye path (nr of segments = nr of nodes - 1)
int BiDirTracer::trace_eye_path(class EyeNode* e)
{
  eyepath[0] = e;                       // store pointer to head of path

  int i=1;
  class ScatteringNode *n = e->expand(&eyesurfnodes[i], &eyebkgnode);
  while (n) {
    eyescatnodes[i] = n;               // store ScatteringNode pointer
    eyepath[i] = n;                     // store PathNode pointer
    i++;                                // expand the path
    n = n->expand(&eyesurfnodes[i], &eyebkgnode);
  }

  return i-1;                           // path length (nr of segments)
}

// Same as trace_eye_path, but for light path starting at the
// emission node l. Results go into lightpath[.], lightscatnodes[.],
// lightsurfnodes[.], and lightbkgnode.
// Returns length of light path.
int BiDirTracer::trace_light_path(class EmissionNode* l)
{
  lightpath[0] = l;

  int i=1;
  class ScatteringNode *n = l->expand(&lightsurfnodes[i], &lightbkgnode);
  while (n) {
    lightscatnodes[i] = n;
    lightpath[i] = n;
    i++;
    n = n->expand(&lightsurfnodes[i], &lightbkgnode);
  }

  return i-1;
}

// Computes the probabilities of sampling the eye path in reverse direction,
// that is: with incident and outgoing direction at the nodes exchanged.
// Result goes into:
// . erdpdf[i]: _D_irection sampling pdf for reverse directions at node i
// . erspdf[i]: unconstrained _S_urvival probability at node i (that is:
//   not taking into account minimum and maximum required path length)
```

```
// . erhpdf[i]: cos / distance squared from node i to node i-1 (_H_it pdf)
// The leading 'e' in the names of the arrays stands for _E_ye path. The
// 'r' for _R_everse.
void BiDirTracer::compute_reverse_eyepath_probs(void)
{
  erdpdf[0] = erspdf[0] = erhpdf[0] = 0.; // no reverse tracing at the eye
  if (eyepathlen == 0)
    return;
  class ScatteringNode* next = eyescatnodes[1];
  erhpdf[1] = 0.;   // chance of hitting eye point is 0 for pinhole camera
  for (int i=1; i<eyepathlen; i++) {
    class ScatteringNode* cur = next;
    next = eyescatnodes[i+1];
    class Vec3 toprevdir(cur->indir);
    class Vec3 tonextdir(-next->indir);
    erspdf[i] = cur->unconstrained_survival_probability(tonextdir);
    cur->eval(tonextdir, toprevdir, 0, 0, &erdpdf[i], 0);

    cur->eval(tonextdir, 0, 0, 0, &erhpdf[i+1]);
    if (!next->at_infinity())
      erhpdf[i+1] /= cur->position.sqdistance(next->position);
  }
  erspdf[eyepathlen] = erdpdf[eyepathlen] = 1.;   // not needed
}
// Same for the light path.
void BiDirTracer::compute_reverse_lightpath_probs(void)
{
  // no reverse tracing at the light source
  lrdpdf[0] = lrspdf[0] = lrhpdf[0] = 0.;
  if (lightpathlen == 0)
    return;
  class ScatteringNode* next = lightscatnodes[1];
  lightnode->eval(-next->indir, 0, 0, 0, &lrhpdf[1]);
  if (!lightnode->at_infinity() && !next->at_infinity())
    lrhpdf[1] /= lightnode->pos().sqdistance(next->position);
  for (int i=1; i<lightpathlen; i++) {
    class ScatteringNode* cur = next;
    next = lightscatnodes[i+1];
    class Vec3 toprevdir(cur->indir);
    class Vec3 tonextdir(-next->indir);
    lrspdf[i] = cur->unconstrained_survival_probability(tonextdir);
    cur->eval(tonextdir, toprevdir, 0, 0, &lrdpdf[i], 0);

    cur->eval(tonextdir, 0, 0, 0, &lrhpdf[i+1]);
    if (!next->at_infinity())
      lrhpdf[i+1] /= cur->position.sqdistance(next->position);
  }
  lrspdf[lightpathlen] = lrdpdf[lightpathlen] = 1.;   // not needed
}

// #define WEIGHT(w) (w)      // balance heuristic
#define WEIGHT(w) (w*w)   // power 2 heuristic
```

```
// Computes weight associated with the combined eye sub path up to
// eyepath[e] and light sub path up to lightpath[l].
// Requires that e>=0 and l>=0. Weighting for e==-1 or l==-1
// (empty sub-path) is special because there is no connecting path
// segment (nor visibility test), see eyepath_on_light() and
// lightpath_on_camera().
float BiDirTracer::weight(int e, int l,
        const Vec3& ltoedir, float ltoepdf, float etolpdf)
{
  class PathNode* en = eyepath[e];
  class PathNode* ln = lightpath[l];

  // weight of "this" strategy is proportional to product of
  // the pdfs of sampling the connected eye and light sub paths.
  // If e<=0, we are dealing with pure light path tracing (see
  // join_lightpath_with_eye() and an additional multiplication by
  // the total nr of light paths being traced is needed (= nr of pixels
  // since we trace one light path per pixel).
  double lpdf = ln->pdf * (e<=0 ? nrparticles : 1.);
  double epdf = en->pdf;
  double thisw = WEIGHT(lpdf * epdf);

  // compute sum of weights associated with all possible combinations
  // of shorter/longer eye/light sub-paths leading to the same path between
  // lightpath[0] and eyepath[0].
  double sumw = thisw;        // sum of weights
  int i, j;

  // shorter eye sub-paths / longer light sub-paths
  i = e; j = l;
  lpdf = ln->pdf;             // prolonged light sub-path pdf
  while (i>=0 && j<PathNode::max_light_path_depth) {
    double lxpdf = 0.;        // light path transition pdf
    if (j == l) {
      // transition probability for light path at lightpath[l]
      // going towards eyepath[e]. Probability is given as an
      // argument to this function.
      // i == e
      lxpdf = ltoepdf;
    } else if (j == l+1) {
      // evaluate transition probability for light path arriving at
      // eyepath[e] from lightpath[l] and going towards eyepath[e-1].
      // i == e-1
      class ScatteringNode* escat = eyescatnodes[e];
      float spdf = j < PathNode::min_light_path_depth   // survival pdf
        ? 1.
        : escat->unconstrained_survival_probability(-ltoedir);
      float dpdf;                                       // direction selection pdf
      escat->eval(-ltoedir, escat->indir, 0, 0, &dpdf, 0);
      lxpdf = spdf * dpdf * erhpdf[e];   // third factor is cosine/dist^2
    } else {
      // transition probability for light path at eyepath[i+1]
```

```
    // from eyepath[i+2] and going towards eyepath[i]. Use
    // precomputed probabilities for reverse eye path).
    // i<e-1
    float spdf = j < PathNode::min_light_path_depth
      ? 1.
      : erspdf[i+1];
    lxpdf = spdf * erdpdf[i+1] * erhpdf[i+1];
  }
  lpdf *= lxpdf;
  // The light sub-path now ends at eyepath[i]. Consider connection
  // with eye sub-path ending at eyepath[i-1].
  i--; j++;
  double w = (i>=0) ? eyepath[i]->pdf * lpdf : lpdf;
  if (i<=0) w *= nrparticles;    // pure light path tracing case
  sumw += WEIGHT(w);
}

// shorter light sub-paths / longer eye sub-paths
i = e; j = 1;
epdf = en->pdf;              // prolonged eye sub-path pdf
while (j>=0 && i<PathNode::max_eye_path_depth) {
  double expdf = 0.;      // eye path transition pdf
  if (i == e) {
    // transition probability for eye path at eyepath[e]
    // going towards lightpath[1]
    // j == 1
    expdf = etolpdf;
  } else if (i == e+1) {
    // evaluate transition probability for eye path arriving at
    // lightpath[1] from eyepath[e] and going towards lightpath[1-1]
    // j == l-1
    class ScatteringNode* lscat = lightscatnodes[1];
    float spdf = i < PathNode::min_eye_path_depth
      ? 1.
      : lscat->unconstrained_survival_probability(ltoedir);
    float dpdf;
    lscat->eval(ltoedir, lscat->indir, 0, 0, &dpdf, 0);
    expdf = spdf * dpdf * lrhpdf[1];
  } else {
    // transition probability for eye path at lightpath[j+1]
    // from lightpath[j+2] and going towards lightpath[j]. Use
    // precomputed probabilities for reverse light path.
    // j < l-1
    float spdf = i < PathNode::min_eye_path_depth
      ? 1.
      : lrspdf[j+1];
    expdf = spdf * lrdpdf[j+1] * lrhpdf[j+1];
  }
  epdf *= expdf;
  // The eye sub-path now ends at lightpath[j]. Consider connection
  // with light sub-path ending at lightpath[j-1].
  j--; i++;
```

```
    double w = (j>=0) ? lightpath[j]->pdf * epdf : epdf;
    sumw += WEIGHT(w);
  }

  return thisw / sumw;
}


// e==0 and l==0: join eye node with light source node
// (adds self-emitted radiance from a light source node to the
// image). This is handled by eyepath_on_light() for eye nodes
// of depth 1.
const Spectrum BiDirTracer::join_light_eye(void)
{
  return Spectrum(0.);
}


const EmissionNode* BiDirTracer::convert_to_lightnode(int e)
{
  if (eyescatnodes[e] == &eyebkgnode) {
    // scattering node is background node
    // convert to background emission node
    eeb = BackgroundEmissionNode(eyebkgnode);
    return &eeb;
  } else {
    // scattering node is surface node
    // convert to surface emission node
    ees = SurfaceEmissionNode(eyesurfnodes[e]);
    return &ees;
  }
}


// e>0 && l==-1: eye path arriving on a light source (that is:
// we check for every surface hit, whether it is a light source
// or not and take its self-emitted radiance into the incident
// direction into account if it is a light source.)
const Spectrum BiDirTracer::eyepath_on_light(const int e)
{
  class ScatteringNode* es = eyescatnodes[e];

  if (!es->on_light_source()) {
    return Spectrum(0.);
  }

  if (e==1) {
    // this is the complementary strategy of join_light_eye(), but
    // join_light_eye() does nothing, so this strategy gets full weight.
    return es->source_radiance() * es->value / es->pdf;
  }

  // Convert the scattering node into a corresponding emission node
  const EmissionNode* ee = convert_to_lightnode(e);
  class Spectrum Le;       // self-emitted radiance
```

```
    float spdf, dpdf;         // light path survival and direction s. pdf
    ee->eval(es->indir, &Le, &spdf, &dpdf, 0);

    // Compute weight of this strategy
    double thisw = WEIGHT(es->pdf);    // pdf of the eye path

    // Compute sum of weights of all equivalent strategies. This is
    // different from the other cases, because there is no connecting
    // path segment here (for the same reason, there's no
    // additional visibility test for this strategy.)
    double sumw = thisw;
    int i=e, j=0;
    double lpdf = ee->pdf; // pdf of the same position using emission sampling
    while (i>=0 && j<PathNode::max_light_path_depth) {
      double lxpdf = 0.;
      if (j==0) {
        lxpdf = spdf * dpdf * erhpdf[e];
      } else {
        double spdf = j<PathNode::min_light_path_depth
          ? 1.
          : erspdf[i];
        lxpdf = spdf * erdpdf[i] * erhpdf[i];
      }
      i--; j++;
      double w = (i>=0) ? eyepath[i]->pdf * lpdf : lpdf;
      if (i<=0) w *= nrparticles;
      sumw += WEIGHT(w);
      lpdf *= lxpdf;
    }

  return Le * es->value * (thisw / (es->pdf * sumw));
}

// e>0, l==0: join eye path vertex e>0 with light source node
// = standard path tracing
const Spectrum BiDirTracer::join_eyepath_with_light(const int e)
{
  if (eyescatnodes[e] == &eyebkgnode ||
      !visible(eyescatnodes[e], lightnode))
    return Spectrum(0.);

  class SurfaceNode *en = &eyesurfnodes[e];
  class EmissionNode *ln = lightnode;
  float ecos, lcos, espdf, lspdf, edpdf, ldpdf, dist;
  class Spectrum efr, Le;
  const Vec3 ltoedir = ln->dirto(en, &dist);
  en->eval(-ltoedir, &efr, &espdf, &edpdf, &ecos);
  ln->eval( ltoedir, &Le, &lspdf, &ldpdf, &lcos);
  double invdist2 = 1. / (dist * dist);
  float etolpdf = espdf * edpdf * lcos * invdist2;
  float ltoepdf = lspdf * ldpdf * ecos * invdist2;
  double G = ecos * lcos * invdist2;
```

```
  float w = weight(e, 0, ltoedir, ltoepdf, etolpdf);
  return en->value * efr * Le * (G / (en->pdf * ln->pdf) * w);
}


// e==-1, l>0: corresponds with a light path node arriving on the
// surface of the camera. Since we are using a pinhole camera,
// this can not happen.
const Spectrum BiDirTracer::lightpath_on_camera(const int l)
{
  return Spectrum(0.);
}


// e==0, l>0: Join light path vertex with eye node
// = standard light particle tracing
// Score contributes to different pixel than the one through
// which the eye path was traced. Therefore we add the score
// directly to the screen buffer and we return a null spectrum here.
const Spectrum BiDirTracer::join_lightpath_with_eye(const int l)
{
  if (lightscatnodes[l] == &lightbkgnode)
    return Spectrum(0.);

  // find pixel through which the light path node is visible.
  class SurfaceNode* ln = &lightsurfnodes[l];
  double dist;
  class Vec3 ltoedir = ln->position.dirto(scrn->eye, &dist);

  float i, j;
  if (!scrn->getPixelCoord(-ltoedir, &i, &j) ||
      !visible(&eyenode, ln))
    return Spectrum(0.);

  class EyeNode e(i, j);          // EyeNode for pixel
  class Spectrum We;              // pixel measurement value
  float espdf, edpdf, ecos, lcos; // path survival/dir.sel. pdf and cos.
  e.eval(-ltoedir, &We, &espdf, &edpdf, &ecos);
  class Spectrum score = ln->scatter(ltoedir, &lcos);
  float invdist2 = 1./(dist*dist); // inverse square distance
  score *= We * (ecos * lcos * invdist2);
  float etolpdf = espdf * edpdf * lcos * invdist2;
  float ltoepdf = 0.;   // no chance of hitting eye point (pinhole cam)
  float w = weight(0, 1, ltoedir, ltoepdf, etolpdf);

  scrn->addPixel(i, j, score * (w / nrparticles));
  return Spectrum(0.);
}


// e>0, l>0: join eye and light sub-path at intermediate nodes
const Spectrum BiDirTracer::join_intermediate(const int e, const int l)
{
  if (eyescatnodes[e] == &eyebkgnode ||
      lightscatnodes[l] == &lightbkgnode ||
```

```
        !visible(eyescatnodes[e], lightscatnodes[l]))
      return Spectrum(0.);

  class SurfaceNode *en = &eyesurfnodes[e];   // eye sub-path end
  class SurfaceNode *ln = &lightsurfnodes[l]; // light sub-path end
  double dist;                                // dist. and dir. between en/ln
  class Vec3 ltoedir = (en->position - ln->position).normalized(&dist);
  float ecos, lcos, espdf, lspdf, edpdf, ldpdf;// cos., surv,pdf, dir.sel.pdf
  class Spectrum efr, lfr;                     // BSDF at eye/light node
  en->eval(en->indir, -ltoedir, &efr, &espdf, &edpdf, &ecos);
  ln->eval(ln->indir,  ltoedir, &lfr, &lspdf, &ldpdf, &lcos);
  float invdist2 = 1. / (dist * dist);        // inverse square distance
  float G = ecos * lcos * invdist2;           // geometric factor
  float etolpdf = espdf * edpdf * lcos * invdist2;  // transition pdf en->ln
  float ltoepdf = lspdf * ldpdf * ecos * invdist2;  // transition pdf ln->en

  float w = weight(e, l, ltoedir, ltoepdf, etolpdf);
  return en->value * efr * lfr * ln->value * (G / (en->pdf * ln->pdf) * w);
}

// joins the eye sub-path vertex of depth e with light sub-path
// vertex of depth l. e or l equal to -1 means empty sub-path.
const Spectrum BiDirTracer::joinat(const int e, const int l)
{
  class Spectrum score(0.);
  if (e==0 && l==0)
    score = join_light_eye();
  else if (e<=0 && l<=0)      // eye point on light or light node on camera
    score = Spectrum(0.);     // or both sub-paths empty: can't happen
  else if (e==-1)
    score = lightpath_on_camera(l);
  else if (l==-1)
    score = eyepath_on_light(e);
  else if (e==0)
    score = join_lightpath_with_eye(l);
  else if (l==0)
    score = join_eyepath_with_light(e);
  else
    score = join_intermediate(e, l);
  return score;
}

const Spectrum BiDirTracer::join(void)
{
  // pre-calculate probabilities of sampling the eye and light path
  // in reverse direction.
  compute_reverse_eyepath_probs();
  compute_reverse_lightpath_probs();

  class Spectrum score(0.);

  // t is total combined path length: length of the eye sub-path +
```

```
    // length of the light sub-path + 1 for the connecting segment.
    // A length of '-1' indicates an empty path (no nodes)
    for (int t=1; t<=eyepathlen+lightpathlen+1
                 && t<=max_combined_path_length; t++) {
      for (int e=-1; e<=eyepathlen; e++) {  // e is eye sub-path length
        int l=t-e-1;                        // l is light sub-path length
        if (l>=-1 && l<=lightpathlen)
          score += joinat(e, l);
      }
    }

    return score;
}

const Spectrum BiDirTracer::tracepixel(const int i, const int j)
{
    // trace eye path
    eyenode = EyeNode(i,j);
    eyepathlen = trace_eye_path(&eyenode);

    // sample light sources and trace light path
    lightnode = 0;
    while (!lightnode) lightnode = lightsampler->sample(&senode, &benode);
    lightpathlen = trace_light_path(lightnode);

    // join eye and light paths
    return join();
}

// pre-calculates constants and allocates memory for arrays needed
// for rendering a frame.
void BiDirTracer::setup(int orgi, int orgj, int di, int dj)
{
    PathNode::min_light_path_depth = min_light_path_length;
    PathNode::max_light_path_depth = max_light_path_length;
    PathNode::min_eye_path_depth = min_eye_path_length;
    PathNode::max_eye_path_depth = max_eye_path_length;

    eyesurfnodes = new class SurfaceNode [PathNode::max_eye_path_depth+1];
    lightsurfnodes = new class SurfaceNode [PathNode::max_light_path_depth+1];
    eyescatnodes = new class ScatteringNode* [PathNode::max_eye_path_depth+1];
    lightscatnodes = new class ScatteringNode* [PathNode::max_light_path_depth+1];
    lightpath = new class PathNode* [PathNode::max_light_path_depth+1];
    eyepath = new class PathNode* [PathNode::max_eye_path_depth+1];
    erdpdf = new float [PathNode::max_eye_path_depth+1];
    lrdpdf = new float [PathNode::max_light_path_depth+1];
    erspdf = new float [PathNode::max_eye_path_depth+1];
    lrspdf = new float [PathNode::max_light_path_depth+1];
    erhpdf = new float [PathNode::max_eye_path_depth+1];
    lrhpdf = new float [PathNode::max_light_path_depth+1];

    int npixx = scrn->width;
```

```
  int npixy = scrn->height;
  nrparticles = npixx * npixy;
}


// undoes the effects of setup().
void BiDirTracer::cleanup(void)
{
  delete [] eyesurfnodes;
  delete [] lightsurfnodes;
  delete [] eyescatnodes;
  delete [] lightscatnodes;
  delete [] lightpath;
  delete [] eyepath;
  delete [] erdpdf;
  delete [] lrdpdf;
  delete [] erspdf;
  delete [] lrspdf;
  delete [] erhpdf;
  delete [] lrhpdf;
}


void BiDirTracer::trace(void)
{
  setup();
  for (int j=0; j<scrn->height; j++) {
    for (int i=0; i<scrn->width; i++) {
      scrn->addPixel(i, j, tracepixel(i, j));
    }
  }
  cleanup();
}
```

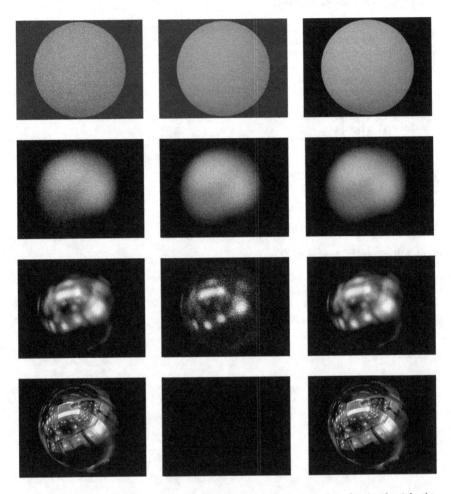

Figure A.2. Multiple importance light source sampling results obtained with the implementation shown in this section: The spheres on top are diffuse. They become more and more mirror-like towards the bottom. The left column of pictures was generated using BSDF sampling only. BSDF sampling works well for specular-like surfaces. The middle column shows results obtained with light sampling only. Light sampling is at its best for diffuse surfaces. The right column shows that combining BSDF sampling and light sampling using multiple importance sampling [201] yields better results overall. (See Plate XVII.)

Hemispherical Coordinates

B.1 Hemispherical Coordinates

In photorealistic rendering, one often wants to work with functions defined over a hemisphere (one-half of a sphere), centered around a surface point. A hemisphere consists of all the directions in which one can look when standing at the surface point: one can look from the horizon all the way up to the zenith and all around. A hemisphere is therefore a two-dimensional space, in which each point on the hemisphere defines a direction. Spherical coordinates are a useful way of parameterizing the hemisphere.

In the spherical coordinate system, each direction is characterized by two angles (Figure B.1). The first angle, φ, represents the azimuth and is measured with regard to an arbitrary axis located in the tangent plane at x; the second angle, θ, gives the elevation, measured from the normal vector N_x at surface point x. Writing directions using capital Greek letters, we can express direction Θ as the pair (φ, θ).

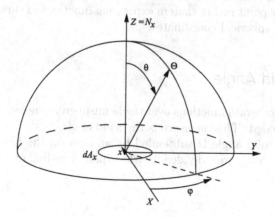

Figure B.1. Hemispherical coordinates.

The values for the angles φ and θ belong to the intervals

$$\varphi \in [0, 2\pi],$$
$$\theta \in [0, \pi/2].$$

So far, we have defined directions (or points) on the hemisphere. If we want to specify every three-dimensional point in space (not only points on the hemisphere), a distance r along the direction Θ is added. Any three-dimensional point is then defined by three coordinates (φ, θ, r). The transformation between Cartesian coordinates and spherical coordinates (place x at the origin, N_x is parallel to the Z-axis, and at the X-axis the angle $\varphi = 0$) is straightforward using some elementary trigonometry:

$$x = r \cos\varphi \sin\theta,$$
$$y = r \sin\varphi \sin\theta,$$
$$z = r \cos\theta,$$

or also

$$r = \sqrt{x^2 + y^2 + z^2},$$
$$\tan\varphi = y/x,$$
$$\tan\theta = \frac{\sqrt{x^2 + y^2}}{z}.$$

In most rendering algorithms, usually only hemispherical coordinates without the distance parameter r are used. This is because we are interested in integrating functions that are defined over directions incident at a given surface point rather than in expressing functions in three-dimensional space in full spherical coordinates.

B.2 Solid Angle

In order to integrate functions over the hemisphere, a measure on the hemisphere is needed. That measure is the solid angle.

A finite solid angle Ω subtended by an area on the hemisphere is defined as the total area divided by the squared radius of the hemisphere (Figure B.2):

$$\Omega = \frac{A}{r^2}.$$

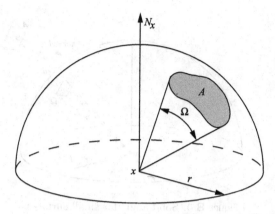

Figure B.2. Solid angle.

If the radius $r = 1$, the solid angle is simply the area on the hemisphere. Since the area of the hemisphere equals $2\pi r^2$, the solid angle covered by the entire hemisphere equals 2π; the solid angle covered by a complete sphere equals 4π. Solid angles are dimensionless but are expressed in *steradians* (sr). Note that the solid angle is not dependent on the shape of surface A, but is only dependent on the total area.

To compute the solid angle subtended by an arbitrary surface or object in space, we first project the surface or object on the hemisphere and compute the solid angle of the projection (Figure B.3). Note that two objects different in shape can still subtend the same solid angle.

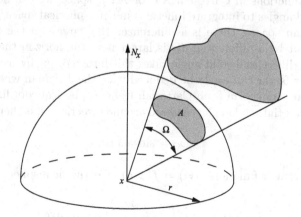

Figure B.3. Solid angle subtended by an arbitrary object.

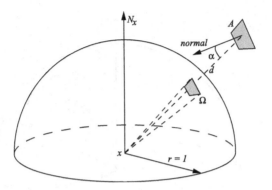

Figure B.4. Solid angle for small surfaces.

For small surfaces, the following approximation can be used to compute the solid angle subtended by a surface or object (Figure B.4):

$$\Omega = \frac{A \cos \alpha}{d^2}.$$

$A \cos \alpha$ is an approximation for the projected surface area.

B.3 Integrating over the Hemisphere

Just as we can define differential surface areas or differential volumes to integrate functions in Cartesian XY or XYZ space, we can define differential solid angles to integrate functions in hemispherical space. Compared to Cartesian spaces, there is a difference: the "area" on the hemisphere "swept" out by a differential $d\Theta$ is larger near the horizon than near the pole. The differential solid angle takes this into account by using a $\sin(\theta)$ factor (this factor can easily be deduced from the Jacobian when applying a coordinate transform from Cartesian to hemispherical coordinates).

A differential solid angle, centered around direction Θ, is then written as

$$d\omega_\Theta = \sin\theta d\theta d\varphi.$$

Integrating a function $f(\Theta) = f(\varphi, \theta)$ over the hemisphere is then expressed as

$$\int_\Omega f(\Theta)d\omega_\Theta = \int_0^{2\pi} \int_0^{\pi/2} f(\varphi, \theta) \sin\theta d\theta d\varphi.$$

Example 1 (Computing the area of the hemisphere.) Computing the area of the hemisphere can be achieved by simply integrating the differential solid angle over the entire integration domain:

$$
\int_\Omega d\omega_\Theta = \int_0^{2\pi} d\varphi \int_0^{\pi/2} \sin\theta d\theta
$$
$$
= \int_0^{2\pi} d\varphi [-\cos\theta]_0^{\pi/2}
$$
$$
= \int_0^{2\pi} 1 \cdot d\varphi
$$
$$
= 2\pi.
$$

Example 2 (Integrating a cosine lobe.) Integrating a cosine lobe over the hemisphere is useful when working with certain BRDF models that use cosine lobes as their fundamental building blocks (e.g., the Phong or Lafortune models). A cosine lobe, centered around N_x, to the power N, can be integrated in a straightforward manner:

$$
\int_\Omega \cos^N(\Theta, N_x) d\omega_\Theta = \int_0^{2\pi} d\varphi \int_0^{\pi/2} \cos^N \theta \sin\theta d\theta
$$
$$
= \int_0^{2\pi} d\varphi [-\frac{\cos^{N+1}\theta}{N+1}]_0^{\pi/2}
$$
$$
= \int_0^{2\pi} \frac{1}{N+1} \cdot d\varphi
$$
$$
= \frac{2\pi}{N+1}.
$$

B.4 Hemisphere-Area Transformation

In rendering algorithms, it is sometimes more convenient to express an integral over the hemisphere as an integral over visible surfaces seen from x. For example, if we want to compute all incident light at a point due to a distant light source, we can integrate over all directions within the solid angle subtended by the light source, or we can integrate over the actual area of the light source. To transform a hemispherical integral into an area integral, the relationship between a differential surface and a differential solid angle must be used:

$$
d\omega_\Theta = \frac{\cos\theta_y dA_y}{r_{xy}^2}.
$$

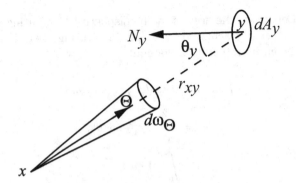

Figure B.5. Area to solid angle conversion.

The differential solid angle $d\omega_\Theta$ around direction Θ is transformed to a differential surface dA_y at surface point y (Figure B.5). Therefore, any integral over the hemisphere can also be written as an integral over each visible differential surface dA_y in each direction Θ:

$$\int_\Omega f(\Theta) d\omega_\Theta = \int_A f(y) \frac{\cos \theta_y}{r_{xy}^2} dA_y.$$

C

Theoretical Analysis of Stochastic Relaxation Radiosity

In this appendix, we show how the variance of the incremental shooting iterative algorithm of Section 6.3 can be analyzed, and demonstrate how a number of practical results can be derived from it. The analysis of the other algorithms is very similar and is a recommended exercise for the interested reader.

We start with the derivation of the variance of the incremental shooting iterative algorithm. The first thing to point out is that the resulting radiosities are obtained as the sum of increments computed in several iteration steps. We first derive the variance of a single iteration and next show how the variance on the converged results is composed from the single-iteration variances.

Variance of a single incremental shooting iteration. The variance of a single incremental shooting iteration can be derived by straightforward application of the definition of Monte Carlo summation variance:

$$S = \sum_{i=1}^{n} a_i \qquad \text{sum to be computed (n terms),}$$

$$S \approx \frac{a_{i_s}}{p_{i_s}} \qquad \text{single-sample estimate,}$$

$$V[\hat{S}] = \sum_{i=1}^{n} \frac{a_i^2}{p_i} - S^2 \qquad \text{single-sample variance.}$$

For N samples, the variance is $V[\hat{S}]/N$.

The sum to be estimated here is given in Equation 6.11. The probabilities p for picking terms from the sum are in Equation 6.12. The resulting single-sample variance of the kth incremental shooting iteration is

$$V[\Delta \hat{P}_i^{(k+1)}] = \rho_i \Delta P_T^{(k)} \Delta P_i^{(k+1)} - \left(\Delta P_i^{(k+1)} \right)^2. \qquad (C.1)$$

The latter term is usually negligible compared to the former ($\Delta P_i^{(k+1)} \ll \Delta P_T^{(k)}$).

Variance of a sequence of incremental shooting iterations until convergence.
The solution P_i is eventually obtained as a sum of increments $\Delta P_i^{(k)}$ computed in each iteration step. The single-sample variance on each increment $\Delta P_i^{(k)}$ is given above in Equation C.1. Assuming that subsequent iterations are independent (which is to good approximation true in practice), and that N_k independent samples are used in the kth iteration, the variance on the result of K iterations will be

$$V[\hat{P}_i] = \sum_{k=1}^{K} \frac{1}{N_k} V[\Delta \hat{P}_i^{(k)}].$$

Optimal allocation of $N = \sum_{k=1}^{K} N_k$ samples over the individual iterations is obtained if $1/N_k$ is inversely proportional to $V[\Delta \hat{P}_i^{(k)}]$ (Section 3.6.5). For all patches i, $V[\Delta \hat{P}_i^{(k)}]$ (Equation C.1) is approximately proportional to $P_T^{(k-1)}$, suggesting that we choose the number of samples in the kth iteration proportional to the total unshot power $\Delta P_T^{(k-1)}$ to be propagated in that iteration:

$$N_k \approx N \frac{\Delta P_T^{(k-1)}}{P_T}.$$

When N_k drops below a small threshold, convergence has been reached. Combining all above results, it can be shown that the variance on the radiosity B_i after convergence is *to good approximation* given by

$$V[\hat{B}_i] \approx \frac{P_T}{N} \frac{\rho_i(B_i - B_i^e)}{A_i}. \tag{C.2}$$

Time complexity. We now turn to the question of how the number of samples N needs to be varied as a function of the number of patches n in order to compute all radiosities B_i to prescribed accuracy ε with 99.7% confidence. According to the central limit theorem (Section 3.4.4), the number of samples N shall be chosen so that

$$3\sqrt{\frac{V[\hat{B}_i]}{N}} \leq \varepsilon$$

for all i. Filling in Equation C.2 then yields

$$N \geq \frac{9P_T}{\varepsilon^2} \cdot \max_i \frac{\rho_i(B_i - B_i^e)}{A_i}. \tag{C.3}$$

This formula allows us to examine how the number of rays to be shot must be increased as a scene to be rendered is "made larger." There are, however, many possible scenarios of how a scene can be "made larger." For instance, new objects can be added, or one can switch to a finer tessellation of the surfaces in the scene without adding new objects. If all patches in a scene are split in two, the required number of rays in order to obtain a given accuracy will need to be doubled, as dividing the patches (asymptotically) has no effect on reflectivities and radiosities. The cost of shooting a ray is often assumed to be logarithmic in the number of polygons. Although the truth is much more complicated, it is often stated that Monte Carlo radiosity algorithms have log-linear complexity. In any case, their complexity is much lower than quadratic. This result is not only valid for incremental stochastic shooting of power but also for other Monte Carlo radiosity algorithms based on shooting [169, 162, 15].

A heuristic for choosing the number of samples N.   We have demonstrated that the number of samples in each incremental shooting iteration shall be chosen proportional to the amount of power to be distributed in that iteration. In other words, each ray to be shot shall propagate the same "quantum" of light energy. We have not yet answered the question of how large the quanta should be, however, or equivalently, how many rays N to choose for a complete sequence of incremental shooting iterations to convergence. That's the point of this paragraph.

Equation C.3 allows us to derive the answer. Suppose one wants to choose N so that with 99.7% confidence, the error ε on any patch i will be less than the average radiosity $B^{\mathrm{av}} = P_T/A_T$ in the scene. The total power P_T in Equation C.3 can then be replaced by $A_T \varepsilon$. Typically, $B_i^e = 0$ for most patches in the scene. Approximating $B_i - B_i^e$ by the average radiosity, and thus by ε, then yields

$$N \approx 9 \cdot \max_i \frac{\rho_i A_T}{A_i}. \qquad (C.4)$$

In practice, it makes a lot of sense to skip, for instance, the 10% of patches in a scene with the largest ratio ρ_i/A_i. Note that a rough heuristic for N suffices: a higher accuracy can always be obtained by averaging the result of several independent runs of the algorithm.

Bibliography

[1] Sameer Agarwal, Ravi Ramamoorthi, Serge Belongie, and Henrik Wann Jensen. "Structured Importance Sampling of Environment Maps." *ACM Transactions on Graphics* 22:3 (2003), 605–612.

[2] L. Alonso, F. Cuny, S. Petit Jean, J.-C. Paul, S. Lazard, and E. Wies. "The Virtual Mesh: A Geometric Abstraction for Efficiently Computing Radiosity." *ACM Transactions on Graphics* 3:20 (2001), 169–201.

[3] Thomas Annen, Jan Kautz, Frdo Durand, and Hans-Peter Seidel. "Spherical Harmonic Gradients for Mid-Range Illumination." In *Rendering Techniques 2004 Eurographics Symposium on Rendering*, pp. 331–336, 2004.

[4] A. Appel. "Some Techniques for Shading Machine Renderings of Solids." In *AFIPS 1968 Spring Joint Computer Conference*, 32, 32, 1968.

[5] J. Arvo. "Backward Ray Tracing." In *SIGGRAPH 1986 Developments in Ray Tracing course notes*, 1986.

[6] J. Arvo. "Stratified Sampling of Spherical Triangles." In *Computer Graphics Proceedings, Annual Conference Series, 1995 (ACM SIGGRAPH '95 Proceedings)*, pp. 437–438, 1995.

[7] Kavita Bala, Julie Dorsey, and Seth Teller. "Interactive Ray-Traced Scene Editing Using Ray Segment Trees." In *Tenth Eurographics Workshop on Rendering*, pp. 39–52, 1999.

[8] Kavita Bala, Julie Dorsey, and Seth Teller. "Radiance Interpolants for Accelerated Bounded-Error Ray Tracing." *ACM Transactions on Graphics* 18:3 (1999), 213–256.

[9] Kavita Bala, Bruce Walter, and Donald P. Greenberg. "Combining Edges and Points for High-Quality Interactive Rendering." *ACM Transactions on Graphics* 23:3 (SIGGRAPH 2003), 631–640.

[10] Kavita Bala. "Radiance Interpolants for Interactive Scene Editing and Ray Tracing." Ph.D. thesis, Massachusetts Institute of Technology, 1999.

[11] Ph. Bekaert and H.-P. Seidel. "A Theoretical Comparison of Monte Carlo Radiosity Algorithms." In *Proc. 6th Fall Workshop on Vision, Modeling and Visualisation 2001 (VMV01), Stuttgart, Germany*, pp. 257–264, 2001.

[12] Ph. Bekaert, L. Neumann, A. Neumann, M. Sbert, and Y. D. Willems. "Hierarchical Monte Carlo Radiosity." In *Proceedings of the 9th. Eurographics Workshop on Rendering, Vienna, Austria*, 1998.

[13] Ph. Bekaert, M. Sbert, and Y. Willems. "The Computation of Higher-Order Radiosity Approximations with a Stochastic Jacobi Iterative Method." In *16th Spring Conference on Computer Graphics, Comenius University, Bratislava, Slovakia*, 2000. 212–221.

[14] Ph. Bekaert, M. Sbert, and Y. Willems. "Weighted Importance Sampling Techniques for Monte Carlo Radiosity." In *Rendering Techniques '2000 (Proceedings of the 11th Eurographics Workshop on Rendering, Brno, Czech Rep.)*, p. 35–46. Springer Computer Science, 2000.

[15] Ph. Bekaert. "Hierarchical and Stochastic Algorithms for Radiosity." Ph.D. thesis, K. U. Leuven, Department of Computer Science, 1999.

[16] Gary Bishop, Henry Fuchs, Leonard McMillan, and Ellen J. Scher Zagier. "Frameless Rendering: Double Buffering Considered Harmful." *Computer Graphics* 28: Annual Conference Series (1994), 175–176.

[17] Ph. Blasi, B. Le Saëc, and C. Schlick. "A Rendering Algorithm for Discrete Volume Density Objects." *Computer Graphics Forum* 12:3 (1993), 201–210.

[18] K. Bouatouch, S. N. Pattanaik, and E. Zeghers. "Computation of Higher Order Illumination with a Non-Deterministic Approach." *Computer Graphics Forum* 15:3 (1996), 327–338.

[19] P. Bratley, B. L. Fox, and H. Niederreiter. "Implementation and Tests of Low-Discrepancy Sequences." *ACM Transactions on Modelling and Computer Simulation* 2:3 (1992), 195–213.

[20] M. Bunnell. "Dynamic Ambient Occlusion and Indirect Lighting." In *GPU Gems 2: Programming Techniques for High-Performance Graphics and General-Purpose Computation*, edited by M. Pharr, pp. 223–233. Reading, MA: Addison-Wesley, 2005.

[21] David Burke, Abhijeet Ghosh, and Wolfgang Heidrich. "Bidirectional Importance Sampling for Direct Illumination." In *Rendering Techniques 2005: 16th Eurographics Workshop on Rendering*, pp. 147–156, 2005.

[22] S. Chandrasekhar. *Radiative Transfer*. Oxford: Oxford University Press, 1950.

[23] S. Chattopadhyay and A. Fujimoto. "Bi-directional Ray Tracing." In *Computer Graphics 1987 (Proceedings of CG International 1987)*, edited by Tosiyasu Kunii, pp. 335–43. Tokyo: Springer-Verlag, 1987.

[24] S. E. Chen, H. E. Rushmeier, G. Miller, and D. Turner. "A Progressive Multi-Pass Method for Global Illumination." In *Computer Graphics (SIGGRAPH '91 Proceedings)*, pp. 165–174, 1991.

[25] P. H. Christensen, D. H. Salesin, and T. D. DeRose. "A Continuous Adjoint Formulation for Radiance Transport." In *Fourth Eurographics Workshop on Rendering*, pp. 95–104, 1993.

[26] P. H. Christensen, E. J. Stollnitz, and D. H. Salesin. "Global Illumination of Glossy Environments Using Wavelets and Importance." *ACM Transactions on Graphics* 15:1 (1996), 37–71.

[27] Petrik Clarberg, Wojciech Jarosz, Tomas Akenine-Möller, and Henrik Wann Jensen. "Wavelet Importance Sampling: Efficiently Evaluating Products of Complex Functions." *ACM Transactions on Graphics* 24:3 (2005), 1166–1175.

[28] M. F. Cohen and D. P. Greenberg. "The Hemi-Cube: A Radiosity Solution for Complex Environments." *Computer Graphics (SIGGRAPH '85 Proceedings)* 19:3 (1985), 31–40.

[29] M. F. Cohen and J. R. Wallace. *Radiosity and Realistic Image Synthesis*. Boston, MA: Academic Press Professional, 1993.

[30] M. F. Cohen, D. P. Greenberg, D. S. Immel, and P. J. Brock. "An Efficient Radiosity Approach for Realistic Image Synthesis." *IEEE Computer Graphics and Applications* 6:3 (1986), 26–35.

[31] M. F. Cohen, S. E. Chen, J. R. Wallace, and D. P. Greenberg. "A Progressive Refinement Approach to Fast Radiosity Image Generation." In *Computer Graphics (SIGGRAPH '88 Proceedings)*, pp. 75–84, 1988.

[32] S. Collins. "Adaptive Splatting for Specular to Diffuse Light Transport." In *Fifth Eurographics Workshop on Rendering*, pp. 119–135, 1994.

[33] R. Cook and K. Torrance. "A Reflectance Model for Computer Graphics." *ACM Transactions on Graphics* 1:1 (1982), 7–24.

[34] R. L. Cook, T. Porter, and L. Carpenter. "Distributed Ray Tracing." *Computer Graphics* 18:3 (1984), 137–145.

[35] S. Daly. "Engineering Observations from Spatio-Velocity and Spatiotemporal Visual Models." *IST/SPIE Conference on Human Vision and Electronic Imaging III, SPIE* 3299 (1998), 180–191.

[36] L. M. Delves and J. L. Mohamed. *Computational Methods for Integral Equations.* Cambridge, UK: Cambridge University Press, 1985.

[37] K. Devlin, A. Chalmers, A. Wilkie, and W. Purgathofer. "Tone Reproduction and Physically Based Spectral Rendering." In *Eurographics 2002: State of the Art Reports*, pp. 101–123. Aire-la-Ville, Switzerland: Eurographics Association, 2002.

[38] Kirill Dmitriev, Stefan Brabec, Karol Myszkowski, and Hans-Peter Seidel. "Interactive Global Illumination using Selective Photon Tracing." In *Thirteenth Eurographics Workshop on Rendering*, 2002.

[39] George Drettakis and Francois X. Sillion. "Interactive Update of Global Illumination Using a Line-Space Hierarchy." In *Computer Graphics (SIGGRAPH 1997 Proceedings)*, pp. 57–64, 1997.

[40] Reynald Dumont, Fabio Pellacini, and James A. Ferwerda. "Perceptually-Driven Decision Theory for Interactive Realistic Rendering." *ACM Transactions on Graphics* 22:2 (2003), 152–181.

[41] Ph. Dutré and Y. D. Willems. "Importance-Driven Monte Carlo Light Tracing." In *Fifth Eurographics Workshop on Rendering*, pp. 185–194. Darmstadt, Germany, 1994.

[42] Ph. Dutré and Y. D. Willems. "Potential-Driven Monte Carlo Particle Tracing for Diffuse Environments with Adaptive Probability Density Functions." In *Eurographics Rendering Workshop 1995*, 1995.

[43] S. M. Ermakow. *Die Monte-Carlo-Methode und verwandte Fragen.* Berlin: V.E.B. Deutscher Verlag der Wissenschaften, 1975.

[44] M. Feda. "A Monte Carlo Approach for Galerkin Radiosity." *The Visual Computer* 12:8 (1996), 390–405.

[45] S. Fernandez, K. Bala, and D. Greenberg. "Local Illumination Environments for Direct Lighting Acceleration." *Eurographics Workshop on Rendering 2002*, pp. 7–14, 2002.

[46] Randima Fernando. *GPU Gems: Programming Techniques, Tips, and Tricks for Real-Time Graphics.* Reading, MA: Addison-Wesley Professional, 2004.

[47] J. Ferwerda, S. Pattanaik, P. Shirley, and D. Greenberg. "A model of Visual Adaptation for Realistic Image Synthesis." In *SIGGRAPH 96 Conference Proceedings*, pp. 249–258, 1996.

[48] James A. Ferwerda, Stephen H. Westin, Randall C. Smith, and Richard Pawlicki. "Effects of Rendering on Shape Perception in Automobile Design." In *APGV 2004*, pp. 107–114, 2004.

[49] R. P. Feynman. *QED.* Princeton: Princeton University Press, 1988.

[50] G. E. Forsythe and R. A. Leibler. "Matrix Inversion by a Monte Carlo Method." *Math. Tabl. Aids. Comput.* 4 (1950), 127 – 129.

[51] C. Piatko G. Ward, H. Rushmeier. "A Visibility Matching Tone Reproduction Operator for High Dynamic Range Scenes." *IEEE Transactions on Visualization and Computer Graphics* 3:4 (1997), 291–306.

[52] A. S. Glassner, editor. *An Introduction to Ray Tracing.* London: Academic Press, 1989.

[53] A. S. Glassner. "A Model for Fluorescence and Phosphorescence." In *Proceedings of the Fifth Eurographics Workshop on Rendering*, pp. 57–68, 1994.

[54] A. S. Glassner. *Principles of Digital Image Synthesis.* San Francisco, CA: Morgan Kaufmann Publishers, Inc., 1995.

[55] J. S. Gondek, G. W. Meyer, and J. G. Newman. "Wavelength Dependent Reflectance Functions." In *Proceedings of SIGGRAPH'94*, pp. 213–220, 1994.

[56] C. M. Goral, K. E. Torrance, D. P. Greenberg, and B. Battaile. "Modeling the Interaction of Light Between Diffuse Surfaces." In *SIGGRAPH '84 Conference Proceedings*, pp. 213–222, 1984.

[57] Steven Gortler, Radek Grzeszczuk, Richard Szeliski, and Michael Cohen. "The Lumigraph." In *Computer Graphics (SIGGRAPH 1996 Proceedings)*, pp. 43–54, 1996.

[58] H. Gouraud. "Continuous Shading of Curved Surfaces." *IEEE Transactions on Computers* 20:6 (1971), 623–629.

[59] D. Greenberg, K. Torrance, P. Shirley, J. Arvo, J. Ferwerda, S. Pattanaik, E. Lafortune, B. Walter, S. Foo, and B. Trumbore. "A Framework for Realistic Image Synthesis." In *Proceedings of ACM SIGGRAPH*, pp. 44–53, 1997.

[60] E. A. Haines and D. P. Greenberg. "The Light Buffer: a Shadow Testing Accelerator." *IEEE Computer Graphics & Applications* 6:9 (1986), 6–16.

[61] J. H. Halton. "A Restrospective and Prospective Survey of the Monte Carlo Method." *SIAM Review* 12:1 (1970), 1 – 63.

[62] J. M. Hammersley and D. C. Handscomb. *Monte Carlo Methods.* London: Methuen/Chapman and Hall, 1964.

[63] P. Hanrahan and W. Krueger. "Reflection from Layered Surfaces Due to Subsurface Scattering." In *Proceedings of SIGGRAPH 93*, pp. 165–174, 1993.

[64] P. Hanrahan, D. Salzman, and L. Aupperle. "A Rapid Hierarchical Radiosity Algorithm." In *Computer Graphics (SIGGRAPH '91 Proceedings)*, pp. 197–206, 1991.

[65] D. Hart, Ph. Dutré, and D. P. Greenberg. "Direct Illumination With Lazy Visibility Evaluation." In *Proceedings of SIGGRAPH 99, Computer Graphics Proceedings, Annual Conference Series*, pp. 147–154, 1999.

[66] Milos Hasan, Fabio Pellacini, and Kavita Bala. "Direct-to-Indirect Transfer for Cinematic Relighting." To appear in *SIGGRAPH: ACM Trans. Graph.*, 2006.

[67] X. D. He, K. E. Torrance, F. X. Sillion, and D. P. Greenberg. "A Comprehensive Physical Model for Light Reflection." In *Computer Graphics (SIGGRAPH 1991 Proceedings)*, pp. 175–86, 1991.

[68] E. Hecht and A. Zajac. *Optics.* Reading, MA: Addison-Wesley Publishing Company, 1979.

[69] P. S. Heckbert and J. Winget. "Finite Element Methods for Global Illumination." Technical Report UCB/CSD 91/643, Computer Science Division (EECS), University of California, Berkeley, California, USA, 1991.

[70] P. S. Heckbert. "Adaptive Radiosity Textures for Bidirectional Ray Tracing." *Computer Graphics (SIGGRAPH '90 Proceedings)* 24:4 (1990), 145–154.

[71] P. S. Heckbert. "Discontinuity Meshing for Radiosity." *Third Eurographics Workshop on Rendering*, pp. 203–226.

[72] Wolfgang Heidrich and Hans-Peter Seidel. "Realistic, Hardware-Accelerated Shading and Lighting." In *Proceedings of SIGGRAPH 99, Computer Graphics Proceedings, Annual Conference Series*, pp. 171–178, 1999.

[73] D. Hockney. *Secret Knowledge.* London: Thames and Hudson, 2001.

[74] Piti Irawan, James A. Ferwerda, and Stephen R. Marschner. "Perceptually Based Tone Mapping of High Dynamic Range Image Streams." In *16th Eurographics Workshop on Rendering*, pp. 231–242, 2005.

[75] A. Ishimaru. *Wave Propagation and Scattering in Random Media, Volume 1: Single Scattering and Transport Theory.* New York: Academic Press, 1978.

[76] H. W. Jensen and J. Buhler. "A Rapid Hierarchical Rendering Technique for Translucent Materials." *ACM Transactions on Graphics* 21:3 (2002), 576–581.

[77] H. W. Jensen and N. J. Christensen. "Photon Maps in Bidirectional Monte Carlo Ray Tracing of Complex Objects." *Computers & Graphics* 19:2 (1995), 215–224.

[78] H. W. Jensen and P. H. Christensen. "Efficient Simulation of Light Transport in Scenes with Participating Media using Photon Maps." In *Proceedings of SIGGRAPH'98*, pp. 311–320, 1998.

[79] H. W. Jensen, J. Arvo, M. Fajardo, P. Hanrahan, D. Mitchell, M. Pharr, and P. Shirley. "State of the Art in Monte Carlo Ray Tracing for Realistic Image Synthesis." In *SIGGRAPH 2001 Course Notes (Course 29)*, 2001.

[80] H. W. Jensen, S. R. Marschner, M. Levoy, and P. Hanrahan. "A Practical Model for Subsurface Light Transport." In *Proceedings of ACM SIGGRAPH 2001, Computer Graphics Proceedings, Annual Conference Series*, pp. 511–518, 2001.

[81] H. W. Jensen. "Global Illumination using Photon Maps." In *Eurographics Rendering Workshop 1996*, pp. 21–30. Eurographics, 1996.

[82] H. W. Jensen. "Rendering Caustics on Non-Lambertian Surfaces." In *Proceedings of Graphics Interface 1992*, pp. 116–121. Canadian Information Processing Society, 1996.

[83] H. W. Jensen. *Realistic Image Synthesis Using Photon Mapping*. Wellesley, MA: A K Peters, 2001.

[84] T. Tawara K. Myszkowski, P. Rokita. "Preceptually-Informed Accelrated Rendering of High Quality Walkthrough Sequences." *Proceedings of the 10th Eurographics Workshop on Rendering*, pp. 5–18.

[85] J. T. Kajiya. "The Rendering Equation." *Computer Graphics (SIGGRAPH '86 Proceedings)* 20:4 (1986), 143–150.

[86] M. H. Kalos and P. Whitlock. *The Monte Carlo method. Volume 1: Basics*. J. Wiley and Sons, 1986.

[87] Jan Kautz, Peter-Pike Sloan, and John Snyder. "Fast, Arbitrary BRDF Shading for Low-Frequency Lighting using Spherical Harmonics." In *Eurographgics Rendering Workshop '02*, pp. 291–296, 2002.

[88] Jan Kautz, J. Lehtinen, and T. Aila. "Hemispherical Rasterization for Self-Shadowing of Dynamic Objects." In *Eurographics Symposium on Rendering*, pp. 179–184, 2004.

[89] A. Keller. "The Fast Calculation of Form Factors Using Low Discrepancy Sequences." In *Proceedings of the Spring Conference on Computer Graphics (SCCG '96)*, pp. 195–204, 1996.

[90] A. Keller. "Quasi-Monte Carlo Radiosity." In *Eurographics Rendering Workshop 1996*, pp. 101–110, 1996.

[91] A. Keller. "Instant Radiosity." In *SIGGRAPH 97 Conference Proceedings*, pp. 49–56, 1997.

[92] A. Keller. "Quasi-Monte Carlo methods for photorealistic image synthesis." Ph.D. thesis, Universität Kaiserslautern, Germany, 1997.

[93] A. J. F. Kok and F. W. Jansen. "Sampling Pattern Coherence for Sampling Area Light Sources." In *Third Eurographics Workshop on Rendering*, p. 283, 1992.

[94] A. J. F. Kok. "Ray Tracing and Radiosity Algorithms for Photorealistic Images Synthesis." Ph.D. thesis, Technische Universiteit Delft, The Netherlands, 1994.

[95] C. Kolb, D. Mitchell, and P. Hanrahan. "A Realistic Camera Model for Computer Graphics." In *Computer Graphics Proceedings, Annual Conference Series, 1995 (SIGGRAPH 1995)*, pp. 317–324, 1995.

[96] T. Kollig and A. Keller. "Efficient Multidimensional Sampling." *Computer Graphics Forum* 21:3 (2002), 557–564.

[97] Thomas Kollig and Alexander Keller. "Efficient Illumination by High Dynamic Range Images." In *Eurographics Symposium on Rendering: 14th Eurographics Workshop on Rendering*, pp. 45–51, 2003.

[98] R. Kress. *Linear Integral Equations*. New York: Springer Verlag, 1989.

[99] Frank Suykens-De Laet. "On Robust Monte Carlo Algorithms for Multi-Pass Global Illumination." Ph.D. thesis, Dept. of Computer Science, Katholieke Universiteit Leuven, 2002.

[100] E. P. Lafortune and Y. D. Willems. "Bi-Directional Path Tracing." In *Proceedings of Third International Conference on Computational Graphics and Visualization Techniques (Compugraphics '93)*, pp. 145–153, 1993.

[101] E. P. Lafortune and Y. D. Willems. "The Ambient Term as a Variance Reducing Technique for Monte Carlo Ray Tracing." In *Fifth Eurographics Workshop on Rendering*, pp. 163–171. New York: Springer Verlag, 1994.

[102] E. P. Lafortune and Y. D. Willems. "A Theoretical Framework for Physically Based Rendering." *Computer Graphics Forum* 13:2 (1994), 97–107.

[103] E. P. Lafortune and Y. D. Willems. "A 5D Tree to Reduce the Variance of Monte Carlo Ray Tracing." In *Rendering Techniques '95 (Proceedings of the Eurographics Workshop on Rendering, Dublin, Ireland*, pp. 11–20, 1995.

[104] E. P. Lafortune and Y. D. Willems. "Rendering Participating Media with Bidirectional Path Tracing." In *Eurographics Rendering Workshop 1996*, pp. 91–100, 1996.

[105] E. P. Lafortune, Sing-Choong Foo, K. Torrance, and D. Greenberg. "Non-Linear Approximation of Reflectance Functions." In *Computer Graphics (SIGGRAPH '97 Proceedings), Annual Conference Series*, pp. 117–126, 1997.

[106] E. Languenou, K. Bouatouch, and P. Tellier. "An Adaptive Discretization Method for Radiosity." *Computer Graphics Forum* 11:3 (1992), C205–C216.

[107] Greg Ward Larson and Rob Shakespeare. *Rendering with Radiance: The Art and Science of Lighting Visualization*. San Fransisco, CA: Morgan Kaufmann Books, 1998.

[108] Patrick Ledda, Alan Chalmers, Tom Troscianko, and Helge Seetzen. "Evaluation of Tone Mapping Operators using a High Dynamic Range Display." *ACM Transactions on Graphics* 24:3 (2005), 640–648.

[109] H. P. A. Lensch, M. Goesele, Ph. Bekaert, J. Kautz, M. A. Magnor, J. Lang, and Hans-Peter Seidel. "Interactive Rendering of Translucent Objects." In *Proceedings of Pacific Graphics*, pp. 214–224, 2002.

[110] Mark Levoy and Pat Hanrahan. "Light Field Rendering." In *Computer Graphics (SIGGRAPH 1996 Proceedings)*, pp. 31–42, 1996.

[111] D. Lischinski, F. Tampieri, and D. P. Greenberg. "Discontinuity Meshing for Accurate Radiosity." *IEEE Computer Graphics and Applications* 12:6 (1992), 25–39.

[112] D. Lischinski, B. Smits, and D. P. Greenberg. "Bounds and Error Estimates for Radiosity." In *Proceedings of SIGGRAPH '94*, pp. 67–74, 1994.

[113] Xinguo Liu, Peter-Pike Sloan, Heung-Yeung Shum, and John Snyder. "All-Frequency Precomputed Radiance Transfer for Glossy Objects." In *Rendering Techniques 2004 Eurographics Symposium on Rendering*, 2004.

[114] Thurstone L.L. "The Method of Paired Comparisons for Social Values." *Journal of Abnormal and Social Psychology* :21 (1927), 384–400.

[115] G. Meyer M. Bolin. "A Perceptually Based Adaptive Sampling Algorithm." *SIGGRAPH 98 Conference Proceedings*, pp. 299–310.

[116] D. Greenberg M. Ramasubramanian, S. Pattanaik. "A Perceptually Based Physical Error Metric for Realistic Image Synthesis." *SIGGRAPH 99 Conference Proceedings*, pp. 73–82.

[117] Yang J.N. Maloney L.T. "Maximum Likelihood Difference Scaling." *Journal of Vision* 3:8 (2003), 573–585.

[118] Vincent Masselus. "A Practical Framework for Fixed Viewpoint Image-based Relighting." Ph.D. thesis, Dept. of Computer Science, Katholieke Universiteit Leuven, 2004.

[119] N. Metropolis, A. W. Rosenbluth, M. N. Rosenbluth, H. Teller, and E. Teller. "Equations of State Calculations by Fast Computing Machines." *Journal of Chemical Physics* 21:6 (1953), 1087–1092.

[120] Tomas Möller and Eric Haines. *Real-Time Rendering.* Natcik, MA: A K Peters, 1999.

[121] K. Myszkowski. "Lighting Reconstruction Using Fast and Adaptive Density Estimation Techniques." In *Eurographics Rendering Workshop 1997*, pp. 251–262, 1997.

[122] K. Myszkowski. "The Visible Differences Predictor: Applications to Global Illumination Problems." *Proceedings of the Ninth Eurographics Workshop on Rendering*, pp. 223–236.

[123] L. Neumann, M. Feda, M. Kopp, and W. Purgathofer. "A New Stochastic Radiosity Method for Highly Complex Scenes." In *Fifth Eurographics Workshop on Rendering*, pp. 195–206. Darmstadt, Germany, 1994.

[124] L. Neumann, W. Purgathofer, R. Tobler, A. Neumann, P. Elias, M. Feda, and X. Pueyo. "The Stochastic Ray Method for Radiosity." In *Rendering Techniques '95 (Proceedings of the Sixth Eurographics Workshop on Rendering)*, 1995.

[125] L. Neumann, R. F. Tobler, and P. Elias. "The Constant Radiosity Step." In *Rendering Techniques '95 (Proceedings of the Sixth Eurographics Workshop on Rendering)*, pp. 336–344, 1995.

[126] A. Neumann, L. Neumann, Ph. Bekaert, Y. D. Willems, and W. Purgathofer. "Importance-Driven Stochastic Ray Radiosity." In *Eurographics Rendering Workshop 1996*, pp. 111–122, 1996.

[127] L. Neumann, A. Neumann, and Ph. Bekaert. "Radiosity with Well Distributed Ray Sets." *Computer Graphics Forum* 16:3.

[128] L. Neumann. "Monte Carlo Radiosity." *Computing* 55:1 (1995), 23–42.

[129] Ren Ng, Ravi Ramamoorthi, and Pat Hanrahan. "All-Frequency Shadows using Non-Linear Wavelet Lighting Approximation." *ACM Transactions on Graphics* 22:3 (2003), 376–381.

[130] Ren Ng, Ravi Ramamoorthi, and Pat Hanrahan. "Triple Product Wavelet Integrals for All-Frequency Relighting." *ACM Transactions on Graphics* 23:3 (2004), 477–487.

[131] F. E. Nicodemus, J. C. Richmond, J. J. Hsia, I. W. Ginsberg, and T. Limperis. "Geometric Considerations and Nomenclature for Reflectance." In *Monograph 161*. National Bureau of Standards (US), 1977.

[132] H. Niederreiter. *Random Number Generation and Quasi-Monte Carlo Methods*, CBMS-NSF regional conference series in Appl. Math., 63. Philadelphia: SIAM, 1992.

[133] T. Nishita and E. Nakamae. "Continuous Tone Representation of 3-D Objects Taking Account of Shadows and Interreflection." *Computer Graphics (SIGGRAPH '85 Proceedings)* 19:3 (1985), 23–30.

[134] Marc Olano, John C. Hart, Wolfgang Heidrich, and Michael McCool. *Real-Time Shading*. Natick, MA: A K Peters, 2001.

[135] Guilford J. P. *Psychometric Methods*. New York: McGraw-Hill, 1954.

[136] E. Paquette, P. Poulin, and G. Drettakis. "A Light Hierarchy for Fast Rendering of Scenes with Many Lights." *Eurographics 98* 17:3 (1998), pp. 63–74.

[137] Steven Parker, William Martin, Peter-Pike Sloan, Peter Shirley, Brian Smits, and Chuck Hansen. "Interactive Ray Tracing." In *Interactive 3D Graphics (I3D)*, pp. 119–126, 1999.

[138] S. N. Pattanaik and S. P. Mudur. "Computation of Global Illumination by Monte Carlo Simulation of the Particle Model of Light." *Third Eurographics Workshop on Rendering*, pp. 71–83.

[139] S. N. Pattanaik and S. P. Mudur. "The Potential Equation and Importance in Illumination Computations." *Computer Graphics Forum* 12:2 (1993), 131–136.

[140] S. N. Pattanaik and S. P. Mudur. "Adjoint Equations and Random Walks for Illumination Computation." *ACM Transactions on Graphics* 14:1 (1995), 77–102.

[141] S. Pattanaik, J. Tumblin, H. Yee, and D. Greenberg. "Time-Dependent Visual Adaption for Fast Realistic Image Display." *Proceedings of SIGGRAPH 2000*, pp. 47–54.

[142] M. Pellegrini. "Monte Carlo Approximation of Form Factors with Error Bounded A Priori." In *Proc. of the 11th. annual symposium on Computational Geometry*, pp. 287 – 296. New York: ACM Press, 1995.

[143] F. Perez-Cazorla, X. Pueyo, and F. Sillion. "Global Illumination Techniques for the Simulation of Participating Media." In *Proceedings of the Eighth Eurographics Workshop on Rendering*. Saint Etienne, France, 1997.

[144] Matt Pharr and Randima Fernando. *GPU Gems 2: Programming Techniques for High-Performance Graphics and General-Purpose Computation*. Reading, MA: Addison-Wesley Professional, 2005.

[145] M. Pharr and P. M. Hanrahan. "Monte Carlo Evaluation Of Non-Linear Scattering Equations For Subsurface Reflection." In *Proceedings of ACM SIGGRAPH 2000, Computer Graphics Proceedings, Annual Conference Series*, pp. 75–84, 2000.

[146] Matt Pharr, Craig Kolb, Reid Gershbein, and Pat Hanrahan. "Rendering Complex Scenes with Memory-Coherent Ray Tracing." In *Computer Graphics (SIGGRAPH 1997 Proceedings)*, pp. 101–108, 1997.

[147] Bui-T. Phong and F. C. Crow. "Improved Rendition of Polygonal Models of Curved Surfaces." In *Proceedings of the 2nd USA-Japan Computer Conference*, 1975.

[148] A. J. Preetham, P. Shirley, and B. Smits. "A Practical Analytic Model for Daylight." In *SIGGRAPH 99 Conference Proceedings, Annual Conference Series*, pp. 91–100, 1999.

[149] W. H. Press, S. A. Teukolsky, W. T. Vetterling, and B. P. Flannery. *Numerical Recipes in FORTRAN*, Second edition. Cambridge, UK: Cambridge University Press, 1992.

[150] Paul Rademacher, Jed Lengyel, Ed Cutrell, and Turner Whitted. "Measuring the Perception of Visual Realism in Images." In *Rendering Techniques 2001: 12th Eurographics Workshop on Rendering*, pp. 235–248, 2001.

[151] Ravi Ramamoorthi and Pat Hanrahan. "An Efficient Representation for Irradiance Environment Maps." In *SIGGRAPH '01: Proceedings*

of the 28th annual conference on Computer graphics and interactive techniques, pp. 497–500, 2001.

[152] Alexander Reshetov, Alexei Soupikov, and Jim Hurley. "Multi-Level Ray Tracing Algorithm." *SIGGRAPH: ACM Trans. Graph.* 24:3 (2005), 1176–1185.

[153] R. Y. Rubinstein. *Simulation and the Monte Carlo method.* New York: J. Wiley and Sons, 1981.

[154] H. E. Rushmeier and K. E. Torrance. "The Zonal Method for Calculating Light Intensities in the Presence of a Participating Medium." In *Computer Graphics (Proceedings of SIGGRAPH 87)*, pp. 293–302, 1987.

[155] L. Santaló. *Integral Geometry and Geometric Probability.* Reading, Mass: Addison-Welsey, 1976.

[156] Mirko Sattler, Ralf Sarlette, Thomas Mücken, and Reinhard Klein. "Exploitation of Human Shadow Perception for Fast Shadow Rendering." In *APGV 2005*, pp. 131–134, 2005.

[157] M. Sbert, X. Pueyo, L. Neumann, and W. Purgathofer. "Global Multipath Monte Carlo Algorithms for Radiosity." *The Visual Computer* 12:2 (1996), 47–61.

[158] M. Sbert, A. Brusi, R. Tobler, and W. Purgathofer. "Random Walk Radiosity with Generalized Transition Probabilities." Technical Report IIiA-98-07-RR, Institut d'Informàtica i Aplicacions, Universitat de Girona, 1998.

[159] M. Sbert, A. Brusi, and Ph. Bekaert. "Gathering for Free in Random Walk Radiosity." In *Rendering Techniques '99 (Proceedings of the 10th Eurographics Workshop on Rendering, Granada, Spain)*, pp. 97–102. Springer Computer Science, 1999.

[160] M. Sbert. "An Integral Geometry Based Method for Fast Form-Factor Computation." *Computer Graphics Forum* 12:3 (1993), C409–C420.

[161] M. Sbert. "The Use of Global Random Directions to Compute Radiosity—Global Monte Carlo Techniques." Ph.D. thesis, Universitat Politècnica de Catalunya, Barcelona, Spain, 1996.

[162] M. Sbert. "Error and Complexity of Random Walk Monte Carlo Radiosity." *IEEE Transactions on Visualization and Computer Graphics* 3:1 (1997), 23–38.

[163] M. Sbert. "Optimal Source Selection in Shooting Random Walk Monte Carlo Radiosity." *Computer Graphics Forum* 16:3 (1997), 301–308.

[164] P. Schröder. "Numerical Integration for Radiosity in the Presence of Singularities." In *4 th Eurographics Workshop on Rendering, Paris, France*, pp. 177–184, 1993.

[165] Peter Shirley and Kenneth Chiu. "A Low Distortion Map Between Disk and Square." *Journal of Graphics Tools* 2:3 (1997), 45–52.

[166] P. Shirley, B. Wade, Ph. M. Hubbard, D. Zareski, B. Walter, and Donald P. Greenberg. "Global Illumination via Density Estimation." In *Rendering Techniques '95 (Proceedings of the Sixth Eurographics Workshop on Rendering)*, pp. 219–230, 1995.

[167] P. Shirley. "A Ray Tracing Method for Illumination Calculation in Diffuse–Specular Scenes." In *Graphics Interface '90*, pp. 205–212, 1990.

[168] P. Shirley. "Radiosity via Ray Tracing." In *Graphics Gems II*, edited by J. Arvo, pp. 306–310. Boston: Academic Press, 1991.

[169] P. Shirley. "Time Complexity of Monte Carlo Radiosity." In *Eurographics '91*, pp. 459–465, 1991.

[170] P. Shirley. *Realistic Ray Tracing*. Natick, MA: A K Peters, 2000.

[171] F. Sillion and C. Puech. "A General Two-Pass Method Integrating Specular and Diffuse Reflection." In *Computer Graphics (SIGGRAPH '89 Proceedings)*, pp. 335–344, 1989.

[172] F. Sillion and C. Puech. *Radiosity and Global Illumination*. San Francisco: Morgan Kaufmann, 1994.

[173] F. Sillion, J. Arvo, S. Westin, and D. Greenberg. "A Global Illumination Solution for General Reflectance Distributions." *Computer Graphics (SIGGRAPH '91 Proceedings)* 25:4 (1991), 187–196.

[174] F. Sillion. "A Unified Hierarchical Algorithm for Global Illumination with Scattering Volumes and Object Clusters." *IEEE Transactions on Visualization and Computer Graphics* 1:3 (1995), 240–254.

[175] B. W. Silverman. *Density Estimation for Statistics and Data Analysis*. London: Chapman and Hall, 1986.

[176] Maryann Simmons and Carlo H. Séquin. "Tapestry: A Dynamic Mesh-based Display Representation for Interactive Rendering." In *Eleventh Eurographics Workshop on Rendering*, pp. 329–340, 2000.

[177] Peter-Pike Sloan, Jan Kautz, and John Snyder. "Precomputed Radiance Transfer for Real-Time Rendering in Dynamic, Low-Frequency Lighting Environments." In *SIGGRAPH '02*, pp. 527–536, 2002.

[178] Peter-Pike Sloan, Jesse Hall, John Hart, and John Snyder. "Clustered Principal Components for Precomputed Radiance Transfer." *ACM Transactions on Graphics* 22:3 (2003), 382–391.

[179] Peter-Pike Sloan, Xinguo Liu, Heung-Yeung Shum, and John Snyder. "Bi-Scale Radiance Transfer." *ACM Trans. Graph.* 22:3 (2003), 370–375.

[180] Peter-Pike Sloan, Ben Luna, and John Snyder. "Local, Deformable Precomputed Radiance Transfer." *ACM Trans. Graph.* 24:3 (2005), 1216–1224.

[181] B. Smits, J. Arvo, and D. Salesin. "An Importance-Driven Radiosity Algorithm." In *Computer Graphics (SIGGRAPH '92 Proceedings)*, pp. 273–282, 1992.

[182] B. Smits, J. Arvo, and D. Greenberg. "A Clustering Algorithm for Radiosity in Complex Environments." In *SIGGRAPH '94 Proceedings*, pp. 435–442, 1994.

[183] J. Spanier and E. M. Gelbard. *Monte Carlo Principles and Neutron Transport Problems*. Reading, MA: Addison-Wesley, 1969.

[184] J. Stam and E. Languenou. "Ray Tracing in Non-Constant Media." In *Proceedings of the 7th Eurographics Workshop on Rendering*, pp. 225–234, 1996.

[185] J. Stam. "Multiple Scattering as a Diffusion Process." In *Proceedings of the 6th Eurographics Workshop on Rendering*, pp. 51–58, 1995.

[186] J. Stam. "Diffraction Shaders." In *SIGGRAPH 99 Conference Proceedings, Annual Conference Series*, pp. 101–110, 1999.

[187] William A. Stokes, James A. Ferwerda, Bruce Walter, and Donald P. Greenberg. "Perceptual Illumination Components: A New Approach to Efficient, High Quality Global Illumination Rendering." *ACM Transactions on Graphics* 23:3 (2004), 742–749.

[188] I. E. Sutherland. "Sketchpad–A Man-Machine Graphical Communication System." Technical Report 296, MIT Lincoln Laboratory, 1963.

[189] L. Szirmay-Kalos and W. Purgathofer. "Global Ray-bundle Tracing with Hardware Acceleration." In *Ninth Eurographics Workshop on Rendering*. Vienna, Austria, 1998.

[190] L. Szirmay-Kalos and W. Purgathofer. "Analysis of the Quasi-Monte Carlo Integration of the Rendering Equation." In *WSCG '99 (Seventh International Conference in Central Europe on Computer Graphics, Visualization and Interactive Digital Media)*, pp. 281–288, 1999.

[191] L. Szirmay-Kalos, T. Foris, L. Neumann, and C. Balasz. "An Analysis of Quasi-Monte Carlo Integration Applied to the Transillumination Radiosity Method." *Computer Graphics Forum (Eurographics '97 Proceedings)* 16:3. 271–281.

[192] L. Szirmay-Kalos, C. Balasz, and W. Purgathofer. "Importance-Driven Quasi-Random Walk Solution of the Rendering Equation." *Computers and Graphics* 23:2 (1999), 203–211.

[193] L. Szirmay-Kalos. "Stochastic Iteration for Non-Diffuse Global Illumination." *Computer Graphics Forum* 18:3 (1999), 233–244.

[194] Whitted T. "An Improved Illumination Model for Shaded Display." *Communications of the ACM* 23:6 (1980), 343–349.

[195] Justin Talbot, David Cline, and Parris Egbert. "Importance Resampling for Global Illumination." In *Rendering Techniques 2005: 16th Eurographics Workshop on Rendering*, pp. 139–146, 2005.

[196] Seth Teller, Kavita Bala, and Julie Dorsey. "Conservative Radiance Interpolants for Ray Tracing." In *Seventh Eurographics Workshop on Rendering*, pp. 258–269, 1996.

[197] R. Tobler, A. Wilkie, M. Feda, and W. Purgathofer. "A Hierarchical Subdivision Algorithm for Stochastic Radiosity Methods." In *Eurographics Rendering Workshop 1997*, pp. 193–204, 1997.

[198] Parag Tole, Fabio Pellacini, Bruce Walter, and Donald Greenberg. "Interactive Global Illumination." In *Computer Graphics (SIGGRAPH 2002 Proceedings)*, 2002.

[199] J. Tumblin and H. E. Rushmeier. "Tone Reproduction for Realistic Images." *IEEE Computer Graphics and Applications* 13:6 (1993), 42–48.

[200] E. Veach and L. J. Guibas. "Bidirectional Estimators for Light Transport." In *Fifth Eurographics Workshop on Rendering*, pp. 147–162. Darmstadt, Germany, 1994.

[201] E. Veach and L. J. Guibas. "Optimally Combining Sampling Techniques for Monte Carlo Rendering." In *SIGGRAPH 95 Conference Proceedings*, pp. 419–428, 1995.

[202] Eric Veach and Leonidas J. Guibas. "Metropolis Light Transport." In *Computer Graphics Proceedings, Annual Conference Series, 1997 (SIGGRAPH 1997)*, 1997.

[203] E. Veach. "Non-Symmetric Scattering in Light Transport Algorithms." In *Eurographics Rendering Workshop 1996*, pp. 81–90, 1996.

[204] E. Veach. "Robust Monte Carlo Methods for Light Transport Simulation." Ph.D. thesis, Stanford university, Department of Computer Science, 1997.

[205] Edgar Velzquez-Armendriz, Eugene Lee, Bruce Walter, and Kavita Bala. "Implementing the Render Cache and the Edge-and-Point Image on Graphics Hardware." *Graphics Interface*, 2006.

[206] V. Volevich, K. Myszkowski, A. Khodulev, and E. A. Kopylov. "Using the Visual Differences Predictor to Improve Performance of Progressive Global Illumination Computations." *ACM Transactions on Graphics* 19:2 (2000), 122–161.

[207] Ingo Wald and Philipp Slusallek. "State of the Art in Interactive Ray Tracing." In *State of the Art Reports, EUROGRAPHICS 2001*, pp. 21–42, 2001.

[208] Ingo Wald, Carsten Benthin, Markus Wagner, and Philipp Slusallek. "Interactive Rendering with Coherent Ray Tracing." In *Proc. of Eurographics*, pp. 153–164, 2001.

[209] J. R. Wallace, M. F. Cohen, and D. P. Greenberg. "A Two-Pass Solution to the Rendering Equation: A Synthesis of Ray Tracing and Radiosity Methods." *Computer Graphics (SIGGRAPH '87 Proceedings)* 21:4 (1987), 311–320.

[210] B. Walter, Ph. M. Hubbard, P. Shirley, and D. F. Greenberg. "Global Illumination Using Local Linear Density Estimation." *ACM Transactions on Graphics* 16:3 (1997), 217–259.

[211] Bruce Walter, George Drettakis, and Steven Parker. "Interactive Rendering using the Render Cache." In *Tenth Eurographics Workshop on Rendering*, pp. 19–30, 1999.

[212] Bruce Walter, George Drettakis, and Donald Greenberg. "Enhancing and Optimizing the Render Cache." In *Thirteenth Eurographics Workshop on Rendering*, pp. 37–42, 2002.

[213] Bruce Walter, Sebastian Fernandez, Adam Arbree, Kavita Bala, Michael Donikian, and Donald P. Greenberg. "Lightcuts: A Scalable Approach to Illumination." *SIGGRAPH: ACM Trans. Graph.* 24:3 (2005), 1098–1107.

[214] Bruce Walter, Adam Arbree, Kavita Bala, and Donald P. Greenberg. "Multidimensional Lightcuts." To appear in *SIGGRAPH: ACM Trans. Graph.*, 2006.

[215] Rui Wang, John Tran, and David Luebke. "All-Frequency Relighting of Non-Diffuse Objects Using Separable BRDF Approximation." In *Rendering Techniques 2004 Eurographics Symposium on Rendering*, pp. 345–354, 2004.

[216] Rui Wang, John Tran, and David Luebke. "All-Frequency Interactive Relighting of Translucent Objects with single and multiple scattering." *ACM Trans. Graph.* 24:3 (2005), 1202–1207.

[217] G. J. Ward and P. Heckbert. "Irradiance Gradients." In *Rendering in Computer Graphics (Proceedings of the Third Eurographics Workshop on Rendering)*, pp. 85–98, 1992.

[218] Greg Ward and Maryann Simmons. "The Holodeck Ray Cache: An Interactive Rendering System for Global Illumination." *ACM Transactions on Graphics* 18:4 (1999), 361–398.

[219] G. J. Ward, F. M. Rubinstein, and R. D. Clear. "A Ray Tracing Solution for Diffuse Interreflection." In *Computer Graphics (SIGGRAPH 1988 Proceedings)*, pp. 85–92, 1988.

[220] G. J. Ward. "Real Pixels." In *Graphics Gems II*, edited by James Arvo, pp. 80–83. Boston: Academic Press, 1991.

[221] G. J. Ward. "Measuring and modeling anisotropic reflection." In *Computer Graphics (SIGGRAPH 1992 Proceedings)*, pp. 265–272, 1992.

[222] G. Ward. "A Contrast-Based Scalefactor for Luminance Display." In *Graphics Gems 4*, edited by Paul S. Heckbert, pp. 415–421. Boston: Academic Press, 1994.

[223] G. J. Ward. "Adaptive Shadow Testing for Ray Tracing." In *Photorealistic Rendering in Computer Graphics (Proceedings of the Second Eurographics Workshop on Rendering)*, pp. 11–20, 1994.

[224] W. Wasow. "A Comment on the Inversion of Matrices by Random Walks." *Math. Tabl. Aids. Comput.* 6 (1952), 78–81.

[225] M. Watt. "Light-Water Interaction using Backward Beam Tracing." In *Computer Graphics (SIGGRAPH 1990 Proceedings)*, pp. 377–85, 1990.

[226] A Wilkie, R. Tobler, and W Purgathofer. "Combined Rendering of Polarization and Fluorescence Effects." In *Proceedings of Eurographics Workshop on Rendering 2001*, pp. 11–20, 2001.

[227] Hector Yee, Sumanta Pattanaik, and Donald P. Greenberg. "Spatiotemporal Sensitivity and Visual Attention for Efficient Rendering of Dynamic Environments." *ACM Transactions on Graphics* 20:1 (2001), pp. 39–65.

[228] H. R. Zatz. "Galerkin Radiosity: A Higher Order Solution Method for Global Illumination." In *Computer Graphics Proceedings, Annual Conference Series, 1993*, pp. 213–220, 1993.

[229] Kun Zhou, Yaohua Hu, Stephen Lin, Baining Guo, and Heung-Yeung Shum. "Precomputed Shadow Fields for Dynamic Scenes." *ACM Trans. Graph.* 24:3 (2005), 1196–1201.

[230] K. Zimmerman and P. Shirley. "A Two-Pass Realistic Image Synthesis Method for Complex Scenes." In *Rendering Techniques 1995 (Proceedings of the Sixth Eurographics Workshop on Rendering)*, pp. 284–295. New York: Springer-Verlag, 1995.

Index

Printed in the United States
by Baker & Taylor Publisher Services